Advances in Digital Multimedia Broadcasting

Volume I

Advances in Digital Multimedia Broadcasting Volume I

Edited by **Alicia Witte**

CLANRYE INTERNATIONAL

New Jersey

Published by Clanrye International,
55 Van Reypen Street,
Jersey City, NJ 07306, USA
www.clanryeinternational.com

Advances in Digital Multimedia Broadcasting: Volume I
Edited by Alicia Witte

International Standard Book Number: 978-1-63240-047-5 (Hardback)

Printed in the United States of America.

Contents

Preface

Multimedia is a combination of different types of media such as audio, video, text, animations, graphics, images, and interactive media. This field of computer technology is widespread in the present world due to its use in communication, entertainment, and academics. Multimedia involves presentation of data using multiple principles, concepts, and theories. A very important aspect of multimedia is digital broadcasting, which one can observe on television, internet, radio, cell phone communication etc. Multimedia has gained unimaginable importance over the last few decades. It has gained relevance in the field of computer science, especially in programming and communication technology.

Digital multimedia has also gained considerable importance in medical sciences, engineering, education, entertainment etc. Digital multimedia broadcasting is a technique used to distribute data over a large area by processing and transmitting the data using computer science tools. It converts data into digital forms such as bits, and then transmits the same using tools of electronics and physics.

This book has contributors from several countries, all of them leading experts in their field. All the chapters have been thoroughly written and reviewed, ensuring that the views of the contributors have been preserved in a uniform format. This effort would not have been possible without the kind cooperation of our contributors, who patiently went through revisions of their chapters. I convey my heartfelt thanks to all contributors and to the team at the publishing house for their encouragement and excellent technical assistance as and when required.

Editor

Rate Adaptive Selective Segment Assignment for Reliable Wireless Video Transmission

Sajid Nazir,[1] Dejan Vukobratović,[2] Vladimir Stanković,[1] and Ivan Andonović[1]

[1] Department of Electronic and Electrical Engineering, University of Strathclyde, Glasgow G1 1XW, UK
[2] Department of Power, Electronics and Communication Engineering, University of Novi Sad, 21000 Novi Sad, Serbia

Correspondence should be addressed to Sajid Nazir, nazirsajid@yahoo.com

Academic Editor: Sanjeev Mehrotra

A reliable video communication system is proposed based on data partitioning feature of H.264/AVC, used to create a layered stream, and LT codes for erasure protection. The proposed scheme termed rate adaptive selective segment assignment (RASSA) is an adaptive low-complexity solution to varying channel conditions. The comparison of the results of the proposed scheme is also provided for slice-partitioned H.264/AVC data. Simulation results show competitiveness of the proposed scheme compared to optimized unequal and equal error protection solutions. The simulation results also demonstrate that a high visual quality video transmission can be maintained despite the adverse effect of varying channel conditions and the number of decoding failures can be reduced.

1. Introduction

Reliable real-time wireless video communication is gaining increased importance as novel richer multimedia applications are being deployed. Since wireless channels are prone to errors, it is necessary to provide strong error control mechanisms. Forward Error Correction (FEC) coding is preferable option as retransmission in real-time wireless applications is usually not a viable solution. On the other hand, error resilience video coding schemes generally come at a cost of decreased video performance in error-free environments and increased video coding complexity.

To combat packet drops, Digital Fountain erasure protection codes [1] are proven effective solution. Fountain codes [2, 3] are a recent class of FEC codes originally proposed for multicast/broadcast applications to combat losses of packets in the network. Fountain codes are rateless and in non-time-constraint applications can generate as many encoded packets as needed. The amount of additional packets transmitted is the redundancy that is necessary for decoding to succeed and can be adjusted to combat different channel conditions. In bandwidth-limited wireless networks it is important to keep the introduced redundancy to a minimum. Thus, instead of targeting the worst possible channel conditions,

the redundancy should be adaptively adjusted according to the varying channel conditions via dynamic source-channel coding. LT codes [2] are the first proposed class of practical fountain codes. Although Raptor codes [3] generally provide better performance, the LT codes are used in this paper due to their design and implementation simplicity. Note, however, that LT codes have a higher decoding complexity of $O(k \log_e k)$ per source message (where k is the message length) than Raptor codes, $O(k)$.

H.264 Advanced Video Coding (AVC) [4] is the state-of-the-art video coding standard achieving significant compression efficiency and gaining widespread use in the emerging communications standards and applications. When transmitting H.264/AVC video over a wireless channel, due to significant fluctuations of channel characteristics, the video is encoded at a fixed source rate and the redundancy (i.e., LT coded symbols) is added to avoid error effects. Usually, for simplicity, the entire video block is protected equally using equal error protection (EEP).

An alternative is to classify the encoded content based on the importance to the reconstruction and assign different amount of redundancy to different importance classes using unequal error protection (UEP). For example, intracoded frames can be protected stronger than inter-coded ones.

Another option is to use a higher source coding rate and to continuously adapt the source rate to the varying channel bandwidth by dropping some of the frames, in order to keep the channel coding rate low enough. This joint source channel coding option can be combined with EEP to lead a simple rate adaptive solution or with UEP to provide a more complex, but optimized protection.

In this paper we proposed Rate adaptive selective segment assignment (RASSA) scheme and compare its performance to that of fixed source rate EEP and fixed source rate UEP. We resort to error resilience and concealment features, designed to make the video less vulnerable to the effects of lost data, and then compress the video at a higher source rate allowing for some decoding errors. In particular, in this paper, we study data partitioning and slicing. Data partitioning (DP) [4] is a low-cost error resilience feature, supported by the extended AVC profile, which can be exploited to introduce a layered structure in H.264/AVC. The DP feature of H.264/AVC effectively prioritizes a video stream by partitioning it into classes of different importance to video reconstruction with a very small rate penalty compared to the AVC standard without error resilience.

Besides DP, it is possible to partition a frame into a fixed number of *slices*, which are of different importance to the video reconstruction. Thus, similarly to DPs, the slices can be aggregated into different priority classes, with the higher-priority classes containing slices that have higher contribution to the reconstruction. Such prioritization can make the sliced video data amenable to UEP and rate adaptation.

A lot of work has been done on joint source-channel coding; see [5] for a review. In the domain of rateless source channel coding, in [6], a class of unequal error protection codes, called Expanding Window Fountain (EWF) codes, is used for UEP of scalable video. In [7], unequal protection has been proposed for video communications by duplicating the information symbols and extending the original LT degree distribution to the new set of information symbols. In [8], unequal Growth codes have been proposed where as the number of packets the receiver has increases, the degree for each new encoding symbol needs to increase, hence the name Growth codes. An adaptive rateless coding for DP AVC coded video has been proposed in [9]. The proposed system uses intracoded macroblocks (MBs) in each frame; some additional redundant data is piggybacked onto the ongoing packet stream. In contrast, this study uses an IPPP... structure, where each GOP is treated as a source block for LT coding. The contributions of this study are (1) analysis of optimized EEP and UEP schemes for transmission of DP and sliced H.264/AVC video and their robustness in channel mismatch scenarios and (2) a rate-adaptive optimized solution for bandwidth-limited wireless channels and limited resource devices.

Although LT codes are used in the simulation section, the proposed solution can be applied to other rateless packet loss protection codes. A scheme has been proposed to decode video even when the rateless decoding fails using packetization information. This is made possible by passing a videotable to the decoder containing the DP type and size information. Thus, the DPs with all or part of their data missing are discarded before the H.264 decoder tries to decode the data. It is important to note that without such information the decoding will fail on encountering such missing data.

The segmentation of video data facilitates a layered coded video that might be preferable to the H.264 Scalable Video Coding (SVC) extension [10] in some applications since it complies with the AVC standard and provides scalability, and more robust output to packet losses than SVC. The proposed scheme can be applied in multicast scenarios with heterogeneous receivers, in which case a receiver can terminate reception and decoding of segments after having received data compatible with its processing power and memory.

The rest of the paper is organized as follows. Section 2 covers the background of DP, slicing, and LT erasure protection coding. In Sections 3 and 4, the proposed system and the proposed rate allocation algorithms are described, respectively. The results and analysis are in Section 5. Finally, the conclusion and future research directions are contained in Section 6.

2. Background

In this section we give background on error resilient H.264/AVC and erasure protection coding used. H.264/AVC formats the video data into Network Abstraction Layer (NAL) units enabling it to be transported over various channels. Each video frame is encapsulated in a separate NAL unit. H.264/AVC provides many errorresilience options to mitigate the effect of lost packets during transmission. Next, we briefly outline two options used in this paper.

2.1. Data Partitioning. A low-cost option is the DP [4, 11] which supports the partitioning of a frame/slice in up to three partitions (NAL units), based on the importance of the encoded video syntax elements for video reconstruction (see Figure 1(a)). DP *A* contains the most important data comprising slice headers, quantization parameters, and motion vectors. DP *B* contains the intracoded macroblocks (MB) residual data, and DP *C* contains inter-coded MB residual data. This importance-based partitioning enables assigning different protection levels to different partitions. The decoding of DP *A* is always independent of DP *B* and *C*. However, if DP *A* is lost the remaining partitions cannot be utilized. To make decoding of DP *B* independent of DP *C*, Constrained Intra Prediction (CIP) parameter in the H.264/AVC encoder is set. The loss of an NAL unit can result in error propagation to later frames due to interframe dependence.

2.2. Slicing. Another scheme available in the baseline profile is slicing [4], which enables the partitioning of a frame into two or more independently coded sections, called slices. Each slice in a frame can have either a fixed number of assigned MBs or fixed data rate. Each coded slice is independently

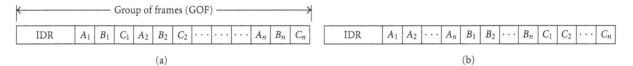

FIGURE 1: (a) Data partitions. (b) Segmented data partitions.

decodable; however, the slices have different contribution (importance) to the video reconstruction. Thus, arranging the slices in decreasing order of their contribution to reconstruction can be used to provide a layered video stream suitable for UEP.

DP has low overhead as its structure is determined in advance, whereas slicing generally requires a slice group map.

2.3. LT Codes. The first practical class of fountain codes are LT codes [2]. The LT encoder can potentially generate an unlimited number of encoded symbols from a limited set of source symbols. Encoded symbol is obtained by selecting uniformly at random d different source symbols and their bitwise XOR-ing. The degree d of each encoded symbol is drawn i.i.d. from a discrete probability distribution $\Omega(d)$ called the degree distribution. LT codes designed using Robust Soliton degree distribution are asymptotically capacity-achieving in combination with the iterative Belief-Propagation LT decoder [2]. It may be worth noting that many implementations of rateless coding, such as systematic 3GPP Raptor code [12], do not use the belief propagation algorithm but employ matrix operations instead.

The LT decoder gathers the received encoded symbols and tries to recover the original source symbols. The decoder needs to know the degree and the location of source symbols, which have been combined together to form the encoded symbol. The decoder keeps on processing the encoded symbols of degree one, recovering a source symbol that is then XOR-ed with all the symbols it is connected to and the corresponding LT code graph edges are removed. This process continues until the decoding succeeds or stops with errors [2].

2.4. UEP Schemes. In order to enable UEP, the video data is divided into two segments/layers according to its importance for video reconstruction. Intuitively, we put the important data, that is, IDR and DP A, always in so-called high-priority layer (HPL). The other layer termed low-priority layer (LPL) contains least important data.

The UEP schemes are based on varying the probability of selection of HPL. Note that the same rateless codes are used for protection of both HPL and LPL, and UEP is achieved by probabilistically selecting at the transmitter for each output symbol whether it should come from the HPL or LPL stream. Thus, instead of two different fixed code rates, we use soft code rates via defined selection probability of HPL. If we increase the selection probability of HPL, we improve its robustness at the price of a decreased robustness of LPL. Also, it is important to take into account the relative sizes of the priority layers. The selection probability of a layer must

at least correspond to its relative size. Moreover, assigning a higher selection probability than required to HPL could be beneficial in cases where more protection to it is required.

3. The Proposed System

In this section we describe the proposed system that segments encoded video and provides equal or unequal error protection. First, we describe a system that forms a layered output using the DP feature. Then, we present the system that exploits slicing instead of DP.

3.1. Protection of DP-Based AVC Video. The video data of each non-IDR frame is divided into three data partitions by the H.264/AVC encoder. IDR frames were not partitioned and they were put always into the HPL. This partitioned data needs to be aggregated together to enable UEP. The structure of a segmented video is shown in Figure 1. The figure shows the DP A, B, and C together with the I frame. (Note that the first non-I frame is denoted as A_1, B_1, C_1, and so forth.) Next, we prioritize the partitions and group all DP As, Bs, and Cs together effectively forming three segments or layers as shown in Figure 1(b). Note that by receiving only the I/Instantaneous decoder refresh (IDR) frame and DP $A_1, \ldots, A_n$, the decoder will still be able to decode all n frames within the group of pictures (GOP), though at reduced quality. Further segmentation is not restricted to be done at the aggregate partition boundaries only. That is, if all IDR and DP A are sent as the first segment, then any number of DP B and DP C partitions can be selected for transmission in the second segment. It is worth noting that this will only work for pre-encoded video.

This gives flexibility that enables a fine-grained layered structure as a large number of reconstruction rate points become available, which can be matched to the channel statistics with a very fine control over video reconstruction quality. The DP B and DP C by virtue of having been aggregated are already in their priority order for reconstruction. The layer with important data (IDR and DP $A \ldots$) is termed HPL, whereas the remaining data is placed in LPL. In the proposed scheme, intra-refresh MBs are not used but instead periodic I frames are assumed.

The segmented data partitions are next protected by FEC codes applied on each GOP independently.

To achieve UEP, each segment should be protected according to its importance using different amount of redundant symbols. The symbol size is 70 bytes. To accomplish that, the FEC encoding process adds an important initial step, that is, to first select a segment from which the encoded symbol is to be generated determined by "selection probability" of a segment, which is a preassigned parameter based on the importance of different segments and the data rate available. After a segment is selected, a conventional encoding is performed over the source packets contained in that particular segment only. Thus, instead of defining a UEP scheme as a set of rates (one for each segment), we equivalently define it by a set of selection probabilities. This resembles the method of [6]. For practical reasons the number of layers in the UEP is usually constrained to two or three.

Note that the UEP scheme allocates redundancies to the segments based on their importance. The optimal rate allocation depends not only on the channel characteristics but also on video data since the importance and sizes of the segments vary from a GOP to a GOP. Thus, the UEP has to be dynamically changed and optimal allocation needs to be found for each GOP, which is practically feasible only for a prerecorded video. Note that in the extreme case when the bandwidth is very scarce or packet loss rate high, which is often in mobile wireless scenarios, the optimal selection probability of low-priority segments would be zero and all redundancy would be allocated to the high-priority segments to ensure their successful decoding.

Motivated by this and targeting wireless applications with limited bandwidth available and high loss rates, we introduce another scheme called the RASSA scheme. The RASSA scheme is a special case of UEP that exploits the flexibility of layered coding of DP and slicing. First, given an estimated packet loss rate and total rate budget, the system calculates the required overhead (and thus also the amount of source data) that will allow for error-free transfer with high probability (w.h.p.). Then, the data is filled starting from leftmost in Figure 1(b), and remaining source data is discarded. This way, the scheme discards some of the lower-priority data by assigning zero selection probability, to increase protection of the more important data.

Thus, this scheme is not constrained in having two or three segments/layers, and any number of DPs/slices can be selected enabling a very flexible rate control. For example, given channel statistics, we can provide enough redundancy for a segment containing DP A and B and part of DP C to be recovered at the decoder w.h.p. The unselected low-priority data (remaining DP Cs) are simply discarded. Note that either the entire sent source block will be decoded, or decoding will fail, in which case the previous GOP is used for reconstruction.

RASSA can be seen as a UEP scheme since it protects only one part of the encoded data and discards the rest, but also as EEP since it provides equal protection of all sent source data. One immediate advantage of this scheme is reduced complexity since only one code is used, where UEP generally requires one code for each layer, and there is no need for complex rate optimization. Indeed, once the channel loss rate is estimated, the required code rate is set, and based on the available bandwidth (total budget) the decision to drop some of the NAL units that cannot fit the total budget is made.

UEP schemes require that the DPs of each type in LPL are aggregated together. To pass this information to the decoder, we propose a video table structure to be created at the encoder. The encoded video generated by the H.264/AVC encoder with DP is used to create a video-table with an entry for each NAL unit and its length. The number of NAL units per GOP is usually small (up to 64), and hence the table can conveniently be passed to the decoder within a header with negligible rate increase. The packet bearing header will be transported with the HPL. If HPL is lost, then anyway no video decoding is possible.

At the receiver side, the video-table structure is used to rearrange the DPs to their original encoding order. The table is also used to discard NAL units with missing data. That is, since one DP/NAL can be sent in multiple packets, if one packet is missing the entire DP is dropped. Also, recovered DP B and DP C of a frame are dropped if DP A for that frame is not recovered properly.

There is negligible latency involved in bringing the DPs to their original order for decoding. The aggregation of DPs is only limited to a priority layer. For instance, if DP A and DP B both are in HPL, then they will remain in their original encoding order.

3.2. Protection of Sliced AVC Video. In our previous work [13], we propose and test a method for segmenting sliced-AVC output into multiple segments based on importance of the slices to reconstruction. For example, we can form two priority classes where more important slices, which contribute to the peak signal-to-noise ratio (PSNR) level above a fixed threshold, are put in the HPL, and all other in LPL. Then, the protection methods described above (EEP, UEP, and RASSA) can be applied to such prioritized data without modification.

We encode a video sequence using slicing with each frame divided into a fixed number of slices. The priority of each slice is obtained by dropping it from the GOP data and measuring the resulting PSNR, as a frame-by-frame average of the entire GOP, by actual decoding. In view of the encoding latency, the scheme is meant for pre-encoded video. This also takes into account the error propagation effect to the subsequent frames due to loss of a slice in an earlier frame. That is, the cumulative PSNR of the GOP is measured by dropping each slice in turn starting at the first P frame. After having obtained the cumulative PSNR values for each slice (as dropped), the difference from the full-decoding PSNR of the GOP is measured. The importance of the slices on total frame-averaged PSNR generally decreases as we move towards the end of the GOP. Thus, we can sort the slices into multiple priority layers and assign a higher degree of protection to the important layers as compared to the layers containing less significant slices. Such layering enables a prioritized data transmission with UEP schemes. Details of assigning slices to different layers can be found in [13].

4. Rate Allocation

In this section we discuss rate allocation optimization for the three proposed schemes. We assume that DP is done; however, in the same way, rate allocation can be done in case of slicing.

Let N be a given total rate budget expressed as the total number of packets/symbols that can be transmitted for each GOP. The video is encoded using DP H.264/AVC forming either four segments, IDR, DP A, DP B, and DP C, or two classes of slices. We assume that each segment can be truncated arbitrarily. Let K be the total number of encoded source packets/symbols.

We consider three schemes: (i) an EEP scheme that generates N packets using all K source packets and transmit them over the network; (ii) a UEP scheme that groups source data into L importance layers starting from IDR; for example, we can have $L = 4$ where each of four segments forms one layer; (iii) an RASSA scheme that takes first $K_{\text{RASSA}} \leq K$ source packets to generate N transmission packets.

Assuming that video is pre-encoded, K is fixed and is not part of the optimization. Then, the EEP scheme always uses an (N, K) code and thus does not require optimization.

An L-layer UEP scheme can be described by L-tuples $\pi = (p_1, p_2, \ldots, p_L)$ and $= (k_1, k_2, \ldots, k_L)$, where p_i and k_i represent the selection probability and the size in packets, respectively, of layer i. Then the optimal rate allocation between the L layers can be found by maximizing the expected PSNR of the reconstruction given by

$$\widehat{\text{PSNR}} = \sum_{i=0}^{L} P_i(\pi, K)\text{PSNR}_i, \qquad (1)$$

where P_0 is the probability that no layer is recovered, P_i is the probability that first i layers can be recovered but not layer $i + 1$, and P_L is the probability that all layers can be recovered successfully. The task is to find L-tuples π^* and K^* that maximize the expected PSNR, over all possible L-tuples π and K. P_i can be obtained experimentally or for some FEC codes estimated analytically for each π, K and each channel condition and are source independent. For simplicity, it is assumed that K is set a priori by the video encoder which is often the case. Indeed, it is natural to group all packets from one segment together. For example, for $L = 3$, IDR and DP A can be placed into one layer, DP B in another, and DP C in the last layer. Note that the sizes of each segment are determined by the video encoder, and are not subject of the optimization. The problem can further be simplified by maximizing the expected received rate instead of PSNR as

$$\hat{R} = \sum_{i=0}^{L} P_i(\pi)K_i, \qquad (2)$$

where K_i is the number of packets in the first i layers and $K_0 = 0$. This way, the optimization is independent of the source content and depends only on the total rate, layer sizes, and channel loss rate. There are many methods proposed to efficiently accomplish the two optimization tasks (see [5, 6] and references therein).

For the RASSA scheme, recall that out of K generated source packets, only K_{RASSA} are selected that are protected by an (N, K_{RASSA}) channel code before transmission. The optimization problem is simplified to the following. Given a total number of transmission packets N and packet loss rate q, the task is to find the number of sent source packets

$K_{\text{RASSA}} \leq K$, such that all K_{RASSA} source packets can be decoded w.h.p. Note that determining K_{RASSA} implies the used channel code (N, K_{RASSA}). Again, the expected PSNR or the expected number of received source packets is maximized, given by

$$\widehat{\text{PSNR}} = (1 - P)\text{PSNR}_0 + P \cdot \text{PSNR}_1,$$
$$\hat{R} = P \cdot K_1, \qquad (3)$$

respectively, where P is the probability of successful decoding and PSNR_0 and PSNR_1 are reconstructed PSNR if decoding fails or is successful, respectively. K_1 denotes the number of source packets sent by the RASSA scheme. Note that P depends on q and K_1 and can be found experimentally or analytically. Indeed, for maximum distance separable codes, P is the probability that the number received packets is at least K_1, and then

$$\hat{R} = \binom{N}{K_1} q^{N-K_1} (1 - q)^{K_1} K_1, \qquad (4)$$

which can be solved numerically.

In the next section, we will compare results of the rate and PSNR-optimized RASSA schemes to that of EEP and optimized UEP schemes.

5. Results and Analysis

We test robustness of the EEP, optimized UEP, and RASSA schemes when packet loss rates q and data rates N vary. We show effectiveness of the proposed approached using both DP and slicing features. Simulations have been performed using the H.264/AVC software JM 16.2 [14]. A GOP size of 16 frames is used with the IPPPP... structure. We report results for two video sequences "Paris" and "Football." Penalty due to DP and slicing for these sequences is up to 0.1 dB.

5.1. DP AVC Transmission. We assume that the video has been pre-encoded at a fixed rate using DP into fixed length segments IDR, DP A, DP B, and DP C. The data in each segment is formed into source symbols/packets of size 70 bytes for the LT coding process, which is a good compromise between performance and complexity. The IDR frame is put in the first NAL unit and it is not partitioned. CIP is used to make the decoding of DP B independent of DP C. Each non-IDR frame is partitioned into DP A, DP B, and DP C.

The partitions with their relative sizes and the PSNR contribution for the first GOP of the CIF format "Paris" and "Football" video sequences are shown in Table 1. We consider a two-layer UEP scheme where the first, HPL, contains selected more important partitions, and the second, LPL, contains the remaining partitions. The UEP schemes are described by UEP(p_1, p_2), where p_1 and p_2 represent the selection probabilities of packets from HPL and LPL, respectively, and the optimal solution can be found as shown in Section 4.

TABLE 1: Partition sizes for the first GOP of "Paris" and "Football" sequences.

Partition	Paris		Football	
	Size	Cum. PSNR	Size	Cum. PSNR
IDR	22281	—	23374	—
DP A	12838	30.13	22823	—
DP B	97	30.32	2893	25.39
DP C	45732	39.16	31731	32.62
Total	80948	39.16	80821	32.62

TABLE 2: Priority class and LT packetization for first GOP of "Paris" sequence.

Class	DP	PSNR	Number of bytes	Number of LT packets
HPL	IDR + DP A	30.13	35119	502
LPL	DP B+ DP C	39.16	45829	655
Total		80,948	39.16	80948	1157

TABLE 3: Priority class and LT packetization for first GOP of "Football" sequence.

Class	DP	PSNR	Number of bytes	Number of LT packets
HPL	IDR + DP A + DP B	25.39	49090	702
LPL	DP C	32.62	31731	453
Total		80,821	32.62	80821	1155

In Tables 2 and 3 we show the classification of the DPs and the resulting LT packets, for the "Paris" and "Football" sequences, respectively.

After FEC coding, one encoded symbol (together with RTP/UDP/IP headers) is placed in an IP packet and is subjected to a uniform and Gilbert loss pattern with average loss rates of 5, 10, 15, and 20%. For the Gilbert model the average burst length is 5. We assume use of header compression, and thus a 4-byte header is considered. The base data rate is set to 1000 kbps, and the successively higher rates are obtained by adding roughly 10% additional symbols, up to a rate 1.5 times higher than the base rate.

The simulations are performed using one slice per frame and a frame rate of 25 frames per second (fps). The selected schemes are simulated with 100 runs for each GOP. In cases where the entire GOP is lost, the PSNR is obtained using the last frame of the previously decoded GOP to replace all frames of the lost GOP.

We report results for the EEP and UEP schemes and compare them to the results obtained with two optimized RASSA schemes: SS-PSNR and SS-Rate schemes. The results with frame-by-frame average PSNR performance of the five selected configurations at 1.1Mbps for selected packet loss rates are shown in Figures 2 and 3, for the "Paris" and "Football" sequences, respectively. "Opt-UEP" denotes the scheme that is optimized for each packet loss rate. As can be seen from Figure 3, the performance of the EEP scheme is the worst. The performance of the UEP schemes gets better with an increase in the protection of HPL. UEP(60,40) performs worse as compared to UEP(80,20) because the protection gets divided over both segments and none is protected enough. SS-PSNR performs the best of all the schemes. For the "Football" sequence performance of the optimized UEP scheme is very close to that of the SS-PSNR. Similar results with the same parameters as Figure 2 are shown in Figure 4 for burst loss.

The results showing PSNR performance of the five selected configurations at 10% packet loss rates for different data rates are shown in Figures 5 and 6, for the "Paris" and "Football" sequences, respectively. The performance of the EEP scheme gets progressively better at higher data rates. SS-PSNR and SS-Rate provide reliable and consistent performance at all the data rates. UEP(80,20) is limited to 30 dB in Figure 5 even at higher rates because the DP C is not getting enough protection. Interestingly, at the highest rate the EEP scheme is better than the optimized UEP scheme,

due to the absence of the performance penalty introduced by DP. In Figure 7 the results for the burst channel model are given.

6. Sliced AVC Transmission

In this section we present our simulation results with the slicing feature. For simplicity, we consider the case of $L = 2$ layers: HPL that contains more important slices and LPL that contains less important slices [13]. The same video parameters are used as in the previous subsection.

The sizes, number of packets, and resulting PSNR values for the "Paris" video sequence are shown in Table 4.

The results are shown in Figures 8 and 9 and confirm the analysis carried out with the DP schemes. SS-PSNR is the best scheme overall. The UEP schemes, except UEP(45,55) in Figure 9, are around 24 dB as they suffer from an overprotection of HPL. This is because the HPL size is only about 43% of the GOP size. This highlights the significance of considering the HPL size while designing UEP schemes. The EEP scheme becomes better than the UEP schemes at high data rates. Figure 10 shows the results for the burst loss model. Similar results are obtained for the "Football" sequence.

7. Discussion and Future Work

Although both DP and slicing have been demonstrated to enable efficient layered video data transmission, the results with DP are seen to be better. The sizes and number of DPs generated are as determined by the encoder. The prioritization of data into various partitions is thus optimum and can easily be used to create different rate points. Slicing, on the other hand, is more flexible as it allows for a finer layered structure. Moreover, in contrast to DP, slicing is available in the baseline AVC profile. However, simulation results show small advantage of the DP-based

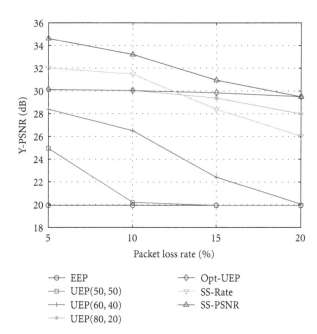

FIGURE 2: PSNR versus PLR at overall data rate of 1.1 Mbps for the "Paris" sequence—uniform loss.

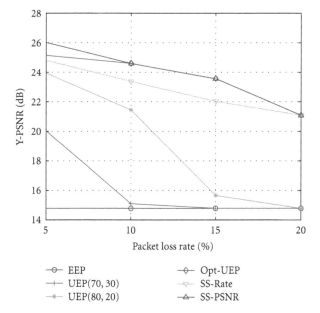

FIGURE 3: PSNR versus PLR at overall data rate of 1.1 Mbps for the "Football" sequence—Uniform Loss.

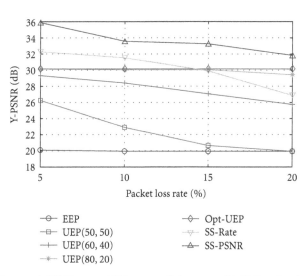

FIGURE 4: PSNR versus PLR at overall data rate of 1.1 Mbps for the "Paris" sequence—burst loss.

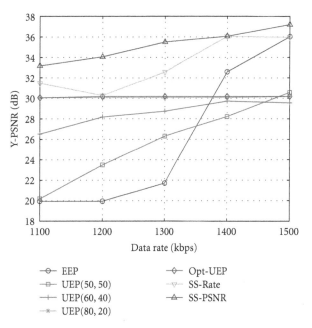

FIGURE 5: PSNR versus data rate at PLR of 10% for the "Paris" sequence—uniform loss.

scheme compared to the slicing-based, especially at high packet loss rates.

The performance of different coding schemes with segmented H.264/AVC video data has been analyzed. The segmented data can be selected to suit the available data rate and channel conditions. The UEP schemes provide better performance over EEP at some rates only. The RASSA scheme can be used to match the available transmission video data to the instantaneous channel conditions. It combines the best of both the EEP and UEP schemes to provide

better and reliable video quality even in the worst channel conditions. The passing of the video-table to the decoder is a low-cost solution to an "all or nothing" decoding. Note that it is assumed that the video is pre-encoded, and thus the best way to match the source rate with the channel rate is to selectively drop some of the DPs, which is done in RASSA. Indeed, the results presented here show that the pure UEP with fixed source rate suffers huge performance loss compared to the scheme that adjusts the source rate. The main advantage of the proposed scheme is a very simple adaptation of the source rate via DP AVC coding. Note that RASSA can be combined with UEP to better match source and channel characteristics. However, that

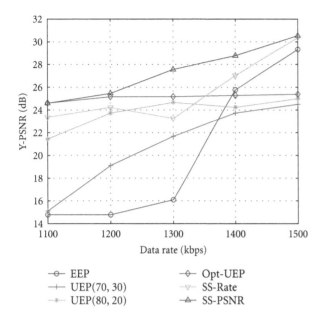

FIGURE 6: PSNR versus data rate at PLR of 10% for the "Football" sequence—uniform loss.

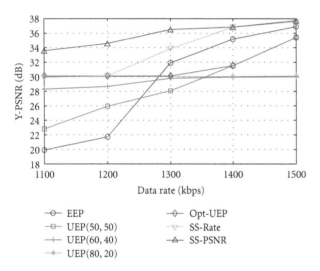

FIGURE 7: PSNR versus data rate at PLR of 10% for the "Paris" sequence—burst loss.

TABLE 4: Priority class and LT packetization for first GOP of "Paris" sequence.

Class	Size (bytes)	Cum. PSNR	Number of LT packets
HPL	34779	24.3	497
LPL	45536	39.08	651
Total	80315	39.08	1148

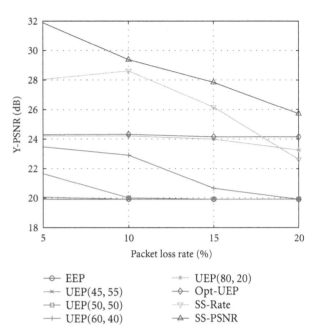

FIGURE 8: PSNR versus PLR at overall data rate of 1.1 Mbps for "Paris" sequence—uniform loss.

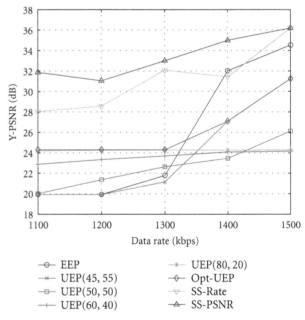

FIGURE 9: PSNR versus Data rate at PLR of 10% for the "Paris" sequence—uniform loss.

would require multiple channel codes, increased complexity, UEP optimization algorithms, and reduction of the channel code length used could worsen channel codes' correction capabilities. This will be part of future work by incorporating expanding window codes [6].

The combined use of FEC and adaptively dropping some DPs to maximize PSNR is thus shown as a practical method to ensure reliable delivery of multimedia data over wireless channels.

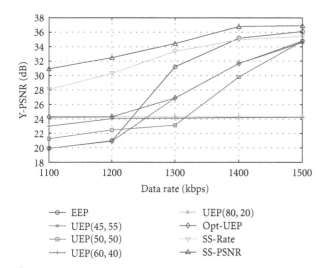

FIGURE 10: PSNR versus data rate at PLR of 10% for the "Paris" sequence—burst loss.

Acknowledgment

D. Vukobratović was supported by a Marie Curie European Reintegration Grant FP7-PEOPLE-ERG-2010 "MMCODE-STREAM" within the 7th European Community Framework Programme.

References

[1] M. Mitzenmacher, "Digital fountains: a survey and look forward," in *Proceedings of the IEEE Information Theory Workshop (ITW '04)*, pp. 271–276, San Antonio, Tex, USA, October 2004.

[2] M. Luby, "LT codes," in *Proceedings of the 43rd Annual IEEE Symposium on Foundations of Computer Science*, pp. 271–280, 2002.

[3] A. Shokrollahi, "Raptor codes," *IEEE Transactions on Information Theory*, vol. 52, no. 6, pp. 2551–2567, 2006.

[4] S. Wenger, "H.264/AVC over IP," *IEEE Transactions on Circuits and Systems for Video Technology*, vol. 13, no. 7, pp. 645–656, 2003.

[5] R. Hamzaoui, V. Stanković, and Z. Xiong, "Optimized error protection of scalable image bit streams," *IEEE Signal Processing Magazine*, vol. 22, no. 6, pp. 91–107, 2005.

[6] D. Vukobratovic, V. Stankovic, D. Sejdinovic, L. Stankovic, and Z. Xiong, "Scalable video multicast using expanding window fountain codes," *IEEE Transactions on Multimedia*, vol. 11, no. 6, pp. 1094–1104, 2009.

[7] S. Ahmad, R. Hamzaoui, and M. M. Al-Akaidi, "Unequal error protection using fountain codes with applications to video communication," *IEEE Transactions on Multimedia*, vol. 13, no. 1, pp. 92–101, 2011.

[8] A. G. Dimakis, J. Wang, and K. Ramchandran, "Unequal growth codes: intermediate performance and unequal error protection for video streaming," in *Proceedings of the 9th IEEE International Workshop on Multimedia Signal Processing (MMSP '07)*, pp. 107–110, Crete, Greece, October 2007.

[9] L. Al-Jobouri, M. Fleury, and M. Ghanbari, "Adaptive rateless coding for data-partitioned video streaming over a broadband wireless channel," in *Proceedings of the 6th Conference on Wireless Advanced (WiAD '10)*, pp. 1–6, June 2010.

[10] H. Schwarz, D. Marpe, and T. Wiegand, "Overview of the scalable video coding extension of the H.264/AVC standard," *IEEE Transactions on Circuits and Systems for Video Technology*, vol. 17, no. 9, pp. 1103–1120, 2007.

[11] R. Razavi, M. Fleury, M. Altaf, H. Sammak, and M. Ghanbari, "H.264 video streaming with data-partitioning and growth codes," in *Proceedings of the 16th IEEE International Conference on Image Processing (ICIP '09)*, pp. 909–912, Cairo, Egypt, October 2009.

[12] ETSI Technical Specification, "Universal mobile telecommunications system (umts); multimedia broadcast/multicast service (mbms); protocols and codecs," ETSI TS 126 346, 2005.

[13] S. Nazir, D. Vukobratovic, and V. Stankovic, "Scalable broadcasting of sliced H.264/AVC over DVB-H network," in *Proceedings of the IEEE International Conference on Networks, Special Session on Robust and Scalable Multimedia Networking (ICON '11)*, Singapore, December 2011.

[14] H.264/AVC Reference Software, http://iphome.hhi.de/suehring/tml/.

Performance Evaluation of an Object Management Policy Approach for P2P Networks

Dario Vieira,[1] Cesar A. V. Melo,[2] and Yacine Ghamri-Doudane[3,4]

[1] LRIE Lab, École d'Ingénieur des Technologies de l'Information et de la Communication (EFREI), 94800 Villejuif, France
[2] Department of Computing Science, Federal University of Amazonas, 69077-000 Manaus, AM, Brazil
[3] École Nationale Supérieure d'Informatique pour l'Industrie et l'Entreprise (ENSIIE), 91025 Evry, France
[4] LIGM Lab, Université Paris-Est, 75420 Champs-sur-Marne, France

Correspondence should be addressed to Dario Vieira, dario.vieira@efrei.fr

Academic Editor: Ivan Lee

The increasing popularity of network-based multimedia applications poses many challenges for content providers to supply efficient and scalable services. Peer-to-peer (P2P) systems have been shown to be a promising approach to provide large-scale video services over the Internet since, by nature, these systems show high scalability and robustness. In this paper, we propose and analyze an object management policy approach for video web cache in a P2P context, taking advantage of object's metadata, for example, video popularity, and object's encoding techniques, for example, scalable video coding (SVC). We carry out trace-driven simulations so as to evaluate the performance of our approach and compare it against traditional object management policy approaches. In addition, we study as well the impact of churn on our approach and on other object management policies that implement different caching strategies. A YouTube video collection which records over 1.6 million video's log was used in our experimental studies. The experiment results have showed that our proposed approach can improve the performance of the cache substantially. Moreover, we have found that neither the simply enlargement of peers' storage capacity nor a zero replicating strategy is effective actions to improve performance of an object management policy.

1. Introduction

The increasing popularity of network-based multimedia applications poses many challenges for content providers to supply efficient and scalable services. Peer-to-peer (P2P) systems have been shown to be a promising approach to provide large-scale video services over the Internet since, by nature, these systems show high scalability and robustness.

One of the essential problems in measuring how these systems perform is the analysis of their properties in the presence of churn, a collective effect created by the independent arrival and departure of peers. Resiliency, key design parameters, and content availability are issues in P2P systems that are influenced by the churn. Hence, the user-driven dynamics of peer participation must be taken into account in both design and evaluation of any P2P system and its related mechanics, such as object management policies. For instance, when peers go off-line, the locally stored data become unavailable

as well. This temporary content unavailability can lead to congestion on backbone links due to the extra traffic generated by requesting to the original content provider.

The main contributions of this paper are as follows.

(1) First, we propose and analyze an object management policy approach for videos' web cache in a P2P context. In this approach we exploit the object's metadata, for example, video popularity, and object's encoding techniques, for example, scalable video coding (SVC). In Section 5, we describe the object management policy based on popularity (POP); that is, we describe how user-generated content is used to define this object management policy. We have carried out set of studies by using three different scenarios so as to analyze our approach with regarding other object management policies. We evaluated how the insertion, replacement, and discarding of videos impacts

the object management policies. Besides, we study as well the effects of the video popularity and the discarding of video layers in the performance of object management policies. In Section 6 we present the numerical results collected from these simulation experiments. We show as well how much our content-oriented web cache mechanism can improve traditional web cache mechanisms. Basically, we have found that our approach outperforms the traditional one and consequently reduce the capacity demand poses over the community output link by increasing the hit rate of community demands and optimizing the network resources available.

(2) Second, we study the impact of the user churn on object management policies. For that, we have used a churn model that is based on a stationary alternating renewal process with its average up and down behavior based on the type of peer (cf. Section 4). By using this churn model, we have evaluated the enlargement of individual peer storage capacity as an action to keep policies performance since the community storage capacity will be affected directly by the churn. In Section 7, we present the numerical results collected from these simulation experiments. We can point that peers will be able to store valuable objects over a long time-scale which could improve content availability. We have noted that the gap among all police performance shrinks due to this enlargement. Nonetheless, this enlargement does not impact linearly the performance of the policies.

(3) Finally, we have evaluated on how much the replicated data affects policies performance by measuring it on a system with and without duplicated data. Indeed, each time a peer leaves the system, it will make chunks of popular content unavailable for other peers. Whenever that peer rejoins the system, its content could have been accessed by other peer. Accordingly, data are naturally replicated into the system due to the churn. This naturally replication has as consequence the decreases of the nominal system storage capacity. So, we have evaluated on how much this replicated data affects policies performance by measuring it on a system with and without duplicated data. In Section 7.1, we present the numerical results collected from these simulation experiments. We have found that the performance of policies is impacted, either positively or negatively, by this replicated data which suggests that content availability could be improved whether the volume of duplicated data is under policy control.

We have used in our experimental studies a YouTube video collection, which records over 1.6 million video's log. In our experiments, each peer can store up to 25 short videos of 4:50 minutes—the average video length identified in the studied video collection. The overall storage capacity, which is defined by the sum of the storage capacity of all peers, is equal to one percent of the video collection storage demand

(cf. Section 3). Different simulated scenarios were defined by scaling up the system storage capacity until 20% of the video collection storage demand.

We have evaluated five policies in our experiments: (i) the context-aware and content-oriented policy (POP), (ii) least recently used (LRU) policy, (iii) least frequently used (LFU) policy, (iv) popularity-aware greedy-dual size (GDSP) policy [1], and (v) proportional partial caching (PARTIAL) policy [2]. The last four policies (described in Section 2) are representative implementations of their classes, that is, recency-based, frequency-based, and cost-based policies.

2. Cache Algorithms

This section gives a short overview of the traditional cache algorithms that we use through this paper. Essentially, these algorithms can be classified into three major flavors of strategies as follows.

Recency-Based Strategies. This kind of approach uses recency as a main factor. Least recently used (LRU) strategy, and all its extensions, is a good example of these strategies. LRU makes use of the locality information to predict future accesses to objects from past accesses. In effect, there are two sorts of locality: (i) temporal locality and (ii) spatial locality. The first one is based on the idea that recently accessed objects are likely to be used again in the future. In the latter approach, the references to some objects suggest accesses to other objects. Recency-based strategies make use of temporal locality; that is, LRU exploits temporal locality. The major disadvantage of these strategies is that they do not consider object size information. Moreover, they do not consider frequency information.

Frequency-Based Strategies. These strategies exploit the frequency as a main factor. They are based on the idea that different objects have different popularity values and this implies that these objects have different frequency values. Accordingly, these values are used for future decisions. The least-frequently used (LFU) is the well-known implementation of these strategies. There are two kinds of implementation of LFU (and its extensions): (i) perfect LFU, which counts all requests to an object. This keeps on across replacement; (ii) in-cache LFU, whose counts are carried out only for cache objects. It should be noted that this does not represent all request in the past. The major disadvantage is that the frequency counts are too static for dynamic environments.

Cost-Based Strategies. In cost-based policies, the importance of an object is defined by a value got from a cost function. When a cache runs out of space, objects are evicted based on their cost; objects with the smallest cost will be evicted first. The greedy-dual size (GDS) policy was the first policy to implement a cost-based cache strategy. It maintains, for each object, a characteristic value H_i which is set in the very first request and calculated every time the object is requested. Improvements on GDS policy have been implemented to

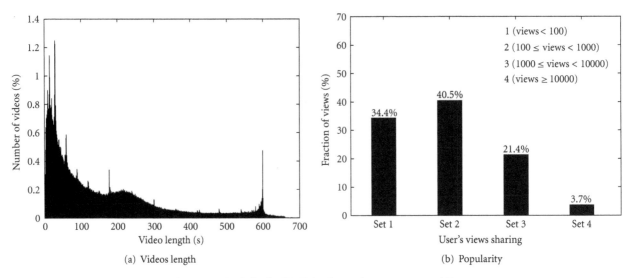

(a) Videos length

(b) Popularity

FIGURE 1: Statistics for YouTube Entertainment category [3].

3. Video Collection

In this section, we present the video collection used so as to carry out our experiments. Our dataset consists of meta-information about user-generated videos from YouTube services. We limited our experiments to the *Entertainment* category collected by [3] owing to the massive scale of YouTube. This collection consists of 1,687,506 videos where each line represents a single video. Furthermore, each video record contains both fixed and time-varying information (e.g., length, views, ratings, stars, and URL), which means

(1) views and ratings stand for the number of times the video has been played and evaluated by users,

(2) stars stand for the average score from rating, and

(3) URL denotes the list of external web pages hyperlinking the video.

We limited the maximum size of cacheable video to 99 minutes; videos with more than this value are considered crawler mistake. Figure 1(a) depicts videos' length distribution in seconds, with video length being equal to 291 seconds.

Figure 1(b) shows the video popularity distribution. By examining the number of requests recorded in our video collection, we grouped those videos in four sets. In the first set we gathered video with less than 100 views. This subset is made of 34.4% of videos in our collection. In the second subset we gathered videos with a number of views into the range of 100 views and 1000 views, which contains 40.5% of videos in our collection. The third subset has videos with a number of views into the range of 1,000 views and 10,000 views and makes up 21.4% of videos recorded in our collection. Finally, in the fourth subset we gathered videos

that recorded over 10.000 views, which contains 3.7% of videos in our collection. Based on our analysis, we see that video requests are highly concentrated on a small set of videos. In fact, the fourth subset has 60% of the total number of views.

This video collection misses individual user requests information; that is, timestamps mark that record when a user dispatched his/her requests. To deploy our simulation studies, we must have such individual user's behavior. Hence, we developed a procedure to simulate the users' behavior based on information gathered from the video collection. Therefore, in order to use this collection, we define a procedure for the generation of requests, as follows.

(1) All requests will be driven by a combination of the video length and the "think time."

(2) For each two nonpopular videos, we picked up three popular videos. This ratio was derived based on the preview analysis carried over our video collection; that is, we determined the number of (non)popular video views recorded.

(3) The pick-up procedure of popular and not popular videos is independent and follows a uniform distribution.

(4) A popular video must be recorded more than 10,000 views.

The rationales behind our procedure are (i) downloaded videos will be watched end-to-end, and users will spend some time looking for related videos, the thinking time, before dispatching a new request; (ii) over the time scale the system is observed, popular and nonpopular videos will keep their status, a reasonable assumption since we are interested only on the effectiveness of popularity as a criterion to manage those videos; (iii) in our collection, videos with more than 10,000 views represent less than 4% of the whole collection but recorded over 60% of the total number of views.

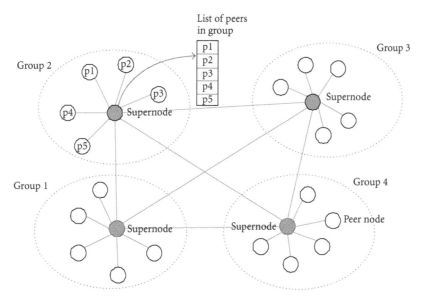

FIGURE 2: Two-tier hierarchy framework.

4. A Hierarchical Content-Oriented Overlay Network

In this section, we present the networking scenario used in our studies. First, the network infrastructure is considered, then we describe how peers are classified and objects are searched in this infrastructure. Finally, the churn model used to characterize peers' dynamics is presented.

4.1. The Network Infrastructure. The network infrastructure is a structured peer-to-peer (P2P) system made by ordinary nodes and supernodes and with peers that are locality-aware clustered into communities or groups. These communities are built around subjects, for example, science, sports, and DIY. Figure 2 illustrates this infrastructure. Peers locality awareness limits content lookups to very few hops into the community. In Crespo and Garcia-Molina [4], similar ideas have been proposed to share music files with overlays being built based on music genres, and lookup operations being bounded to the community.

In this network infrastructure, for each group there is one or more superpeers, which are analogous to gateways routers in hierarchical IP networks. The goal is to use superpeers so as to transmit messages intergroups.

On this networking scenario, the mix of gathered peers defines a community as homogeneous or heterogeneous. Accordingly, peers can be classified based on their up probability and they can be clustered in $\mathcal{T} > 1$ groups. In this paper, we classify and cluster them in four groups (i.e., $\mathcal{T} = 4$) as follows.

(i) *Stable group*, each peer is up with probability big or equal to p.

(ii) *Moderate group*, each peer is up with probability t, but with $p \gg t$.

(iii) *Low group*, each peer is up with probability r, but with $t \gg r$.

(iv) *Unstable group*, each peer is up with probability less or equal to q, but with $r \gg q$.

These peer group's up probabilities are mapped to the peer group's up session duration in our numerical studies as suggested by Wang et al. [5]. Specifically, we studied a community made by peers that fits in a low group behavior; that is, peers up sessions last 28 minutes in average, and a typical YouTube session duration by the time our video collection was collected, according to Wang et al. [5].

4.2. The Churn Model. To model the peers' dynamics, we have exploited a generic churn model defined by Yao et al. [6]. Consider a P2P system with n peers, where each peer i is either UP at time t or DOWN. This behavior can be modeled by a renewal process $\{Z_i(t)\}$ for each peer i:

$$Z_i(t) = \begin{cases} 1, & \text{peer } i \text{ is alive at time } t, \\ 0, & \text{otherwise,} \end{cases} \quad 1 \leq i \leq n. \quad (1)$$

Unlike [6], the UP and DOWN lasting sessions of $\{Z_i(t)\}$ are based on the type of peer i. Therefore, the actual pairs $(F_i(x), G_i(x))$ are chosen randomly from set $\mathcal{F}$ define as follows.

$$\mathcal{F} = \left\{ \left(F^{(1)}(x), G^{(1)}(x) \right), \ldots, \left(F^{(\mathcal{T})}(x), G^{(\mathcal{T})}(x) \right) \right\}, \quad (2)$$

where $\mathcal{T} \geq 1$ is the number of peer types in the system.

Therefore, for each process $\{Z_i(t)\}$, its UP lasting sessions $\{L_{i,c}\}_{c=1}^{\infty}$ have some joint distribution $F_i(x)$, and its DOWN lasting sessions $\{D_{i,c}\}_{c=1}^{\infty}$ have another joint distribution $G_i(x)$, where c stands for cycle number and durations of users and i's UP and DOWN sessions are given by random variables $L_{i,c} > 0$ and $D_{i,c} > 0$, respectively.

Examples of UP/DOWN distributions used throughout this paper are (i) the exponential, defined as

$$F_i' = 1 - e^{-\lambda_i x}, \quad (3)$$

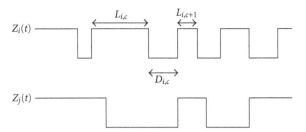

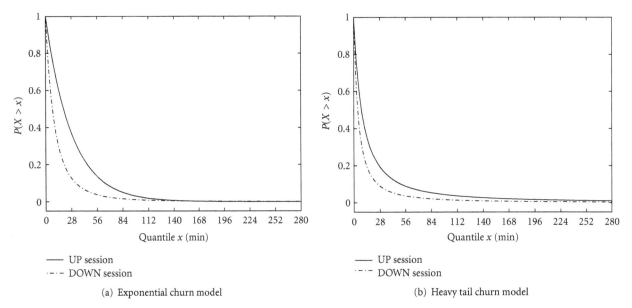

FIGURE 3: Up and down behaviors for peer p_i and p_j. Processes $\{Z_i(t)\}$ and $\{Z_j(t)\}$ are independent.

—— UP session
·-·- DOWN session

(a) Exponential churn model

—— UP session
·-·- DOWN session

(b) Heavy tail churn model

FIGURE 4: Complementary cumulative distribution functions of UP and DOWN session duration used on exponential and heavy tail churn models.

with mean $1/\lambda_i$, and (ii) the Pareto, defined as

$$F_i'' = 1 - \left(1 + \frac{x}{\beta_i}\right)^{\alpha i}, \quad x > 0, \ \alpha_i > 1, \qquad (4)$$

with mean $\beta_i/(\alpha_i - 1)$.

Based on the aforementioned model, the following assumptions are made.

(1) To capture the independent nature of peers, we assume that the set $\{Z_i(t)\}_{i=1}^n$ consists of mutually independent alternating renewal processes, as depicted in the Figure 3. Accordingly, peers behave independently of each other and processes $\{Z_i(t)\}$ and $\{Z_j(t)\}$, for any $i \neq j$, are independent.

(2) Note that l_i, the average UP session duration, and d_i, the average DOWN session duration, are independent and unique for each peer. Once pair $(l_i; d_i)$ is generated for each peer p_i, it remains constant for the entire evolution of the system.

(3) 28-minute YouTube average session duration is set to l_i. In addition, half of the value of l_i is set to d_i. Hence, as regards content availability, a demanding community of peers is expected.

(4) The upprobability of peer i at an arbitrary time instance t is given by

$$p = \lim_{t \to \infty} P(\{Z_i(t)\} = 1) = \frac{l_i}{l_i + d_i}. \qquad (5)$$

Based on previous characterization, two churn models have been used on our studies: heavy tail and exponential. When exponential churn model is applied, the lasting of UP session is driven by $\exp(1/l_i)$ distribution, while the lasting of DOWN session is driven by a *pareto* $(3, d_i)$ distribution, where l_i stands for the expected mean of UP session duration and d_i stands for the expected mean DOWN session duration.

Figure 4(a) shows the complementary cumulative distribution function (CCDF) of the exponential (UP session) and Pareto (DOWN session) distributions when l_i and d_i are set as mentioned previously. For exponential distribution, the probability of chose values greater than the expected ones vanishes after minute 120. However, for Pareto distribution, this probability still exists over large time-scale. This churn pattern can be summarized by the following: peers will stay connected, as they join the community, but will lose interest over time.

```
Require: video_popularity ∨ cache_size ≥ 0
    request_from_community(video);
    if miss_video then
        request_from_outside(video);
    end if
    if video_popularity > threshold then
        insert_cache(video);
    end if
```

ALGORITHM 1: The popularity-based object management policy.

```
Require: video_popularity ∨ cache_size ≥ 0
    if video_popularity > threshold then
        insert_cache(video);
    end if
```

ALGORITHM 2: Considering video popularity.

In the heavy tail churn model, the UP and DOWN sessions are driven by the Pareto distributions. Different from exponential churn model, heavy tail churn model draws probability still significant over time, Figure 4(b), which means that picking a value great than the mean value is highly possible. The churn pattern defined by this heavy tail model can be summarized by the following: peers will keep interest on content over long time-scales.

5. POP: A Content-Oriented Management Policy Based on Popularity

As mentioned in Section 4.1, peers will cooperate and the interesting-oriented community has very useful information to improve the cache system performance. In this context, the probability that a video comes to be accessed again by other members of a community is higher than that in a general case since members inside a community might share common interests. Hence, the question about how much popular a video is inside a community seems to be an important metadata to be considered when implementing an object management policy.

Based on the aforementioned assumptions, we have developed an object management policy [7], that is, the popularity-based (POP) policy. In this object management policy, we keep the most popular video in cache (number of visualizations) based on a predefined threshold. The rationale of our policy is that the majority of video requests is targeted to the popular ones, hence keeping the cache filled by the popular video will probably improve the hit rate and decrease the volume of traffic that flows outside the community link. Algorithm 1 describes this procedure.

As said, the threshold used to identify popular videos is a predefined value and closed related to video collection statistics. In our studies we set the threshold equal to 10,000 visualizations which defines a popular video collection with less than 4% of the whole video collection, at the same time, this popular video collection has over 60% of all visualizations. In summary, the threshold setting procedure will reduce the number of videos that have to be managers, but those videos will receive the majority of requests.

6. Performance Analysis of POP

In this section we show the numerical results collected from our first studies. We evaluated how the insertion, replacement, and discarding of videos impact the object management policies. To evaluate the effectiveness of our proposed policy, we defined a reference scenario and we compared it to three other different scenarios so as to evaluate the performance of the POP. For that, we assume that peers are always connected to the system, a borrowed concept from [5] which identifies and describes the importance of stable peers.

6.1. Numerical Results. We use a trace-driven simulation to evaluate our proposed policy. The simulated P2P network has 10,000 peers, and we assume that there is only one community where each peer can connect to any other peer. Each peer has a cache with capacity to storage up to 1.000 seconds of video. The total number of video requests is 200,000, and we consider that videos with more than a *threshold value* are popular. In our experiments, the threshold value is equal to 10,000 views.

6.2. Reference Scenario. In this scenario, we establish the following conditions: (i) every requested (and not yet cached) video must be added to the cache, (ii) LRU is the object replacement policy implemented by the web cache, and (iii) the whole video will be discarded when the managed cache is full. Taking into consideration these assumptions, we simulated the user requests based on a uniform distribution. As we have pointed out, the results are then compared with three other scenarios, which are described as follows.

6.3. Scenario Number 1. In this scenario, we evaluated the effects of the video popularity on the performance of our web cache. Instead of adding all referenced, and not yet cached videos, we keep only cached videos that are considered popular, that is, videos that have a number of views greater than 10,000. The rationale of our policy is that the majority of video requests is targeted to the popular ones, hence keeping the cache filled by the popular video will probably improve the hit rate and decrease the volume of traffic that flow outside the community link. In summary, in scenario number 1 we cached only popular videos, the object management policy is still the LRU, and the whole video is discarded when the managed cache is full.

Algorithm 2 describes the patched applied to the object management policy; that is, the execution of function *insert_cache(·)* is conditioned to the video popularity. Figures 5 and 6, the first bars, show the improvements, in terms of hit rate (35.2%) and volume of traffic that is saved (36.2%), when that new policy is implemented.

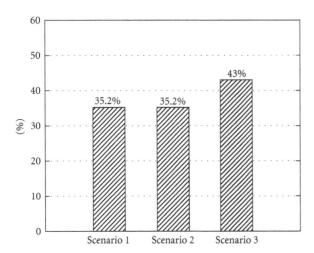

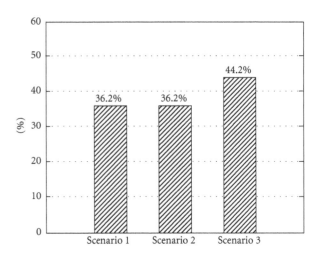

FIGURE 5: Hit rate—based on reference scenario.

FIGURE 6: Traffic volume reduction—based on reference scenario.

```
Require: free_cache_size ∨ video_size
  While free_cache_size < video_size do
    (video,node) ⇐ LRU_video_object();
    nlayers ⇐ discard_highest_layer(video, node);
    if nlayers = 0 then
      nlayers ⇐ discard_highest_layer(video, node);
      remove_reference_DHT(video, node);
    end if
  end while
```

ALGORITHM 3: Discarding layers, the local approach.

```
Require: free_cache_size ∨ video_size
  While free_cache_size < video_size do
    (video, node) ⇐ random_video_object();
    nlayers ⇐ discard_highest_layer(video, node);
    if nlayers = 0 then
      nlayers ⇐ discard_highest_layer(video, node);
      remove_reference_DHT(video, node);
    end if
  end while
```

ALGORITHM 4: Discarding layers, the global approach.

6.4. Scenario Number 2. In this scenario, we evaluated the effects of the video popularity and the discarding of video layers on the performance of our object management policy. Differently to the scenario number 1, we dispose only video layers that are coding to improve the video quality and hence keep those layers that have the minimum amount of data to the receiver reproduce his/her requested video. The least recently used criterion is applied to elect which video must have its layers discarded. Whether the room made available by the discarded layer is still insufficient to store the recently accessed video, a new video is elected and its layer is discarded. This process is repeated until the web cache has sufficient space to store the recently referenced video. The rationale of our policy is to keep as much as possible a popular video cached, even it is a low-quality copy, since references to it are very probable.

Algorithm 3 presents the patch applied to object management policy. Function *LRU_video_object(·)* finds the least recently used cached object and returns both that video and the node that has the object. Function *discard_highest_layer (video, node)* discards the highest layer of the found video. For example, if there are two layers for this video in cache, the second, which has less priority, will be discarded. Additionally, after calling the *discard_highest_layer(·)* function no

layers could remain for that video, hence the reference for this video must be removed from distributed hash table (DHT). Figures 5 and 6, the second bars, show the improvements in term of hit rate (35.2%) and saved traffic (36.2%) when a new policy is implemented.

6.5. Scenario Number 3. In this scenario, we introduce the layer discarding policy associated with a global approach instead of the local one deployed in scenario number 2. In other words, we randomly selected objects in cache and discarded the highest layer of this object. The rationale of our approach is that when a cache run out of space, we have a set of high popular videos cached with all those video showing a high requesting rate. Hence when we apply the discarding policy over the whole set of videos, and not just over the "least" recently used set, we will increase the set of popular videos that can be cached. Consequently, we can observe an improvement over the hit rate. In summary, scenario number 3 has only popular video cached, a random object replacement policy, and video layers are discarded when cache is full.

Algorithm 4 presents the patches applied to the object management policy. Function *random_video_object(·)* picks a cached object and returns both the targeted video and node that has that object.

Figures 5 and 6, the third bars, show the improvements in terms of hit rate (43%) and saved traffic (44.2%) when the new policy is implemented.

6.6. Discussions. Requests to popular video are much more probe than nonpopular videos; over 60% of requests recorded in our video collection are targeted to popular videos. In addition, popular videos made just 3.7% of our video collection. Based on these facts, we tested the video popularity metadata as the criteria to cache or dispose recently accessed videos. As noted from scenario number 1, there was a 30% improvement in the cache hit rate, compared to the traditional approach, reassuring that bringing metadata associated to the objects will save the network resources with server communities that were built around subjects.

Although 30% improvement is remarkable, we learnt that traditional web cache policies do not assume anything about the managed objects. In the scenario number 3, we exploit the fact that videos are distributed in layers. Besides, we use a discarding policy based on those layers instead of discarding the whole video, as implemented on traditional web cache policy. We underline that the discarding of layers does not constrain a web cache to server requests to that video; that is, videos can be served, for instance, in a low definition instead of high definition. As a result, whenever a cache runs out of space and a new object needs to be cached, the number of cached videos increase since the discarding of a whole video will be postponed, at least in the first moment.

An important finding to be explained is how LRU policy and video layers discarding policy are related, as pointed in scenario number 2. In this scenario, we discard video layers that belong to the set of the least recently used videos. Nonetheless, this situation does not offer any improvement in both the number and quality of cached objects. This happens because the group of least used objects is very small (only popular video are cached), which heavily restrict the space where our discarding policy can act to improve the number of cached videos.

We noted as well that bringing video metadata (i.e., video popularity) into an object management policy associated with a global layers discard policy can increase substantially the quality and number of cached videos. Consequently, this improves the cache hit rate and saved traffic measured over the output link. Using these approaches, we got over 40% improvement which could mean to postpone updates over an output link.

7. Numerical Results

In this section, we have carried out some studies so as to evaluate the impact of the churn on object management policies implemented by peers. Accordingly, we have set up a peer-to-peer-assisted video distribution system, compare Section 4, and we have measured the decreasing ratio, that is, on how much the policy performance measured by the hit rate is impacted by the churn. The decreasing ratio is defined by the following equation:

$$\text{HR}_{\text{Decr}} = 1 - \frac{\text{HR}_{\text{With}}}{\text{HR}_{\text{Without}}}, \tag{6}$$

where HR_{With} and $\text{HR}_{\text{Without}}$ are, respectively, the measured hit rates in a system with and without churn. In our experiments, we have employed both exponential and heavy tail churn models (cf. Section 4.2).

As we have pointed out, the accomplishment of an object management policy is affected by the performance metrics taken into account. For instance, the LRU policy can have high hit rate but performs poorly in term of byte hit rate. Therefore, we have studied also the decreasing ratio defined by the byte hit rate collected in a system with and without churn. From a qualitative stand point of view, the impacts measured by the decreasing ratio defined by both, hit rate and byte hit rate, are similar. Hence, we show as well the decreasing ratio defined by (6).

We have evaluated five policies: the context-aware and content-oriented policy (POP) [7], least recently used (LRU) policy, least frequently used (LFU) policy, popularity-aware greedy-dual size (GDSP) policy [1], and proportional partial caching (PARTIAL) policy [2]. The last four policies are representative implementations of their classes, that is, recency-based, frequency-based, and cost-based policies.

In our experiments, each peer can store up to 25 short videos of 4:50 minutes—the average video length identified in the studied video collection. The overall storage capacity, which is defined by the sum of the storage capacity of all peers, is equal to one percent of the video collection storage demand, see Section 3. We have defined different simulated scenarios by scaling up the system storage capacity until 20% of the video collection storage demand.

Figure 7 depicts the impact of the churn in term of decreasing on hit rate, when both exponential and heavy tail models drive the churn. Although their decreasing ratios, defined by (7), have different values, all policies' behavior is as follows: the gap among their performance shrinks as the system storage capacity is enlarged. However, this enlargement does not impact linearly the performance of policies. Specifically, for an enlargement of 20% in the system storage capacity, LFU policy has recorded a variation of 36% (29%) on its decreasing ratio for the exponential (heavy tail) churn model. LRU shows a variation of 34% (27%), while GDSP shows a variation of 33% (24%) and PARTIAL shows variation of 29% (23%).

The performance of POP policy represents an exception in the previous conclusion, specially for heavy tail churn model where the variation on its decreasing ratio is equal to 20%. That is, for the POP policy, the impact of churn is linearly reduced by the system enlargement. The volume of replicated data is the main reason for that performance (cf. Section 7.1).

The enlargement of the system storage capacity impacts policies performance, especially for exponential churn model where variations in the decreasing ratio are more pronounced as this enlargement happens. Figure 8 depicts the decreasing of system size, that is, the shrinking on the number of UP peers, when exponential and heavy tail churn models drive the joining and leaving events. When the churn is driven by the heavy tail model, the maximum decreasing on system size is 39%, whereas for exponential model, this value is 48%. As a general system design observation, we

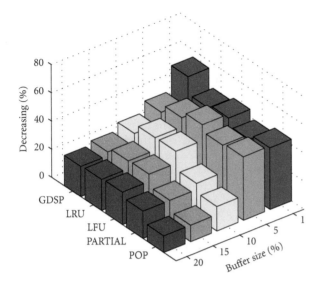

(a) Exponential churn model

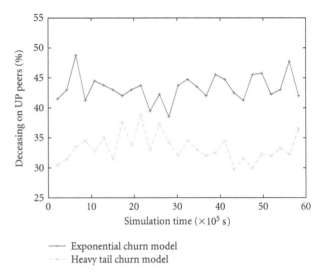

FIGURE 8: The decreasing on number of UP peers.

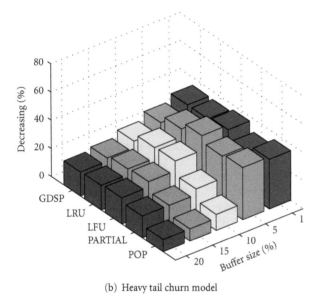

(b) Heavy tail churn model

FIGURE 7: Decreasing ratio of object management policies (see (6)).

have noted that, since strong assumption on peers' storage capacity could jeopardize the system implementation, P2P-assisted systems have to deploy mechanisms to keep, over large time-scales, peers interested on content made available by communities.

7.1. Replicated Data.

Each time a peer leaves the system, it will make chunks of popular content unavailable for other peers. Whenever that peer rejoins the system, its content could have been accessed by an other peer. This dynamic replicates data over peers that share interest and, consequently, decreases the nominal system storage capacity. Figure 9 shows the percentage of data that has been replicated into the system due to the churn.

For LRU, LFU, and GDSP policies, the maximum amount of replicated data demands 20% of storage capacity.

However, for the two other policies, PARTIAL and POP, the amount of replicated data is around 25% and over 45%, respectively. The POP policy can handle twice as much replicated data than other policies. Since the POP policy keeps only objects with certain number of views (10,000 views in our experiments) and this requirement is too restrictive, the amount of replicated data grows rapidly due to the churn.

Resilience to failure is a key property of P2P systems. In this context, every time a peer A fails in delivering a service, which is under its responsibility, another peer will replace the peer A so as to deliver this service. This property has consequences in the proposed video distribution system; that is, the studied policies have to handle replicated data held independently by peers. From the preview results, at least 20% of stored data is replicated ones, this value being greater than 45% when the POP policy is used.

To measure the impact of replicating on policy performance, we have performed experiments by using the following nonreplicating procedure: peers must evict any replicated video every time they rejoin the system.

In this new scenario, we have computed the decreasing ratios as follows:

$$HR_{DecrNorep} = 1 - \frac{HR_{NorepWith}}{HR_{Without}}, \qquad (7)$$

where $HR_{NorepWith}$ is the collected hit rate in a system with churn but without replicated data, and $HR_{Without}$ is the hit rate in a system without churn.

Figure 10 shows the decreasing ratio for all studies' policies. We have noted that in spite of the enlargement of the system storage capacities, the decreasing ratio is around 40% when the exponential churn model drives the joining and leaving dynamics. For peers under the heavy tail churn model, this decreasing ratio is around 20% (see Figure 10(b)).

Compared to results showed in Figure 7, the performance of policies under both churn models reduces by 50%.

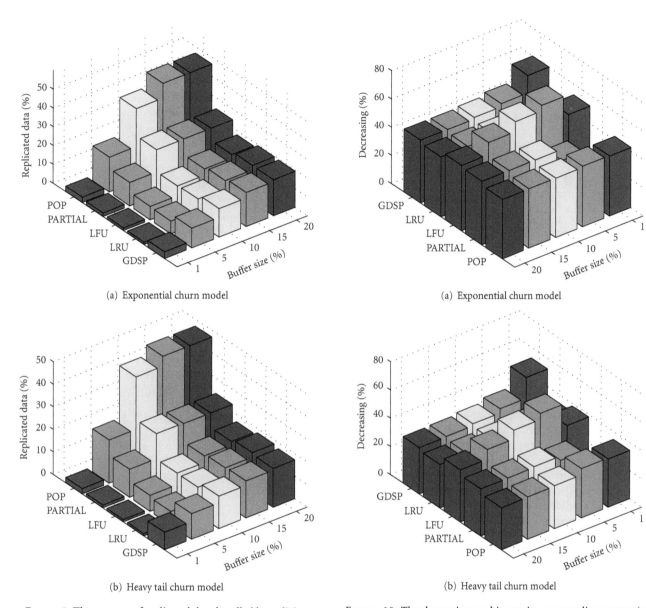

(a) Exponential churn model

(b) Heavy tail churn model

FIGURE 9: The amount of replicated data handled by policies.

(a) Exponential churn model

(b) Heavy tail churn model

FIGURE 10: The decreasing on hit rate in a nonreplica system (see (7)).

This suggests that (i) an enlarged storage capacity has limited impact over policies performance and (ii) a controlled amount of replicated data tends to improve the performance of policies. In fact, it is under evaluation an algorithm to support replicating. Peers that just initiated the leaving procedure will use this algorithm to spread objects' metadata in order to support the decisions made by other peers during the evicting process.

8. Related Work

Several approaches (e.g., [8]) have been proposed in the literature so as to deal with video caching. In these approaches, whether a video or some part of it cannot be found in local proxies, it can be requested from the original central provider. In a P2P video system, however, there is no such central

video server nor does any peer guarantee the availability of any data it caches.

Zink et al. [9] and Cha et al. [3] strongly suggest that metrics such as object popularity has to be considered in-cache object management policies. These studies show that popular and nonpopular videos access ratio is 2 in 3, despite popular video collection is being made of just 3.7% of the whole video collection. Although Zink et al. [9] show that local popularity has a weak correlation with the global popularity, still most of the accessed videos are the local popular ones.

Kulkarni and Devetsikiotis [10] propose the design of a distributed cache similar in principle to a content distribution network (CDN). The goal is to select some of the most valuable objects and bring them closer to the clients requesting them so that redundant load on the network is reduced. Social network analysis techniques were used to identify the most valuable objects that should be cached. While Kulkarni's work focus is to determine the measurements that can be used to define the objects popularity, our goal is to verify the effectiveness of such measurements in the implementation of a cache approach based on P2P systems.

The behavior of P2P system under churn is one of the most fundamental issues of P2P research (e.g., [6, 11, 12]). Several approaches (e.g., [11, 13]) have dealt with churn by investigating its characteristics (e.g., median session length) in large-scale P2P systems. Gummadi et al. [11] measure session lengths by monitoring a router at the University of Washington. Sripanidkulchai et al. [13] study the live streaming workload of a large-content delivery system and present an analysis characterizing popularity, arrival process, and session length.

9. Conclusions

In this paper we studied object management policies in a peer-to-peer network context. While traditional object management policies were built around only three object proprieties, that is, aging, size, and frequency, we built our policy around user-generated content and metadata made available by content providers. We used video popularity and took advantage of video-encoding techniques to build our policy. We have carried out a set of simulation experiments so as to evaluate the performance of our approach. In the first part of our simulation experiments, we have observed that our approach outperforms the traditional one and consequently will reduce the capacity demand poses over the community output link by increasing the hit rate of community demands and optimizing the network resources available.

We have studied as well the impact of the churn on the object management policies. We evaluated the enlargement of peer's storage capacity as an action to keep policies performance since the system storage capacity will be affected by the churn. Though the gap among a policy's performance shrinks as we enlarged the storage capacity, it does not impact proportionally a policy performance.

Also, we have carried out studies to look into how replicated data impact the performance of object management policies. We found that the worst case scenario, in terms of content availability, is for a system without replicated data. Despite the enlargement of the storage capacity, in general, we have not seen improvements on policies performance for such systems. On the other hand, replicating due to the churn improved the performance of policies to a certain level. However, we have shown from the POP policies performance, whether the amount of duplicated data is under policy control, the content availability could be greatly improved.

As future works, we have looked into mechanisms to control the amount of replicated data through the system and investigated whether or not incentive-based peer participating mechanisms, developed for other content distribution systems, could be applied in such hybrid P2P-CDN system.

References

[1] S. Jin and A. Bestavros, "Popularity-aware greedy dual-size web proxy caching algorithms," in *Proceedings of the The 20th International Conference on Distributed Computing Systems (ICDCS '00)*, IEEE Computer Society, Washington, DC, USA, 2000.

[2] M. Hefeeda and O. Saleh, "Traffic modeling and proportional partial caching for peer-to-peer systems," in *Proceedings of the IEEE/ACM Transactions on Networking*, vol. 16, pp. 1447–1460, IEEE Press, Piscataway, NJ, USA, 2008.

[3] M. Cha, H. Kwak, P. Rodriguez, Y. Y. Ahnt, and S. Moon, "I tube, you tube, everybody tubes: analyzing the world's largest user generated content video system," in *Proceedings of the 7th ACM SIGCOMM Internet Measurement Conference (IMC '07)*, pp. 1–14, October 2007.

[4] A. Crespo and H. Garcia-Molina, "Semantic overlay networks for P2P systems," in *Agents and Peer-to-Peer Computing*, vol. 3601 of *Lecture Notes in Computer Science*, pp. 1–13, Springer, Berlin, Germany, 2005.

[5] F. Wang, J. Liu, and Y. Xiong, "Stable peers: existence, importance, and application in peer-to-peer live video streaming," in *Proceedings of the 27th IEEE International Conference on Computer Communications, Joint Conference of the IEEE Computer and Communications Societies (INFOCOM '08)*, pp. 1364–1372, IEEE Computer Society, Phoenix, Ariz, USA, 2008.

[6] Z. Yao, D. Leonard, X. Wang, and D. Loguinov, "Modeling heterogeneous user churn and local resilience of unstructured P2P networks," in *Proceedings of the IEEE International Conference on Network Protocols, (ICNP '06)*, pp. 32–41, Washington, DC, USA, 2006.

[7] A. Bezerra, C. Melo, D. Vieira, Y. Ghamri-Doudane, and N. Fonseca, "A content-oriented web cache policy," in *Proceedings of the IEEE Latin-American Conference on Communications, (LATINCOM '09)*, pp. 1–6, September 2009.

[8] Z. Miao and A. Ortega, "Scalable proxy caching of video under storage constraints," *IEEE Journal on Selected Areas in Communications*, vol. 20, no. 7, pp. 1315–1327, 2002.

[9] M. Zink, K. Suh, Y. Gu, and J. Kurose, "Watch global, cache local: youtube network traffic at a campus network—measurements and implications," in *Proceedings of the Multimedia Computing and Networking Conference, (MMCN '08)*, January 2008.

[10] V. Kulkarni and M. Devetsikiotis, "Communication timescales, structure and popularity: using social network metrics for youtube-like multimedia content distribution," in *Proceedings of the IEEE International Conference on Communications, (ICC '10)*, May 2010.

[11] K. P. Gummadi, R. J. Dunn, S. Saroiu, S. D. Gribble, H. M. Levy, and J. Zahorjan, "Measurement, modeling, and analysis of a Peer-to-peer file-sharing workload," in *Proceedings of the 19th ACM Symposium on Operating Systems Principles, (SOSP '03)*, pp. 314–329, ACM, New York, NY, USA, October 2003.

[12] D. Leonard, Z. Yao, V. Rai, and D. Loguinov, "On lifetime-based node failure and stochastic resilience of decentralized peer-to-peer networks," *IEEE/ACM Transactions on Networking*, vol. 15, no. 3, pp. 644–656, 2007.

[13] K. Sripanidkulchai, B. Maggs, and H. Zhang, "An analysis of live streaming workloads on the internet," in *Proceedings of the ACM SIGCOMM Internet Measurement Conference, (IMC '04)*, pp. 41–54, New York, NY, USA, October 2004.

3

Adjustable Two-Tier Cache for IPTV Based on Segmented Streaming

Kai-Chun Liang and Hsiang-Fu Yu

Department of Computer Science, National Taipei University of Education, Taipei 106, Taiwan

Correspondence should be addressed to Hsiang-Fu Yu, yu@tea.ntue.edu.tw

Academic Editor: Pin-Han Ho

Internet protocol TV (IPTV) is a promising Internet killer application, which integrates video, voice, and data onto a single IP network, and offers viewers an innovative set of choices and control over their TV content. To provide high-quality IPTV services, an effective strategy is based on caching. This work proposes a segment-based two-tier caching approach, which divides each video into multiple segments to be cached. This approach also partitions the cache space into two layers, where the first layer mainly caches to-be-played segments and the second layer saves possibly played segments. As the segment access becomes frequent, the proposed approach enlarges the first layer and reduces the second layer, and vice versa. Because requested segments may not be accessed frequently, this work further designs an admission control mechanism to determine whether an incoming segment should be cached or not. The cache architecture takes forward/stop playback into account and may replace the unused segments under the interrupted playback. Finally, we conduct comprehensive simulation experiments to evaluate the performance of the proposed approach. The results show that our approach can yield higher hit ratio than previous work under various environmental parameters.

1. Introduction

Internet protocol TV (IPTV) is a promising Internet killer application, which integrates video, voice, and data onto a single IP network, and offers viewers an innovative set of choices and control over their TV content. Many major telecommunication companies, such as AT&T, Verizon, and Bell, have announced their IPTV solutions by replacing the copper lines in their networks with fiber optic cables to create sufficient bandwidths for delivering many TV contents. The Bell Entertainment Service in Bell Canada, for example, uses a single VDSL line with a consistent download speed of 20 Mbps and an upload rate of 8 Mbps to provide a converged Internet and television service. The trend is similar in other areas, such as Europe and Asia. Major cities in Japan, for example, already provide high-speed networks which allow customers to obtain video over IP. In Taiwan, the largest telecommunication company, Chunghwa Telecom, offers the multimedia on-demand (MOD) services, which allow clients to watch traditional TV contents over IPTV infrastructures.

A conventional solution to provide IPTV services is through a content distribution network (CDN), in which the service provider installs multiple video servers at different locations to transmit video contents to local customers. In general, multimedia streaming objects are far bigger than web objects. Additionally, real-time transmission is necessary for continuous video playback. A video server thus yields much larger disk load and bandwidth consumption than a web server. Once viewer arrival rate increases significantly, the video server is easily overloaded and reduces service quality. To alleviate the limits, most CDNs are based on cache servers. Figure 1 depicts a popular architecture, which is composed of a video server, cache servers, and clients. Usually, the video server is in WAN, and the cache servers are deployed near clients. An incoming video request is first forwarded to the cache server, instead of the video server. Once receiving the request, the cache server checks whether

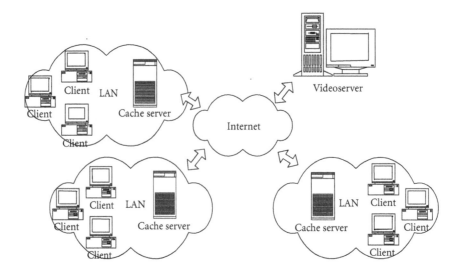

FIGURE 1: Basic streaming cache architecture.

the video data are available in the cache storage. If so, the cache server transmits the data to the client directly. Otherwise, the cache server connects to the video server for the video data, which are then forwarded to the client.

The studies in [1–3] investigated how to allow time-shifted IPTV services, which could enable the end user to watch a broadcasted TV program with a time shift. Wauters et al. [1, 2] proposed a network-based time-shifted television (tsTV) solution using cooperative proxy caches. The study in [3] proposed a hybrid strategy combining genetic algorithms to determine the optimal cache locations for supporting time-shifted IPTV services. Simsarian and Duelk [4] analyzed the bandwidth requirements in metropolitan area networks (MANs) for providing IPTV services and developed a model of the IPTV network to determine the optimum location of the cached video content. The study in [5] introduced the concept of content cacheability and proposed a cache-partition algorithm using the cacheability to serve the maximum amount of video requests subject to constraints on cache memory and throughput. Sofman and Krogfoss [6] indicated that a portion of the video content could be stored in caches closer to clients to reduce the IPTV traffic and further presented an analytical model of hierarchical cache optimization depending on traffic, topology, and cost parameters. A heuristic model [7] was proposed for hierarchical cache optimization in an IPTV network. Chen et al. [8] presented an IPTV system based on a peer-to-peer hierarchical cache architecture. The work [9] devised a caching algorithm that tracked the popularity of objects to make intelligent caching decisions in IPTV services.

A web cache server generally considers a web page an atomic object, and thus caches a complete page. However, caching a complete streaming object is not suitable to a streaming cache server. If a streaming cache server always caches a complete video object, the number of cached videos will be very small because a streaming object is much larger than a web page. When incoming requests increase, cached

videos are easily swapped out because the cached objects are not enough, leading to poor cache performance. In addition, caching an entire video also results in long playback latency because the data transmission time is too large to be ignored. Suppose that a client can download a 100-minute MPEG2 video encoded by 6 Mbps at a bandwidth of 10 Mbps. The video size is $100 * 60 * 6$ bits, and the data transmission time equals 3600 seconds. Clearly, playback after downloading is unrealistic. To alleviate these problems, many studies [10–19] partition a streaming object into multiple smaller segments, which are cached partially. A prefix caching [10] stores the initial frames of popular videos. Upon receiving a video request, the cache server transmits the initial frames to the client and simultaneously requests the remaining frames from the video server. Wu et al. [11, 12] investigate how to partition videos to achieve higher hit ratio. Three video-segmentation approaches—fixed, pyramid, and skyscraper—are proposed. Their simulation results indicate that the pyramid segmentation is the best segmentation approach. Compared with whole video caching, segmentation-based caching is more effective in increased byte-hit ratio. Lazy segmentation approach [13] delays the video partition until a video is accessed. The study in [14] introduces the proxy jitter, which results in playback jitter at the client side due to proxy delay in fetching the uncached segments. The proposed hyperproxy [14] can generate minimum proxy jitter with a low delayed startup ratio and a small decrease of byte-hit ratio. SProxy [15] implements a segment-based streaming cache system on Squid [16]. The study in [17] devises a segment-based cache mechanism to support VCR functions on the client side. extending popularity-aware partial caching algorithm (PAPA) [18], dynamic segment-based caching algorithm (DECA) [19] determines the segment size according to segment popularity.

This paper proposes a two-layer segment-based cache for streaming objects, as shown in Figure 2. The cache server divides the cache storage into two layers—L1 and L2—in

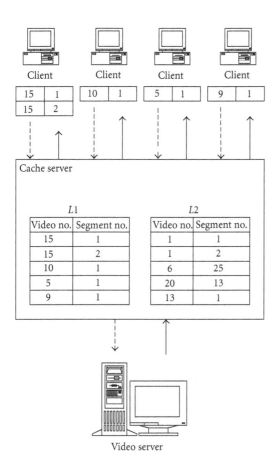

FIGURE 2: The proposed streaming cache.

$$Ratio_{viewing} = C_{viewing}/C_{L1+L2}$$
$$If(Ratio_{viewing} \geq L1\_Cache\_Ratio_{max})\{$$
$$C_{L1\_new\_size} = C_{L1+L2} \cdot L1\_Cache\_Ratio_{max}$$
$$C_{L2\_new\_size} = C_{L1+L2} - C_{L1\_current\_size}\}$$
$$Else\{$$
$$C_{L1\_new\_size} = Ratio_{viewing} \cdot C_{L1+L2}$$
$$C_{L2\_new\_size} = C_{L1+L2} - C_{L1\_new\_size}\}$$

ALGORITHM 1: The algorithm to determine the sizes of caches L1 and L2.

2. The Proposed Cache

The work devises a segment-based two-layer caching approach to increase byte-hit ratio. Suppose that the bandwidth between a video server and a cache server is unlimited, and the bandwidth between the cache server and a client is larger than playback rate. Each video is partitioned into multiple fixed-length segments, as indicated in Figure 2. The proposed approach periodically adjusts the sizes of caches L1 and L2 according to the size of segments accessed, as shown in Figure 3. With the decreasing of the number of the segments currently played, the proposed approach reduces the size of cache L1 and enlarges the size of cache L2, and vice versa. In order to avoid frequent size adjustment, the adjustment is executed periodically, rather than when a segment request arrives. Table 2 lists the parameters to determine the sizes of caches L1 and L2. Algorithm 1 shows how to determine the sizes of caches L1 and L2. The size of cache L1 has an upper bound to avoid the size of cache L2 being zero when many video requests arrive. Upon determining the cache sizes, the cache server adjusts the cache space by moving recently or seldom used segments, as indicated in Algorithm 2.

Besides LRU, the replacement of cache L1 is also based on the observation that a video is played continuously. If a video is played currently, its segments not played yet are very possibly accessed later. Accordingly, cache L1 avoids swapping out these segments. It is well known that the popularity of video data varies with time. The condition that video segments in cache L1 are no longer played may reflect that the segments become less popular. We thus move the segments to cache L2 when cache L1 is full. Figure 4 depicts the complete operation of the proposed approach once cache hits. When a requested segment hits the cache, the segment can be either in cache L1 or in cache L2. If the segment hits cache L1, cache L1 reorders the segment according to LRU and transmits the segment to the requested client. Otherwise, the segment hits cache L2 and is moved to cache L1. If cache L1 has enough space, cache L2 directly moves the segment to cache L1; else, cache L1 swaps cache L2 a played segment for the hit segment.

When a segment is neither in cache L1 nor in cache L2, the segment is missed. Figure 5 shows how to process a missed segment. If cache L1 has enough space, the segment is saved in cache L1 according to LRU. Otherwise, if cache L2 has free space, cache L1 swaps cache L2 a played segment

which cache L1 mainly caches to-be-played segments and cache L2 saves possibly played segments. As the segment access becomes frequent, the proposed approach enlarges cache L1 and reduces cache L2, and vice versa. Once the space of cache L1 is not enough, cache L1 uses LRU to choose a victim, which is then moved to cache L2. If cache L2 also has not enough space, cache L2 first swaps out a selected segment according to LRU-K [20] and saves the segment coming from cache L1. Because requested segments may not be accessed frequently, this work further designs an admission control mechanism to determine whether an incoming segment should be cached or not. The cache architecture takes forward/stop playback into account and may replace the unused segments under the interrupted playback. Table 1 briefly compares the proposed caching architecture with previous approaches. This work conducts a comprehensive simulation to evaluate the proposed cache under various cache size, video popularity, request arrival rate, and playback interrupt rate. In comparison with the segment-based LRU, the video-based LRU, and Wu's approach [12], our approach mostly yields higher hit ratio.

The rest of this paper is organized as follows. Section 2 presents the proposed cache. The simulation results and performance comparisons are shown in Section 3. Brief conclusions are drawn in Section 4.

```
If(Ratio_viewing > C_L1_current_size/C_L1+L2){ // if cache L1 is not enough
    While(C_L1_current_size < C_L1_new_size){
        Select recently-used segments in cache L2 to move to the bottom of cache L1.
        Update current cache sizes of caches L1 and L2. }}
Elsif(Ratio_viewing < C_L1_current_size/C_L1+L2){
    While (C_L1_current_size > C_L1_new_size){
        Select seldom-used segments in cache L1 to move to the top of cache L2.
        Update current cache sizes of caches L1 and L2.}}
```

ALGORITHM 2: The algorithm to adjust the sizes of caches L1 and L2.

TABLE 1: Comparison among related streaming caches.

Approach	Wu's approach	Hyperproxy	SProxy	PAPA	DECA	Segment-based two-layer caching
Segment partition	Pyramid	Lazy	Fixed	Segment prefix	Dynamic segment prefix	Fixed
Cache replacement	Cost function + LRU	Cost function	NA	Cost function	Cost function	LRU + LRU-K
Number of cache layers	2	1	1	1	2	2
Admission control	YES	YES	NA	NA	NA	YES
Precache	NA	YES	YES	NA	NA	NA

TABLE 2: Terms used by the algorithm to determine the cache size.

Term	Definition
C_{L1+L2}	Entire cache size
$C_{L1\_current\_size}$	Current size of cache L1
$C_{L1\_new\_size}$	New size of cache L1
$C_{L2\_current\_size}$	Current size of cache L2
$C_{L2\_new\_size}$	New size of cache L2
$C_{viewing}$	Size of playing segments
$L1\_Cache\_Ratio_{max}$	Maximum ratio of size of cache L1 to entire cache size
$Ratio_{viewing}$	Ratio of playing segments to entire cache size

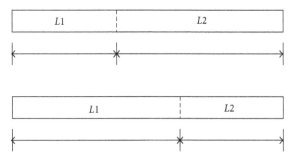

FIGURE 3: Size adjustment on caches L1 and L2.

for the missed segment. If cache L2 is also full, cache L2 performs an admission control to determine whether to cache the segment. If not, the missed segment is not cached and simply transmitted to the client. If so, cache L2 drops a victim segment according to LRU-K. Cache L1 then moves

a segment chosen by LRU to cache L2 and saves the missed segment.

The admission control is based on LRU-K. When both of the caches L1 and L2 are full, the admission control compares the previous Kth access time of a missed segment with that of the victim segment chosen by cache L2. If the access time of the missed segment is later than that of the victim segment cache L2 drops the victim segment and saves the missed segment.

3. Performance Analysis and Comparison

We implemented an event-driven simulator by Perl to evaluate the performance of the proposed cache approach. The simulation settings are listed in Table 3. Suppose that the number of videos equals 2000. Assume that the video size is uniformly distributed between 10 segments and 110 segments, where the length of each segment equals 1 minute. The cache size is expressed in terms of ratio of total videos, and the default value is 0.2. The interarrival time is assumed to follow a Poisson distribution. For each request, it is generated by a Poisson process, which is exponentially distributed with a mean of $1/\lambda$, where λ is the request arrival rate. The default value is 6 requests per minute. The requested videos are drawing from a total of M distinct videos. The popularity of each video follows a Zipf-like distribution $\text{Zipf}(x, M)$ [21]. A Zipf-like distribution contains two parameters, x and M, the former corresponding to the degree of skew. The distribution of each video i equals $p_i = c/i^{1-x}$, where $i \in \{1, \ldots, M\}$ and $c = 1/\sum_{j=1}^{M}(1/j^{1-x})$. Setting $x = 0$ corresponds to a pure Zipf distribution, which is highly skewed. On the other hand, setting $x = 1$ corresponds to a uniform distribution without skew. The default value for x is 0.2 and that for M is 2,000. The popularity of each video changes

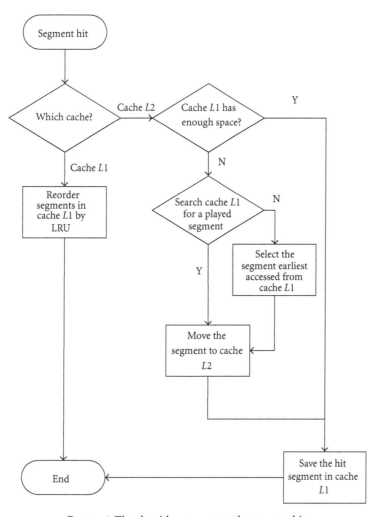

FIGURE 4: The algorithm to process the segment hit.

TABLE 3: Simulation parameters and default values.

Number of videos	2000
Video length	10–110 minutes
Request arrival rate	6 requests per minute
Simulation duration	43200 minutes
Cache size	0.2 (in the percentage of the entire video size)
Video popularity	Zipf-like distribution for video titles, Zipf(0.2, 2000)
Probability of forward/stop playback	0.2
Popularity shift distance	10 videos every 21600 minutes

over time to simulate the scenario that there may be different user groups accessing the videos at different time and their interest may be different. Similar to Wu's study [11], the popularity distribution changes every 21600 minutes, and the shift distance equals 10 videos. The default probability of forward/stop playback is 0.2.

This work compares the proposed approach with the video-based LRU, the segment-based LRU, and Wu's approach [12]. The video-based LRU caches a complete video and selects a replaced video according to LRU. For the segment-based LRU, a video is partitioned into multiple equal-size segments. Wu's approach divides a video into unequal segments under pyramid segmentation. The simulator is installed on FreeBSD 8.0 running on HP ProLiant DL380G6 and HP ProLiant DL320G6.

Figure 6 shows the impact of the cache size on the byte-hit ratio. For a wide range of the cache size, the proposed approach has higher byte-hit ratio than other approaches. The advantage in byte-hit ratio of our approach is more significant for a smaller cache size. For instance, the hit ratio of our approach is 11% higher than that of Wu's approach at the cache size of 0.1, while 26% better than those of the video-based LRU and the segment-based LRU. With the growth of the cache size, all the schemes can cache most videos, and thus their performance is similar.

We next examine the impact of the skew in video popularity on the byte-hit ratio, as indicated in Figure 7. The proposed approach has the higher byte-hit ratio under skewed video popularity. When the video popularity becomes normal distribution, our scheme performs less effectively. For example, the hit ratio of the proposed scheme is 7% better

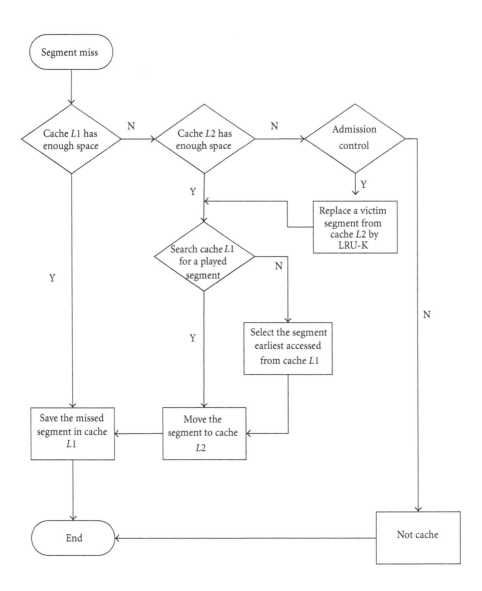

FIGURE 5: The algorithm to process the segment missed.

than that of Wu's approach at the skew factor of 0.2. The scheme also outperforms the video-based LRU and the segment-based LRU. However, when the skew factor is larger than 0.6, Wu's approach performs better than the proposed.

Figure 8 shows the impact of the request arrival rate on the byte-hit ratio. For a wide range of the arrival rate, the proposed approach outperforms other schemes. In comparison with Wu's approach, our approach yields 3–11% higher-hit ratio. The hit ratio of the approach is also 11–13% larger than those of the video-based LRU and the segment-based LRU. The results reflect that the proposed cache performs steadily under various request arrival rates.

Figure 9 depicts the impact of the rate of the forward/stop playback on the byte-hit ratio. The rate indicates the probability that a user performs forward/stop playback during watching a video. The rate of 0.1 represents that one of ten videos happens forward/stop playback. The figure shows that the proposed cache yields 8-9% larger hit ratio than Wu's

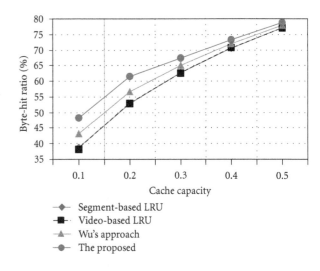

FIGURE 6: Influence of cache size on byte-hit ratio.

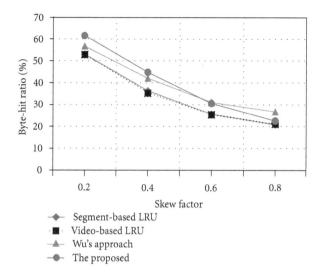

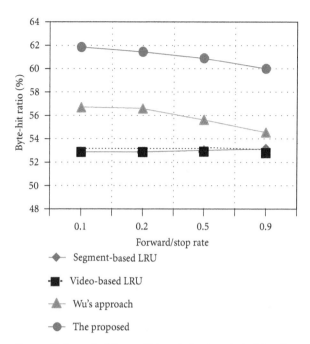

FIGURE 7: Impact of skew in video popularity on byte-hit ratio.

FIGURE 9: Impact of forward/stop playback on byte-hit ratio.

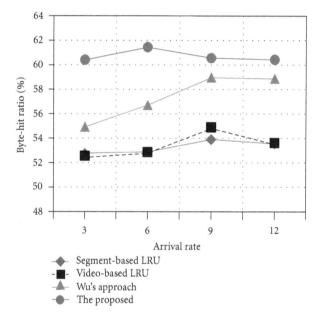

FIGURE 8: Influence of request arrival rate on byte-hit ratio.

L1 is not enough, cache L1 uses LRU to choose a victim, which is then moved to cache L2. If cache L2 also has not enough space, cache L2 first swaps out a selected segment according to LRU-K and saves the segment coming from cache L1. To enlarge the hit ratio, this study also presents an admission control to determine which accessed segments should be cached. The proposed cache further considers the situations that clients may suddenly perform forward/stop playback. This work conducts a comprehensive simulation to evaluate the proposed cache under different cache size, video popularity, request arrival rate, and playback interrupt rate. The simulation results indicate that our approach mostly outperforms the segment-based LRU, the video-based LRU, and Wu's approach under various settings.

Acknowledgment

The work was financially supported by National Science Council, Taiwan under a research Grant no. NSC 100-2221-E-152-005.

References

[1] T. Wauters, W. Van De Meerssche, F. De Turck et al., "Co-operative proxy caching algorithms for time-shifted IPTV services," in *Proceedings of the 32nd Euromicro Conference on Software Engineering and Advanced Applications (SEAA '06)*, pp. 379–386, September 2006.

[2] T. Wauters, W. Van De Meerssche, F. De Turck et al., "Management of time-shifted IPTV services through transparent proxy deployment," in *Proceedings of the IEEE Global Telecommunications Conference (GLOBECOM '06)*, pp. 1–5, December 2006.

[3] Z. Juchao, L. Jun, and W. Gang, "Study of cache placement for time-shifted TV cluster using genetic algorithm," in

approach. In comparison with the video-based LRU and the segment-based LRU, the proposed approach also achieves 13–17% better.

4. Conclusions

Internet protocol TV (IPTV) is a promising Internet killer application, which integrates video, voice, and data onto a single IP network, and offers viewers an innovative set of choices and control over their TV content. To provide high-quality IPTV services, this work proposes a two-layer segment-based cache, which divides the cache storage into caches L1 and L2, and dynamically adjusts their sizes according to video popularity. As the segment access becomes frequent, the proposed approach enlarges cache L1 and reduces cache L2, and vice versa. Once the space of cache

Proceedings of the Genetic and Evolutionary Computation Conference (GEC '09), pp. 781–785, June 2009.

[4] J. E. Simsarian and M. Duelk, "IPTV bandwidth demands in Metropolitan Area Networks," in *Proceedings of the 15th IEEE Workshop on Local and Metropolitan Area Networks (LANMAN '07)*, pp. 31–36, June 2007.

[5] L. B. Sofman, B. Krogfoss, and A. Agrawal, "Optimal cache partitioning in IPTV network," in *Proceedings of the 11th Communications and Networking Simulation Symposium (CNS '08)*, pp. 79–84, April 2008.

[6] L. B. Sofman and B. Krogfoss, "Analytical model for hierarchical cache optimization in IPTV network," *IEEE Transactions on Broadcasting*, vol. 55, no. 1, pp. 62–70, 2009.

[7] B. Krogfoss, L. B. Sofman, and A. Agrawal, "Hierarchical cache optimization in IPTV networks," in *Proceedings of the IEEE International Symposium on Broadband Multimedia Systems and Broadcasting (BMSB '09)*, pp. 1–10, May 2009.

[8] L. Chen, M. Meo, and A. Scicchitano, "Caching video contents in IPTV systems with hierarchical architecture," in *Proceedings of the IEEE International Conference on Communications (ICC '09)*, pp. 1–6, June 2009.

[9] D. De Vleeschauwer and K. Laevens, "Performance of caching algorithms for IPTV on-demand services," *IEEE Transactions on Broadcasting*, vol. 55, no. 2, pp. 491–501, 2009.

[10] S. Sen, J. Rexford, and D. Towsley, "Proxy prefix caching for multimedia streams," in *Proceedings of the 18th Annual Joint Conference of the IEEE Computer and Communications Societie (INFOCOM '99)*, pp. 1310–1319, New York, NY, USA, March 1999.

[11] K. L. Wu, P. S. Yu, and J. L. Wolf, "Segment-based proxy caching of multimedia streams," in *Proceedings of the International Conference on World Wide Web (WWW '01)*, Hongkong, May 2001.

[12] K. L. Wu, P. S. Yu, and J. L. Wolf, "Segmentation of multimedia streams for proxy caching," *IEEE Transactions on Multimedia*, vol. 6, no. 5, pp. 770–780, 2004.

[13] S. Chen, H. Wang, X. Zhang, B. Shen, and S. Wee, "Segment-based proxy caching for Internet streaming media delivery," *IEEE Multimedia*, vol. 12, no. 3, pp. 59–67, 2005.

[14] S. Chen, B. Shen, S. Wee, and X. Zhang, "Segment-based streaming media proxy: modeling and optimization," *IEEE Transactions on Multimedia*, vol. 8, no. 2, pp. 243–256, 2006.

[15] S. Chen, B. Shen, S. Wee, and X. Zhang, "SProxy: a caching infrastructure to support internet streaming," *IEEE Transactions on Multimedia*, vol. 9, no. 5, pp. 1062–1072, 2007.

[16] http://www.squid-cache.org/.

[17] J. Z. Wang and P. S. Yu, "Fragmental proxy caching for streaming multimedia objects," *IEEE Transactions on Multimedia*, vol. 9, no. 1, pp. 147–156, 2007.

[18] L. Shen, W. Tu, and E. Steinbach, "A flexible starting point based partial caching algorithm for video on demand," in *Proceedings of the IEEE International Conference on Multimedia and Expo (ICME '07)*, pp. 76–79, Beijing, China, July 2007.

[19] W. Tu, E. Steinbach, M. Muhammad, and X. Li, "Proxy caching for video-on-demand using flexible starting point selection," *IEEE Transactions on Multimedia*, vol. 11, no. 4, pp. 716–729, 2009.

[20] E. J. O'Neil, P. E. O'Neil, and G. Weikum, "LRU-K page replacement algorithm for database disk buffering," in *Proceedings of the ACM SIGMOD International Conference on Management of Data*, pp. 297–306, May 1993.

[21] G. K. Zipf, *Human Behavior and the Principles of Least Effort*, Addison-Wesley, Cambridge, Mass, USA, 1949.

4

QoS Supported IPTV Service Architecture over Hybrid-Tree-Based Explicit Routed Multicast Network

Chih-Chao Wen and Cheng-Shong Wu

Department of Electrical Engineering, National Chung Cheng University, Chia-Yi 62102, Taiwan

Correspondence should be addressed to Chih-Chao Wen, ccwen@ccu.edu.tw

Academic Editor: János Tapolcai

With the rapid advance in multimedia streaming and multicast transport technology, current IP multicast protocols, especially PIM-SM, become the major channel delivery mechanism for IPTV system over Internet. The goals for IPTV service are to provide two-way interactive services for viewers to select popular program channel with high quality for watching during fast channel surfing period. However, existing IP multicast protocol cannot meet above QoS requirements for IPTV applications between media server and subscribers. Therefore, we propose a cooperative scheme of hybrid-tree based on explicit routed multicast, called as HT-ERM to combine the advantages of shared tree and source tree for QoS-supported IPTV service. To increase network utilization, the constrained shortest path first (CSPF) routing algorithm is designed for construction of hybrid tree to deliver the high-quality video stream over watching channel and standard quality over surfing channel. Furthermore, the Resource Reservation Protocol-Traffic Engineering (RSVP-TE) is used as signaling mechanism to set up QoS path for multicast channel admission control. Our simulation results demonstrated that the proposed HT-ERM scheme outperforms other multicast QoS-based delivery scheme in terms of channel switching delay, resource utilization, and blocking ratio for IPTV service.

1. Introduction

As the rapid growth of broadband network applications with streaming transport over Internet, the Internet Protocol Television (IPTV) system has been widely deployed to provide multimedia service anywhere at any time. This is because IPTV enables digital service convergence of communications, computing, and media content over IP network with desired QoS guarantee [1]. From the perspective of the quality of experience (QoE), IPTV system operates as the same with broadcasting TV service, which would deliver the watching and surfing programs over different channels. However, the most difference is that IPTV works in a two-way interactive communications between service providers and subscribers. We need to consider the effective channel and delivery control problem to achieve video streaming with desired quality over Internet.

To efficiently satisfy multiple viewers' own quality requirements, IP multicast is considered a promising solution for IPTV application. Nevertheless, quality of service

(QoS) support to IPTV system still poses challenging issues for multicast channel delivery and resource utilization through IP networks. The QoS-supported IPTV multicast service architecture is to deploy an efficient multicast transmission system via IP multicast delivery tree with the integration of resource provisioning and channel admission control. The IP multicast delivery has the merit of efficient bandwidth saving; however, it is difficult to assign effective multicast channel to meet QoS requirements in consideration of multicast channel state labeling and channel switching delay [2]. Therefore, the original IP multicast is not designed for multimedia application to transport time-sensitive packet streaming with bandwidth reservation and QoS gurantee along point-to-multipoint (P2MP) multicast path for large amount of IPTV channel subscribers.

From the perspective of QoS requirement, IPTV channel change will impair the content quality of video streaming to speed up the surfing streams transmission. It usually depends on the group of picture (GOP) size between Intracoded frames (I-frames) in video stream sequence to determine the quality of watching channel and surfing channel. According to high quality video coding, a typical high definition (HD) video stream requires at least 10 Mbps of I-frames transfer rate for IPTV watching channels, while a standard definition (SD) video stream requires 2–5 Mbps for lower quality video stream in IPTV surfing channels upon channel change [3].

From the perspective of network transmission performance, current IP multicast protocols can be enhanced by different multicast QoS routing mechanisms. The QoS-aware multicast routing protocol (QMRP) [4] was first to propose feasible multicast paths computation based on QoS metric for single path or multipath. Afterwards, the protocol independent multicast (PIM) protocol is based on receiver initiated routing decision to find the shortest path regardless of underlying unicast routing. For example, the typical PIM protocols are represented by source specific multicast (SSM) [5], and PIM-sparse mode (SM) [6]. Those two multicast protocols are integrated by QoS routing algorithm with traffic control to construct source tree, shared tree, and even hybrid-tree structures. Especially, this hybrid-tree multicast can be an alternative to improve IPTV QoS and achieve load balance of multicast traffic by combining advantages of above two multicast tree types: shared tree and source tree.

As the previous paper mentioned in [7], the hybrid-tree multicast is considered as a suitable solution for IPTV channel control and delivery to satisfy multicast QoS requirements. However, existing core functionality of PIM-SM protocol in rendezvous point (RP) node still lacks the efficient control mechanism for hybrid-tree switchover operations to realize IPTV QoS multicast during channel change period. The reasons are explained as follows.

(i) *High-level traffic control mechanism*: RP router will aggregate all channel source streaming into the single shared tree until the link efficient bandwidth is over-threshold. The status report is a high-level control message detected by receivers. Therefore, the reaction time may be too slow to deal with unexpected QoS degradation and traffic congestion.

(ii) *Two-pass switchover control operation*: for channel change, multicast tree switchover is executed by RP node after receiver member-leave and rejoin request. By using two-pass switchover operation, RP node suspends the traffic aggregation from the specified source node; then channel traffic can be changed to new source node inefficiently.

Therefore, IPTV service provider must provide a cost-effective multicast network control mechanism as an efficient channel delivery solution. In this paper, we propose the enhanced hybrid-tree-based multicast delivery scheme with explicit routed multicast, called as HT-ERM. To improve performance of QoS-supported IPTV multicast channel, our HT-ERM routing algorithm is designed based on constrained shortest path first (CSPF) [8], and HT-ERM channel admission control is employed by RSVP-TE mechanism [9]. In performance evaluation, the proposed HT-ERM scheme can improve IPTV delivery and channel control as compared with the other QoS multicast schemes.

The rest of this paper is organized as follows. We summarize past works of multicast QoS for IPTV in Section 2. In Section 3, we made assumptions of hybrid-tree multicast in related IPTV models. The Section 4 describes the HT-ERM control algorithm and multicast channel operations. Section 5 presents simulation results for IPTV service, and in Section 6 we give conclusions.

2. Related Works

QoS-supported IPTV services need to consider QoS guarantee, which involves with multicast delivery through core network, and channel selective control in user access network. Most of researches focus IPTV multicast QoS on two crucial subjects: multicast network resource control for IPTV watching channels and multiple surfing channel change delay control.

2.1. IPTV Multicast Channel Delivery and Change. The analysis of IPTV channel control for content delivery and channel change depends on those factors such as command processing time, network transmission delay time, streaming switchover delay time, and video-decoding time [10–12]. The most important key factors for channel control are affected by content transmission and streaming switchover through networks. In [11], the authors proposed multicast proxy IGMP scheme for channel prejoining to the expected IPTV channels by bulk delivery the popular watching channels and other subscribers can filter watching channel and switchover surfing channels in the same local network.

2.2. IPTV Multicast Network Resource Control. Many QoS multicast routing algorithms are proposed to compute the feasible multicast tree, so that can reduce traffic transmission delay and achieve efficient resource utilization. In traditional IP multicast network, the multicast routing algorithm lacks QoS control for network P2MP connections and traffic load balancing. Recently, QoS-aware multicast approaches, such as ECMP [13] and QMRP [4], are developed to solve scalability and resource allocation when a large amount of different multicast streams transmit to heterogeneous receivers through Internet.

The modified multicast equal-cost multipath (ECMP) scheme [13] has been applied in shared tree to enhance PIM-SM or SSM-related IP multicast protocols. To achieve traffic balancing, multiple paths with equal cost are constructed to split the traffic from RP-shared tree. The centralized multicast traffic control approach is usually utilized by RP node to aggregate multicast traffic into the shared tree for IPTV watching channels and adjacent surfing channels together.

The QMRP is a well-known QoS-aware multicast routing control approach [4], which can compute optimal tree-path in single-path or multi-path mode to join multiast tree for IPTV channel delivery. When the traffic load on multicast tree link is over threshold, the multipath traffic distribution will be activated to diverse the traffic load, and thus switchover to the specific multicast path.

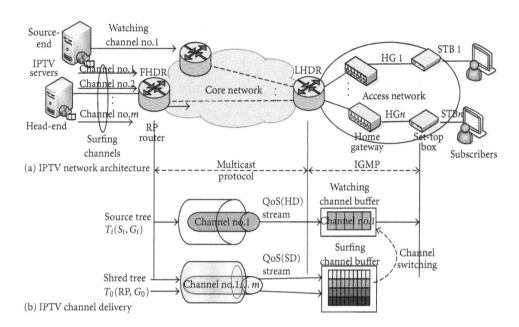

FIGURE 1: IPTV multicast network architecture consists of (a) core network and access network; IPTV channel delivered by (b) hybrid-tree based channel distribution scheme.

Furthermore, the proposed HT-ERM algorithm is to improve the overall IPTV channel delivery with efficient network resource utilization and fast channel change. The hybrid-tree-based multicast HT-ERM protocol integrates with hybrid multicast advantages to enhance functionality of current IP multicast protocol for IPTV QoS channel delivery control.

3. IPTV System Model

We use the IPTV system model to simplify the complicated service interaction between application level and network level. The IPTV channel quality states are assumed to abstract the channel dynamic behavior so as to introduce the proposed HT-ERM scheme in following sections.

3.1. Network Architecture for IPTV Service. The IPTV network architecture consists of multicast core network for channel distribution and local network for channel access as shown in Figure 1(a). In core network, IPTV channels are distributed and delivered by multicast protocol from first-hop designated router (FHDR) to last-hop designated router (LHDR). In local access network, the subscribers with terminal devices access IPTV channels via set-top box (STB) through home gateway (HG). For IPTV media service provider, the head-end (HE) server is to aggregate different basic quality channels for viewers' channel surfing and change behavior. The source-end server is to supply high quality program stream as a unique watching channel.

We model the IPTV system over IP multicast network. Assume that IPTV media servers can provide IPTV channels with source streams denoted by $S_i = \{S_1, \ldots, S_m\}$, and the subscriber members $M_i = \{M_1, \ldots, M_n\}$ can join any watching or surfing channel from its attached LHDR node R_i to form the channel group $G_i = \{R_1, \ldots, R_n\}$. The collection of IPTV channels are delivered through multipoint-to-multipoint (MP2MP) connections (S_i, G_i) between FHDR and LHDR over core network.

3.2. State Parameters for IPTV QoS Channel. In Figure 1(b), IPTV multicast channels are distributed between FHDR and LHDR. The source tree T_i links carry the multiple high quality streams from their specific sources to the corresponding group. Each watching stream is transferred from watching channel buffer to STB. The surfing channel is aggregated by surfing streams over RP-based shared tree T_0 links with low quality. Each surfing channel is extracted from surfing channel buffer for fast channel switching during channel change.

The QoS-supported IPTV channel state is defined by two types of video quality: high definition (HD) and standard definition (SD). The HD video stream is paid per channel for high quality watching program, and SD video stream is normal quality used for fast channel surfing and free watching. Accordingly, the channel stream with higher QoS level is assigned to source-based multicast channel, and lower QoS level stream is delivered by shared multicast channel.

For QoS-supported IPTV channel state, the QoS level with HD is in steady-state function, and SD is in dynamic

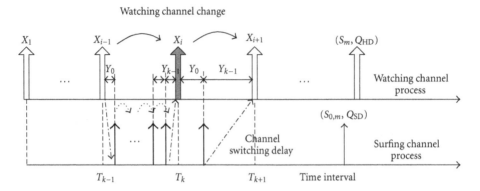

FIGURE 2: IPTV channel change process between watching and surfing channel state.

state. The IPTV QoS channel state can be represented by multicast tree symbol with QoS level $T(S, G, Q)$, which is characterized by

$$T(S, G, Q) = \begin{cases} T_{\text{watch}}\left(S_i, G_i, Q_q\right), & i = 1, \ldots, m; \ q = \text{hd}, \\ T_{\text{surf}}\left(S_{i,j}, G_0, Q_q\right), & i = 0; \ j = 1, \ldots, m, \\ & q = \text{sd}, \end{cases} \tag{1}$$

where the parameter S denotes the source nodes of IPTV channel, G denotes the group identification for receiver joining, and Q denotes the required stream QoS level with HD/SD. The G_i is the multicast group joining to the specified source S_i for watching channel no. i, and G_0 is the shared multicast group joining to the common source $S_{i,j}$ with RP router for aggregated surfing channels. In other words, the watching channel set is delivered by source tree $T_i(S_i, G_i, Q_{\text{hd}})$ for HD quality stream. The surfing channel is delivered by RP shared tree $T_0(S_{0,j}, G_0, Q_{\text{sd}})$ for SD quality stream.

3.3. IPTV Channel Change Behavior. According to the definition of channel state, IPTV QoS channel can be obtained by watching state T_{watch} and channel surfing state T_{surf} in channel change process. Assume that viewers usually stay in watching channel X_i with the state parameters (S_i, Q_{HD}), and the last surfing channel state with the state parameters $(S_{0,m}, Q_{\text{SD}})$ will stop before next watching channel.

As the viewer making multiple channel changes, the random behavior of channel changing in surfing state can be modeled by a terminating renewal process [3]. Once channel change is occurred, the surfing state is zapping between surfing channels in transition state with random time interval $Y_i, i = 0, 1, 2, \ldots$. channel switching process as shown in Figure 2. When channel change is stopped, we observed that the events X_i of watching channel state always stay in steady state within the time interval $[T_k, T_{k+1}]$, where $T_k = Y_0 + Y_1 + \cdots + Y_{k-1}$.

As IPTV channel change is a random process, the channel state may occur either in watching states or surfing states at any given time. We can figure out the joint channel state probability density function by

$$P_T = p(k, q), \tag{2}$$

where index k is the channel number depending on program popularity, and index q is the QoS stream quality distributed ratio over core network.

The channel popularity is the preference to the desired watching channel for most of viewers. According to Zipf's law [2], the probability Z_k that a viewer will choose the kth most popular channel is given by

$$Z_k = \frac{c}{k^s}, \tag{3}$$

where c is a constant to make the probabilities sum to 1, and exponent s is set to 1. The selection of watching channel is first determined by Zipf's law. Then, the watching channel changes are occurred by poison process and terminated at next watching channel from surfing channel selection.

4. The HT-ERM Scheme for IPTV Channel Delivery

The proposed HT-ERM scheme has efficient hybrid-tree multicast operation for IPTV channel control and delivery as compared with the function of PIM-SM protocol.

4.1. HT-ERM Protocol Design. As shown in flow chart of Figure 3, we design the HT-ERM algorithm for multicast IPTV channels, including the hybrid-tree initialization, shared tree aggregation, source tree switchover and multicast admission control in following subsections.

4.1.1. Channel Initialization and Join. The RP node is initialized by IPTV channel aggregation for surfing channel joining requests in random process before watching channel selection. In additions, the initial parameters setting are shared tree T_0, shared group G_0, channel quality Q, and resource allocation threshold BW_{th}.

While receiving the channel request message, RP node checks the control message types (Join or Switchover) by source node (rp or s) and group member ($g0$ or gi). The RP node is channel concentrator to update the surfing channel states through the shared tree T_0. The explicit routes of shared tree T_0 can be derived by computing CSPF (constrain

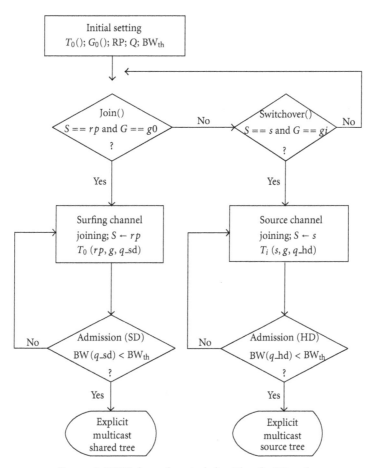

FIGURE 3: IPTV channel control algorithm for RP node.

shortest path first). The group source mapping table is generated. The surfing channels are expressed by explicit routed states in core routers as the multicast branching toward members. The more different IPTV channels are joined, the more network resource is utilized by multicast packet delivery.

4.1.2. Channel Change by Hybrid-Tree Switchover. As mentioned in Section 2, the channel change is a random process for viewer's behavior to select preferable watching channel. To reduce IPTV channel change time, the switchover control message is fast operated between RP shared tree and source tree simultaneously. The fast switchover mechanism, which is considered by link bandwidth utility and channel change time, can insert temporary SD quality stream from the same RP-aggregated shared tree as soon as possible to HD quality stream buffer for watching channel. After the new source tree switchover is finished, the HD quality media stream is delivered by specific source tree.

When the channel change request is occurred, the RP node executes switchover process for group members. After being informed by switchover control message, the source node computes the explicit routes for source tree T_i by CSPF and then updates the channel states for watching stream delivery.

4.1.3. Channel Setup with Multicast Admission Control. According to the group member joining request with QoS requirements, the HT-ERM admission control will check the link bandwidth status for multicast hybrid tree. To guarantee QoS for multicast stream delivery, the upper bound of link utilization is defined by *bandwidth threshold* (BW_{th}) for efficient resource allocation that IPTV channel can carry the media streams through specific source tree T_i and shared tree T_0. The bandwidth threshold (BW_{th}) is to maximize the bandwidth usage for the total watching channel demands and additional channel change bandwidth estimation for network links.

Because the RSVP-TE is explicit routed signaling protocol, the admission control is used to reserve resource for hybrid-tree-based multicast. The surfing channel joining and watching channel switchover are admitted by comparing between available resource and bandwidth threshold (BW_{th}). When the total bandwidth of T_i and T_0 exceed the threshold BW_{th}, the blocking ratio for joining requests will be increasing due to detection of bandwidth overthreshold.

4.2. Channel Delivery Operational Differences between HT-ERM and PIM-SM. The differences between proposed HT-ERM and PIM-SM multicast protocol for channel delivery are listed as follows.

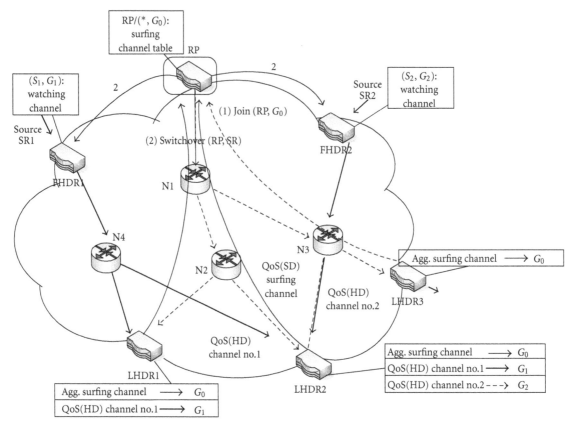

FIGURE 4: IPTV channel delivery through HT-ERM operations.

(1) *Source group mapping table*: because PIM-SM multicast routing is based on reverse path check, it is difficult to make accurate QoS estimation for bandwidth allocation from FHDR router of source node (or RP node) to multiple LHDR routers. The proposed HT-ERM scheme is based on mapping table to compute the source multicast explicit routed path forwarding toward all joining multicast group members.

(2) *The modified control messages*: Join/Leave (RP, G_0) and Switchover (RP, SR_i) are adopted by the extended multicast protocol message of PIM-SM for IPTV channel setup and change. The control messages of HT-ERM are operated to enhance delivery performance between FHDR and LHDR.

To explain the HT-ERM protocol operations, we take an illustrative example in Figure 4. Firstly, the source node SR1 and SR2 will register to RP for surfing streams aggregation in RP shared tree. All group members distributed in LHDR nodes request RP to join to group G_0 for surfing channels. Secondly, upon receiving the join requests from LHDR 1–3, the RP function performs multicast channel initialization, and the group-source mapping table is updated by shared tree for surfing stream aggregation from SR1 and SR2. By information collecting from all sources and group members, the shared tree in hybrid multicast tree can be computed by CSPF for the explicit multicast routes of surfing channels.

In the scenario of LHDR1, the switchover message is completed to request new watching channel no. 1 from node SR1 via RP. However, in the scenario of LHDR2, not only one viewer requests watching the channel no. 1, one of views desires to change channel from the channel no. 1 to new channel no. 2. Instead of rejoining to SR2 for new channel no. 2 (S2, G2), RP can relay the control message *Switchover* (RP, SR) to inform old source node SR1 to retain the routes of subpath to LHDR2 for channel no. 1. The new source node SR2 is admitted to submit the media stream from channel no. 2 to LHDR2 by using the explicit routes with available bandwidth over (S2 and G2) source tree through core router N3. As for the scenario of LHDR3, the viewer is still in surfing state without decision making for specific watching channel.

5. Performance Evaluation

The performance measures of the proposed HT-ERM scheme for IPTV service are in terms of blocking ratio of admission control, resource utilization, and channel change delay over multicast core network and access network employed as performance. As compared with two underlying protocols, PIM-SM with ECMP algorithm and QMRP with QSPF algorithm, the HT-ERM with CSPF algorithm will be verified as a valid QoS supported IPTV multicast approach.

5.1. Simulation Parameters Setup. The simulation is conducted over two different network topologies. The first one is the random graph RandNet with 100-node and 294-link, generated by GT-ITM [14] network topology generator. The other is the fixed backbone graph NSFNet [15], which is abstracted from a real network model with 14 nodes and 42 bidirectional links. The multicast core network environment is setup by sources and receivers randomly attached to any network edge node as the designated router. In experiments, the number of join requests is measured from 500 to 5000 per 500 increasing step, to join different multicast channels. The group size is proportional to the total number of group member, and the joining requests from each node are uniformly distribution. From the aspect of viewer's random behavior, channel change joint state probability equals to the relationship with channel switching ratio (α) and channel popularity. The popular channels are usually assumed to stay within HD quality stream distribution ratio (β). According to the empirical estimation by Zipf's law in (3), the cumulative probability of channel popularity is over 50% when β is set to 0.2 (i.e., top 10 popular channels over total 50 channels). In our IPTV channel test scenario, those simulation parameters are summarized in Table 1.

5.2. Performance Metrics.
In HT-ERM channel control simulation, the performance evaluations for hybrid-tree-based multicast scheme with different multicast routing algorithms are employed by PIM-like protocols. Table 2 lists hybrid multicast with three different multicast routing algorithms. The proposed HT-ERM scheme is used by CSPF algorithm. The conventional PIM-SM multicast scheme can be adopted by the equal cost multi-path (ECMP) algorithm. The QoS-aware multicast routing protocol (QMRP) is used as PIM-like protocol based on QoS shortest path first (QSPF or QoS-SPF). The proposed HT-ERM scheme is source initial explicit routed multicast based on available bandwidth. The other schemes, multicast ECMP and multicast QSPF algorithms, are receiver-based multicast tree join by traversing the single path and/or multiple shortest path computations according to the link cost.

The performance metrics for multicast network delivery and QoS channel control are defined as following.

(i) Multicast Tree Setup Ratio.
The multicast tree is computed by the specific on-tree node in RP node or source node. The tree setup ratio can be represented as the average number of multicast source and shared trees for multicast channel (S, G) established by the joining requests from group members.

(ii) Multicast Forwarding Entries.
The total number of multicast forwarding entries can be represented by the number of forwarding entries in multicast routing table per multicast router and the number of multicast router on multicast distribution tree T with group member g. The number of multicast forwarding entries ε is calculated by

$$\varepsilon(T, g) = N_e \times N_T = (N_s + N_b + N_t + N_l) \times N_T \quad (4)$$

where N_e is the total number of forwarding entries in multicast routing table, that is, the total number of (S, G) entries

TABLE 1: IPTV multicast simulation parameters.

IPTV channel delivery test conditions	Parameter
Total number of IPTV channels	50
Channel switching ratio α	0.25, 0.5, 0.8
HD QoS stream distribution ratio β	0.2
HD/SD QoS stream bitrate	10/2 Mbps
Bandwidth threshold	80%
Link bandwidth capacity	500 Mbps

TABLE 2: Hybrid multicast scheme with routing algorithms.

Hybrid-tree protocol	Multicast routing algorithm
PIM-SM	Equal cost multipath (ECMP)
QMRP	QoS shortest path first (QSPF)
HT-ERM	Constrained shortest path first (CSPF)

in all multicast nodes for distribution tree T, including the root node number N_s, branching node number N_b, transit node number N_t, and leaf node number N_l. The number of multicast tree is denoted by N_T.

(iii) Maximum Multicast Resource Usage.
The ratio of the utilized bandwidth is calculated in most traffic-congested link over multicast tree. The metric of resource usage U is the total bandwidth consumption BW for QoS channels with HD and SD streams through multicast tree T from joining requests of group member g by

$$U(Q, T) = \sum_{i \in T, q \in Q} \frac{BW(i, q)}{C_T}, \quad (5)$$

where C_T is the total tree link capacity over multicast network, and $BW(i, q)$ is the reserved bandwidth for HD stream and SD stream over each link i through distributed tree T.

(iv) Blocking Ratio.
The ratio of rejection service request is divided by total requests under the admission control with bandwidth threshold BW_{th}. The metric of blocking ratio B is defined

$$B(Q, G) = \sum_{g \in G} \frac{N_R}{N_g}, \quad (6)$$

where N_g is the number of join requests from group member G for available IPTV channels, and N_R denotes the number of rejected member requests for specified QoS channel by admission control.

(v) Multicast Channel Change Delay.
it is considered by channel processing delay, watching channel stream transmission, and surfing channel switching delay over multicast trees

T with group member size g. The metric of total switching delay time D can be summed up by

$$D(T,g) = D_{1,\text{channel processing delay}}$$
$$+ D_{2,\text{surfing channel switching delay}} \quad (7)$$
$$+ D_{3,\text{watching channel transmission delay}},$$

where D_1 denotes channel processing delay, D_2 denotes surfing channel switching delay, and D_3 denotes watching channel transmission delay.

5.3. Comparisons of Multicast Network Delivery. We carried out following simulations over 100-node and 294-link random graph RanNet to evaluate the performance for multicast routing algorithms such as multicast ECMP, receiver-based QMRP- and RP-based HT-ERM scheme.

(1) Multicast Tree Setup Ratio Comparisons. The *multicast tree setup ratio* is measured by the average number of multicast source and shared trees computed by specific on-tree nodes per joining requests from group members. The main effect of multicast tree computation is determined by the number of active joining requests during channel change. The popular channel ratio β with HD QoS stream distribution is set to 0.2. With incremental channel switching ratio α by 0.25, 0.5, and 0.8, we observed the setup trend of multicast tree for multicast channel (S, G) computed by proposed HT-ERM routing schemes in RP and source nodes. Figure 5 shows the results for multicast tree setup ratio versus the average number of group member requests that compared HT-ERM scheme with CSPF, PIM-SM protocol with ECMP, and PIM-SSM protocol with QSPF. We found that the lowest setup ratio of multicast tree for ECMP scheme can afford for large amount of new channel change requests to diverse traffic flows into multiple links of shared tree. It means more multicast tree setup leads to more computation and delivery resource consumption. We also derive that multicast trees setup is almost identical to channel switching ratio in HT-ERM scheme with parameter $\alpha = 0.25, 0.5, 0.8$. When the switching ratio is increasing to 0.8, the multicast tree setup ratio of HT-ERM scheme still outperforms that of QMRP. That is because RP node uses HT-ERM with CSPF algorithm to gain the minimum hybrid-tree setup ratio with shared and source tree, instead QMRP is based on receiver multipath for source trees setup.

(2) Multicast Forwarding Entry Comparisons. Multicast *forwarding entry* is represented as the control overhead of multicast channel state maintenance in multicast forwarding table for network delivery through the multicast delivery tree. The total number of forwarding entries (S, G) consists of root node number, branching node number, transit node number, and leaf node number over the distribution tree with group member. The increasing size of multicast forwarding entries is proportional to the number of group member joining requests because of grafted subpath from multicast branching node. Therefore, the performance for forwarding entry scalability may be affected by routing control scheme.

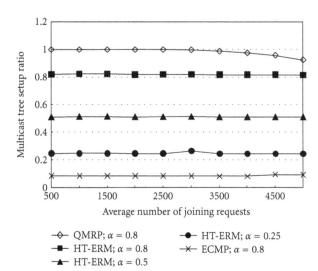

FIGURE 5: Multicast tree setup ratio versus group member joining requests.

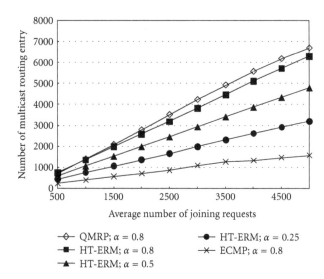

FIGURE 6: Comparisons of multicast forwarding entry size.

Figure 6 shows the comparison of ECMP, QMRP, and HT-ERM scheme with number of the forwarding entry number versus the average number of group joining requests. We found that the number of multicast forwarding entries for HT-ERM is increasing largely from 3,199 to 6,301 (i.e., the raising ratio is over 50%) in condition of HD QoS stream distribution ratio ($\beta = 0.2$) and multicast channel switching ratio ($\alpha = 0.8, 0.5$ and 0.25), when group joining member requests are more than 5000 times. When switching ratio is set to 0.8, the growth of forwarding entry size computed by QMRP is a little greater than that of HT-ERM. In contrast, HT-ERM uses the explicit routes in RP-shared tree that can reduce more forwarding entries in multicast trees. However, ECMP is used to compute the unique shared tree, so that forwarding entry size is almost the same.

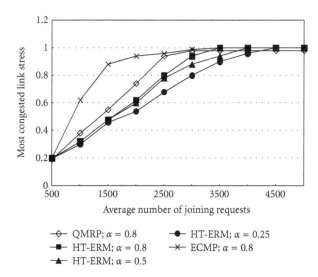

$-\diamond-$ QMRP; $\alpha = 0.8$ $-\bullet-$ HT-ERM; $\alpha = 0.25$
$-\blacksquare-$ HT-ERM; $\alpha = 0.8$ $-\times-$ ECMP; $\alpha = 0.8$
$-\blacktriangle-$ HT-ERM; $\alpha = 0.5$

FIGURE 7: Multicast tree link resource usage versus group joining requests.

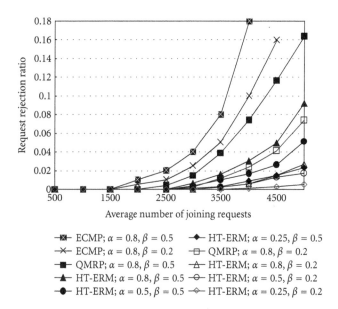

$-\boxtimes-$ ECMP; $\alpha = 0.8, \beta = 0.5$ $-\blacklozenge-$ HT-ERM; $\alpha = 0.25, \beta = 0.5$
$-\times-$ ECMP; $\alpha = 0.8, \beta = 0.2$ $-\boxminus-$ QMRP; $\alpha = 0.8, \beta = 0.2$
$-\blacksquare-$ QMRP; $\alpha = 0.8, \beta = 0.5$ $-\triangle-$ HT-ERM; $\alpha = 0.8, \beta = 0.2$
$-\blacktriangle-$ HT-ERM; $\alpha = 0.8, \beta = 0.5$ $-\ominus-$ HT-ERM; $\alpha = 0.5, \beta = 0.2$
$-\bullet-$ HT-ERM; $\alpha = 0.5, \beta = 0.5$ $-\diamond-$ HT-ERM; $\alpha = 0.25, \beta = 0.2$

FIGURE 8: Request rejection ratio versus group joining requests.

(3) Multicast Tree Link Resource Usage Comparisons. In multicast resource usage comparison, the multicast tree link stress is estimated by summation with the various channel switching ratio (α = 0.8, 0.5, and 0.25), under the HD QoS stream distribution ratio (β = 0.2). In Figure 7, we observed that HT-ERM achieves the best resource efficiency utilized on the most congested multicast tree link as compared with ECMP and QMRP approach before link resource is overutilized by at the number of joining requests up to 4000. In other words, the resource usage control of the proposed HT-ERM scheme is efficient by using CSPF algorithm because the explicated multicast routing can limit bandwidth threshold to redistribute heavy traffic loads between the shared tree and source trees over entire network topology.

(4) Joining Request Rejection Ratio Comparisons. The blocking for joining request is caused by insufficient resource allocation and high-level QoS request. The admission control can detect the available bandwidth in advance before accepting the joining requests with channel access. On the other hand, high-level QoS request may be rejected by either source node or RP node when multicast tree is switching over the specific links of source tree. By adjusting the various channel switching ratio (α = 0.8, 0.5, and 0.25) and HD QoS stream distribution ratio (β = 0.2, 0.5), we evaluate the performance for large amount of joining requests for multicast tree setup by comparing multicast routing algorithm with ECMP, QMRP, and HT-ERM. We found that the rejection ratio of each routing algorithm is increasing by large amount of the joining requests from group members at higher channel switching ratio (α = 0.8) and higher QoS stream distributed ratio (β = 0.5), as shown in Figure 8. Especially, even in the worst conditions of channel switching ratio (α = 0.8) and HD QoS distribution ratio (β = 0.5), the performance of rejection ratio for HT-ERM routing algorithm is better than that of ECMP and QMRP routing algorithm. As the result,

we can prove that the CSPF algorithm of proposed HT-ERM can achieve efficient resource allocation and effective admission control for QoS requirements.

5.4. Comparisons of IPTV Channel Control. We carried out following simulations over real backbone network NSFNet with 14-node and 42-link to evaluate the performance for different IPTV multicast protocols PIM-SM, QMRP, and HT-ERM applied by associated channel control scheme.

(1) Channel Change Delay. In metric definition (7), the major channel delay effects are caused by surfing channel switching delay D_2, and watching channel transmission delay D_3. We simulated a large amount of groups to receive different IPTV watching channels over NSFNet topology and obtained the results of channel change delay. The Figure 9 demonstrates comparisons among different multicast tree construction for successful channel change from 10 to 50 at each access node.

The traditional RP-shared tree setup with ECMP algorithm leads to the largest transmission delay during channel change. The traffic of multipath is separated on the shared tree links so as to result in the large switching control delay; however, the multi-path can reduce the traffic load. As the QRMP approach constructs the source tree by QoS routing algorithm (i.e., QSPF), the IPTV channel traffic distribution can be diversified by different source tree links. The proposed HT-ERM can construct hybrid multicast tree based on CSPF algorithm to reduce the switching latency by source and shared tree switchover. As compared by QSPF routing algorithm, the proposed CSPF of HT-ERM scheme improves the performance for channel change delay. The importance of this simulation result indicates that the source-initiated QoS routing algorithm can achieve better channel switching

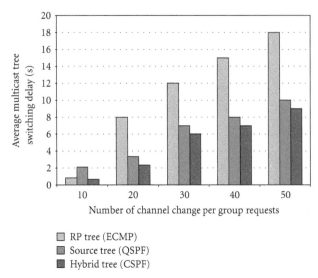

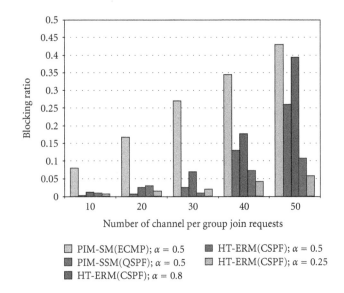

FIGURE 9: Channel change delay comparisons by multicast tree switching and transmission.

FIGURE 10: Comparisons of blocking ratio for channel control.

control performance than that of the receiver-initiated routing algorithm. Therefore, the proposed HT-ERM scheme can reduce the channel change delay by enhancing the hybrid-tree operation with efficient switchover mechanism for RP-centralized control.

(2) Channel Blocking Ratio. To simulate the blocking ratio for practical IPTV channel service, multicast routing protocols are employed by using different routing algorithm for number of IPTV channel request per group joining. By adjusting the channel switching ratios (α = 0.25, 0.5, and 0.8) for different test scenarios, the HD QoS IPTV channels are requested to join per group member using PIM-SM with ECMP, QMRP with QSPF, and the proposed HT-ERM with CSPF. The results of Figure 10 indicate that the HT-ERM scheme with CSPF outperforms the other two QSPF and ECMP algorithm beneath the average switch ratio (α = 0.5), while the number of channel joining requests is increasing from 10 to 50. We observe that the traditional PIM-SM multicast using ECMP resulted in the highest blocking ratio due to the traffic aggregation over shared tree with the same routing path, regardless of the multiple parallel links. In additions, note that the channel blocking ratio of HT-ERM is rising sharply by admission control at higher switching ratio α = 0.8.

(3) Channel Resource Usage. Figure 11 shows the results of resource usage for delivering watching streams over the requested IPTV channels using different multicast approaches. The resource consumptions are nearly even with those multicast approaches: PIM-SM (ECMP), QMRP (QSPF), and proposed HT-ERM (CSPF) at any channel switching ratio (α = 0.8, 0.5, 0.25). For the effect of traffic load balancing, QMRP and HT-ERM scheme can achieve the better link usage performance as compared by PIM-SM while the number of channel joining is increasing to 50. Because

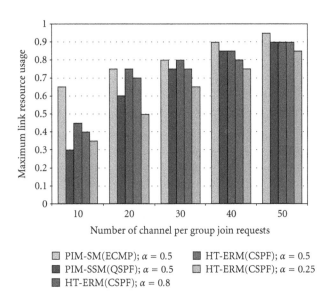

FIGURE 11: Comparisons of resource usage for IPTV channels.

the QSPF routing algorithm is based on receiver's multiple tree-nodes joining decision, the channel traffic distribution can perform better than that of the proposed HT-ERM at lower channel joining requests of 10 and 20. However, the maximum link utilization of HT-ERM performs nearly the same resource usage at higher channel joining requests more than 30. This is the cross-effect caused by network congestion and traffic control. Therefore, the proposed HT-ERM scheme can operate hybrid-tree efficiently via enhanced RP functionality which makes better resource management for HD/SD channel stream utilization and traffic load distribution by hybrid-tree multicast channel service.

6. Conclusions

As the killer application in future Internet, IPTV service needs to provide the effective and efficient operations for channel delivery and control. The hybrid-tree-based multicast IPTV has been validated to supply watching channels and surfing channel services. However, we need to overcome the drawbacks in RP functionality and switchover mechanism to achieve effectiveness and efficiency in hybrid-tree multicast channel control and delivery. To solve the QoS degradation problems of multicast network utilization and IPTV channel change delay, the hybrid-tree-based explicit routed multicast (HT-ERM) scheme is proposed to enhance current multicast protocols for QoS-supported IPTV service. The main contributions focus on performance improvement for multicast network delivery and IPTV channel control, including the reduction of maximum link resource utilization, fast switchover mechanism for channel change delay, and admission for multicast QoS channel setup. In network-layer level, HT-ERM provides flexible approach to design hybrid-tree-based IPTV multicast for IP multicast protocols. We also validate multicast solution to QoS-supported IPTV channel control and delivery by simulation. The result shows that the proposed HT-ERM outperforms existing QoS multicast approaches applied by PIM-related protocols while retaining QoS guarantee.

References

[1] Y. Xiao, X. Du, J. Zhang, F. Hu, and S. Guizani, "Internet protocol television (IPTV): the killer application for the next-generation internet," *IEEE Communications Magazine*, vol. 45, no. 11, pp. 126–134, 2007.

[2] W. Sun, X. Luo, K. Lin, and Y. Guan, "Performance analysis of a finite duration multichannel delivery method in IPTV," *IEEE Transactions on Broadcasting*, vol. 54, no. 3, pp. 419–429, 2008.

[3] D. E. Smith, "IP TV bandwidth demand: multicast and channel surfing," in *Proceedings of the 26th IEEE International Conference on Computer Communications (INFOCOM '07)*, pp. 2546–2550, Anchorage, Alaska, USA, May 2007.

[4] S. Chen, K. Nahrstedt, and Y. Shavitt, "QoS-aware multicast routing protocol," *IEEE Journal on Selected Areas in Communications*, vol. 18, no. 12, pp. 2580–2592, 2000.

[5] H. Holbrook and B. Cain, "RFC 4607: Source-Specific Multicast for IP," Internet Engineering Task Force, August 2006.

[6] B. Fenner, M. Handley, H. Holbrook, and I. Kouvelas, "Protocol Independent Multicast-Sparse Mode (PIM-SM): Protocol Specification (Revised)," RFC 4601, August 2006.

[7] C. C. Wen, C. S. Wu, and M. T. Yang, "Hybrid tree based explicit routed multicast for QoS supported IPTV service," in *Proceedings of the IEEE Global Telecommunications Conference (GLOBECOM '09)*, December 2009.

[8] M. Bag-Mohammadi, N. Yazdani, and S. Samadian-Barzoki, "On the efficiency of explicit multicast routing protocols," in *Proceedings of the 10th IEEE Symposium on Computers and Communications (ISCC '05)*, pp. 679–685, June 2005.

[9] S. Yasukawa, M. Uga, H. Kojima, and K. Sugisono, "Extended RSVP-TE for Multicast LSP Tunnels," IETF draft, June 2003.

[10] C. Sasaki, A. Tagami, T. Hasegawa, and S. Ano, "Rapid channel zapping for IPTV broadcasting with additional multicast stream," in *Proceedings of the IEEE International Conference on Communications (ICC '08)*, pp. 1760–1766, May 2008.

[11] Y. Kim, J. K. Park, H. J. Choi et al., "Reducing IPTV channel zapping time based on viewer's surfing behavior and preference," in *Proceedings of the IEEE International Symposium on Broadband Multimedia Systems and Broadcasting (BMSB '08)*, April 2008.

[12] H. Joo, H. Song, D. B. Lee, and I. Lee, "An effective IPTV channel control algorithm considering channel zapping time and network utilization," *IEEE Transactions on Broadcasting*, vol. 54, no. 2, pp. 208–216, 2008.

[13] Cisco Technical Support Module, *Load Splitting IP Multicast Traffic over ECMP*, Cisco Systems, 2007.

[14] B. Chinoy and H.-W. Braun, "The national science foundation network," Technical Report GA-A210029, SDSC, 1992.

[15] K. L. Calvert, E. W. Zegura, and S. Bhattacharjee, "How to model an internetwork," in *Proceedings of the 1996 15th Annual Joint Conference of the IEEE Computer and Communications Societies (INFOCOM '96)*, pp. 594–602, March 1996.

5

Monitoring Accessibility Services in Digital Television

Francisco Utray,[1, 2] **Mercedes de Castro,**[1, 3] **Lourdes Moreno,**[4] **and Belén Ruiz-Mezcua**[1, 4]

[1] *Spanish Centre of Captioning and Audio Description (CESyA), Avenida de Gregorio Peces-Barba 1, 28918 Madrid, Spain*
[2] *Research Group TECMERIN, Journalism and Audiovisual Communication Department, Universidad Carlos III de Madrid,*
   C/Madrid 126, 28903 Getafe, Madrid, Spain
[3] *Telematic Department, Universidad Carlos III de Madrid, Avenida de la Universidad 30, 28911 Leganés, Madrid, Spain*
[4] *Computer Science Department, Universidad Carlos III de Madrid, Avenida de la Universidad 30, 28911 Leganés, Madrid, Spain*

Correspondence should be addressed to Lourdes Moreno, lmoreno@inf.uc3m.es

Academic Editor: Thomas John Owens

This paper addresses methodology and tools applied to the monitoring of accessibility services in digital television at a time when the principles of accessibility and design are being considered in all new audiovisual media communication services. The main objective of this research is to measure the quality and quantity of existing accessibility services offered by digital terrestrial television (DTT). The preliminary results, presented here, offer the development of a prototype for automatic monitoring and a methodology for obtaining quality measurements, along with the conclusions drawn by initial studies carried out in Spain. The recent approval of the UN Convention on the Rights of Persons with Disabilities gives special relevance to this research because it provides valuable guidelines to help set the priorities to improve services currently available to users.

1. Introduction

The Convention on the Rights of Persons with Disabilities, adopted on 13 December 2006 by the UN General Assembly, is an important milestone for technological developments related to people with disabilities. Article 6 of this convention establishes that

To enable persons with disabilities to live independently and participate fully in all aspects of life, states parties shall take appropriate measures to ensure to persons with disabilities access, on an equal basis with others, to the physical environment, to transportation, to information and communications, including information and communications technologies and systems.

The UN Convention thus recognises the right of people with disabilities to access communication and cultural information. As a supporting instrument, the G3ict initiative defines and maintains an index of accessibility and digital inclusion, which provides a measure of the degree to which countries meet the requirements for providing accessibility to information and communication technologies (ICT).

Worldwide, this situation has led to new legislation to enforce the provision of accessibility. As far as accessibility to television is concerned, the different laws focus on subtitling, audio description, sign language interpretation, and accessible interactive services; these aspects will be addressed below. Television operators are among the entities affected by these service requirements. Governments in many countries have taken initiatives to promote and regulate accessibility services to multimedia television contents. This is the case in Spain [1, 2], UK [3], France, Italy, Germany, and other countries in Europe [4]. Current regulations establish minimum levels of availability of accessible multimedia in DTT as well as in the fast growing IPTV networks.

Once these regulations are established, it is necessary to measure and qualify the actual contents of subtitling and audio description services. Television operators need to evaluate the real presence of accessibility services. While users' organisations are also interested parties, it is the duty of regulators to monitor what providers are really offering. The UN Convention, in Article 33 entitled "National implementation and monitoring", states that state parties and civil society shall designate and establish "... a framework, including one or more independent mechanisms, as appropriate, to promote, protect and monitor implementation of the present Convention ...", and civil society "shall be involved and participate fully in the monitoring process."

To measure the degree of compliance with obligations related to the above requirements imposed on television operators, new tools and research methodologies are necessary to monitor both the quantity and quality of the provided services. This challenge has been addressed within the Hermes-TDT project, the preliminary results of which are presented in this paper.

After this introduction, Section 2 includes a background on the subject and related work. Section 3 offers a study on accessibility monitoring services in digital television in Spain. DTT accessibility services are explored in Section 4. The methodology proposed for monitoring accessibility services in digital television is presented in Section 5. The Hermes-TDT approach is presented in Section 6. As a resource, Section 7 offers a checklist, and finally some conclusions are given.

2. Background

Accessibility to digital television systems is a topic that has received a major boost in recent years as a result of studies utilising a new multidisciplinary research perspective [5], which has departed from studies limited to a linguistic scope [6], incorporating new disciplines into the research field [7–9]. Research networks that have included this new perspective include the Cepacc network (http://www.cepacc.net/) in Spain and the international networks transmedia (http://www.transmediaresearchgroup.com/) and Intercultural Studies Group (http://isg.urv.es/isg.htm).

Studies in the areas of communication sciences [10], audiovisual translation [6, 11, 12], linguistics [13, 14], and telecommunications engineering [15], conducted in collaboration with leading companies and international experts [16], have led to significant, high-quality technological developments in Europe and particularly in Spain.

Based on the above-mentioned research and consultations with the organisations that represent people with disabilities (EDF (http://www.edf-feph.org/), CERMI (http://www.cermi.es/en-US/Pages/Portada.aspx), and RNIB (http://www.rnib.org.uk/), we can highlight some of the most important requirements for accessibility services in television according to the specific disabilities of users.

Thus, we can state that people with hearing disabilities require

(i) subtitles available for 100% of the broadcast content,

(ii) the use of Sign Language in newscasts, documentaries, and education programmes [17],

(iii) a clean audio service [18] available for dramatic or fictional contents.

For people with visual impairments, the audio description service is essential for fiction programmes and documentaries. However, this group also requires that interactive services, such as the electronic program guide (EPG), be accessible by means of audio navigation systems [19, 20]. People with residual vision also require enhanced graphical user interfaces.

People with physical disabilities have also defined their user requirements for television, focusing on the need for interactive navigation systems and the ergonomics of hardware and software to be adapted to the great heterogeneity of their needs.

The elderly and people with intellectual disabilities can benefit from applications that address any of the requirements mentioned above, provided these applications follow a "design for all" strategy [16]. This approach postulates that if products and environments are designed and developed taking into consideration the demands of people with special needs, all users can benefit from the usability and quality of these products.

3. Previous Study of the Monitoring Accessibility Services in the Spanish DTT

For users and regulators the quantity of accessibility services is the most relevant of all aspects related to television accessibility. In this research, a procedure has been designed to measure the amount of time during which subtitling, audio description and sign language are available in IPTV or DTT channels. For this reason, the first objective considered is to verify if broadcasters are complying with the percentage of accessible programming defined by the regulator.

Ever since January 2011, it is incumbent on Spanish Audiovisual Authorities to ascertain that television operators have indeed complied with the established regulation by the end of December 2010 regarding the provision of accessibility services pursuant to the General Law on Audiovisual Communication (LGCA) [2]. To that purpose, subtitle, audio description, and sign language interpretation services need to be measured in a homogeneous and reliable manner for each television channel.

Two bodies in Spain have dealt with such measurements: the Spanish Telecommunications Market Commission (CMT) (http://www.cmt.es/) and the Ministry of Industry, Tourism and Trade. For the time being, official and public information on the availability of accessibility services emanates from the CMT and is based on the questionnaires that television operators provide it with since 2008. In addition, in 2006 the Ministry of Industry, Tourism and Trade commissioned the Kantar Media (http://www.kantarmedia.es/) company to collect data on accessibility service provision in the main DTT channels.

We have carried out a comparative analysis of both sources. The result has yielded significantly different results in measurements, proving that the margin of error is high and that the methodologies employed by the two bodies are not consistent.

In Figure 1, we compare annual subtitling average percentages in the CMT report with the data collected by Kantar Media. Figures provided by operators to the CMT are

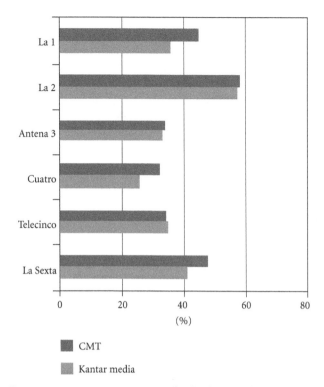

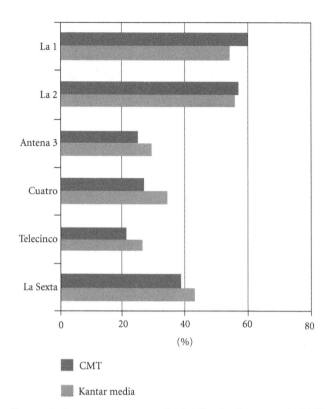

Figure 1: Average percentages of subtitling in the main DTT channels in Spain in 2009. Comparison of sources: CMT and Kantar Media (elaborated by the authors).

Figure 2: Average percentages of subtitling in the two main DTT channels in Spain during the first semester of 2010. Comparison of sources: CMT and Kantar (elaborated by the authors).

almost always higher than those measured by Kantar Media (except for "Telecinco" channel). The gaps are considerable in "La 1," "La Sexta," and "Cuatro," ranging from 9 to 6 percentage points. However, for "Telecinco," "Antena 3," and "La 2" channels, the gaps are more reasonable, coming to approximately one per cent.

Available data for the first semester of 2010 (see Figure 2) shows that the differences between the two sources ranging from −7 to 6 percentage points, but we cannot reasonably explain the evolution of the gap for each one of the channels in the two years analysed.

With the data available for the two periods, the maximum gap ranges between 9% for "La 1" channel in 2009 and 7% for "Cuatro" channel in 2010.

We thus consider that, in order to carry out reliable and verifiable measurements in Spain, it is imperative to establish a permanent observation laboratory, as well as to implement the methodology introduced in the present paper for quality assessment. The system developed in the Hermes-TDT project may be the best technology for this purpose.

4. Analysis of Requirements for Accessibility Services in Digital Television

This section explores DTT accessibility services. The first issue addressed within the HERMES-TDT project was an analysis of the requirements needed by the different services that provide accessibility to television content. Once these requirements have been identified, an assessment method

is developed. Conclusions on how to address the service tracking/monitoring process are provided.

4.1. Subtitling Service. Subtitling for the deaf and hard of hearing is a written summary of dialogues, music, and sound effects that is displayed on screen simultaneously as sound is being emitted [11].

The European standard for digital terrestrial television (DTT) offers two types of subtitles: DVB subtitling and Teletext. Some European broadcasters such as the BBC in the United Kingdom and CRTVE in Spain use both technologies simultaneously, while other broadcasters have chosen to use just one of them.

In both cases, subtitle signalling in the television's signal transport stream (TS) is an important parameter. It needs to be analysed to verify interoperability and to ensure the technical quality of the reception.

All digital receivers and television sets sold in Europe should support both types of subtitles. This is a demanding regulation, and not all of the receivers in the market presently comply with this rule. A thorough analysis of the accessibility of the set-top boxes and television sets in Spain revealed that equipment that is not fully accessible can still be found in the market [10].

In addition to the regulatory obligations to adapt all related equipment to the needs of different users and to broadcast a given number of hours of subtitled programmes, there are also codes of best practices for subtitling that identify a range of quality indicators related to the use of language, synchronisation with sound, presentation speed [23], and size and position, as well as typographical issues [24]. However, most of these quality parameters cannot be analysed in a fully automated way and require human intervention by an expert researcher for their evaluation.

Therefore, a combination of both manual and automated verification methods is needed for a comprehensive evaluation of the quality of a subtitling service.

4.2. Audio Description Service.

The audio description provides a narrative of the visual elements of an audiovisual programme to visually impaired people [25].

The approach used in Europe is to provide this accessibility service through an alternate audio channel that offers a mix of the original soundtrack and the audio description. In the United Kingdom, a system of local mixing in the receiver, also recognised by the DVB digital television standard [26], is available as an alternative.

A relevant aspect of this research is the analysis of audio description signalling within the transport stream. Signalling, defined by the standard mentioned above, is not homogeneously used in the different countries of the European Union; there are even different interpretations of the standard within the countries themselves.

As in the previous category, along with the technical quality and related signalling parameters, there are codes of best practices in the field of audio description that address issues such as language use, quality of diction (intonation and interpretation), sound mix, and adequacy in fulfilling needs of users [27]. All these parameters require the intervention of domain experts in the evaluation process.

Therefore, a manual method carried out by experts was needed for a comprehensive evaluation of an audio description service.

4.3. Sign Language Service.

Sign Language is a linguistic communication system traditionally used by the deaf and deafblind signers [17].

Although combinations of Sign Language and different technologies have been widely studied [17, 28], the use of Sign Language in television is currently limited to the incorporation of an interpreter in the image, either by integrating her/him in the original television staging or by using a dedicated on-screen window.

The development and integration of a Sign Language option that users could enable or disable using the remote control is still pending.

Therefore automatic monitoring of this service is restricted because, at present, Sign Language interpretation services are embedded in the video signal and are not identified as such in the transmission flow.

4.4. Clean Audio Service.

A clean audio service provides the end user with a sound mix that favours dialogue over sound effects and music, thereby optimising the understanding of verbal audio content [18].

Incorporating this accessibility service into the DVB standard has been contemplated; however, regular broadcasting of this service has not started yet in Europe, and the need to move forward on this issue has only been pointed out in research circles.

Therefore, monitoring for this service has been postponed until its future development.

4.5. Accessibility to Interactive Services.

Accessibility to the interactive services of digital television is another key factor in the nondiscrimination of people with disabilities. However, the technological innovations required in this field are oriented primarily toward manufacturers of receiving equipment and are beyond the scope of this research, which is limited to monitoring the provision of accessibility services by broadcasters.

The multimedia home platform (MHP) interactivity system (http://www.etsi.org/), whose implementation in Europe has been tried in the 2000–2010 decade, has failed to raise consumer demand. A new model of interactivity based on Internet connectivity in television receivers is currently being defined. The definition of accessibility verification models for this emerging technology requires more data than is currently available.

5. Methodology Approach for Monitoring of Accessibility Services in Digital Television

One goal of the HERMES-TDT project is to define indicators and methods for evaluating the accessibility of services in digital television. As discussed in Section 4, the methodology must provide support to evaluation through a combination of automatic, semiautomatic, and manual processes.

Just as previously indicated, the tools and procedures for measuring and classifying these services must take into account both the aspects that can be automatically measured and those that can only be measured through human intervention.

(i) The elements that can be automatically monitored include the existence of an audio stream for audio description, existence of subtitle streams, actual presence of subtitles in television channels, EPG content, coherence between subtitle presence and signalling data, colour use in subtitles, and subtitle speed.

(ii) Human intervention is required for advertisement detection in video streams (which in some scenarios can be automated), actual content of the audio description streams, literality, and subtitling of audio effects. By measuring these parameters, it is possible to analyse the existence, quantity, and quality of services.

6. Hermes-TDT Project

The research lines within the Hermes-TDT project address the accessibility of audiovisual media in digital terrestrial television for people that are visually or hearing impaired.

The main objectives are (1) to provide the knowledge and equipment required to monitor the actual accessible audiovisual content in the DTT signal transmission in Spain and (2) to measure the real audience for these accessibility aids and their perceived usefulness.

To achieve such goals, the project has developed a technology. This technology includes two tools for measuring the broadcast and audience of accessibility services in digital terrestrial television (DTT).

The first system (called DTV signal sniffer) samples the DTT signal in a particular geographical location and extracts relevant information. The second system (called TDT audience sniffer) automatically monitors the audience's use of accessibility services in DTT channels.

This work focuses on the first system, designed to monitor subtitling and audio description in the DTT broadcast.

6.1. Hermes-TDT Signal Sniffer. Within the Spanish Hermes-TDT project, the signal sniffer system automatically analyses the signals transmitted by broadcasters by extracting data and analysing the signalling related to the services mentioned above. This system, which is in a prototype phase, provides quantitative measurements of the services and also verifies the adequacy of signalling in regard to applicable television broadcasting quality standards.

Thus, the Hermes-TDT Signal Sniffer recovers and processes critical information through automated methods following the methodology described above.

The Hermes-TDT signal sniffer is a distributed system that is able to continuously monitor relevant information from the DTT signal in various geographic positions according to the coverage maps of national and regional channels (see "Hermes-TDT signal sniffer at location 1 and 2" in Figure 3).

The TDT signal sniffer is a configurable system (see "remote management" in Figure 3), which enables the user to configure a number of useful parameters by remote control via a web interface. The configurable parameters include the number of channels sampled, the frequency of signal sampling, and the extraction of video sample (duration, frequency, etc.) among others. Once the user has selected the desired options, the system generates a configuration file. This file is sent to the remote configuration subsystems and to the control system included in the TDT signal sniffer. Afterwards the system will begin operating following the configuration file.

This system operates in two phases: information extraction, in which DTT signals are captured in real time, and a second stage in which an offline analysis of the stored information is carried out.

(1) In the first step: "*Capture and store*", the system extracts the relevant data necessary for an evaluation of accessibility and transfers it to a database. Each Hermes-TDT signal sniffer node explores the DTT signal. New information detected is time-stamped and stored in the database. The following data recovery processes are executed

(i) Extracting programming data from the event information table (EIT).

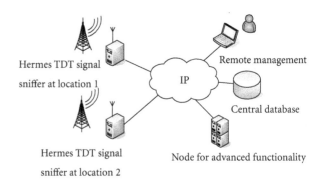

FIGURE 3: Hermes TDT signal sniffer.

(ii) Detecting the actual presence of subtitling and audio descriptions for each programming event described in the electronic programming guide (EPG).

(iii) Obtaining signalling data, including composition of every channel (e.g., video, audio, subtitles, Teletext, MPH application), signalling related to the accessibility services available in each channel, and timing information required for further processing.

(iv) Extracting the subtitles themselves from the transmission flow, that is, retrieving and storing the entire subtitle contents. Because of the differences between subtitles used in Teletext and DVB, two formats for extraction are defined:

(a) Teletext subtitles: information regarding the text, presentation time, colour information, and position on the screen is stored,

(b) DVB subtitles: the rendered images of subtitles and their corresponding time codes, along with the position information on the screen, are stored. Textual information in this case can be recovered in a further process by using optical character recognition (OCR) technology.

(v) Recording full DTT signals of one or more channels. This permits further offline research in areas that require human intervention.

All this information is stored in a "central database" (see Figure 3). Relevant data is time-stamped to provide a complete information history.

(2) As a second step: "*Analyze*", the system can automatically extract quality-of-service indicators from the central database. Stored data is postprocessed with the combination of automatic, semiautomatic, and manual methods described in Section 4.

The extracted data can also be used as a source for further research based on manual measurements of those aspects that cannot be automated. The manual and human-based analysis of stored data are speech and subtitle synchronization, subtitle colour for the identification of speakers, literality of subtitles, and verification of subtitle adequacy for the deaf and the hard of hearing among others. The processes to be performed are manual screening; we provide more detailed information in the next section.

Additional analyses of stored data can be automatic. Among the measurements or reports automatically provided by the system are the following:

(i) subtitle presence/absence,

(ii) total subtitling time including advertising,

(iii) coherence between EPG and actual subtitles,

(iv) subtitle colours,

(v) subtitle speed,

(vi) characters per line in the subtitles,

(vii) EPG historical data.

Through automatic analysis, the system generates reports on the total time of availability for each service in each channel and on the consistency of signalling.

With regard to audio description monitoring, it is necessary to highlight the fact that it is not possible to automatically verify whether any of the audio streams associated with a television channel actually contains an audio description or not. However, when an audio description is known to exist, it is possible to verify the presence of correct signalling (according to DVB standards).

During the preliminary research for this project, it was found that in the few television channels in Spain that broadcast audio description (channels owned by "RTVE" or "TV3"), signalling is not in line with the DVB standard: the audio stream containing the audio description is signalled just like any of the other audio streams that convey alternative audio in other languages. This precludes any signalling-based automated monitoring.

As a consequence, quantitative measurements of the number of hours of audio description of a given television channel is only possible by human-based analyses of recordings obtained for this purpose; these analyses can be scheduled using television programme guides available in different media (i.e., newspapers, Teletext, and Internet).

6.2. Manual Method for Evaluation of the Quality of the Broadcast Accessibility Services. The extracted subtitle files are also used for quality-of-service analyses that require manual intervention by an expert researcher. The analysis parameters have been defined using the most relevant professional best practice codes in Europe as a basis [3, 29, 30]. The analysis parameters, identified as being applicable to subtitling, have been considered when defining the methodology. These parameters are classified into three groups: those concerning aspects of the presentation of the texts, those related to the correct use of language, and those related to the synchronisation of subtitles with audio. Relevant parameters in each group are indicated below:

(i) presentation attributes: text font size, position on the screen, and use of colours to identify different speakers,

(ii) language: spelling and syntactical correctness,

(iii) synchronisation: literality, verbosity, and presentation speed.

On the other hand, the recordings of the video, audio, and subtitle streams allow further research regarding the availability of signalling for accessibility services, as well as on the correctness of the EPG in relation to the actual content of the broadcast. Among the indicators that are manually evaluated, the most relevant are

(i) correct name in the event-name field of the EPG,

(ii) EPG updated in sync. to actual programme changes,

(iii) existence and consistency of subtitle signalling,

(iv) existence of Teletext subtitles,

(v) existence of DVB subtitles,

(vi) interference of subtitles with other informative captions,

(vii) subtitle position on the screen,

(viii) number of subtitle lines in prerecorded programmes,

(ix) number of subtitle lines in live programmes,

(x) usage of colours in subtitles.

As an aid resource for professionals, the next section provides a checklist of guidelines that include the many indicators that need to be considered in a subtitling service.

When analysing the parameters for the audio description, the most relevant indicators are

(i) how the language is used,

(ii) the quality of intonation and interpretation,

(iii) sound mixing quality,

(iv) how user needs are met.

6.3. Results of Hermes-TDT Project. Following the methods and using the technology shown in the Hermes-TDT project, the following conclusions are derived from verification work in the fourth quarter of 2009.

The analysis has been executed over a sample of television clips obtained from 20 television channels. The samples were recorded in 35 min slots interleaved with 30 min pauses; the recordings took place over four different weeks during November and December 2009. Sample analysis produced a set of questionnaires for 170 different programs, including top audience leaders and covering different genres. The main conclusions of this preliminary research are as follows.

(i) With regard to subtitling services, it has been verified that subtitle generation is, in general, driven by literality and follows the conventions established by the UNE 153010 standard [29].

(ii) Similarly, we can assert that the technology most widely used in Spain for the transmission of this service is Teletext, with the use of the DVB standard for subtitling being limited to only a few channels.

TABLE 1: Checklist of checkpoints and evaluation guidelines defined for the manual verification of subtitling in television programmes.

N	Checkpoint	Checking-guideline
1	Programme name in EPG	Check if name in EPG corresponds with programme name
2	EPG synchronisation	Check if EPG information is updated when a programme starts, within a predetermined time window
3	Subtitle signalling	Check that subtitle icons appear in the on-screen display of the television set
4	Presence of subtitles	Activate Teletext subtitles and check whether they appear on the screen
		Activate DVB subtitles and check whether they appear on the screen
5	Subtitle position on screen	Check that speech subtitles are centred and in the lower part of the screen
		Check the position of sound effect subtitles
		Check that no overlays occur when open captions appear on screen
6	No. of lines of text in a subtitle	Get the maximum number of lines simultaneously displayed on the screen in prerecorded programmes
		Get the maximum number of lines simultaneously displayed on the screen in live programmes
7	Colour usage	Check whether colours are used to identify different characters in the programme
		Check if colour allocation is consistent throughout the entire programme
8	Subtitling speed	Check the time in which individual subtitles are displayed and their length to obtain maximum and average subtitling speeds
9	Subtitle grammatical correctness	Evaluate the level of orthographical and syntactical correctness of text
10	Subtitle literality	Evaluate how close subtitle and speech contents are
11	Subtitle synchronisation	Measure subtitle presentation times relative to corresponding speech fragments to obtain maximum and average offsets both in prerecorded and live programmes

(iii) There is no uniformity in the signalling of subtitling services.

(iv) We have detected that, with certain exceptions, broadcasters do not dynamically signal changes in the availability of subtitling.

(v) The fact that audio description services are almost nonexistent in Spain must be emphasised. Few audio-described programmes are broadcasted on public television networks, and private entities have not yet begun to provide this service.

(vi) Regarding the accuracy of the EPG, the results show important discrepancies between EPG contents and actual broadcasts for all television channels in Spain. This is an important issue, as a reliable EPG is essential for users requiring accessibility services.

7. Checklist for Manual Verification of Subtitling in Television Programmes

Tools and algorithms defined within the Hermes-TDT project allow for the automated capture and manual post-processing of an important subset of checkpoints, the most remarkable being subtitle presence, speed, number of lines, and position on screen, colour presence, and subtitle signalling.

As a helpful resource for evaluators, Table 1 shows the checkpoints that were defined for manual analysis. The unit of analysis that was used is the television programme.

Each checkpoint listed below represents an independent variable and can be measured separately. The evaluation

of the overall quality and adequacy of a given television programme from the accessibility point of view must take into account the fact that some of these parameters may be interrelated. The correlation between such parameters is beyond the scope of this research project.

8. Conclusions

This research work provides an overview of the accessibility requirements taken into account when assessing the accessibility services in digital television and offers an overview of the situation in Spain. It also provides a methodological approach as a resource on how to carry out follow-up processes and evaluation of the accessibility of digital TV services, which can be extrapolated to other countries.

The indicators required and guidelines for the measurements presented in this paper are themselves a significant contribution to knowledge on this subject.

As the provision of accessibility services is inseparable from television content in future multimedia networks, the legislative developments should come together with the creation of supervision and enforcement methodologies like the technology and methods of the Hermes-TDT project, which monitor compliance with the requirements stated by the UN Convention and by local legislation. These entities need appropriate tools to carry out their function, an activity that, in order to evaluate service provision from both quantitative and qualitative points of view, will also require appropriate analytical methodologies. This paper has presented a practical procedure and a methodology summarized in Table 2, to accomplish this task. The results obtained can

TABLE 2: Additional: Hermes-TDT method summary.

Accessibility services in digital TV	Methods	Monitoring process		Manual evaluation to guarantee quality (parameters)
		Step 1: capture and store	Step 2: analysis process	
Subtitles	Automated and manual methods	(i) EPG information	(i) Subtitle presence/absence	(i) Correct name in the event-name field of the EPG
		(ii) DTT channel composition	(ii) Audio description presence/absence	(ii) EPG updated in sync to actual programme changes
		(iii) Detecting subtitling for each programming event in the EPG.	(iii) Total subtitling time including spots	(iii) Existence and consistency of subtitle signalling
		(iv) Subtitles themselves	(iv) Coherence between EPG and actual subtitles	(iv) Existence of Teletext subtitles
		(a) Teletext: presentation time, speed, colour information, and position on the screen	(v) Subtitle colors	(v) Existence of DVB subtitles
		(b) DVB: the rendered images and time codes, speed, along with the position information on the screen	(vi) Subtitle speed	(vi) Interference of subtitles with other informative captions
			(vii) Character per line in the subtitles	(vii) Subtitle position on the screen
			(viii) Historic EPG	(viii) Number of subtitle lines in prerecorded programmes
				(ix) Number of subtitle lines in live programmes
				(x) Usage of colours in subtitles (follow checklist of Table 1)
Audio description	Semiautomatic and manual method	(i) Detecting audio descriptions for each programming event described in the EPG	(i) Audio description presence/absence	(i) Used language
		(ii) Extracting the audio description themselves according to DVB standards	(*) Some exception of the audio streams that can contain an audio description or not	(ii) Quality of intonation and interpretation
		(*) Some exception of the audio streams that can contain an audio description or not		(iii) Sound mixing quality
				(iv) How user needs are met

be utilised by regulatory entities and broadcasters to measure both quantity and quality of the accessibility services offered to users.

Technological developments may open a new door to research in the field of accessibility; however, the identification of objective criteria to define quality indicators is a very complex task that will undoubtedly spark debate and discussion.

Acknowledgments

This research work is supported by the Spanish Ministry of Industry, Tourism and Trade (Avanza I+D programme) and The Spanish Centre of Captioning and Audio Description (see http://www.cesya.com/).

References

[1] *Spanish Digital Television Technical Forum, WG 5 for accessibility*, Spanish Ministry of Industry, Tourism and Trade, 2006.

[2] Spanish Government, "Law 7/2010, de 31 de marzo, General Law on Audiovisual Communication," Spain: BOE, 2010, http://boe.es/boe/dias/2010/04/01/pdfs/BOE-A-2010-5292.pdf.

[3] OFCOM, *Code on Television Access Services*, Office of Communication, London, UK, 2008.

[4] OSI/EU Monitoring and Advocacy Programme, "Television across Europe: Regulation, policy and independence," Hungary: Open Society Institute, 2005, http://www.soros.org/initiatives/media/articles_publications/publications/eurotv_20051011.

[5] A. Pereira and V. Arnáiz, "A comprehensive bibliography on subtitling for the deaf and hard of hearing from a multidisciplinary approach," in *Listening to the Subtitles*, A. Matamala and P. Orero, Eds., pp. 219–228, Peter Lang, Frankfurt, Germany, 2010.

[6] Y. Gambier, "Multimodality and Audiovisual Translation," in *Audiovisual Translation Scenarios (MuTra '06)*, EU–High–Level Scientific Conference Series, Copenhagen, Denmark, 2006.

[7] G. D'Ydewalle and W. De Bruycker, "Eye movements of children and adults while reading television subtitles," *European Psychologist*, vol. 12, no. 3, pp. 196–205, 2007.

[8] C. Eugeni, "Respeaking the BBC news: a strategic analysis of respeaking on the BBC," *The Sign Language Translator and Interpreter*, vol. 3, pp. 29–68, 2009.

[9] T. Häikiö, R. Bertram, J. Hyönä, and P. Niemi, "Development of the letter identity span in reading: evidence from the eye movement moving window paradigm," *Journal of Experimental Child Psychology*, vol. 102, no. 2, pp. 167–181, 2009.

[10] F. Utray, *Accesibilidad a la TDT en España, para personas con discapacidad sensorial (2005–2007)*, Real Patronato sobre Discapacidad, Madrid, Spain, 2009.

[11] J. Díaz Cintas, Ed., *The Didactics of Audiovisual Translation*, John Benjamins, Philadelphia, Pa, USA, 2008.

[12] Y. Gambier, "Challenges in research on audiovisual translation," in *Translation Research Projects 2*, A. Pym and A. Perekrestenko, Eds., pp. 17–25, Intercultural Studies Group, Tarragona, Spain, 2009.

[13] S. Ramos Pinto, "Theatrical texts vs subtitling: linguistic variation in a polymedial context," in *Audiovisual Translation Scenarios (MuTra '06)*, Copenhagen, Denmark, 2006.

[14] Y. Zhang and J. Liu, "Subtitle translation strategies as a reflection of technical limitations: a case study of Ang Lee's films," Asian Social Science, 5, 2009, http://www.ccsenet.org/journal/index.php/ass/article/view/545.

[15] F. deJong, "Access Services for Digital TV," in *Sociedad, integración y televisión en España*, R. Pérez-Amat and A. Pérez-Ugena, Eds., pp. 331–344, Laberinto, Madrid, Spain, 2006.

[16] P. O. Looms, "Digital television for some or for all?" in *Listening to the Subtitles*, A. Matamala and P. Orero, Eds., pp. 19–25, Peter Lang, Frankfurt, Germany, 2010.

[17] A. Pereira, "Including Spanish sign language in subtitles for the deaf and hard of hearing," in *Listening to the Subtitles*, A. Matamala and P. Orero, Eds., pp. 103–115, Peter Lang, Frankfurt, Germany, 2010.

[18] B. Shirley and P. Kendrick, "The Clean Audio project: Digital TV as assistive technology," *Technology and Disability*, vol. 18, no. 1, pp. 31–41, 2006.

[19] J. Greening, "Development of audio description in the UK," in *Sociedad, integración y televisión en España*, R. Pérez-Amat and Á. Pérez-Ugena, Eds., Laberinto, Madrid, Spain, 2006.

[20] C. Schmidt and T. Wlodkowski, *A developer's guide to creating talking menus for set–top–boxes and DVDs*, WGBH Educational Foundation, Boston, Mass, USA, 2003.

[21] N. Tanton and P. Weitzel, "DVB subtitleling in an open environment," in *Proceedings of the International Broadcasting Conference (IBC '99)*, 1999.

[22] J. Clark, "How standardization solves problems in captioning and beyond," in *Proceedings of the NAB Broadcast Engineering Conference*, 2004.

[23] P. Romero-Fresco, "More haste less speed: Edited versus verbatim respoken subtitles," *Vigo International Journal of Applied Linguistics*, vol. 6, no. 1, pp. 109–133, 2009.

[24] F. Utray, B. Ruiz, and J. A. Moreiro, "Maximum font size for subtitles in standard definition digital television (SDTV): Tests for a font magnifying application," in *Listening to the Subtitles*, A. Matamala and P. Orero, Eds., pp. 59–69, Peter Lang, Frankfurt, Germany, 2010.

[25] F. Utray, A. M. Pereira, and P. Orero, "The present and future of audio description and subtitling for the deaf and hard of hearing in spain," *Meta*, vol. 54, no. 2, pp. 248–263, 2009.

[26] G. Stallard, "Standardisation requirements for access to digital TV and interactive services by disabled people," Final report to CENELEC on TV for ALL, 2003.

[27] P. Orero, "Audio description: professional recognition, practice and standards in Spain," *Translation Watch Quarterly*, vol. 1, pp. 7–18, 2005.

[28] I. C. Báez and S. Fernández, "Spanish deaf people as recipients of closed captioning," in *Listening to the Subtitles*, A. Matamala and P. Orero, Eds., pp. 25–44, Peter Lang, Frankfurt, Germany, 2010.

[29] AENOR Spanish technical standards, "Standard UNE 153010: 2003: Subtitled through teletext," http://www.aenor.es/.

[30] AENOR Spanish technical standards, "Standard UNE 153020: 2005: Requirements for audiodescription," http://www.aenor.es/.

6

Efficient Wireless Broadcasting through Joint Network Coding and Beamforming

Monchai Lertsutthiwong, Thinh Nguyen, and Bechir Hamdaoui

School of EECS, Oregon State University, Corvallis, OR 97331, USA

Correspondence should be addressed to Thinh Nguyen, thinhq@eecs.oregonstate.edu

Academic Editor: Manzur Murshed

We develop a framework that exploits network coding (NC) and multiple-input/multiple-output (MIMO) techniques, jointly together, to improve throughput of downlink broadcast channels. Specifically, we consider a base station (BS) equipped with multiple transmit antennas that serves multiple mobile stations (MSs) simultaneously by generating multiple signal beams. Given the large number of MSs and the small number of transmit antennas, the BS must decide, at any transmission opportunity, which group of MSs it should transmit packets to, in order to maximize the overall throughput. We propose two algorithms for grouping MSs that take advantage of NC and the orthogonality of user channels to improve the overall throughput. Our results indicate that the proposed techniques increase the achievable throughput significantly, especially in highly lossy environments.

1. Introduction

In recent years, multiple-input/multiple-output (MIMO) has been recognized as a key enabling technology for improving the performance of wireless communication systems. Unlike traditional communications, MIMO techniques rely on multiple antennas to transmit and/or receive signals. The number of antennas that a device can be equipped with can be limited due to spatial constraints. For example, in a cellular network, while there may be no limit on the number of antennas that the base station (BS) can be equipped with, there is a limit on that number when it comes to mobile station (MS) due to size and/or cost constraints. MIMO capabilities can be exploited to enable the spatial division multiple access (SDMA) technique, which basically allows multiple simultaneous transmissions from the BS to multiple MSs, thereby achieving higher overall data throughput [1–3]. Specifically, the BS exploits MIMO to generate radiation patterns that simultaneously target different groups of MSs [4, 5]; this is known as beamforming (BF). Mathematically, the signal beam from each antenna is coded and multiplied independently by a BF weight vector to control its shape and direction. A BF weight vector is determined by MSs locations as well as the characteristics of channels between the BS and

MSs. Assuming that the BF weight vectors are available, an optimal SDMA scheme consists then of selecting the set of MSs whose signal-to-interference plus noise ratios (SINRs) are maximized.

A BS with M transmit antennas can form and transmit a signal with at most M beams [6, 7]. Therefore, assuming that one beam is allocated for each MS, when the number of MSs, K, exceeds the number of transmit antennas, M, the BS selects the best M MSs, that is, those whose SINRs are maximized [8]. An efficient scheduling algorithm is then required at the BS to map the MSs with these beams. For example, given 10 MSs ($z_1, z_2, \ldots, z_{10}$) and one BS equipped with 2 antennas, an efficient scheduler may select (z_2, z_4) in the first time slot for transmission, (z_1, z_5) in the second time slot, (z_7, z_9) in the third time slot, and so on. After five time slots, the BS completes then transmitting all packets to their intended MSs. The key challenge in designing these scheduling algorithms lies in grouping the MSs in such a way that interference among MSs is minimized; that is, a transmitted beam intended for one MS should create no or minimal interference to any other MSs in the group. One way to achieve this objective is to group together MSs whose channel vectors are somewhat orthogonal to one another.

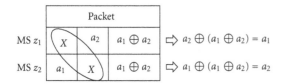

X lost packet

FIGURE 1: Illustrative example of NC technique.

Network coding (NC) is another effective technique that is also well recognized for its great network throughput potentials and has received a considerable attention due to its practical simplicity [9]. In single-hop wireless networks, such as cellular networks, NC can be used to significantly reduce the number of transmission/retransmission attempts required to successfully deliver data packets [10]. Consider the example of Figure 1 for the purpose of illustration. Instead of immediately retransmitting a lost packet a_1 for an MS, for example, z_1, the BS waits until there is another lost packet a_2 for another MS, for example, z_2. Due to spatial proximity of z_1 and z_2, it is possible that a_1, although intended for z_1, may be received and cached successfully by z_2; likewise, a_2 may also be cached successfully by z_1. In that case, the BS only needs to retransmit a single packet $a_1 \oplus a_2$, which is a bitwise exclusive-OR (XOR) of packets a_1 and a_2. (Here, all packets are assumed to have the same bit length so as to be able to perform the XOR operation.) If this packet is successfully received by both z_1 and z_2, then z_1 can recover a_1 as $a_2 \oplus (a_1 \oplus a_2) = a_1$ and z_2 can recover a_2 as $a_1 \oplus (a_1 \oplus a_2) = a_2$. Thus, one retransmission allows both MSs to recover their lost packets, resulting in a reduced number of retransmissions or, equivalently, in an increased throughput efficiency.

In this paper, we develop scheduling algorithms that exploit NC and BF techniques jointly together to maximize the overall throughput achievable on a wireless broadcast downlink channel. Specifically, we consider a BS with multiple transmit antennas that simultaneously serves multiple MSs by generating multiple signal beams with well-defined beamforming weight vectors, where each MS corresponds to a particular beam. Given a large number of MSs and a small number of transmit antennas, the BS must decide, at any transmission opportunity, which group of MSs it should transmit packets to, in order to maximize the overall throughput. In this work, we prove that the group formation problem is NP-hard and propose two scheduling heuristics that take advantage of NC capabilities and the orthogonality of user channels to improve the overall throughput on broadcast transmissions. Our simulation results show that the proposed techniques achieve greater throughput than that achievable under existing techniques, especially in highly lossy environments.

The outline of our paper is as follows. First, we present a literature review in Section 2. Then, we overview NC techniques and discuss our joint BF-NC framework in Sections 3 and 4, respectively. In Section 5, we describe our proposed joint BF-NC-based scheduling algorithms. We show the simulation results for the proposed techniques in Section 6 and conclude the paper in Section 7.

2. Related Work

Simultaneous service support of multiple MSs through BF techniques can be very challenging due to interference incurred by different active signal beams. Therefore, several efficient scheduling algorithms and proper BF strategies have been proposed to reduce interference among multiple beams. To maximize the sum capacity, the scheduled MSs are typically selected through an exhaustive search, which can be very costly or even infeasible for a large MS pool. For example, Shad et al. [11] proposed an algorithm for selecting the MSs for each time slot over SDMA/TDMA networks by considering the largest SINR margin of scheduled MSs with respect to some SINR thresholds. Choi et al. [12] provided a scheduling algorithm, which relies on the feedback from MSs during each time slot to determine a subset of MSs in such a way to maximize the sum capacity. Ravindran et al. [13] studied the performance of zero-forcing BF techniques under limited channel feedback in line of sight (LOS) channels. Their results show that a zero-forcing BF technique performs well especially when the system has reliable channel state information (CSI) from MSs. Furthermore, Yoo and Goldsmith [7] considered the orthogonality of CSIs among the MSs to schedule the MSs while minimizing the overall interference. In particular, their technique greedily selects a set of MSs while assuming that the BS knows CSIs of all MSs in the system.

Another traditional technique, yet efficient, is to use a BF codebook containing a set of all possible coefficients (or codewords) to form a BF beam. In general, the codebook is generated offline and consists of a fixed number of codewords, which do not depend on statistical characteristics of channel conditions [14]. Most codebooks are fixed and designed for a specific transmitter. For example, Love and Heath [15] proposed a way to generate a codebook that cannot adaptively change as the channel changes. By using their technique, both BS and MSs have full knowledge of a codebook. Amiri et al. [16] provided an efficient algorithm to adaptively change a codebook based on new feedback information at the BS. However, their technique is complex because the BS needs to frequently evaluate new feedback information, and, hence, the technique may not be suitable for systems with a large number of MSs. Huang et al. [17] showed the performance of orthogonal BF techniques by selecting a codeword for each MS in such a way to reduce the interference among all active beams. More specifically, their technique consists of finding a set of codewords from a fixed codebook for all active beams by relying on MSs CSIs.

Most of these reported works consider associating/ allocating one BF beam for each intended MS. However, MSs within a close proximity often experience similar channel conditions and have similar SINR levels. Therefore, considering grouping and associating these MSs together under one BF beam not only allows to support more MSs but also enables effective use of NC techniques, thus improving throughput even further. This work proposes a framework that takes into consideration the proximity in SINRs and CSI orthogonality when grouping MSs and forming BF beams. We first prove that the group formation problem is NP-hard (the proof is given in the appendix) and then propose two heuristic techniques: a greedy-selection-based technique and a codebook-based technique, which are described later in Section 5.

3. Network Coding and Broadcasting

For notational convenience, throughout this paper, upper-case boldface letters are used for matrices and lowercase boldface letters are used for vectors, and $\mathbf{X}^*$, $\mathbf{X}^T$, $\tilde{\mathbf{X}}$, $|\mathbf{X}|$, and $\|\mathbf{X}\|$ denote conjugate transpose, transpose, normalized, size or magnitude, and L-2 norm of $\mathbf{X}$, respectively.

In this section, we briefly describe the use of NC technique over wireless broadcast channels. We consider K MSs (as receivers) and one BS (as the sender). Without loss of generality, we assume that each data packet can be transmitted in one time slot (all time slots are of a fixed duration). We also assume that MSs use either positive or negative acknowledgements (ACK/NAK) to let the BS know about the status of receiving each packet. Traditionally, an MS immediately sends a NAK if the packet is not successfully received. When using an XOR NC technique, instead of immediately retransmitting a lost packet to a certain MS right after receiving a NAK, the BS waits for a fixed interval of time (in time slots) before retransmitting starts. With NC enabled, the BS then retransmits an XOR-coded packet for each set of multiple lost packets. For this to happen, the BS maintains a list of all lost packets as well as their corresponding MSs for some time (i.e., waiting period) during retransmission phase. The number of lost packets that can be coded at once is then at most equal to the number of MSs, K, one lost packet from each MS. Any successful packets received by any of the K MSs will not be included in the coded packet to be retransmitted. The BS keeps retransmitting coded packets of lost packets until all MSs receive all packets successfully.

Consider a broadcast transmission example of a cellular network, where all BS packet transmissions are assumed to reach all MSs. For a system with two MSs, that is, z_1 and z_2, we consider the pattern of lost packets shown in Figure 2 as an example, where a cross X and an oval O, respectively, represent a lost and a coded packet. Since $K = 2$, the coded packets generated by the BS and intended for the two MSs, z_1 and z_2, are $(a_1 \oplus a_2)$, $(a_3 \oplus a_4)$, and a_5. Packet a_6 is only intended for MS z_2 because MS z_1 has already received it successfully. Note that if some coded packets cannot be correctly received by any of the intended MSs, the BS will update the lost packet table and determine the best coded packet for the next retransmission opportunity.

Without loss of generality, for a system with K MSs, we assume that $PER_i \le PER_j$ if $i \le j$ for any $i, j \in \{1, 2, \ldots, K\}$ where PER_i is the packet error rate for MS z_i. Recall that the BS will generate a coded packet combining as many lost packets as possible, and the MS with the highest *PER* dominates the performance of the system. Let z_K be this MS.

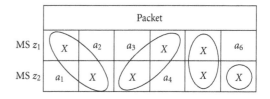

X   lost packet

◯   coded packet

FIGURE 2: An example of a pattern of lost packets at MSs z_1 and z_2.

Let X_i be a random variable representing the number of lost packets of MS z_i after a certain number N, transmissions. When N approaches infinity and each transmission follows a Bernoulli trial, X_i will follow the Binomial random variable. Therefore, we have

$$E\left[\max_{i \in \{1,2,\ldots,K\}} \{X_i\}\right] \approx E[X_K]. \tag{1}$$

With N transmitted packets to K MSs, the expected number of transmissions can be written as

$$
\begin{aligned}
N + E[X_K] &= N + \frac{N \times \max_{i \in \{1,2,\ldots,K\}} \{PER_i\}}{1 - \max_{i \in \{1,2,\ldots,K\}} \{PER_i\}} \\
&= \frac{N}{1 - \max_{i \in \{1,2,\ldots,K\}} \{PER_i\}}.
\end{aligned} \tag{2}
$$

Note that the NC technique described in this section considers that packets will be broadcast to all MSs. Thus, packets sent by the BS can be heard either by all MSs or by none.

4. Joint Beamforming and Network Coding

In this work, we consider broadcast transmissions in a downlink channel of a cellular network, where data packets sent by the BS are intended for and reach all MSs in the network. When data packet transmission is not successful, the BS keeps retransmitting until the lost/unsuccessful packet is delivered to all MSs successfully. We assume that the BS needs to broadcast D packets to the MSs.

After the first transmission, one or more MSs may not receive the packets. When this happens, one simple way to ensure successful delivery of packets is for the BS to retransmit/broadcast each lost packet to all MSs again (e.g., Figure 3(a)). Another retransmission technique is to use beamforming to retransmit the lost packets only to those MSs that did not receive the packets. In this paper, we investigate and develop techniques that rely on MIMO to form BF beams so as to direct transmission towards a set of MSs only, that is, those MSs that did not receive the packets (e.g., Figure 3(b)). In addition to BF techniques, our proposed techniques rely on and incorporate network coding (NC) to further improve throughput performances of broadcast channels.

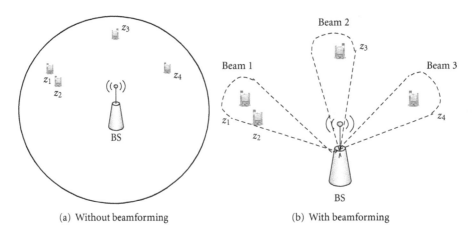

(a) Without beamforming   (b) With beamforming

FIGURE 3: NC example.

Simply broadcasting lost packets to all MSs, instead of using BF technique, can be very inefficient for the following reasons. First, MSs are often located at different positions with various distances from the BS, leading to high variations of MSs received signal strengths. With this, different MSs are likely to experience different packet success rates. Second, without directing the transmitted signals, power could be wasted when signals are sent in directions/regions that happen to have no MSs. Let us consider the example shown in Figure 3, where there are 3 groups of MSs: $\{z_1, z_2\}$, $\{z_3\}$, and $\{z_4\}$. In this example, transmitting packets to a location that does not contain any of the groups will be a waste of energy resources. By using a BF technique as in Figure 3(b), the BS can direct BF beams in such a way to increase the signal quality reaching the intended MSs. Note that the BS may use multiple time slots for transmitting a packet to everyone if all MSs are located apart from each other. The challenge as well as the novelty of the proposed BF technique lies in grouping all MSs into multiple clusters each corresponding to one beam in such a way to enhance broadcast throughput while minimizing power consumption.

We now describe how to combine NC and BF to further improve broadcast network throughput. Figures 4(a) and 4(b) illustrate the use of NC to broadcast a stream of packets in the network, respectively, shown in Figure 3(a) (without beamforming) and Figure 3(b) (with beamforming). In this example, there are 4 MSs (i.e., z_1, z_2, z_3, z_4). The BS needs to deliver 7 packets (i.e., $a_1, a_2, \ldots, a_7$) to all MSs and can generate at most 3 beams at once. Recall that the best strategy to generate a coded packet is to maximize the number of lost packets that can be coded at once. Therefore, we use 3 time slots to generate and send coded packets. In the first time slot, when not using a BF technique, the coded packet to be sent to all MSs is $(a_1 \oplus a_2 \oplus a_3 \oplus a_4)$, whereas, when using a BF technique, the three coded/uncoded packets, $(a_1 \oplus a_2)$, a_3, and a_4, are to be sent on beams 1, 2, and 3, respectively. In the second time slot, the BS generates coded packets that combine the lost packets a_5 and a_6 and sends them to MSs z_1, z_2, and z_4. When not using a BF technique, the coded packet $(a_5 \oplus a_6)$ is then to be sent to all MSs. Whereas, when using a

BF technique, the coded packet $(a_5 \oplus a_6)$ and uncoded packet a_6 are to be transmitted through beams 1 (for z_1 and z_2) and 3 (for z_4), respectively. In the third time slot, the BS needs to transmit only packet a_7 to MS z_4. In this case, it is obvious that there is no need to broadcast a packet a_7 to everyone. Hence, when using a BF technique, the signal quality sent to MS z_4 can be improved by allocating all transmit power to beam 3, thereby increasing the packet success rate and/or reducing energy consumption.

In the first time slot, note that the coded packet combining the first 4 lost packets (i.e., without BF) when sent to all MSs exactly suffices as it enables each of the 4 MSs to recover its lost packet (i.e., a_i for z_i). Thus, this may seem to be the best strategy. Likewise, the BF technique also suffices; that is, sending $(a_1 \oplus a_2)$, a_3, and a_4 on three different beams 1, 2, and 3, respectively, also enables all MSs to recover their lost packets. The difference between the two techniques lies, however, on the fact that the BF technique can make received signals stronger, thus decreasing the packet error rates by increasing the chance of correctly decoding received packets.

Note that there is a tradeoff in grouping MSs when using a BF technique. Grouping a large number of MSs under the same beam may reduce the number of coded packets but this would also lead to lesser chances of successfully receiving coded packets by an intended MS. Let us consider the example with 4 MSs as shown in Figure 5. As can be seen in Figure 5(a), with one beam, the BS can simply use one coded packet for all 4 intended MSs. On the other hand, forming multiple groups of MSs (e.g., 2 MSs per beam as in this example) requires generating more coded packets, but MSs are more likely to receive higher signal quality, resulting in higher chances to successfully receive coded packets. Referring to Figure 5(b) again for illustration, the BS uses 2 coded packets: one for MSs z_1 and z_2 and the other for MSs z_3 and z_4. Note that the BS here can transmit 2 coded packets at the same time or at two successive time slots. One strategy to determine the sizes/groups of MSs for BF techniques is to minimize the variance of MSs lost packets in each group. This would allow the BS to efficiently generate coded packets while all MSs in each group can successfully receive all required packets at the same time.

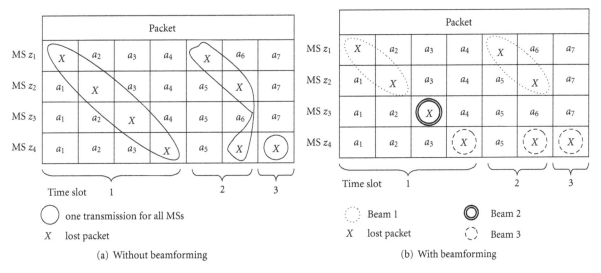

(a) Without beamforming

(b) With beamforming

FIGURE 4: Retransmission techniques.

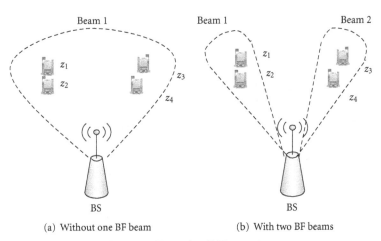

(a) Without one BF beam

(b) With two BF beams

FIGURE 5: Example of MS grouping.

Therefore, efficient grouping algorithms that can determine the best sizes/groups are needed. In this paper, we develop and propose two efficient algorithms for grouping MSs.

We assume that the BS is equipped with multiple antenna systems that enable it to simultaneously generate multiple transmitted beams. We also assume that the BS knows all channel vectors $\mathbf{h}_i$ associated with each MS z_i for all i through feedback channels. Let P_i be the power allocated to beam i by the BS. For each beam i, we assign a group of MSs V_i where $V_i \subseteq V$, $V_i \cap V_j = \varnothing$ for any $i, j \in \{1, 2, \ldots, M\}$, and V is a set of all MSs. Groups are formed in such a way that all MSs belonging to the same group are likely to experience the same packet losses, reducing then the number of transmissions at the BS via bitwise XOR operations.

The objective is to minimize the time T for the BS to successfully deliver all D packets to each MS. Note that minimizing the time T is equivalent to maximizing the overall throughput under some fairness constraints. However, if a particular MS is far away from the BS such that it cannot receive packets, then clearly $T = \infty$. In this work, we do not consider this degenerated case, and such an

MS is likely to be serviced by a neighboring BS. Furthermore, we assume that the BS uses a round-robin transmission style and the channels at MSs are stationary. Thus, each MS will receive a fair share of transmission packets and the expected achievable throughput would reflect the performance of the considered system.

Recall that the signal quality at MSs can be assessed/quantified via SINR. In particular, SINR_{ij} for MS z_j in beam i can be computed as

$$\text{SINR}_{ij} = \frac{P_i \left| \mathbf{h}_j \mathbf{w}_i \right|^2}{\sum_{k=1(k \neq i)}^{M} P_k \left| \mathbf{h}_j \mathbf{w}_k \right|^2 + \sigma^2}, \qquad (3)$$

where P_i, $\mathbf{w}_i$, $\mathbf{h}_j$, σ^2, and M are transmit power, weight vector for beam i, channel vector for MS z_j, noise power, and number of beams, respectively. If all transmitted beams are pairwise orthogonal such that $|\mathbf{w}_i \mathbf{w}_k|^2 = 0$ and $|\tilde{\mathbf{h}}_j \mathbf{w}_i|^2 = 1$ (assume that $\mathbf{h}_j$ is normalized as $\tilde{\mathbf{h}}_j$ so as to check its orthogonality), where $z_j \in V_i \setminus V_k$, then $|\mathbf{h}_j \mathbf{w}_k|^2 = 0$. Thus, (3) would reduce to $\text{SINR}_{ij} = P_i|\mathbf{h}_j \mathbf{w}_i|^2/\sigma^2$ (signal-to-noise ratio (SNR)). If all scheduled MSs have high SINR (or SNR), the equal power allocation is close to an optimal water-filling method [17]. Thus, the allocated transmit powers for all beams are all equal. Given a fixed total transmit power $\mathbb{P}$ at the BS, this implies that the transmit power allocated for each beam j is $P_j = \mathbb{P}/M$ where M is the number of active beams during that time.

Let n_j be a set of lost packets for MS z_j. The number of transmissions for broadcast schemes over a group V_i depends on the combination of all lost packets from all MSs in V_i. Therefore, a set of coded and uncoded lost packets in V_i can be considered as $N_{V_i} = \cup_{\forall_j} n_j$, where n_j belongs to z_j and $z_j \in V_i$. Each group V_i is independent of any other group V_j for $i \neq j$. This implies that the combination process of group V_i is totally independent of that of group V_j. Within each beam, the MS with the highest packet error rate would dominate the performance of that beam. For each beam i, the expected number of transmissions can be formulated as

$$\frac{N_{V_i}}{1 - \max_j\left\{x(i,j)\text{PER}_{ij}\right\}}, \tag{4}$$

where N_{V_i} is a set of coded/uncoded lost packets based on the NC technique applied to beam i, PER_{ij} is packet error rate for MS z_j in beam i, and $x(i,j)$ is an assignment binary variable for MS z_j in beam i defined as

$$x(i,j) = \begin{cases} 1 & \text{if MS } z_j \text{ is in beam } i, \\ 0 & \text{otherwise.} \end{cases} \tag{5}$$

Furthermore, each MS can only belong to one beam; that is, $\sum_i x(i,j) = 1$. For simplicity of analysis, we do not use any error correcting code. Therefore, PER_{ij} can be computed in terms of bit error rate (BER_{ij}) such that $\text{PER}_{ij} = 1 - (1 - \text{BER}_{ij})^\alpha$, where α is a packet size in bits. Assume BPSK is used. Thus,

$$\text{BER}_{ij} = 0.5\left[1 - \text{erf}\left(\sqrt{\text{SINR}_{ij}}\right)\right], \tag{6}$$

where $\text{erf}(\gamma) \approx (2/\sqrt{\Pi})\left[\gamma - (\gamma^3/3) + (\gamma^5/10)\right]$ and $\gamma = \sqrt{\text{SINR}_{ij}}$ [18]. The expected number of transmissions for this system is the time that the BS spends until all MSs successfully receive all of their required packets.

Without lost of generality, (4) can be written as

$$\left\{\frac{N_{V_i}}{1 - \max_j\left\{x(i,j)\text{PER}_{ij}\right\}}\right\}_{l_q}, \tag{7}$$

where l_q is the index of sets of BF beams. For each set l_q, the BS requires to successfully transmit all lost packets over a set of all BF beams before moving forward to the next set of BF beams, that is, l_{q+1}. Assume there are Q sets of BF beams to be used at the BS. By taking into account all Q sets of

BF beams, our goal is then to minimize the total number of transmissions; that is,

$$\textbf{minimize} \quad \sum_q\left\{\max_i\left\{\frac{N_{V_i}}{1 - \max_j\left\{x(i,j)\text{PER}_{ij}\right\}}\right\}_{l_q}\right\},$$
$$\textbf{s.t.} \quad \sum_i x(i,j) = 1, \tag{8}$$
$$x(i,j) \in \{0,1\},$$

where $q = \{1, 2, \ldots, Q\}$. The solution to this optimization problem will be $x(i,j)$ assignments that minimize the total number of transmissions. However, we prove that this assignment problem is NP-hard (we provide the proof of NP-hardness in the appendix), and, instead, we propose two heuristics/techniques that solve this group formation problem by taking advantage of NC capabilities and the orthogonality of user channels. One proposed technique uses greedy selection based on SINR levels, whereas the other technique uses a predefined codebook to generate a set of orthogonal BF beams. Let $L = \{l_1, l_2, \ldots, l_Q\}$ denote the Q sets of M orthogonal beams. For example, $l_i = 1$ means the BS uses the ith set of M orthogonal beams in a codebook, otherwise $l_i = 0$. Next, we describe our two proposed scheduling techniques.

5. Proposed Scheduling Algorithms

Because our assignment problem is NP-hard, we propose to use two techniques to design heuristic algorithms that efficiently solve it. The first technique schedules and groups MSs based on their SINRs, and the second one uses a predefined codebook that first generates multiple sets of orthogonal BF beams and then assigns each MS to the beam whose SINR is maximized. The details of the proposed techniques will be described next.

5.1. Technique 1: Greedy-Selection-Based Scheduler. We first describe and formulate the group formation problem, which basically tries to find the optimal set of MSs that maximizes the overall throughput and then proposes a scheduling algorithm that solves it. The scheduling algorithm improves overall throughput through joint exploitation of both BF and NC techniques. Given an M-transmit antenna BS and K one-receive antenna MSs located within the communication range of the BS, the BS can choose to transmit packets to a selected set of MSs that are located far apart from each other and whose quality levels are above a certain threshold. Note that the use of linear, equally spaced antenna arrays limits the number of concurrent signal beams to a certain number. We denote this number by M^{opt}, where $M^{\text{opt}} \leq M$.

When the number of MSs, K, exceeds M^{opt}, the BS chooses the best M^{opt} (or fewer) MSs with the highest SINRs. We consider spatial separation among MSs by using the orthogonality in channel vectors, described in [7]. Below, we describe our greedy-selection-based scheduling algorithm.

The details of our proposed algorithm are described as follows: in step 1, $\mathcal{T}_i$ is a set of all available MSs and $\mathcal{S}$

---

step 1: Initialization

$i = 1$

$\mathcal{T}_i = \{1, 2, \ldots, K\}$

$\mathcal{S} = \varnothing$ (empty set)

step 2: For each MS $k \in \mathcal{T}_i$, compute $\mathbf{g}_k$ where $\mathbf{g}_k$ is determined by $\mathbf{h}_k$ semiorthogonal to the subspace $\{\mathbf{g}_1, \ldots, \mathbf{g}_{i-1}\}$

$\mathbf{g}_k = \mathbf{h}_k \left(\mathbf{I} - \sum_{j=1}^{i-1} \mathbf{g}_j^* \mathbf{g}_j / \|\mathbf{g}_j\|^2 \right)$

{Note that when $i = 1$, assume $\mathbf{g}_k = \mathbf{h}_k$}

step 3: Select the ith MS such that

$\pi_{(i)} = \arg \max_{k \in \mathcal{T}_i} \|\mathbf{g}_k\|$

$\mathcal{S} := \mathcal{S} \cup \{\pi_{(i)}\}$

$\mathbf{h}_i = \mathbf{h}_{\pi_{(i)}}$

$\mathbf{g}_i = \mathbf{g}_{\pi_{(i)}}$

step 4: Find a cluster of MSs whose SINRs are greater than some threshold Ω. We denote that cluster by $\mathcal{G}(\pi_{(i)})$ where $\pi_{(i)} \in \mathcal{G}(\pi_{(i)})$ and $\mathcal{G}(\pi_{(i)}) \subset \mathcal{T}_i$

step 5: If $|\mathcal{S}| < M^{\text{opt}}$, compute $\mathcal{T}_{i+1}$ as follows:

$\mathcal{T}_{i+1} := \{k\}$

where $k \in \mathcal{T}_i, k \notin \mathcal{G}(\pi_{(i)})$, and $\dfrac{|\mathbf{h}_k \mathbf{h}_i^*|}{\|\mathbf{h}_k\| \|\mathbf{h}_i\|} \leq \alpha$

$i = i + 1$

{Note that if $\mathcal{T}_{i+1} \neq \varnothing$ and $|\mathcal{S}| < M^{\text{opt}}$ then go to step 2. Otherwise, the algorithm terminates and returns a set of scheduled MSs}

ALGORITHM 1: Greedy-selection-based algorithm.

is a set of scheduled MSs where i represents the current iteration number. Thus, $\mathcal{S}$ is initially empty and $\mathcal{T}_i$ is equal to $\{1, 2, \ldots, K\}$. In step 2, we compute $\mathbf{g}_k$, the component of channel vector $\mathbf{h}_k$ for each k in $\mathcal{T}_i$, orthogonal to previously determined subspace spanned by $\{\mathbf{g}_1, \ldots, \mathbf{g}_{i-1}\}$. Note that when $i = 1$, we assume $\mathbf{g}_k = \mathbf{h}_k$ for each MS k. In step 3, we select the MS, denoted by $\pi_{(i)}$, whose norm $\|\mathbf{g}_k\|$ is maximized (i.e., best MS) over each $k \in \mathcal{T}_i$. After that we update the values of $\mathcal{S}$, $\mathbf{h}_i$, and $\mathbf{g}_i$, consecutively. In step 4, after finding the best MS $\pi_{(i)}$, we further determine a cluster of MSs whose SINRs are greater than some threshold Ω. We denote this cluster by $\mathcal{G}(\pi_{(i)})$. Note that the value of Ω depends on MSs channel gain as well as their spatial distribution within a BS coverage area. Finally, in step 5, we determine $\mathcal{T}_{i+1}$ for next iteration by eliminating all MSs in $\mathcal{G}(\pi_{(i)})$ and all MSs whose channel vectors are not semiorthogonal to $\pi_{(i)}$ within a certain threshold α. If $\mathcal{T}_{i+1}$ is not an empty set and $|\mathcal{S}| < M^{\text{opt}}$, then go to step 2. Otherwise, the algorithm terminates and returns a set of $\pi_{(i)}$ with their corresponding cluster $\mathcal{G}(\pi_{(i)})$.

Note that Algorithm 1 requires two thresholds Ω and α. In practice, one can try multiple thresholds in order to select/determine the one that minimizes the number of total transmissions. We now propose our second technique.

5.2. Technique 2: Codebook-Based Scheduler. The second technique, as described in the pseudocode shown below, uses two algorithms: Algorithm 2, which determines the best beam for each MS whose SINR is maximized and Algorithm 3, which further minimizes the number of transmissions. The outcome will be a set of MSs in $V_1, V_2, \ldots, V_{Q \times M}$, an optimized codebook L, and the expected number of transmissions T_Q.

Pseudocode for technique 2

$V = \{z_1, z_2, \ldots, z_K\}$

$V_1 = V_2 = \cdots = V_{Q \times M} = \varnothing$ (empty set)

begin

Run Algorithm 2

{determine the best beam for each MS}

Run Algorithm 3

{further minimize the number of transmissions}

end

return a set of MSs in $V_1, V_2, \ldots, V_{Q \times M}$, an optimized codebook L, and the expected number of transmissions T_Q.

Algorithm 2 is described as follows: in step 1, V represents the set of all K MSs and $Q \times M$ represents the number of all possible beams in a codebook. V_i is the set of all assigned MSs in beam i and is initially empty where $i \in \{1, 2, \ldots, Q \times M\}$. In step 2, we select beam i^* for MS z_j whose SINR is maximized (the best assigned beam) over all possible beams. In step 3, we update the value of V and V_{i^*}. Finally, in step 4, if V is not an empty set, then go to step 2. Otherwise, the algorithm terminates, and returns a set of MSs in $V_1, V_2, \ldots, V_{Q \times M}$. If some set of MSs (e.g., V_i for beam i) is an empty set, this implies that the BS will not transmit any packets over that beam whose power allocation is zero. Note that Algorithm 2 minimizes the variance of SINRs of all MSs in each beam.

---

step 1: Initialization

$$V = \{z_1, z_2, \ldots, z_K\}$$
$$V_1 = V_2 = \ldots = V_{Q \times M} = \varnothing \quad \text{(empty set)}$$

step 2: For each MS z_j in V, compute SINR_{ij} over all possible $Q \times M$ beams. Then, assign MS z_j to beam i^* that maximizes SINR_{ij} such that

$$i^* = \arg\max_i \{\text{SINR}_{ij}\}$$

{Note that if MS z_j is assigned to beam i^* in set l_q of a codebook, the interference will come from all other beams in set l_q, except beam i^* }

step 3: Update

$$V = V - \{z_j\}$$
$$V_{i^*} = V_{i^*} \cup \{z_j\}$$

step 4: If $V \neq \varnothing$ then go to step 2. Otherwise, the algorithm terminates and returns a set of MSs in $V_1, V_2, \ldots, V_{Q \times M}$.

ALGORITHM 2: Codebook-based allocation algorithm.

---

step 1: Initialization

$$L = \{l_1, l_2, \ldots, l_Q\}$$
$$\text{Given } V_1, V_2, \ldots, V_{Q \times M}$$
$$\text{compute } T_Q$$

step 2: For each set l_q of a codebook where $q \in \{1, 2, \ldots, Q\}$, compute the maximum value of PERs over all MSs assigned to a set l_q such that

$$X_{l_q} = \max_i \{\max_j \{\text{PER}_{ij}\}\}_{l_q}$$

step 3: Eliminate a set l_q^* over all existing sets such that

$$l_q^* = \arg\min_{l_q} \{X_{l_q}\}$$

step 4: For each MS z_j in a set l_q^*, compute SINR_{ij} over all existing beams i except all beams in a set l_q^*. Then, assign MS z_j to beam i^* that maximizes SINR_{ij} such that

$$i^* = \arg\max_i \{\text{SINR}_{ij}\}$$

step 5: Compute T_{Q-1}

step 6: If $T_{Q-1} \leq T_Q$,

update $V_1, V_2, \ldots, V_{(Q-1) \times M}$
$$L = L - \{l_q^*\}$$
$$Q = Q - 1$$

then go to step 2

step 7: The algorithm terminates, then returns a set of MSs in $V_1, V_2, \ldots, V_{Q \times M}$, an optimized codebook L, and the expected number of transmissions T_Q.

ALGORITHM 3: Optimized codebook algorithm.

Using all Q sets, a codebook may not be the best solution. In other words, using a large number of sets of a codebook implies that the BS spends an amount of time to successfully retransmit all lost packets while all MSs most likely have high SINR levels. However, when we lower SINR values for a certain set of MSs by eliminating some sets of a codebook and assigning these MSs to the remaining sets, the overall number of transmissions can be reduced. Therefore, we propose an algorithm to further minimize the number of transmissions as shown in Algorithm 3.

Algorithm 3 works as follows: in step 1, we have the original sets of a codebook $L = \{l_1, l_2, \ldots, l_Q\}$ and the groups of MSs in each $V_1, V_2, \ldots, V_{Q \times M}$. Then, we compute the expected number of transmissions T_Q where Q is the number of sets of a codebook. In step 2, we determine the maximum PER over all MSs assigned to each set l_q of a codebook denoted by X_{l_q}. The best set of a codebook (l_q^*), that is, the set that has the lowest value of the maximum PERs among all sets of a codebook, is determined in step 3. Because the set with the highest value of maximum PERs dominates the transmission performance in the system, when we eliminate the set l_q^*, the number of transmissions is likely to decrease. Then, we assign all MSs in the set l_q^* to all other existing sets as done in step 4. In step 5, we compute the expected number of transmissions T_{Q-1} after eliminating the set l_q^*. In step 6, if $T_{Q-1} \leq T_Q$, then we go to step 2 for further codebook optimization. Otherwise, the algorithm returns the optimized codebook together with a set of MSs in $V_1, V_2, \ldots, V_{Q \times M}$ and the expected number of transmissions T_Q as described in step 7.

6. Performance Evaluation

We consider a downlink channel consisting of one BS and multiple MSs. The BS and each MS are, respectively,

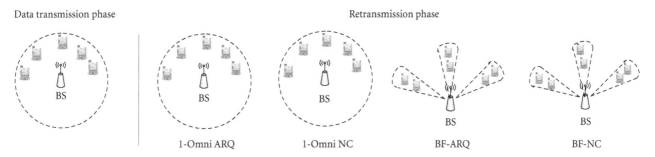

Data transmission phase   Retransmission phase

1-Omni ARQ   1-Omni NC   BF-ARQ   BF-NC

FIGURE 6: Broadcast transmission/retransmission schemes.

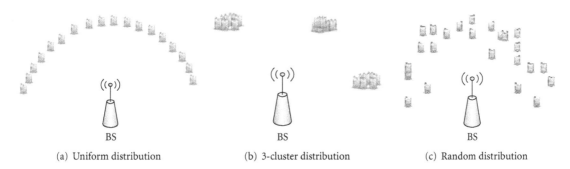

(a) Uniform distribution   (b) 3-cluster distribution   (c) Random distribution

FIGURE 7: Simulated network topology scenarios with different MS distributions.

equipped with 4-transmit antenna elements and a 1-receive antenna element. The system parameters are set as follows: maximum number of concurrent signal beams is $M^{\mathrm{opt}} = 3$; operation frequency is 5 GHz; antenna array spacing at the BS is $\Delta x = \lambda/2$ where λ is the wavelength; noise power is $\sigma^2 = 1$; packet size is 1000 Bytes; number of transmitted packets per MS is 100 packets; modulation technique is BPSK. To be fair to all MSs, we assume that the BS adopts the round-robin transmission scheduling policy. The simulation is implemented with MATLAB.

In broadcast scenarios, the BS transmits a packet to all MSs at once. One example of broadcast transmissions is digital TV broadcasting, where all MSs watch the same TV channel at the same time. Therefore, the BS needs only to transmit data packets omnidirectionally, which makes them reach all MSs. We assume that the BS uses one antenna to do so, and there is no need for applying BF techniques during data transmissions.

For the purpose of evaluating the performance of our proposed scheduling algorithms, we consider evaluating four retransmission schemes: 1-Omni ARQ (i.e., traditional retransmission technique), 1-Omni NC (i.e., traditional with NC only), BF-ARQ (i.e., BF with traditional retransmission technique), BF-NC with SINR (proposed technique 1: greedy-selection-based scheduler), and BF-NC with codebook (proposed technique 2: codebook-based scheduler). Both 1-Omni ARQ- and 1-Omni NC-based retransmission schemes use one transmit antenna element, and retransmissions of lost packets are respectively done with ARQ and NC techniques only. BF-ARQ-based retransmission scheme is to use BF to retransmit lost packets to a group of MSs with ARQ techniques. The group formation for BF-ARQ is based

on technique 1 (Algorithm 1). The proposed BF-NC-based retransmission schemes use either technique 1 (Algorithm 1) or technique 2 (Algorithms 2 and 3). A graphical illustration of these schemes is given in Figure 6.

6.1. Uniform MS Distribution on a Circle. First, we study the broadcast scenario shown in Figure 7(a), where there are 120 uniformly distributed MSs, all having the same channel gain.

Recall that the BS uses one transmit antenna during the data transmission phase, making signals/packets (transmitted omnidirectionally) reach all MSs. In Figure 8(a), we show the average loss rate of packet transmissions during these omnidirectional transmissions as a function of the transmit power. Figures 8(b) and 8(c) show the total number of transmitted packets and throughput gain, respectively, as a function of power for all simulated retransmission schemes.

Figure 8(b) shows that 1-Omni NC-based retransmission scheme performs the best in this network scenario when compared with all the other retransmission schemes, followed by the BF-NC with codebook, the BF-NC with SINR, the 1-Omni ARQ, and then the BF-ARQ. The achieved performances of the 1-Omni NC scheme are expected in this network topology, since all MSs experience the same channel gain and signal strength. We will see later that this is no longer the case when considering more realistic scenarios where MSs may experience different gains. For the BF-NC with SINR (i.e., with greedy selection) scheme, SINR thresholds are set to 3 levels (6.75, 7.25, and 8.00) for grouping MSs in each beam. For completeness and to assess the impact of incorporating the NC technique, we also measure and plot in Figure 8(c) the throughput gains of the 1-Omni NC, the BF-ARQ, the BF-NC with SINR,

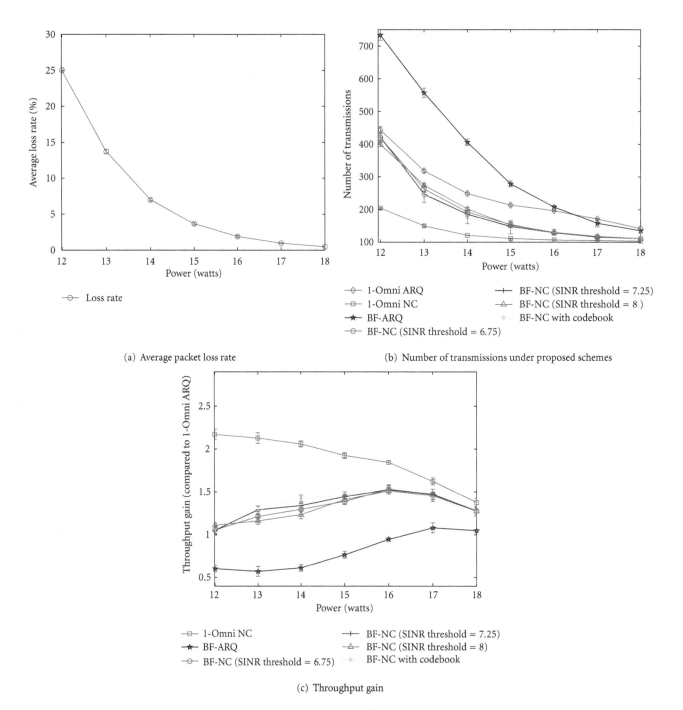

(a) Average packet loss rate

(b) Number of transmissions under proposed schemes

(c) Throughput gain

FIGURE 8: Simulation results for network topology scenario of Figure 7(a) with 120 uniformly distributed MSs.

and the BF-NC with codebook over the 1-Omni ARQ-based retransmission scheme. In all figures, a throughput gain of ratio 1 means that both retransmission schemes use the same number of total transmissions. The figure shows that the 1-Omni NC- and the BF-NC-based retransmission schemes reach throughput gains of ratio 2.2 (i.e., 120% gain) and 1.5 (i.e., 50% gain), respectively. Even though both of the proposed BF-NC-based retransmission schemes have similar results, we lean towards the codebook-based one since it does not require multiple levels of SINR thresholds while still achieving similar performances.

6.2. Clustered MS Distribution on a Circle. In this section, we consider studying a network topology with a clustered MS distribution. Specifically, we consider the network topology scenario of Figure 7(b), where 60 MSs are grouped into 3 clusters each having 20 MSs.

All MSs in each cluster are close to one another, and the channel gains for all MSs belonging to the same cluster are the same (or close). Figure 9(a) shows the average loss rate of omnidirectional packet transmissions (without including retransmissions) as function of the transmit power. In Figure 9(b), we show the number of

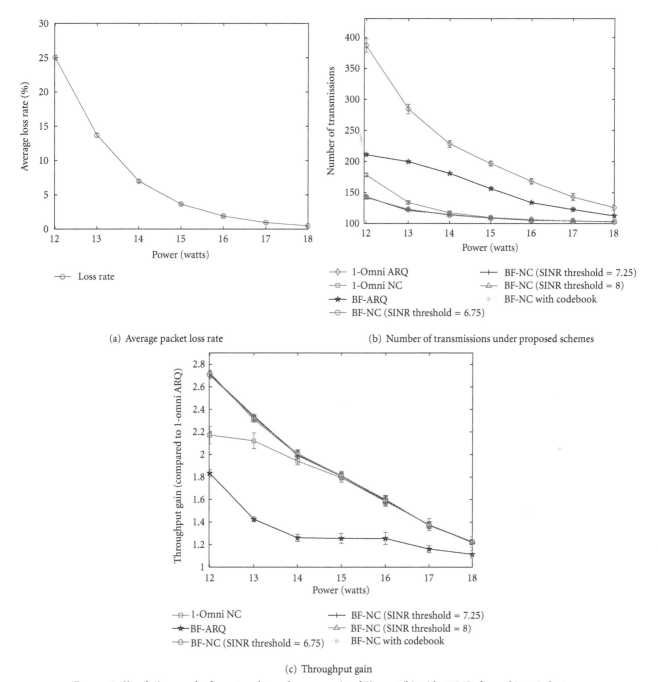

(a) Average packet loss rate

(b) Number of transmissions under proposed schemes

(c) Throughput gain

FIGURE 9: Simulation results for network topology scenario of Figure 7(b) with 60 MSs formed into 3 clusters.

total transmissions (including retransmissions) under each of the studied retransmission schemes as function of the transmit power. First, observe that unlike the case when MSs are uniformly distributed (as illustrated in Section 6.1), when MSs are not uniformly distributed, the proposed retransmission schemes (both BF-NC with SINR and BF-NC with codebook) outperform not only the traditional retransmission scheme (i.e., 1-Omni ARQ and BF-ARQ), but also the traditional scheme with NC (i.e., 1-Omni NC scheme). The total number of transmissions needed under the proposed schemes is substantially lesser than that needed under the 1-Omni ARQ and the 1-Omni NC, especially for low transmit power levels. This is because the BS can

now efficiently allocate the power to a set of active BF beams instead of spreading the power in all directions, strengthening then the signals received at intended MSs, and as a consequence, increasing MSs SINRs.

The second observation that we can draw from the figure is that both proposed techniques achieve very similar performances in terms of the total number of transmissions. This is because when all MSs in the same cluster have similar channel gain, each coded packet most likely comes from all MSs whose packet loss rates are similar. In other words, this maximizes the number of lost packets to be coded at once.

We now plot the throughput gains of the proposed schemes and the 1-Omni NC scheme when compared with

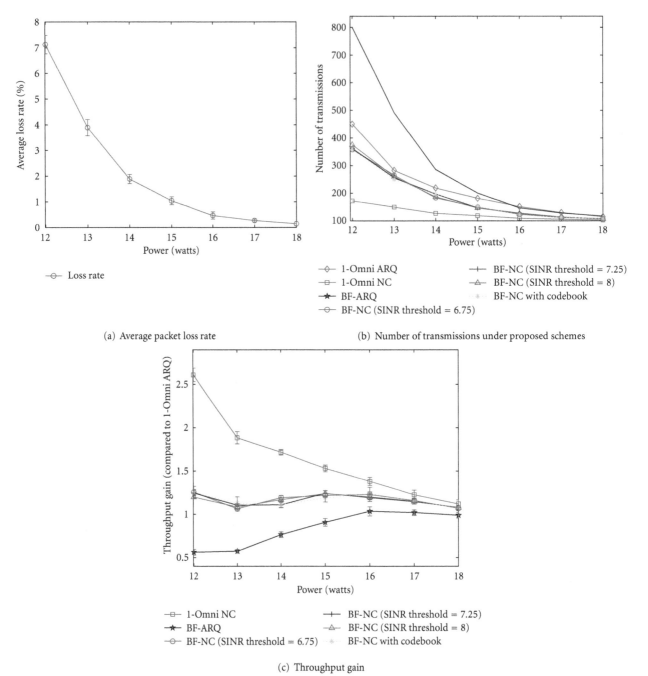

(a) Average packet loss rate

(b) Number of transmissions under proposed schemes

(c) Throughput gain

FIGURE 10: Simulation results for network topology scenario of Figure 7(c) with 120 randomly distributed MSs inside a circle.

the traditional scheme (i.e., 1-Omni ARQ). As shown in Figure 9(c), the throughput gains for the 1-Omni NC- and the BF-NC-based retransmission schemes can reach up to 120% (ratio of 2.2) and 175% (ratio of 2.75), respectively. Note that the incorporation of NC into the 1-Omni scheme results in almost halving the number of total transmissions, whereas the incorporation of these same NC techniques into BF-based schemes (whether SINR or codebook based) reduces the number of total transmissions by almost a third.

6.3. Random MS Distribution inside the Circle. Finally, we study a network topology with a random MS distribution.

In particular, we consider the network topology scenario of Figure 7(c), where 120 MSs are randomly distributed at distances from the base station such that their channel gains are uniformly distributed between 0.7 and 1.3. Furthermore, the angles are normally distributed with the mean of 90 and standard deviation of 30 degrees. Any station located outside the range of [0, 180] degrees ignored.

The average loss rate of packet transmissions during these omnidirectional transmissions is shown in Figure 10(a). The performance of BF-based retransmission schemes in this case is under that of the 1-Omni NC scheme as in Figure 10(b). Specifically, the 1-Omni NC scheme has

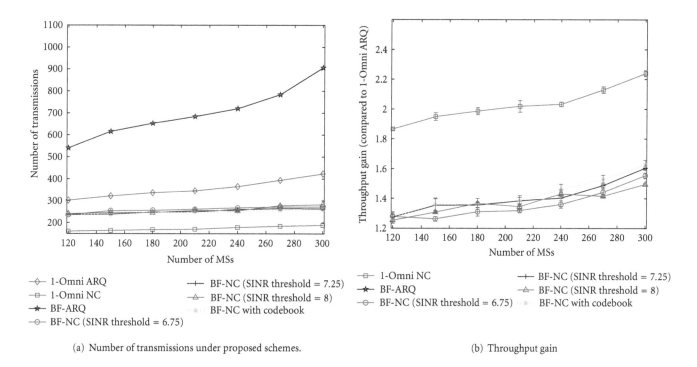

(a) Number of transmissions under proposed schemes.

(b) Throughput gain

FIGURE 11: Simulation results for network topology scenario of Figure 7(a) when varying the number of MSs.

the best result followed by NC-based retransmissions (i.e., BF-NC with SINR or codebook), the 1-Omni ARQ, and the BF-ARQ, respectively. Finally, Figure 10(c) shows the throughput gain with respect to the 1-Omni ARQ scheme. This is intuitively plausible as when mobile stations are dispersed too much, beamforming becomes less effective. In this case, omnitransmission makes sense and NC provides additional benefit with fewer retransmissions. Thus, 1-Omni NC transmission scheme performs the best.

6.4. Impact of Number of MSs. In this section, we want to study the impact of the number of MSs on the performance behaviors. In this simulation, we use the network topology of Figure 7(a), where the number of MSs is varied from 120 to 300. In all scenarios, all MSs have the same channel gains. Figure 11(a) shows how the number of transmissions changes as the number of MSs is varied for each of the proposed retransmission schemes. As expected, when increasing the number of MSs, the BS tends to spend more time to successfully retransmit all lost packets to all corresponding MSs. The number of transmissions when using the BF-NC with codebook retransmission scheme is less than that of the BF-NC with greedy selection (with SINR) retransmission scheme. Note that the number of MSs affects the throughput gain of both BF-NC-based retransmission schemes; this is shown in Figure 11(b). The higher the number of MSs, the higher the chances of combining more lost packets before retransmitting, thus leading to higher throughput gains (lesser transmissions).

7. Conclusion

This paper proposes two joint BF/NC-based scheduling algorithms for wireless broadcast downlink channels. The first algorithm relies on greedy selection of MSs based on their SINRs, whereas the second algorithm uses codebook to group and schedule MSs. The greedy selection approach consists of using MSs orthogonality and their physical locations to maximize their signal quality over a wireless network. The codebook-based approach, on the other hand, uses a predefined codebook to generate multiple sets of orthogonal beams.

Our results show that both of the proposed techniques/algorithms increase the overall throughput by minimizing the number of transmission attempts.

Our simulations indicate that our techniques reduce the number of retransmission attempts significantly, resulting in achieving high throughput gain of up to 175% of broadcast transmissions when compared to that of traditional ARQ retransmission approaches.

Appendix

In this section, we prove that our BF-NC scheduling problem is NP-hard. First of all, we know that the well-known problem "scheduling unrelated parallel machines (SUPM)" is NP-hard [19]. To prove that our BF-NC-based scheduling problem is NP-hard, we need to show the reduction from the SUPM problem to our problem. In the SUPM problem, there is a set of K' jobs denoted by $J = \{p_1, p_2, \ldots, p_{K'}\}$ and a set of M parallel machines with their related speed factors denoted by $S = \{s_1, s_2, \ldots, s_M\}$. For generalization of identical machines, they can run at different speeds but do so uniformly. For each machine i with a speed factor s_i, the processing time for job j (p_j) on machine i denoted by p_{ij} can be computed as $p_{ij} = p_j/s_i$. Note that each machine i can process only one job at a time. Therefore, the total time on machine i is $\sum_j p_{ij}$. The goal is to find a scheduler that minimizes the makespan such that

$$
\begin{aligned}
\textbf{minimize} \quad &\max_i \left\{ \sum_j x(i,j) p_{ij} \right\}, \\
\textbf{s.t.} \quad &\sum_i x(i,j) = 1, \\
&x(i,j) \in \{0,1\},
\end{aligned}
\tag{A.1}
$$

where $i \in \{1, 2, \ldots, M\}$ and $j \in \{1, 2, \ldots, K'\}$. Formally, an instance of an SUPM problem is a 3-tuple problem as follows:

$$
\langle \{p_1, p_2, \ldots, p_{K'}\}, \{s_1, s_2, \ldots, s_M\}, \{x(1,1), \ldots, x(M, K')\} \rangle.
\tag{A.2}
$$

Given an instance of an SUPM problem, we can construct the following version of our BF-NC-based scheduling problem by reduction as follows. All MSs are in a set V. A set of lost packets belonging to MS z_k is p_k. In particular, the job p_k in original problem is reducible to our problem as a set of lost packets n_k for MS z_k (i.e, $n_k \leftarrow p_k$). For each beam i, we randomly assign MS z_k with a set of lost packets p_k to a group of MSs V_i over all M groups as shown in Figure 12, where $V = \cup_{\forall j} V_i$ and $i \in \{1, 2, \ldots, M\}$. In this case, we set $x(i,k) = 1$ for assigning a set of lost packets p_k to a group V_i (for beam i). Note that this reduction is the special case of our BF-NC-based scheduling problem when all lost packets in each group cannot be combined. Therefore, the reduction for variables p_k to n_k can be done in $O(1)$.

Suppose we have the optimal solution to solve a BF-NC-based scheduling problem. To be complete, we can show that the optimal solution to our BF-NC-based scheduling problem is the optimal solution to an SUPM problem as follows. First, we use only one set of orthogonal BF beams from a given codebook. For example, the BS uses only the qth set, then we set $l_q = 1$ and $l_p = 0$ in (8) where $p \neq q$. Therefore, we have

$$
\begin{aligned}
\textbf{minimize} \quad &\max_i \left\{ \frac{N_{V_i}}{1 - \max_j \{ x(i,j) \mathrm{PER}_{ij} \}} \right\}, \\
\textbf{s.t.} \quad &\sum_i x(i,j) = 1, \\
&x(i,j) \in \{0,1\},
\end{aligned}
\tag{A.3}
$$

where N_{V_i} and PER_{ij} are a set of coded/uncoded lost packets based on an NC technique in beam i and packet error rate for MS z_j in beam i, respectively. Recall that all lost packets in each beam i cannot be combined in this special case. Thus,

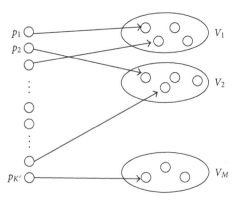

FIGURE 12: Illustration of the reduction from an SUPM problem to a BF-NC-based scheduling problem.

a set of lost packets n_j for MS z_j strictly depends on PER_{ij}, where $n_j \subseteq N_{V_i}$. In such case, we can rewrite (A.3) as follows:

$$
\begin{aligned}
\textbf{minimize} \quad &\max_i \left\{ \sum_j x(i,j) \frac{n_j}{1 - \mathrm{PER}_{ij}} \right\}, \\
\textbf{s.t.} \quad &\sum_i x(i,j) = 1, \\
&x(i,j) \in \{0,1\}.
\end{aligned}
\tag{A.4}
$$

In (A.4), the time to successfully retransmit all lost packets in N_{V_i} is the summation of the time to retransmit all n_j where $n_j \subseteq N_{V_i}$.

Comparing (A.1) to (A.4) and assuming there exists a function for reduction from $p_{ij} = p_j/s_i$ to $n_j/(1 - \mathrm{PER}_{ij})$, all instances of an SUPM problem are correctly reducible to our BF-NC-based scheduling problem. That is

$$
\begin{aligned}
\textbf{minimize} \quad &\max_i \left\{ \sum_j x(i,j) \frac{p_j}{s_i} \right\}, \\
\Longleftrightarrow \textbf{minimize} \quad &\max_i \left\{ \sum_j x(i,j) \frac{n_j}{1 - \mathrm{PER}_{ij}} \right\}.
\end{aligned}
\tag{A.5}
$$

The solution to (A.4) is a set of $x(i,j)$ for all i and j. From (A.5), both objective functions can be reducible to each other and vice versa. That means the optimal solution to our BF-NC-based scheduling problem in (A.4) is the optimal solution to an SUPM problem in (A.1). Furthermore, the SUPM problem can be reducible to our problem in polynomial time. This concludes that our problem is NP-hard.

References

[1] P. Viswanath and D. N. C. Tse, "Sum capacity of the vector Gaussian broadcast channel and uplink-downlink duality," *IEEE Transactions on Information Theory*, vol. 49, no. 8, pp. 1912–1921, 2003.

[2] K. Huang, R. W. Heath, and J. G. Andrews, "Space division multiple access with a sum feedback rate constraint," *IEEE Transactions on Signal Processing*, vol. 55, no. 7, pp. 3879–3891, 2007.

[3] W. Choi, A. Forenza, J. G. Andrews, and R. W. Heath, "Opportunistic space-division multiple access with beam selection," *IEEE Transactions on Communications*, vol. 55, no. 12, pp. 2371–2380, 2007.

[4] B. D. Van Veen and K. M. Buckley, "Beamforming: a versatile approach to spatial filtering," *IEEE ASSP Magazine*, vol. 5, no. 2, pp. 4–24, 1988.

[5] G. Dimić and N. D. Sidiropoulos, "On downlink beamforming with greedy user selection: performance analysis and a simple new algorithm," *IEEE Transactions on Signal Processing*, vol. 53, no. 10, pp. 3857–3868, 2005.

[6] T. Yoo and A. Goldsmith, "Optimality of zero-forcing beamforming with multiuser diversity," in *Proceedings of the IEEE International Conference on Communications (ICC '05)*, vol. 1, pp. 542–546, May 2005.

[7] T. Yoo and A. Goldsmith, "On the optimality of multiantenna broadcast scheduling using zero-forcing beamforming," *IEEE Journal on Selected Areas in Communications*, vol. 24, no. 3, pp. 528–541, 2006.

[8] H. Yin and H. Liu, "Performance of Space-division Multiple-access (SDMA) with scheduling," *IEEE Transactions on Wireless Communications*, vol. 1, no. 4, pp. 611–618, 2002.

[9] R. Ahlswede, N. Cai, S. Y. R. Li, and R. W. Yeung, "Network information flow," *IEEE Transactions on Information Theory*, vol. 46, no. 4, pp. 1204–1216, 2000.

[10] D. Nguyen, T. Tran, T. Nguyen, and B. Bose, "Wireless broadcast using network coding," *IEEE Transactions on Vehicular Technology*, vol. 58, no. 2, pp. 914–925, 2009.

[11] F. Shad, T. D. Todd, V. Kezys, and J. Litva, "Indoor SDMA capacity using a smart antenna basestation," in *Proceedings of the 6th International Conference on Universal Personal Communications (ICUPC '97)*, vol. 2, pp. 868–872, October 1997.

[12] W. Choi, A. Forenza, J. G. Andrews, and R. W. Heath, "Capacity of opportunistic space division multiple access with beam selection," in *Proceedings of the IEEE Global Telecommunications Conference*, pp. 1–5, November-December 2006.

[13] N. Ravindran, N. Jindal, and H. C. Huang, "Beamforming with finite rate feedback for LOS MIMO downlink channels," in *Proceedings of the 50th Annual IEEE Global Telecommunications Conference (GLOBECOM '07)*, pp. 4200–4204, November 2007.

[14] V. Raghavan, A. M. Sayeed, and N. Boston, "Near-optimal codebook constructions for limited feedback beamforming in correlated MIMO channels with few antennas," in *Proceedings of the IEEE International Symposium on Information Theory (ISIT '06)*, pp. 2622–2626, July 2006.

[15] D. J. Love and R. W. Heath, "Grassmannian beamforming on correlated MIMO channels," in *Proceedings of the IEEE Global Telecommunications Conference*, pp. 106–110, November-December 2004.

[16] K. Amiri, D. Shamsi, B. Aazhang, and J. R. Cavallaro, "Adaptive codebook for beamforming in limited feedback MIMO systems," in *Proceedings of the 42nd Annual Conference on Information Sciences and Systems (CISS '08)*, pp. 994–998, March 2008.

[17] K. Huang, J. G. Andrews, and R. W. Heath, "Performance of orthogonal beamforming for SDMA with limited feedback," *IEEE Transactions on Vehicular Technology*, vol. 58, no. 1, pp. 152–164, 2009.

[18] A. Goldsmith, *Wireless Communications*, Cambridge University Press, 2005.

[19] K. Jansen and L. Porkolab, "Improved approximation schemes for scheduling unrelated parallel machines," in *Proceedings of the 31st Annual ACM Symposium on Theory of Computing (FCRC '99)*, pp. 408–417, May 1999.

7

A Seamless Broadcasting Scheme with Live Video Support

Zeng-Yuan Yang,[1] Yi-Ming Chen,[2] and Li-Ming Tseng[1]

[1] Department of Computer Science and Information Engineering, National Central University, Jhongli 32001, Taiwan
[2] Department of Information Management, National Central University, Jhongli 32001, Taiwan

Correspondence should be addressed to Zeng-Yuan Yang, yzy@dslab.csie.ncu.edu.tw

Academic Editor: Hsiang-Fu Yu

Broadcasting schemes, such as the fast broadcasting and harmonic broadcasting schemes, significantly reduce the bandwidth requirement of video-on-demand services. In the real world, some history events are very hot. For example, every year in March, thousands of people connect to Internet to watch the live show of Oscar Night. Such actions easily cause the networks contested. However, the schemes mentioned previously cannot alleviate the problem because they do not support live broadcasting. In this paper, we analyze the requirements for transferring live videos. Based on the requirements, a time skewing approach is proposed to enable the broadcasting schemes to support live broadcasting. However, the improved schemes require extra bandwidth for live broadcasting once the length of live shows exceeds the default. Accordingly, we proposed a scalable binomial broadcasting scheme to transfer live videos using constant bandwidth by increasing clients' waiting time. When the scheme finds that the length of a video exceeds the default, it doubles the length of to-be-played segments and then its required bandwidth is constant.

1. Introduction

With the growth of broadband networks, the video-on-demand (VOD) [1] becomes realistic. Many studies start investigating VOD. One of important areas is to explore how to distribute the top ten or twenty so-called hot videos more efficiently. Broadcasting is one of the promising solutions. It transfers each video according to a fixed schedule and consumes constant bandwidth regardless of the presence or absence of requests for the video. That is, the system's bandwidth requirement is independent of the number of users watching a given video. A basic broadcasting scheme is the batch scheme [2], which postpones the users' requests for a certain amount of time and serves these requests in batch so that its bandwidth consumption is reduced. However, the batch scheme still requires quite large bandwidth for a hot video. For example, given a video of 120 minutes, if the maximum clients' waiting time equals 10 minutes, the required bandwidth is 12b, where b is the video playout rate.

Many broadcasting schemes were proposed to further reduce the bandwidth requirement by using a set-top box (STB) at the client end. The schemes include the fast broadcasting (FB) [3, 4], pagoda broadcasting (PB) [5], new pagoda broadcasting (NPB) [5], recursive-frequency splitting (RFS) [6], staircase broadcasting (SB) [7], and harmonic broadcasting (HB) [8, 9] schemes, which divide a video into multiple segments and distribute them through several independent data channels. As well, these schemes require the STB to receive the segments from the channels when users start watching the video. The schemes substantially reduce the bandwidth requirements for hot videos. For example, if a video server allocates 4 video channels to transmit a 120-minute video by FB, then its maximum waiting time is merely 8 minutes. The FB scheme, in comparison with the batch scheme, reduces the bandwidth requirements and waiting time remarkably.

In the real world, some history events are very hot. For example, every year in March, many people connect to Internet to watch the live show of Oscar Night. Such actions easily cause the networks congested. However, the schemes, such as PB, NPB, SB, RFS, and HB, cannot broadcast live programs to alleviate the congestion. In order to overcome this obstacle, we analyzed the requirements for live broadcasting and proposed an approach, called time skewing, to enabling these schemes to distribute live shows. However, the improved schemes require extra bandwidth for

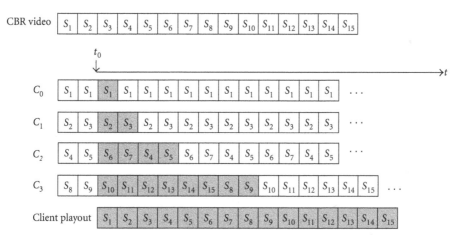

FIGURE 1: The FB scheme ($N = 15$ and $k = 3$).

live broadcasting once the length of live shows exceeds the default. Accordingly, a scalable binomial broadcasting scheme was proposed to demonstrate how to transfer live videos at the constant bandwidth regardless of video length.

The remainder of the paper is as follows. Section 2 analyzes the requirements of live broadcasting. This section also introduces the time skewing and the scalable binomial broadcasting scheme. An analysis and comparison is presented in Section 3. Finally, we make a brief conclusion in Section 4.

This work briefly introduces the FB and HB first. Suppose that there is a video with length L (e.g., 120 minutes). The consumption rate of the video is b (e.g., 10 Mbps). The size of the video is $S = L * b$ (e.g., 9 Gbytes). Suppose that the desired viewer's waiting time is less than $l = L/N$, where N is a positive integer. Both schemes involve the following steps.

(1) The video is equally divided into N segments. Suppose that S_i is the ith segment of the video. The concatenation ($\bullet$) of all the segments, in the order of increasing segment numbers, constitutes the whole video, $S = S_1 \bullet S_2 \bullet \cdots \bullet S_N$.

(2) On the server side, the FB and HB schemes involve the following steps, respectively.

2. The Live Broadcasting Schemes

2.1. Background.

(a) For FB, there exists an integer k such that $\sum_{i=0}^{k-1} 2^i < N \leq \sum_{i=0}^{k} 2^i$. The server then periodically transfers segments S_{2^i} to $S_{2^{i+1}-1}$ on channel C_i, where $0 \leq i \leq k$, as shown in Figure 1. Hence, the total bandwidth allocated for the video is $B = (k+1) * b$.

(b) For HB, the server further equally divides segment S_i into i subsegments $\{S_{1,i}, S_{2,i}, \ldots, S_{i,i}\}$. The subsegments of segment S_i are then broadcast on channel C_i, where $1 \leq i \leq N$, as indicated in Figure 2. The bandwidth of C_i thus

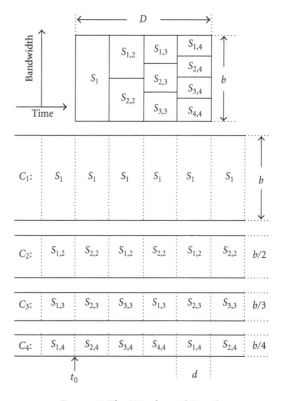

FIGURE 2: The HB scheme ($N = 4$).

equals b/i. The total bandwidth for the video equals $B = \sum_{i=1}^{N} b/i = H_N * b$, where $H_N = \sum_{n=1}^{N} 1/n$ is the harmonic number of N.

(3) At the client end, suppose that there are enough buffer spaces to store data segments of a video. The steps to watch a video include the following.

(a) The client downloads the first data segment at the first occurrence on the first channel and then downloads other related data segments from other channels concurrently.

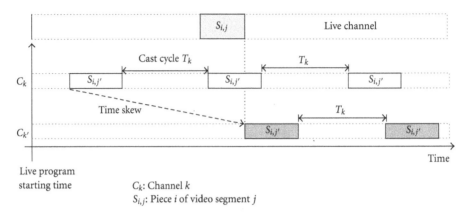

C_k: Channel k
$S_{i,j}$: Piece i of video segment j

FIGURE 3: An illustration of time skewing.

(b) Once finishing the downloading of the first segment, the client starts to play the video with its normal speed in the order of $S_1 \bullet S_2 \bullet \cdots \bullet S_N$.

(c) The client stops loading from channels when all data segments are received.

2.2. The Requirements of Live Broadcasting. The section describes three important requirements for live broadcasting.

(R1) *The data transfer rate of a channel must be less or equal to media production rate.* In the case of live broadcasting, the new media are produced at constant speed such that the broadcasting schemes transferring data on a channel at a higher rate than media production rate are unable to support live broadcasting.

(R2) *The broadcasting schemes cannot transmit the rearward and unavailable video segments in advance.*

(R3) *A live broadcasting scheme has to tolerate the varying length of live videos.* In the real world, live shows often end either early or late, rarely on time. Most current broadcasting schemes [3–9] assume that the length of a video is known and fixed. In the case of early ending, such schemes simply free the allocated channels or repeat the last or blank video segments. Hence, the viewer watching the video is not affected. However, in the case of late ending, the schemes require additional bandwidth to handle the situation of program elongation. If the bandwidth is not available, the live broadcasting will be interrupted.

Being subject to the aforementioned requirements, we examine whether several proposed broadcasting schemes support live-program broadcasting. First, the pyramid broadcasting [10] scheme violates the requirement R1 because it uses multifold bandwidth channels to distribute video segments. Second, HB and SB conflict with the requirement R2 because they attempt to broadcast the nonexistent rearward video segments. Third, all of the mentioned broadcasting schemes cannot satisfy the requirement R3. They need to allocate additional channels to transfer the over length of a live video. Hence, they cannot distribute live videos using constant bandwidth. Accordingly, we proposed

the time skewing to enable the schemes to satisfy the requirement R2. Furthermore, a scalable binomial broadcasting, based on FB, was proposed to demonstrate how to fulfill the requirement R3.

2.3. Time Skewing. Suppose that a broadcasting scheme schedules a subsegment $S_{i,j}$ of segment S_j onto channel C_k in a constant cycle time T_k. That is, subsegment $S_{i,j}$ will appear once on channel C_k every time T_k. This work also assumes that in the beginning of broadcasting the video, segment S_j is not available yet. Hence, the video server must put off the transmission of segment S_j until the segment is available. Once receiving segment S_j from a video source, such as a video camera, the video server transfers the deferred subsegment $S_{i,j}$ via channel C_k as it does for prerecorded videos. We call this postponement as time skewing. Figure 3 shows the differences between a regular broadcasting scheme on C_k and a broadcasting scheme with the time skewing.

The time skewing is a general approach. If a broadcasting scheme cannot be rescheduled to fit time skewing, then it cannot support live broadcasting. In the paper, we merely demonstrate how HB takes the advantage of the approach to support live broadcasting. This is because HB was proved to require the minimum bandwidth under the same average waiting time in [9].

Live Harmonic Broadcasting. Suppose that the default length of a live video is L and the maximum user's waiting time is $L/5$. According to HB, the video is equally divided into five segments, and the jth segment is further divided into j subsegments. With the time skewing, we put off the transmission of the posterior video segments until they are available. Figure 4 displays the scenario.

The channel C_L broadcasts the live video sequentially. Meanwhile, the other channels, that is, C_1 to C_5, distribute the recorded segments of live program with time skewing. Whenever the entire live video is recorded, it is distributed over the HB scheme.

2.4. The Scalable Binomial Broadcasting. The time skewing successfully allows the previous broadcasting schemes [3–9] to distribute live videos; however, it does not address

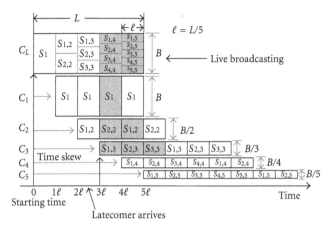

FIGURE 4: Live harmonic broadcasting scheme.

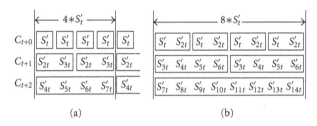

FIGURE 5: The binomial relations on the fast broadcasting scheme.

the over-length problem. For example, in Figure 4, if the live program's length is longer than L, we must allocate an additional channel C_6 to transmit the excess part of the video. If the bandwidth is unavailable, the system has to stop video distribution. To overcome this obstacle, we develop a scalable binomial broadcasting that broadcasts a live video using constant bandwidth, regardless of its length.

The idea comes from the binomial relationship of FB [3]. The FB scheme reveals the binomial relationship between two conjunctive channels (Figure 5(a)). For channel C_{t+1}, the length of basic cycle unit $(S'_{2t} + S'_{3t})$ is twice larger than that (S'_t) of channel C_{t+0}. The binomial relationship is independent of the length of each video segment. Therefore, the server can broadcast a video of double length on the same number of channels by doubling the length of basic cycle unit (Figure 5(b)). Namely, by increasing the length of the cyclic unit on demand, the over-length part of a live video can be broadcast via preallocated channels.

The work then presents how to seamlessly lively broadcast an over-length video at a constant bandwidth.

(1) Schedule the allocated channels by regular FB.

(2) When the last timeslot of a basic cycle unit on the highest numbered channel (S'_{7t} on C_{t+2} in Figure 6(a)) is allocated and no addition channel is available for the live video, the elongation process of the basic cycle unit starts. The process doubles the length of basic cycle unit of each channel ($2 * S'_t$ on channel C_{t+0}, $4 * S'_t$ on channel C_{t+1}, and $8 * S'_t$ on channel C_{t+2}). As well, the starting segment $S'_{t+i} = S'_w$ of basic

cycle unit on each channel C_{t+i} is derived based on the following formula:

if $i = 0$, then $w = 1$;

$$\text{else } w = 1 + \sum_{n=1}^{i} 2^k \times 2^{n-1}, \tag{1}$$

where k is the times which the elongation process is applied to. (As shown in Figure 6(b), the starting segments of channel C_t, C_{t+1}, and C_{t+2} are S'_{1t}, S'_{3t}, and S'_{7t}, resp.).

(3) If the starting segment S'_w has been broadcasted via this channel, the VOD server scans backward one by one till to the first occurrence of S'_w and mark it as a new run of broadcasting cycle.

(4) If a new data cycle has been broadcasted completely and the live video is not over yet, then the video server jumps back to Step 2 and begins a new elongation process (Figure 6(c)). Otherwise, the video server cyclically broadcasts the double length of basic cycle unit as usual.

By the scalable binomial broadcasting, a video server can distribute live videos using a constant number of channels. The cost of the scheme is that the latecomers' waiting time and buffer requirements grow in the power of two.

3. Analysis and Comparison

This section presents the requirements of network bandwidth, buffer size, and I/O load on client sides with respect to each live broadcasting scheme. The assumptions include the following. Let L be the video length. (1) The media playback rate is b. (2) The length of a segment is l. (3) The number of video segments is N. The media size of the live video is blN bytes. The over-length portion is M. (4) A playing time slot denotes n.

3.1. Bandwidth Requirements. When the length of the live video is longer than L, the broadcasting scheme must allocate extra channels to distribute the over-length portion, as mentioned in Section 2.3. The bandwidth requirements of each broadcasting scheme are listed as follows.

(i) *Live Harmonic Broadcasting* (LHB). Its bandwidth requirements include a channel for live broadcast C_L and multiple channels C_n for clients (Figure 4). Since the bandwidth of each channel is a harmonic series [8], the bandwidth requirement (β_h) is

$$\beta_h = \left(1 + \sum_{x=1}^{n-1} \frac{1}{x}\right) \times B, \quad \text{where } 1 \leqq n \leqq N + M. \tag{2}$$

Equation (2) represents the bandwidth requirement when the live video is not over:

$$\beta_h = \left(\sum_{x=1}^{N+M} \frac{1}{x}\right) \times B, \quad \text{where } N + M < n. \tag{3}$$

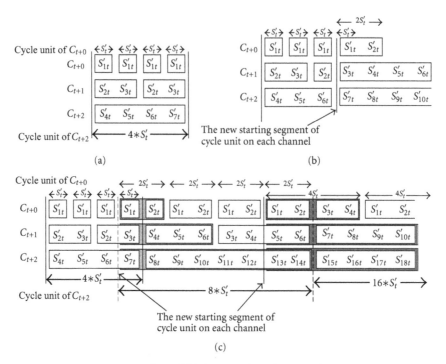

(a)

(b)

(c)

FIGURE 6: The scalable binomial broadcasting scheme.

The equation represents the bandwidth requirement when the live video is over, and the channel C_L is released.

(ii) *Live Staircase Broadcasting* (LSB). In comparison with the regular staircase broadcasting [7], this scheme requires an additional channel C_L for live broadcasting. Hence, the bandwidth requirement (β_s) is

$$\beta_s = \left(1 + c + m\left(\frac{1}{2^c}\right)\right) \times B, \qquad (4)$$

where $c = \lfloor \log_2 n \rfloor$, $m = n - 2^c$, and $1 \leq n \leq N + M$:

$$\beta_s = \left(c + m\left(\frac{1}{2^c}\right)\right) \times B, \qquad (5)$$

where $c = \lfloor \log_2(N + M + 1) \rfloor$, $m = N + M - 2^c$, and $N + M < n$.

(iii) *Live Fast Broadcasting* (LFB. Its bandwidth requirement β_f can be obtained from [3]; it is

$$\beta_f = \left(1 + \lceil \log_2 n \rceil\right) \times B, \quad \text{where } 1 \leq n \leq N + M, \quad (6)$$

$$\beta_f = \left(1 + \lfloor \log_2(N + M) \rfloor\right) \times B, \quad \text{where } N + M < n. \quad (7)$$

(iv) *Scalable Binomial Broadcasting*. Since the scalable binomial broadcasting scheme transfers a live video at a constant number of channels, its bandwidth requirement β_b is

$$\beta_b = \left(1 + \lfloor \log_2 N \rfloor\right) \times B. \qquad (8)$$

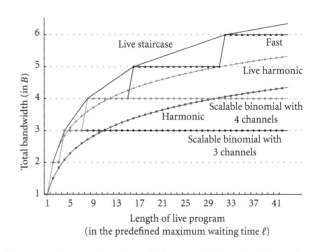

FIGURE 7: The required bandwidth versus the length of live videos.

Figure 7 depicts the bandwidth requirements of each broadcasting scheme. In [9], we proved that the optimal broadcasting scheme is harmonic scheme. However, in the study, we find that when the length of the live video is less than 16l, LFB becomes the optimal live broadcasting scheme, as shown in Figure 7. This is because LHB requires an additional channel, the live channel CL, to broadcast the live program. Furthermore, when the length exceeds 16l, LHB can be proved to be the optimal scheme by following the same deduction process revealed in [9]. Finally, Figure 7 displays that the scalable binomial broadcasting works with constant number of channels at the cost of doubling the maximum waiting time.

3.2. The Minimum Disk Transfer Rate Requirement.

In the broadcasting schemes, the video segments are written to clients' disk as they need to be buffered. When clients need to consume the segments, they need to read them from disk. The disk transfer rate (Φ) is the sum of the read transfer rate (r_{read}) and write transfer rate (r_{write}). In order to ensure smooth playback, the minimum read transfer rate is the playback rate B. As well, the minimum write transfer rate must be large enough to save the need-to-be-buffered segments in time. It depends on which time slot a client receives video segments at. The following discusses the required disk transfer rate of each broadcasting schemes.

(i) *LHB.* From (2) and (3), we can find that the bandwidth requirement is maximum when $n = N + M$. The bandwidth requirement β at the time slot is $\beta = (1 + \sum_{x=1}^{N+M-1} 1/x) \times B$, and the server distributes maximum data at the time slot. In order to save video segments completely, the minimum write transfer rate at clients ($r_{\text{min\_write}}$) must equal the bandwidth requirement. Accordingly, the minimum disk transfer rate ($\Phi_{\min}$) is the sum of $r_{\text{min\_read}}$ and $r_{\text{min\_write}}$. That is,

$$\Phi_{\min} = r_{\text{min\_read}} + r_{\text{min\_write}} = \left(2 + \sum_{x=1}^{N+M-1} \frac{1}{x}\right) \times B. \quad (9)$$

(ii) *LSB.* Like the LHB, when $n = N + M$, the bandwidth requirement is maximum. Thus,

$$\Phi_{\min} = \left(2 + c + m\left(\frac{1}{2^c}\right)\right) \times B, \quad (10)$$

where $c = \lfloor \log_2(N + M) \rfloor$, and $m = N + M - 2^c$.

(iii) *LFB.* From (6), we can derive the maximum bandwidth requirement when $n = N + M$. Thus,

$$\Phi_{\min} = \left(2 + \lceil \log_2(N + M) \rceil\right) \times B. \quad (11)$$

(iv) *Scalable Binomial Broadcasting.* Owing to the constant bandwidth requirement, the disk transfer rate is also constant and equal to

$$\Phi_{\min} = \left(2 + \lfloor \log_2 N \rfloor\right) \times B. \quad (12)$$

Figure 8 shows the maximum I/O load Φ of each broadcasting scheme.

3.3. Maximum Client Buffer Requirements.

Based on the previous discussion, we find that the client's video incoming rate ($r_{\text{live}} + r_{\text{filling}}$) is greater than video playback rate (r_{playback}). The unconsumed video segments will be saved on the client's auxiliary storage. Because media playback rate is equal to the live broadcasting rate ($r_{\text{playback}} = r_{\text{live}} = B$), the rate to fill the missing segments mainly contributes to the buffer accumulation, as indicated in Figure 9.

Suppose that the filling process of missing segments ends at T_f and the live video ends at T_e. Thus the integration

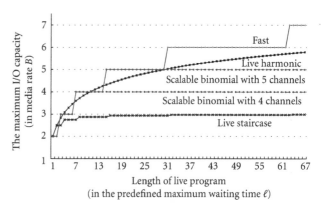

FIGURE 8: The maximum I/O load on clients versus the length of live videos.

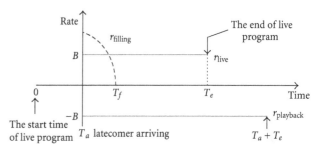

FIGURE 9: A media rate diagram of a client on LHB.

$\int_{T_a}^{T_f} r_{\text{filling}} dt$ is the size of missing video segments. If T_f is before T_e, as shown in Figure 9, the maximum buffer requirement (Z) is equal to the size of missing video segments $Z = \int_{T_a}^{T_f} r_{\text{filling}} dt$. In order to satisfy the continuous playback constraint, the time to fill the missing segments must be shorter than the time to play the missing segments. Therefore, if a client arrives in the first half of the live broadcasting, the buffered video size is always equal to the size of missing video segments. On the contrary, if a client arrives after the midpoint of a live show, the maximum buffer requirement varies with the adopted live broadcasting schemes. Suppose that the length of a live video is $1024l$. Figure 10 illustrates the relationship between the buffer requirements and the client's arrival time.

Suppose that a client arrives at the nth time slot and the live video length is N. For the live broadcasting schemes, their maximum buffer (Z) requirements are listed as follows.

(i) *LHB.* Its maximum buffer requirement is

$$Z_h = \left(\sum_{i=n+1}^{N+n} \zeta^i\right) \times \ell B \quad \text{when } \zeta^i \geq 0, \quad (13)$$

where $\zeta^i = r_{\text{live},i} + \phi^i - r_{\text{playback},i}$. The ϕ^i is the sum of the $(i-n)$th column of filling rate matrix in (6) when $i \leq n + n$; others $\phi^i = 0$. (The $r_{\text{live},i} = 0$, when $i > N$; others $r_{\text{live},i} = r_{\text{playback},i} = B$.)

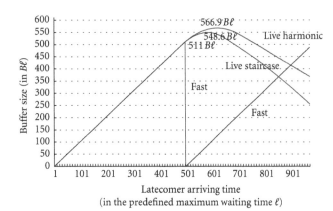

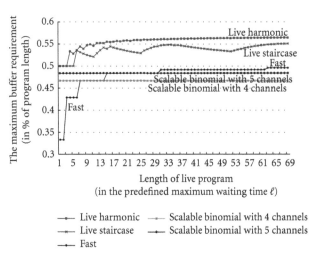

FIGURE 10: The relation between the buffer requirement and the client's arrival time.

FIGURE 11: The maximum buffer requirements of each live broadcasting scheme.

(ii) *LSB*. Its maximum buffer requirement is

$$Z_s = \left(\sum_{i=n+1}^{N+n} \zeta^i \right) \times \ell B \quad \text{when } \zeta^i \geq 0, \qquad (14)$$

where $\zeta^i = r_{\text{live},i} + \phi^i - r_{\text{playback},i}$. The ϕ^i is the sum of the $(i-n)$th column of filling rate matrix in (9) when $i \leq n + n$; others $\phi^i = 0$. (The $r_{\text{live},i} = 0$, when $i > N$; others $r_{\text{live},i} = r_{\text{playback},i} = B$.)

(iii) *LFB*. Its maximum buffer requirement can be obtained from [3]

$$Z_F = \left(\frac{(2^{c-1} - 1)}{(2^c - 1)} \right) \times \ell B, \qquad (15)$$

where c is the number of channels, and $c = (1 + \lfloor \log_2 N \rfloor)$.

(iv) *Scalable Binomial Broadcasting*. Its maximum buffer requirement is identical to that of live fast broadcasting:

$$Z_B = \left(\frac{(2^{c-1} - 1)}{(2^c - 1)} \right) \times \ell B, \qquad (16)$$

where C is a constant number of the preallocated channels.

According to (13) to (16), Figure 11 illustrates the maximum buffer requirements of the previous live broadcasting in the percentage of the video length.

4. Conclusions

Live program distribution is an important service on Internet. However, most current broadcasting schemes, such as PB, NPB, SB, and HB, cannot support live broadcasting. In this paper, we analyze the requirements for broadcasting live programs. In addition, the time skewing approach is proposed to allow traditional the VOD broadcasting schemes to distribute live programs. We also develop the scalable binomial broadcasting to distribute a live program with varying length in constant bandwidth consumption, however, at the cost of longer waiting time. The analyses and comparisons indicate that the scalable binomial broadcasting provides a reasonable performance than other live broadcasting schemes with respect to bandwidth requirements, I/O capacity, and receiver's buffer size.

References

[1] T. D. Little and D. Venkatesh, "Prospects for interactive video-on-demand," *IEEE Multimedia*, vol. 1, no. 3, pp. 14–24, 1994.

[2] T. C. Chiueh and C. H. Lu, "Periodic broadcasting approach to video-on-demand service," in *Integration Issues in Large Commercial Media Delivery Systems*, vol. 2615 of *Proceedings of SPIE*, pp. 162–169, October 1995.

[3] L. S. Juhn and L. M. Tseng, "Fast data broadcasting and receiving scheme for popular video service," *IEEE Transactions on Broadcasting*, vol. 44, no. 1, pp. 100–105, 1998.

[4] L. S. Juhn and L. M. Tseng, "Adaptive fast data broadcasting scheme for video-on-demand service," *IEEE Transactions on Broadcasting*, vol. 44, no. 2, pp. 182–185, 1998.

[5] J.- F. Paris, S. W. Carter, and D. E. Long, "A hybrid broadcasting protocol for video-on-demand," in *Proceedings of the Multimedia Computing and Networking Conference*, pp. 317–326, San Jose, Calif, USA, January 1999.

[6] Y. C. Tseng, M. H. Yang, and C. H. Chang, "A recursive frequency-splitting scheme for broadcasting hot videos in VOD service," *IEEE Transactions on Communications*, vol. 50, no. 8, pp. 1348–1355, 2002.

[7] L. S. Juhn and L. M. Tseng, "Staircase data broadcasting and receiving scheme for hot video service," *IEEE Transactions on Consumer Electronics*, vol. 43, no. 4, pp. 1110–1117, 1997.

[8] L. S. Juhn and L. M. Tseng, "Harmonic broadcasting for video-on-demand service," *IEEE Transactions on Broadcasting*, vol. 43, no. 3, pp. 268–271, 1997.

[9] Z. Y. Yang, L. S. Juhn, and L. M. Tseng, "On optimal broadcasting scheme for popular video service," *IEEE Transactions on Broadcasting*, vol. 45, no. 3, pp. 318–324, 1998.

[10] S. Viswanathan and T. Imielinski, "Metropolitan area video-on-demand service using pyramid broadcasting," *Multimedia Systems*, vol. 4, no. 4, pp. 197–208, 1996.

8

A Gain-Computation Enhancements Resource Allocation for Heterogeneous Service Flows in IEEE 802.16 m Mobile Networks

Wafa Ben Hassen and Meriem Afif

Mediatron: Research Unit on Radio Communication and Multimedia Networks, Higher School of Communication of Tunis (Sup'com), Carthage University, Cité Technologique des Communications, Route de Raoued Km 3.5, 2083 El Ghazala, Ariana, Tunisia

Correspondence should be addressed to Wafa Ben Hassen, wafa.benhassen@hotmail.fr and Meriem Afif, mariem.afif@supcom.rnu.tn

Academic Editor: Yifeng He

This paper deals with radio resource allocation in fourth generation (4G) wireless mobile networks based on Orthogonal Frequency Division Multiple Access (OFDMA) as an access method. In IEEE 802.16 m standard, a contiguous method for subchannel construction is adopted in order to reduce OFDMA system complexity. In this context, we propose a new subchannel gain computation method depending on frequency responses dispersion. This method has a crucial role in the resource management and optimization. In a single service access, we propose a dynamic resource allocation algorithm at the physical layer aiming to maximize the cell data rate while ensuring fairness among users. In heterogeneous data traffics, we study scheduling in order to provide delay guaranties to real-time services, maximize throughput of non-real-time services while ensuring fairness to users. We compare performances to recent existing algorithms in OFDMA systems showing that proposed schemes provide lower complexity, higher total system capacity, and fairness among users.

1. Introduction

In fourth Generation (4G) wireless cellular networks, increasing demands for higher speed data rates transmission, mobility, and multiservice access, have imposed staggering challenges. Therefore, IEEE 802.16 standards propose the use of Orthogonal Frequency Division Multiple Access (OFDMA) among multiple alternatives. OFDMA has become one of the most interesting developments in the area of new broadband wireless networks due to its powerful capability to mitigate Inter-Symbol Interference (ISI), provide high spectral efficiency and immunity of multipath fading.

Looking at wireless networks literature, several researches focus on adaptive resource allocation algorithms for single service required by users, in order to achieve some objectives aimed either to minimize total power under data rate constraint, called Margin Adaptive (MA) problem [1–3], or to maximize the total system throughput under power constraints referred as Rate Adaptive (RA) problem [4–6]. However, in practice how to efficiently allocate resources in multiservice wireless networks is not well-explored, nowadays. To

resolve this challenge, recent multiservice transmission researches in wireless networks are paid more attention [7–9]. To handle a multiservice access network of heterogeneous traffic, the resource management scheme that can efficiently allocate subchannels to different users and services is essential.

The major characteristics of resource allocation algorithms consist of their running time, computational complexity, and efficiency. Generally, optimal resource allocation algorithms are classified as Nondeterministic Polynomial-time Hard (NP-Hard) problems, making them unsuitable for real-time applications such as video call. Therefore, literature tackles such problems by proposing suboptimal algorithms and heuristic methods in order to close optimal solution with low complexity and face real-time and channel variations constraints.

In this work, we propose two complementary methods in order to guarantee an efficient resource allocation policy. The first method gives new approach, in context of contiguous subchannel method, for subchannel gain computation using frequency responses dispersion. Our goal in this study is to increase the number of bit per symbol subject to maintain lower BLoc Error Rate (BLER) in mobility and high-mobility context. The main objective in this second contribution is to resolve resource assignment to mobile users' problem, in order to take into account the trade-off between maximizing resources' use and fairness. In this context, a new dynamic heuristic algorithm is proposed. After that, we bring out multiservice feature of fourth generation wireless networks by proposing an adaptive resource allocation algorithm in OFDMA systems to support a variety of Quality-of-Service- (QoS-) sensitive applications such as streaming multimedia.

The remainder of this paper is organized as follows, In Section 2, system model is introduced and problem for resource allocation is formulated. In Section 3, a new method for subchannel gain is presented. Then, an adaptive subchannel allocation scheme is proposed. After that, a multi-QoS-based adaptive resource allocation algorithm is introduced in Section 5. Finally, numerical results are provided in Section 6.

2. System Model and Problem Formulation

In this work, we consider an OFDMA system for mobile wireless networks, based on IEEE 802.16 m standard. The system consists of a single Base Station (BS) that servers K users and N represents the number of subchannels composed by a group of M adjacent subcarriers in a single subchannel with $N = L/M$ and L is the total number of adjacent subcarriers. Considering $h_{k,n}$ as the channel gain of the kth user on nth subchannel, it following the complex Gaussian distribution and its magnitude, called fading factor, following Rayleigh distribution [10]. In fact, intercell interference occurs at a Mobile Station (MS), when the BSs of neighbouring cells transmit data over a subchannel used by its serving cell. The intercell interference phenomenon depends on user locations and mobilities, frequency reuse factor interfering cells as it is expressed by (2). We should notice that our considered cell in this work is not isolated. The downlink quality can be measured by the Signal-to-Interference plus Noise Ratio (SINR) and expressed as

$$\text{SINR}_{e,k} = \frac{P_e}{(I_{e,k} + \Delta f N_0)} |h_{k,n}|^2, \tag{1}$$

where P_e and Δf are, respectively, the total transmit power and subchannel spacing. N_0 presents the Additive White Gaussian Noise (AWGN) variance. The average downlink interference per subchannel $I_{e,k}$ for the MS k served by BS e [11] is expressed as follows:

$$I_{e,k} = \sum_{s \neq e} \Lambda(e,s) \chi_s \left(\frac{P_s G_{s,k}}{L_{s,k}} \right), \tag{2}$$

where

(i) P_s is the transmit power per subchannel of BS s;

(ii) $G_{s,k}$ is the antenna gain;

(iii) $L_{s,k}$ is the path-loss between BS s and MS k;

(iv) χ_s is the probability that the same subchannel used by the mobile k is used in the same time by another MS served by the BS s;

(v) $\Lambda(e,k)$ denotes the interference matrix, where the coefficient $\Lambda(e,k)$ equals 1 if cells e and s use the same band and zero otherwise.

The system capacity, C_{syst}, is given by the following equation:

$$C_{\text{syst}} = \sum_{t=1}^{T} \sum_{k=1}^{K} \sum_{n=1}^{N} \alpha_{k,n} C_{\text{SC}_{t,k,n}}. \tag{3}$$

If the subchannel n is allocated to user k at the subframe t, $\alpha_{k,n}$ is equal to 1 and zero otherwise. The Parameter $C_{\text{SC}_{t,k,n}}$ is the capacity of subchannel n allocated to user k at the subframe t and is presented by

$$C_{\text{SC}_{t,k,n}} = \sum_{m=1}^{M} C_{\text{sbcr}_m}, \tag{4}$$

where C_{sbcr_m} is the transmitted information quantity of subcarrier in a subframe time. Assuming that all sub-carriers in each subchannel use the same AMC, (4) becomes

$$\begin{aligned} C_{\text{SC}_{t,k,n}} &= M \cdot C_{\text{sbcr}_m}, \\ C_{\text{sbcr}_m} &= N_{\text{AMC}_{k,n}} \cdot N_{\text{sym/SF}}, \end{aligned} \tag{5}$$

where $N_{\text{AMC}_{k,n}}$ and $N_{\text{sym/SF}}$ represent, respectively, the number of bits per symbol and the number of symbols per subframe. They depend on the modulation choice type.

Thus, the total system capacity is obtained as follows:

$$C_{\text{syst}} = \sum_{t=1}^{T} \sum_{k=1}^{K} \sum_{n=1}^{N} \alpha_{k,n} \cdot M \cdot N_{\text{AMC}_{k,n}} \cdot N_{\text{sym/SF}}. \tag{6}$$

The Bit Error Rate (BER) for QPSK and M-QAM modulations are determined by formulas approximations presented in Table 1. In order to measure efficiency of the proposed method, we have introduced the Jain fairness index [13], given as

$$J_{\text{Fair Index}} = \frac{\left(\sum_{k=1}^{K} R_{k,\text{mean}} \right)^2}{K \cdot \sum_{k=1}^{K} \left(R_{k,\text{mean}} \right)^2}, \tag{7}$$

where $R_{k,\text{mean}}$ is the mean data rate of user k in a simulation time. This indicator is given by the following formula:

$$R_{k,\text{mean}} = \frac{1}{b} \sum_{i=1}^{b=T/T_{\text{SF}}} R_{k,i}, \tag{8}$$

where $R_{k,i}$ is the data rate of MS k in subframe i.

In this work, equal power is allocated to subchannels in downlink sense in order to reduce computational complexity.

TABLE 1: Approximate BER for coherent modulations [12].

Modulation	Formula
QPSK	$P_b \approx Q(\sqrt{2\gamma_b})$
M-QAM	$P_b \approx \dfrac{4(\sqrt{M}-1)}{\sqrt{M}\log_2 M}Q\left(\sqrt{\dfrac{3\overline{\gamma}_b\log_2 M}{(M-1)}}\right)$

Having the target to maximize the system capacity, the objective function is formulated as follows:

$$
\begin{aligned}
\text{Maximize} \quad & C_{\text{syst}} = \sum_{t=1}^{T}\sum_{k=1}^{K}\sum_{n=1}^{N}\alpha_{k,n}\cdot M \\
& \qquad\qquad \cdot N_{\text{AMC}_{k,n}}\cdot N_{\text{sym/SF}} \\
& J_{\text{Fair Index}} = \frac{\left(\sum_{k=1}^{K}R_{k,\text{mean}}\right)^2}{K\cdot\sum_{k=1}^{K}\left(R_{k,\text{mean}}\right)^2} \\
\text{Subject to} \quad & \text{C1: } \alpha_{k,n}\in\{0,1\},\quad \forall k\in\Psi, n\in\Gamma \\
& \text{C2: } \sum_{k=1}^{K}\alpha_{k,n}=1,\quad \forall n\in\Gamma \\
& \text{C3: } \sum_{n=1}^{N}\alpha_{k,n}\leq 1,\quad \forall k\in\Psi.
\end{aligned}
\tag{9}
$$

The two constraints C1 and C2 are on subchannel allocation to ensure that each subchannel is assigned to only one user where Ψ and Γ denote, respectively, the set of active users and subchannels in the cell. The constraint C3 denotes that one MS could have only one subchannel at the same time.

3. Efficiency of Sliding Window Gain Computation Method

In IEEE 802.16 m systems, the total sub-carriers of one bandwidth are grouped into subchannels in order to reduce the computational complexity and the signalling overhead [14–16]. Each subchannel is presented by a global channel gain that has a crucial role in the subchannels allocation policy in the case of multiuser wireless OFDMA systems.

In order to compute the global subchannel gain, different methods are described in [17–19]. In [18], a conservative estimation at the channel quality is made by choosing the most unfavorable channel of each group to represent that group's channel quality. Similarly, in [20, 21], the minimum channel gain approach is selected and considered as intuitive from an information-theoretic framework to ensure error-free transmission on all sub-carriers contained in the subchannel. However, if there are several sub-carriers with high channel gain, then the minimum sub-carriers gain method degrades the total system capacity and the maximum subchannel capacity is not being reached. In other works, the subchannel is denoted by an average channel gain for the corresponding set of sub-carriers. In [17], the channel magnitude response for each user is divided into a number of partitions where each partition is represented by the average channel gain. The same approach is adopted in [22] that allocates a subset of blocks with highest average channel gains to the corresponding user. In this case, sub-carriers with high channel gain are penalized by those with bad channel gain even though these sub-carriers represent a minority compared to those with high channel gain. Then, existing methods degrade the total system capacity.

In this section, we propose a new method to compute the subchannel's gain depending on frequency responses. The idea here is to close the channel quality based on dispersion probability and average channel gain. We can define the sub-carrier gain array as

$$
H = \begin{pmatrix} h_{1,1} & h_{1,2} & \cdots & h_{1,L} \\ h_{2,1} & h_{2,2} & \cdots & h_{2,L} \\ \cdot & \cdot & \cdot & \cdot \\ \cdot & \cdot & \cdot & \cdot \\ \cdot & \cdot & \cdot & \cdot \\ h_{K,1} & h_{K,2} & \cdots & h_{K,L} \end{pmatrix},
\tag{10}
$$

where K and L represent, respectively, the number of users and the number of available sub-carriers in the system. $h_{k,l}$ is the channel gain of the lth sub-carrier for the kth user. We assume that a subchannel is composed by M adjacent sub-carriers where $N = L/M$. When sub-carriers are grouped into subchannels, the subchannel gain array is obtained as

$$
H' = \begin{pmatrix} h'_{1,1} & h'_{1,2} & \cdots & h'_{1,N} \\ h'_{2,1} & h'_{2,2} & \cdots & h'_{2,N} \\ \cdot & \cdot & \cdot & \cdot \\ \cdot & \cdot & \cdot & \cdot \\ \cdot & \cdot & \cdot & \cdot \\ h'_{K,1} & h'_{K,2} & \cdots & h'_{K,N} \end{pmatrix}.
\tag{11}
$$

Our proposed "Sliding Window" method is a recursive scheme that depends on the average of sub-carriers gain and the dispersion probability. It gathers sub-carriers into three groups presented by a quality coefficient Q that may vary from a type of service to another with $0.5 \leq Q \leq 1$.

  (i) The number of sub-carriers with high channel gain is greater than that with bad channel gain: $P > Q$.

 (ii) The number of sub-carriers with bad channel gain is greater than that with high channel gain: $P < (1-Q)$.

(iii) The number of sub-carriers with bad and high gain is almost the same: $P \in [1-Q, Q]$.

Our proposed method is described as in Algorithm 1.

After computing the available subchannels gain, let us move to the subchannel allocation scheme in a single-service context.

4. A New Heuristic Method for Subchannel Allocation in Loaded System

In a loaded system, the number of users K is greater than the number of available subchannels N. Here, the BS may assign to each user only one subchannel and a subchannel is allocated to only one user during a subframe. Our proposed resource allocation scheme consists of 3 steps: (1) *Initialization step*. Vectors and matrices that will be used later in the algorithm are initialised. (2) *Users ordering step*. Users are

BEGIN
for $k = 1$ **to** K **do**
 for $n = 1$ **to** N **do**
(i) *Initialization*
  $vect \leftarrow \{h_{k,1}, h_{k,2}, \ldots, h_{k,M}\}$; $\forall l \in \{1, 2, \ldots, L\}$;
  $\forall m \in \{1, 2, \ldots, M\}$; $vect_{\max} \leftarrow \phi$; $vect_{\min} \leftarrow \phi$.
(ii) *Subchannel Gain Computation*
  Step (1):
  Calculate the average channel gain avg based on
  the sub-carriers frequency responses where $avg \leftarrow$
  $average(vect)$.
  Step (2):
  Calculate the probability p where $p \leftarrow \sum_{m=1}^{M} x_m / M$, with
  $\sum_{m=1}^{M} x_m \leq M$ and
$$x_m = \begin{cases} 1 & \text{if } h_{k,m} > avg, \\ 0 & \text{if not.} \end{cases}$$
  if $p > Q$ **then**
   for $m = 1$ **to** M **do**
    if $h_{k,m} > avg$ **then**
     $vect_{\max} = vect_{\max} + \{h_{k,m}\}$.
    end if
   end for
   if $length\,(vect_{\max}) = 1$ **then**
    return $gain \leftarrow vect_{\max}(1)$.
   else
    $vect \leftarrow vect_{\max}$; Jump to Step (1).
   end if
  end if
  if $p < (1 - Q)$ **then**
   for $m = 1$ **to** M **do**
    if $h_{k,m} < avg$ **then**
     $vect_{\min} = vect_{\min} + \{h_{k,m}\}$.
    end if
   end for
   if $length(vect_{\min}) = 1$ **then**
    return $gain \leftarrow vect_{\min}(1)$.
   else
    $vect \leftarrow vect_{\min}$; Jump to Step (1)
   end if
  end if
  if $p \in [1 - Q, Q]$ **then**
   for $m = 1$ **to** M **do**
    if $h_{k,m} < avg$ **then**
     $vect_{\min} = vect_{\min} + \{h_{k,m}\}$.
    end if
   end for
   if $length(vect_{\min}) = 1$ **then**
    return $gain_{\min} \leftarrow vect_{\min}(1)$.
   else
    $vect \leftarrow vect_{\min}$; Jump to Step (1)
   end if
   for $m = 1$ **to** M **do**
    if $h_{k,m} > avg$ **then**
     $vect_{\max} = vect_{\max} + \{h_{k,m}\}$.
    end if
   end for
   if $length(vect_{\max}) = 1$ **then**
    return $gain_{\max} \leftarrow vect_{\max}(1)$.
   else

ALGORITHM 1: Continued.

$vect \leftarrow vect_{max}$; Jump to Step (1).
    end if
      return $gain \leftarrow average(gain_{max}, gain_{min})$.
   end if
   $h'_{k,n} \leftarrow gain$.
  end for
 end for
END

ALGORITHM 1: Our sliding window scheme.

sorted in decreasing order depending on their best subchannel gain given by Algorithm 1. (3) *Subchannels allocation step.* Here, two cases are defined as it is depicted in Algorithm 2. Firstly, if only the selected user has this order, then we verify if its best subchannel is free. If yes, we allocate it and update the rate. If not, we search for the next free and best subchannel. Secondly, if two users or more have the same order, we verify if they require the same subchannel. If yes, we choose the user with the minimum second subchannel gain because it has a low chance to get a good subchannel (Algorithm 2).

Computational Complexity. Let us recall that K refers to the users number and N is the subchannels number. The users ordering step (2) sorts subchannels in descending order for each user. The sorting process requires $(N\log_2(N))$ operations for each user. Sorting subchannels in decreasing order for K users requires then $KN\log_2(N)$. Thus, the asymptotic complexity is $O(KN\log_2(N))$. As proportional fairness method [23] includes a remaining subchannels allocation phase to ensure fairness criterion, computational complexity is equal to $O(KN\log_2(N)+K(N-K)\log_2(N-K))$. Alternative factor method [24] includes two steps: (1) Subchannels ordering step requires $KN\log_2(N)$ operations. (2) Users ordering step requires $K\log_2(K)$ operations. Alternative factor computation requires (KN) operations. These steps pertain to subchannel allocation and the asymptotic complexity is equal to $O(KN\log_2(N) + K\log_2(K) + (KN))$. Then, we conclude that our suboptimal resource allocation scheme provides lower complexity than other existing methods and may be adopted for real-time applications. However, the key feature of 4G mobile network is its capability to support multiservice access when a user requires different service types, as it is well underlined in the next section.

5. Multi-QoS-Based Adaptive Resource Allocation Algorithm

We consider three Classes of Service (CoS) which are realtime Polling Service (rtPS), non-real-time Polling Service (nrtPS), and Best Effort (BE). For each CoS, the QoS satisfaction has a distinct definition [7]. The proposed algorithm consists of three steps: resource distribution step, calculation of each user's priority step, and resource allocation step.

5.1. Resource Distribution. We assume that N_{rtPs}, N_{nrtPs}, and N_{BE} represent, respectively, the number of subchannels

reserved to rtPS, nrtPS, and BE classes and are determined by the following equations: $N_{rtPs} = \alpha N$, $N_{nrtPs} = \beta N$, and $N_{BE} = \gamma N$, where α, β and $\gamma \in [0,1]$ and $\alpha + \beta + \gamma = 1$. Let NC_{rtPS}, NC_{nrtPS}, NC_{BE} represent and, respectively, rtPS connections number, nrtPS connections number and BE connections number, and NC denotes the total connections number. Proportional parameters are initially determined by $\alpha = (NC_{rtPS}/NC)$, $\beta = (NC_{nrtPS}/NC)$, and $\gamma = (NC_{BE}/NC)$. They are dynamically updated depending on the system availability. If necessary, a class, as rtPS-class, may reserve free subchannels from lower prior classes as nrtPS and BE classes and the opposite case is not allowed.

5.2. Calculation of User's Priority. For each user, a queue is used for buffering arrival packets in the proposed BS scheduler. We design the scheduling priority of each connection based on its channel quality, QoS satisfaction and service type priority.

5.2.1. Real-Time Traffic. For rtPS traffic of user k on subchannel n, the scheduling priority $P_{k,n}$ is defined as [25]

$$P_{k,n} = \begin{cases} \beta_{rtPS}\left(\dfrac{R_{k,n}}{R_{max}}\right)\left(\dfrac{1}{F_k}\right) & \text{if } F_k > 1, R_{k,n} \neq 0, \\ \beta_{rtPS}\left(\dfrac{R_{k,n}}{R_{max}}\right) & \text{if } F_k \leq 1, R_{k,n} \neq 0, \\ 0 & \text{if } R_{k,n} = 0, \end{cases} \quad (12)$$

where $\beta_{rtPS} \in [0,1]$ is the rtPS class coefficient as defined in [25] and F_k is the delay satisfaction indicator and is defined as

$$F_k = \frac{T_k - 2T_F}{W_k}, \quad (13)$$

where

(i) $R_{k,n}$ is the information bits that can be carried by user k on the subchannel n in one OFDM symbol,

(ii) R_{max} is the most bits per symbol that can be allocated when the most efficient AMC mode is selected,

(iii) W_k is the longest packet waiting time of user k,

(iv) T_k is the maximum packet latency of user k,

(v) T_F is the frame duration.

BEGIN

(i) *Initialization*

Equal power is allocated to groups

$\Gamma = \{1, 2, \ldots, N\}$; $\Psi = \{1, 2, \ldots, K\}$; $h_{k,n}, \forall k \in \Psi, \forall n \in \Gamma$; $\alpha_{k,n} = 0, \forall k \in \Psi, \forall n \in \Gamma$; $R_k = 0, \forall k \in \Psi$.

(ii) *Users Ordering*

for $k = 1$ to K **do**

    Sort $h_{k,n}$ in decreasing order.

    Order user k according to its best channel gain $h_{k,1}$.

end for

(iii) *Subchannels Allocation*

for $k = 1$ to K where $order\ (k) \leq order\ (k + 1)$ **do**

    $n \leftarrow$ find the subchannel n where the user k has its best channel gain.

    Step (1):

    if $(uniqueorder = 1)$ **then**

        {% only user k has this order}.

        Sub-step (1.a):

        if $\alpha_{1 \rightarrow K,n} = 0$ **then**

            {% the subchannel n is not allocated}

            $\alpha_{k,n} \leftarrow 1$ {% allocate the subchannel n}

            $\Gamma \leftarrow \Gamma - \{n\}$; Updated data rate R_k

        end if

        Sub-step (1.b):

        if $\alpha_{1 \rightarrow K,n} = 1$ **then**

            {% the subchannel n is allocated}

            repeat

                $j = j + 1$ {% search the next free subchannel}

            until $\alpha_{1 \rightarrow K,j} = 0$ **or** $h_{k,j} < h_{k^*,j}$ {k^* is the user less priority than the actual one and $k^* \in [k + 1, K]$.}

            Jump to Sub-step (1.a)

        end if

    end if

    Step (2):

    if $(uniqueorder = 0)$ **then**

        {% two or more users have the same order}.

        Sub-step (2.a):

        if $(uniquesubchannel = 0)$ **then**

            {% users with the same order do not require the same subchannel}

            jump to Sub-step (1.a) or Sub-step (1.b)

        end if

        Sub-step (2.b):

        if $(uniquesubchannel = 1)$ **then**

            {% these users require the same subchannel}

            if $\alpha_{1 \rightarrow K,n} = 0$ **then**

                $\hat{k} \leftarrow$ determine the user that has the minimum second best sub-channe {% this user has a low chance to get a good subchannel}.

                Jump to Sub-step (1.a)

            end if

            if $\alpha_{1 \rightarrow K,n} = 1$ **then**

                $\hat{k} \leftarrow$ determine the user that has the minimum second best subchannel; Jump to Sub-step (*1.b*)

            end if

         end if

        end if

end for

END

ALGORITHM 2: An adaptive resource allocation scheme.

We should notice that in this rtPS-class, the packet should be immediately sent if its deadline expires before the next frame is totally served. The ratio $(R_{k,n}/R_{\max})$ denotes the normalized channel quality. If $W_k \geq T_k - 2T_F$ we set the highest priority to the corresponding packet. When $R_{k,n} = 0$, the channel is in deep fade and this connection should not be served.

5.2.2. Non-Real-Time Traffic. For the nrtPS connection of user k on subchannel n, the scheduling priority is defined as [25]

$$P_{k,n} = \begin{cases} \beta_{\mathrm{nrtPS}}\left(\dfrac{R_{k,n}}{R_{\max}}\right)\left(\dfrac{1}{F_k}\right) & \text{if } F_k \geq 1, R_{k,n} \neq 0, \\ \beta_{\mathrm{nrtPS}}\left(\dfrac{R_{k,n}}{R_{\max}}\right) & \text{if } F_k < 1, R_{k,n} \neq 0, \\ 0 & \text{if } R_{k,n} = 0, \end{cases} \quad (14)$$

where $\beta_{\mathrm{nrtPs}} \in [0,1]$ is the nrtPS class coefficient as defined in [25] and F_k is the ratio of the average transmission rate $\overline{r}_k$ over minimum reserved rate r_k, representing the rate satisfaction indicator. If $F_k \geq 1$ the rate requirement is satisfied. If not, representing the case within the queue will be full, packets of user k should be then sent as soon as possible.

5.2.3. Best Effort Traffic. For the BE service of user k on subchannel n, the scheduling priority is defined as [26]

$$P_{k,n} = \beta_{\mathrm{BE}}\left(\frac{R_{k,n}}{R_{\max}}\right), \quad (15)$$

where $\beta_{\mathrm{BE}} \in [0,1]$ is the BE-class coefficient as defined in [25]. In fact for the BE service, the scheduling priority depends only on the channel quality.

We should notice that the role of β_{rtPS}, β_{nrtPS}, and β_{BE}, is to provide different priorities for different QoS classes, then $\beta_{\mathrm{rtPS}} > \beta_{\mathrm{nrtPS}} > \beta_{\mathrm{BE}}$ [25]. The purpose behind this idea is that the QoS of connections in a high-priority QoS class can be satisfied prior to those of low-priority QoS class.

After calculating the priority of each user k on each subchannel n, we define a Priority Function that represents the user's priority and is described as

$$P_k = \max P_{k,n}, \quad \forall n \in \{1, \ldots, N\}. \quad (16)$$

5.3. Resource Allocation Scheme. We should notice that in this study, each user requires a single service at the same time and packets buffered in the same queue follow a First In First Out (FIFO) scheduler. Let k^* denote the selected serving user, where

$$k^* = \max P_k, \quad \forall k \in \{1, \ldots, K\}. \quad (17)$$

After that, the user k^* picks its best subchannel n^* where

$$n^* = \max\left(\frac{R_{k^*,n}}{R_{\max}}\right), \quad \forall n \in \{1, \ldots, N\}. \quad (18)$$

The number of OFDMA symbols allocated for each user is calculated under the assumption that the minimum reserved rate r_k and maximum latency T_k should be satisfied for rtPS-class and only the minimum reserved rate r_k for nrtPS-class. For each connection, a minimum data rate r_k should be guaranteed and expressed by the following inequality:

$$r_k \leq \overline{r}_k(m+1), \quad (19)$$

where $\overline{r}_k(m+1)$ is the average service data rate of user k at frame $(m+1)$. It is estimated over a windows size T_c as [26]

$$\overline{r}_k(m+1) = \overline{r}_k(m)\left(1 - \frac{1}{T_c}\right) + \frac{\Delta_k(m+1)/T_F}{T_c}, \quad (20)$$

where $\Delta_k(m+1)$ is the number of information bits that should be sent during the frame $(m+1)$ of user k, where [26]

$$\Delta_k(m+1)$$
$$= \begin{cases} (r_k - \overline{r}_k(m))\, T_c + \overline{r}_k(m)T_F & \text{if } \overline{r}_k(m) < r_k. \\ 0 & \text{if } \overline{r}_k(m) \geq r_k. \end{cases} \quad (21)$$

The number of slots required to carry $\Delta_k(m+1)$ information bits on subchannel n equals

$$N_{\mathrm{sub},k}(m+1) = \left\lceil \frac{\Delta_k(m+1)}{M \cdot R_{k,n}} \right\rceil. \quad (22)$$

For rtPS connection, there is one more step to calculate the number of information bit to be sent. We examine the waiting time of packets in the queue of connection from the head of line until the first packet whose waiting time is longer than $(T_k - 2T_F)$ is encountered. We denote $\Delta_k'(m+1)$ the sum of bits of packets from the head of line to the finding packet. The number of information bits allocated to rtPS connection of user k is given by [26]

$$\hat{\Delta}_k(m+1) = \max\left\{\Delta_k(m+1), \Delta_k'(m+1)\right\}. \quad (23)$$

The number of slots required to carry $\hat{\Delta}_k(m+1)$ information bits on subchannel n equals

$$N_{\mathrm{sub},k}(m+1) = \left\lceil \frac{\hat{\Delta}_k(m+1)}{M \cdot R_{k,n}} \right\rceil. \quad (24)$$

If the available slot on subchannel n is less than $N_{\mathrm{sub},k}$, the second best subchannel for that user is selected and the remaining bits are allocated.

6. Simulation Results

In this work, the channel is modelled as a Rayleigh Channel with four multipaths. The simulated system consists of a single cell that uses 1024 sub-carriers for communications. In order to consider the mobility, the channel state changes every subframe delay and the simulation window is equal to 10000 subframes. Simulation parameters are described in Table 2.

TABLE 2: OFDMA parameters for IEEE 802.16 M.

Parameter	Symbol	Value
Subchannels number	N	48
Subcarriers number per subchannel	M	18
Number of subframes per frame		7
Sub-carriers spacing	Δf	7.813 KHz
Super frame delay		20 ms
Frame delay	T_F	5 ms
Subframe delay		714,286 μs

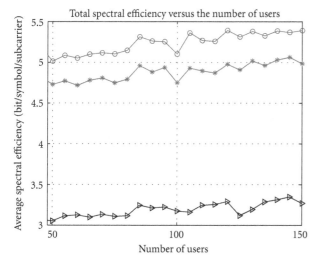

FIGURE 1: Total spectral efficiency versus the number of users in loaded systems.

TABLE 3: Variation intervals in terms of total spectral efficiency.

	[48, 75[	[75, 100[	[100, 125[	[125, 150]
TSEVI$_{Pag}$ (bit/sym)	0.197	0.193	0.250	0.246
TSEVI$_{Pmi}$ (bit/sym)	1.823	1.883	1.899	1.923

6.1. Proposed Sliding Window Method Performances. We show the performance of our sliding window method compared to the minimum [18] and average [19] method.

Figure 1 compares the average spectral efficiency per subcarrier versus the number of users. The total spectral efficiency is determined by (6).

Table 3 shows variation intervals in terms of total spectral efficiency. Let TSEVI$_{Pag}$ and TSEVI$_{Pmi}$ denote the total spectral efficiency for different variation user intervals. These values are computed based on, respectively, the mean difference between sliding window and average channel gain method and the mean difference between sliding window and minimum channel gain method. As TSEVI$_{Pag}$ > 0 and TSEVI$_{Pmi}$ > 0, for all intervals, it is obvious that the proposed method provides greater spectral efficiency, because it computes a subchannel gain that closes the channel quality.

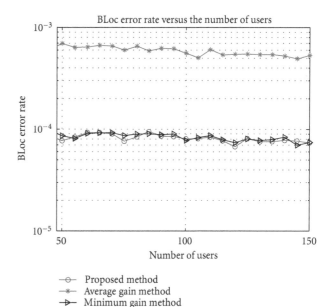

FIGURE 2: BLoc Error Rate (BLER) versus the number of users.

TABLE 4: Variation intervals in terms of BLER.

	[48, 75[	[75, 100[	[100, 125[	[125, 150]
BVI$_{Pag}$10^{-4} (dB)	−5.718	−5.320	−4.724	−4.535
BVI$_{Pmi}$10^{-6} (dB)	−1.371	−3.870	−2.233	−0.977

Figure 2 illustrate the average Bloc Error Rate (BLER) versus the number of users.

Table 4 shows variation intervals in terms of BLER. Let BVI$_{Pag}$ and BVI$_{Pmi}$ denote the average BLER for different variation user intervals. These values are computed based on, respectively, the mean difference between sliding window and average channel gain method and the mean difference between sliding window and minimum channel gain method. As BVI$_{Pag}$ < 0 and BVI$_{Pmi}$ ≤ 0, for all intervals, our proposed method provides lower BLER than the average gain method and quasisimilar BLER compared to minimum gain method, because our scheme closes the channel quality.

6.2. Proposed Subchannels Allocation Algorithm Performances in a Single Service Context. Our proposed resource allocation algorithm is compared with the suboptimal existing solutions [23, 24]. The reason for this comparison is as follows. Shen et al. [23] formulates the problem of maximizing the total system capacity with proportional rate constraints. It uses the subchannel with high SINR for each user. Hwang et al. [24] proposes a heuristic for channel allocation. In this work, an alternative factor is defined for subchannel allocation. It aims to increase the downlink system capacity while maintaining sufficient fairness.

Figure 3 compares the average spectral efficiency per subcarrier versus the number of users.

Table 5 shows variation intervals in terms of total spectral efficiency. Let SEVI$_{PAF}$ and SEVI$_{PPF}$ denote the average spectral efficiency in different variation user intervals. These

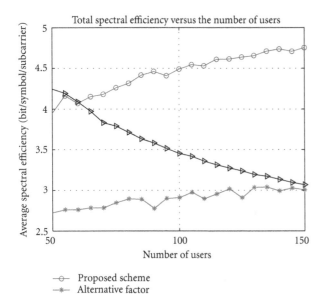

FIGURE 3: Total spectral efficiency in loaded systems.

TABLE 5: Variation intervals in terms of total spectral efficiency.

	[50,60]	]60,75[	[75,100[	[100,125[	[125,150]
SEVI$_{PAF}$ (bit/s)	1.31	1.38	1.51	1.60	1.70
SEVI$_{PFF}$ (bit/s)	−0.11	0.26	0.72	1.19	1.55

TABLE 6: Variation intervals in terms of Jain Fairness Index.

	[50,75[	[75,100[	[100,125[	[125,150]
JFIVI$_{PAF}$	0.183	0.420	0.549	0.639
JFIVI$_{PPF}$	0.057	0.103	0.128	0.145

values are computed based on, respectively, the mean difference between proposed scheme and alternative factor method [24] and the mean difference between proposed scheme and proportional fairness method [23]. As SEVI$_{PAF}$ > 0 and SEVI$_{PPF}$ > 0, when the number of users $K \in\,]60,150]$, our proposed method provides greater spectral efficiency, because it covers the loaded system case when the number of available resources is lower than the number of users requiring access to the cell. However, when $K \in [50,60]$, the proposed scheme provides lower SE than the proportional fairness method as SEVI$_{PPF}$ < 0. Hence, the contribution of our proposed scheme performs better when the number of users in the cell is important which is close to the practical case.

To better examine the fairness of these algorithms for different number of users, their performance is shown in Figure 4. The Jain Fairness Index is expressed by (7). It is obvious that the proposed method provides a fairness index close to 1.

Table 6 shows variation intervals in terms of average Jain Fairness Index. Let JFIVI$_{PAF}$ and JFIVI$_{PPF}$ denote the Jain Fairness Index for different variation user intervals. These values are computed based on, respectively, the mean

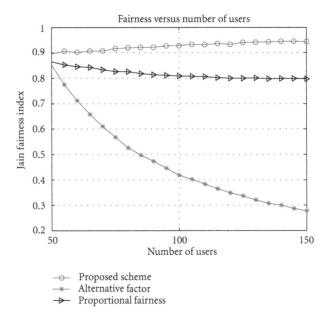

FIGURE 4: Jain Fairness Index versus the number of users in loaded systems.

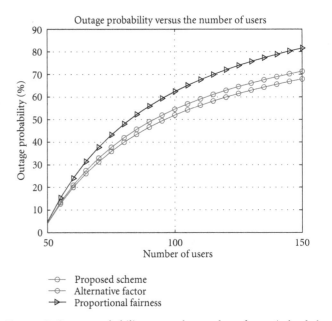

FIGURE 5: Outage probability versus the number of users in loaded systems.

difference between proposed scheme and alternative factor method described in [24] and the mean difference between proposed scheme and proportional fairness method proposed in [23]. As JFIVI$_{PAF}$ > 0 and JFIVI$_{PPF}$ > 0, for all intervals, it is obvious that the proposed method provides more fairness among active users than the alternative factor and proportional fairness method as each user may reserve only a single subchannel at any given time as it is expressed by constraint C3 in our optimisation problem formulation.

Figure 5 shows the outage probability versus the number of users where the outage probability represents the rejected

TABLE 7: Variation intervals in terms of outage probability.

	[50, 75[	[75, 100[	[100, 125[	[125, 150]
OPVI$_{PAF}$ (%)	−0.943	−2.156	−2.809	−3.247
OPVI$_{PPF}$ (%)	−3.772	−8.626	−11.236	−12.991

TABLE 8: Variation intervals in terms of total spectral efficiency in unloaded systems.

	[10, 12]	]12, 15[	[15, 20[	[20, 25[	[25, 30]
USEVI$_{PMM}$ (bit/s)	−0.231	0.237	0.687	1.123	1.458
USEVI$_{PPF}$ (bit/s)	−0.087	0.265	0.709	1.132	1.466

users percentage. When a user does not get its required subchannel, the number of rejected users increases by one. Then, the outage probability is the ratio of the number of rejected users and the total number of active users in a loaded system.

Table 7 shows variation intervals in terms of outage probability. Let OPVI$_{PAF}$ and OPVI$_{PPF}$ denote the Outage probability for different users variation intervals. These values are computed based on, respectively, the average of difference between proposed scheme and alternative factor method described in [24] and the average of difference between proposed scheme and proportional fairness method proposed in [23]. As OPVI$_{PAF}$ < 0 and OPVI$_{PPF}$ < 0, for all intervals, it is obvious that the proposed scheme provides lower outage probability than other methods. We should notice that in this case, as it is shown by Table 7, the difference between the proposed heuristic and existing methods [23, 24] increases when the number of users rises, meaning that the proposed scheme satisfies a greater number of users than other existing methods [23, 24] in a loaded system case, because it covers the inefficiency resource case by allocating to each user its second best and free subchannel.

For unloaded system case, the performance of our proposed algorithm is compared with the algorithms proposed in [23, 27]. The reason for this comparison is as follows. Authors in [23] aim to maximize the total system capacity while maintaining proportional fairness among active users. The principle of this suboptimal subchannel algorithm is to use the subchannels with high SINR for each user. For remaining subchannels, the user with the lowest proportional capacity has the option to pick which subchannel to use in order to achieve proportional fairness. Resource allocation algorithm proposed in [27] aims to assign to each user a subchannel in which the user has the best channel conditions. For the remaining subchannels, the user with the lowest amount of capacity is selected and its best subchannel is allocated to him in order to reach a sufficient fairness among users.

Figure 6 compares the average spectral efficiency per subcarrier versus the number of users.

Table 8 shows variation intervals in terms of total spectral efficiency for proposed. Let USEVI$_{PMM}$ and USEVI$_{PPF}$ denote the average total spectral efficiency for different users variation intervals in unloaded systems. These values are computed based on, respectively, the mean difference between proposed scheme and max-min method described in [27]

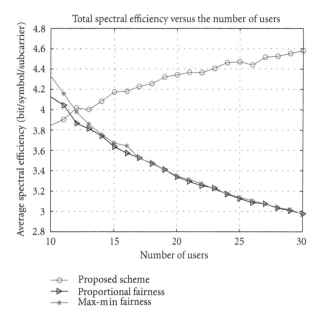

FIGURE 6: Total spectral efficiency versus the number of users in unloaded systems.

and the mean difference between proposed scheme and proportional fairness method proposed in [23]. As USEVI$_{PMM}$ > 0 and USEVI$_{PPF}$ > 0, when $K \in]12, 30]$, it is obvious that the proposed method provides greater spectral efficiency than the max-min and proportional fairness method. We should notice that in this case, as it is shown by Table 8, the difference between the proposed method and existing methods [23, 27] increases when the number of users rises. Then, the proposed method operates well the multiusers diversity. However, when $K \leq 12$, the existing method in [23, 27] provides better performance in terms of total spectral efficiency as USEVI$_{PMM}$ < 0 and USEVI$_{PPF}$ < 0 when $K \in [10, 12]$, because they introduce a remaining subchannel allocation phase. So, one user may have more than one subchannel as it is described above. Hence, the contribution of our proposed scheme performs better when the number of users in the cell is important which is generally close to the practical case when good subchannels are not yet available.

6.3. Proposed Subchannels Allocation Scheme Performances in a Heterogeneous Traffics System. The performance of the Multi-QoS-based adaptive resource allocation proposed algorithm is compared to two existing algorithms that are proposed in [28, 29] in terms of rtPS average Packet Loss Rate (PLR) and nrtPS Packet Satisfaction Ratio (PSR). On one hand, Maximum-Carrier-to-Interference and Noise Ratio (MAX-CINR) scheme [28] allocates resources to the user with the maximum receiver CINR and then only the users' link qualities are concerned and the QoS requirements are totally ignored. On the other hand, Modified Proportional Fair (MPF) scheduling algorithm proposed in [29] is taken into account with QoS guaranteed to users in the system. In order to evaluate the performance of various QoS services, we use the Near Real Time Video (NRTV) traffic model for

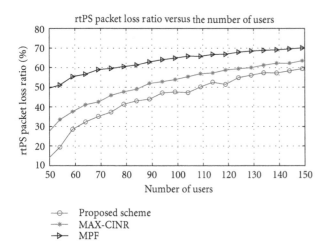

FIGURE 7: Average rtPS packet loss ratio versus the number of users.

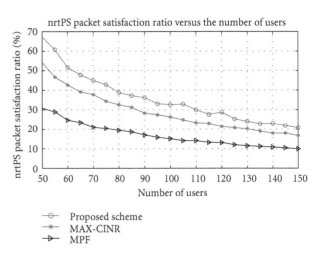

FIGURE 8: Average nrtPS packet satisfaction ratio versus the number of users.

TABLE 9: Variation intervals in terms of rTPS packet loss ratio.

	$[50, 75[$	$[75, 100[$	$[100, 125[$	$[125, 150]$
HPLRVI$_{PMCI}$(%)	−20.88	−13.78	−9.204	−8.351
HPLRVI$_{PMPF}$(%)	−24.84	−16.72	−14.21	−10.33

TABLE 10: Variation intervals in terms of nrTPS packet satisfaction ratio.

	$[50, 75[$	$[75, 100[$	$[100, 125[$	$[125, 150]$
HPSRVI$_{PMCI}$ (%)	9.078	5.994	5.740	3.631
HPSRVI$_{PMPF}$ (%)	27.21	18.32	15.57	11.32

rtPS service, FTP model for nrtPS service [30]. Here we heuristically define length of rtPS packets 1024 bits, nrtPS 2048 bits, and BE 4096 bits and we set the QoS class coefficients as $\beta_{rtPS} = 1.0$, $\beta_{nrtPS} = 0.8$ and $\beta_{BE} = 0.6$. Moreover, we assume that packet arrival process is Poisson distributed, each connection with its own average arrival rate. We suppose that there are 150 users in the system where each one requires a single service at the same time. For rtPS connection, the minimum reserved rate and maximum latency of each connection are set to 500 kbps and 20 ms, respectively. For nrtPS connection, the minimum reserved rate is set as 1 Mbps. For BE connection, the buffer size is 5000 packets with 512 bytes each.

Figure 7 shows the average Packet Loss Ratio (PLR) of the rtPS connection across different number of users. The average PLR is defined as the ratio of the number of the lost rtPS packets to the total packets' number.

Table 9 shows variation intervals in terms of rtPS Packet Loss Ratio. Let HPLRVI$_{PMCI}$ and HPLRVI$_{PMPF}$ denote the PLR in different variation user intervals in heterogeneous services system. These values are computed based on, respectively, the average of difference between proposed scheme and MAX-CINR method described in [28] and the average of difference between proposed scheme and modified proportional fairness method proposed in [29]. As HPLRVI$_{PMCI}$ < 0 and HPLRVI$_{PMPF}$ < 0, for all intervals, it is obvious that the proposed method satisfies more rtPS users than the MAX-CINR and modified proportional fairness method, because our scheduler gives the priority to rtPS-class to ensure an adequate resource allocation.

In Figure 8, we investigate the average nrtPS Packet Satisfaction Ratio (PSR) which is defined as the ratio of the number of the connections guaranteeing the minimum reserved rate to the total connections number. Table 10 shows variation intervals in terms of nrtPS Packet Satisfaction Ratio. Let HPSRVI$_{PMCI}$ and HPSRVI$_{PMPF}$ denote the PSR in different variation user intervals in heterogeneous services systems. These values are computed based on, respectively, the mean difference between proposed scheme and MAX-CINR method [28] and the mean difference between proposed scheme and modified proportional fairness method [29]. As HPSRVI$_{PMCI}$ > 0 and HPSRVI$_{PMPF}$ > 0, for all intervals, it is obvious that the proposed method satisfies more nrtPS users than the MAX-CINR and MPF method, due to our proposed reservation phase that reserves subchannels to rtPS, nrtPS, and BE services according to proportional parameters depending on system resources availability. For other methods, there are no resource reservation phase, which can increase the nrtPS calls rejection.

6.4. Concluding Remarks. Simulation results demonstrate that our sliding window method increases the system capacity and decreases the BLER effectively compared the minimum and the average channel gain methods. In loaded systems, simulation results show that the proposed algorithm permits to achieve a better trade-off between fairness and efficiency use of resources compared to other recent methods [23, 24]. Moreover, our proposed resource allocation scheme proves efficient in unloaded system than other existing methods. In addition to this contribution, the new heuristic algorithm present a low complexity and may be adopted for real-time and mobile applications. In a heterogeneous services context, simulation results illustrate that our proposed scheme can simultaneously satisfy the QoS requirements of various classes services: rtPS, nrtPS, and BE.

7. Conclusion

In order to reduce the OFDMA system complexity, available sub-carriers are grouped into equal groups of contiguous sub-carriers, where each group is called a subchannel. The adaptive modulation and coding scheme, AMC, is used in order to maximize the number of bit per symbol. In this paper, we have firstly proposed a new method for subchannel gain computation based on the frequency responses dispersion. Secondly, we have proposed a new heuristic method for subchannels allocation problem in the context of WiMAX release 2.0, IEEE 802.16 m. An adaptive method for subchannels allocation was necessary in order to exploit the multi-user diversity, to respect real-time constraints and to maximize the system capacity. The idea of this method was based on the statistic parameters, mean, variance, root mean square, or RMS of the frequency response channel gain for every mobile station. Finally, we proposed a multi-QoS-based resource allocation algorithm for OFDMA systems. We defined a priority function for each user according to the QoS satisfaction degree and its corresponding subchannel qualities. Simulation results showed that proposed algorithms provide a better trade-off between total system capacity, fairness, and complexity compared to other existing methods. For future work, we are interested to validate the present proposition in a multiservice context in order to develop an efficient radio resources management policy for Long-Term Evolution (LTE) network.

References

[1] C. Y. Wong, R. S. Cheng, K. B. Letaief, and R. D. Murch, "Multiuser OFDM with adaptive subcarrier, bit, and power allocation," *IEEE Journal on Selected Areas in Communications*, vol. 17, no. 10, pp. 1747–1758, 1999.

[2] W. Rhee and J. M. Cioffi, "Increase in capacity of multiuser ofdm system using dynamic subchannel allocation," in *Proceedings of the 51st Vehicular Technology Conference (VTC '00)*, vol. 2, pp. 1085–1089, 2000.

[3] W. Yu and R. Lui, "Dual methods for non-convex spectrum optimization of multi-carrier systems," *IEEE Transactions on Communications*, vol. 54, no. 7, pp. 1310–1322, 2006.

[4] J. Jang and K. B. Lee, "Transmit power adaptation for multiuser OFDM systems," *IEEE Journal on Selected Areas in Communications*, vol. 21, no. 2, pp. 171–178, 2003.

[5] M. Fathi and H. Taheri, "Utility-based resource allocation in orthogonal frequency division multiple access networks," *IET Communications*, vol. 4, no. 12, pp. 1463–1470, 2010.

[6] H. Zhu and J. Wang, "Adaptive chunk-based allocation in multiuser ofdm systems," in *Proceedings of the IEEE Wireless Communications and Networking Conference (WCNC '10)*, pp. 1525–3511, 2010.

[7] W. Lihua, M. Wenchao, and G. Zihua, "A cross-layer packet scheduling and subchannel allocation scheme in 802.16e ofdma system," in *Proceedings of the Wireless Communications and Networking Conference (WCNC '07)*, pp. 1865–1870, 2007.

[8] K. Juhee, K. Eunkyung, and S. K. Kyung, "A new efficient B S scheduler and scheduling algorithm in WiBro systems," in *Proceedings of the 8th International Conference Advanced Communication Technology (ICACT '06)*, pp. 1467–1470, 2006.

[9] Y. F. Yu, H. Ji, and G. X. Yue, "A novel wireless IP packets scheduling algorithm with QoS guaranteeing based on OFDM system," *Journal of Beijing University of Posts and Telecommunications*, vol. 29, no. 3, pp. 61–65, 2006.

[10] Z. Huiling and J. Wang, "Adaptive chunk-based allocation in multiuser OFDM systems," in *Proceedings of the Wireless Communications and Networking Conference (WCNC '10)*, pp. 1–6, IEEE, 2010.

[11] R. Nasri and Z. Altman, "Handover adaptation for dynamic load balancing in 3gpp long term evolution systems," in *Proceedings of the MoMM*, pp. 145–154, 2007.

[12] A. Goldsmith, *Wireless Communications*, vol. 572, Cambridge University Press, 2005.

[13] R. K. Jain, D. W. Chiu, and W. R. Hawe, "A quantitative measure of fairness and discrimination for resource allocation in shared computer system," Tech. Rep. 301, DEC, 1984.

[14] D. Marabissi, D. Tarchi, R. Fantacci, and A. Biagioni, "Adaptive subcarrier allocation algorithms in wireless OFDMA systems," in *Proceedings of the IEEE International Conference on Communications (ICC '08)*, pp. 3475–3479, Beijing, China, May 2008.

[15] A. Gotsis, D. Komnakos, and P. Constantinou, "Dynamic subchannel and slot allocation for OFDMA networks supporting mixed traffic: upper bound and a heuristic algorithm," *IEEE Communications Letters*, vol. 13, no. 8, pp. 576–578, 2009.

[16] S. H. Paik, S. Kim, and H. B. Park, "A resource allocation using game theory adopting AMC scheme in multi-cell OFDMA system," in *Proceedings of the 2nd International Conference on Future Computer and Communication (ICFCC '10)*, vol. 2, pp. 344–347, 2010.

[17] T. C. H. Alen, A. S. Madhukumar, and F. Chin, "Capacity enhancement of a multi-user OFDM system using dynamic frequency allocation," *IEEE Transactions on Broadcasting*, vol. 49, no. 4, pp. 344–353, 2003.

[18] Q. Wang, D. Xu, J. Xu, and Z. Bu, "A grouped and proportional-fair subcarrier allocation scheme for multiuser OFDM systems," in *Proceedings of the 25th IEEE International Performance, Computing, and Communications Conference (IPCCC '06)*, pp. 97–101, April 2006.

[19] U. Kim, H. Nam, and B. F. Womack, "An adaptive grouped-subcarrier allocation algorithm using comparative superiority," in *Proceedings of the Military Communications Conference (MILCOM '05)*, vol. 2, pp. 963–969, October 2005.

[20] R. Agarwal, R. Vannithamby, and J. M. Cioffi, "Optimal allocation of feedback bits for downlink OFDMA systems," in *Proceedings of the IEEE International Symposium on Information Theory*, pp. 1686–1690, 2008.

[21] J. Chen, R. A. Berry, and M. L. Honig, "Performance of limited feedback schemes for downlink OFDMA with finite coherence time," in *Proceedings of the IEEE International Symposium on Information Theory*, pp. 2751–2755, 2007.

[22] L. Xiaowen and Z. Jinkang, "An adaptive subcarrier allocation algorithm for multiuser OFDM system," in *Proceedings of the IEEE 58th Vehicular Technology Conference (VTC '03)*, pp. 1502–1506, October 2003.

[23] Z. Shen, J. G. Andrews, and B. L. Evans, "Adaptive resource allocation in multiuser OFDM systems with proportional rate constraints," *IEEE Transactions on Wireless Communications*, vol. 4, no. 6, pp. 2726–2736, 2005.

[24] S. Hwang, J. Park, Y. S. Jang, and H. S. Cho, "A heuristic method for channel allocation and scheduling in an OFDMA system," *ETRI Journal*, vol. 30, no. 5, pp. 741–743, 2008.

[25] L. Qingwen, W. Xin, and G. B. Giannakis, "A cross-layer scheduling algorithm with QoS support in wireless networks," *IEEE Transactions on Vehicular Technology*, vol. 55, no. 3, pp. 839–847, 2006.

[26] Z. Xinning, H. Jiachuan, Z. Song, Z. Zhimin, and D. Wei, "An adaptive resource allocation scheme in OFDMA based multiservice WiMAX systems," in *Proceedings of the 10th International Conference on Advanced Communication Technology*, pp. 593–597, February 2008.

[27] D. Marabissi, D. Tarchi, R. Fantacci, and A. Biagioni, "Adaptive subcarrier allocation algorithms in wireless OFDMA systems," in *Proceedings of the IEEE International Conference on Communications*, pp. 3475–3479, 2008.

[28] S. Ryu, B. Ryu, H. Seo, and M. Shin, "Urgency and efficiency based packet scheduling algorithm for OFDMA wireless system," in *Proceedings of the IEEE International Conference on Communications (ICC '05)*, pp. 2779–2785, May 2005.

[29] T.-D. Nguyen and Y. Han, "A dynamic channel assignment algorithm for OFDMA systems," in *Proceedings of the IEEE Vehicular Technology Conference (VTC '06)*, pp. 1273–1277, 2006.

[30] cdma2000 evaluation methodology, 3gpp2 contribution c.r1002-0. 1, December 2004.

9

Client-Driven Joint Cache Management and Rate Adaptation for Dynamic Adaptive Streaming over HTTP

Chenghao Liu,[1] **Miska M. Hannuksela,**[2] **and Moncef Gabbouj**[1]

[1] *Department of Signal Processing, Tampere University of Technology, 33720 Tampere, Finland*
[2] *Nokia Research Center, 33720 Tampere, Finland*

Correspondence should be addressed to Chenghao Liu; chenghao.liu@tut.fi

Academic Editor: Yifeng He

Due to the fact that proxy-driven proxy cache management and the client-driven streaming solution of Dynamic Adaptive Streaming over HTTP (DASH) are two independent processes, some difficulties and challenges arise in media data management at the proxy cache and rate adaptation at the DASH client. This paper presents a novel client-driven joint proxy cache management and DASH rate adaptation method, named CLICRA, which moves prefetching intelligence from the proxy cache to the client. Based on the philosophy of CLICRA, this paper proposes a rate adaptation algorithm, which selects bitrates for the next media segments to be requested by using the predicted buffered media time in the client. CLICRA is realized by conveying information on the segments that are likely to be fetched subsequently to the proxy cache so that it can use the information for prefetching. Simulation results show that the proposed method outperforms the conventional segment-fetch-time-based rate adaptation and the proxy-driven proxy cache management significantly not only in streaming quality at the client but also in bandwidth and storage usage in proxy caches.

1. Introduction

Recently, Hypertext Transfer Protocol (HTTP) [1] has been widely used for the delivery of real-time multimedia content over the Internet, such as in video streaming applications. Unlike Realtime Transport Protocol (RTP) over User Datagram Protocol (UDP), HTTP typically traverses through firewalls and network address translators (NATs), which makes it attractive for multimedia streaming applications. Kim and Ammar [2] reported that short-term transmission rate variation in HTTP/TCP can be smoothed out through buffering at the receiver side. Recently, standardization projects on dynamic adaptive streaming over HTTP have been carried out, which are briefly reviewed next.

Adaptive HTTP streaming (AHS) was first standardized in Release 9 of the packet-switched streaming (PSS) service [3] by the Third Generation Partnership Project (3GPP). The Moving Picture Experts Group (MPEG) took 3GPP AHS Release 9 as a starting point for its newly published MPEG Dynamic Adaptive Streaming over HTTP (DASH) standard [4]. 3GPP continued to work on adaptive HTTP streaming

in communication with MPEG and recently published the 3GP-DASH standard [5]. MPEG DASH and 3GP-DASH have a common core and are therefore collectively referred to as DASH in this paper.

In DASH, a client continuously requests and receives small segments of multimedia content, denoted as media segments. Rate adaptation can be easily supported by requesting media segment encoded at different bitrates. The capability for rate adaptation is one of the key advantages of adaptive HTTP streaming compared to current real-time video services in the Internet, which use a progressive download approach and, hence, may suffer from frequent playback interruptions and suboptimum streaming quality. Nevertheless, DASH standards merely specify the formats for Media Presentation Description and media segments, while client operations, such as rate adaptation, are not normative. However, rate adaptation affects the perceived quality at the client through the selection of the media segments and, hence, the media bitrate to be received as well as the experienced interruption frequency, which also results from the selection of the media segments.

Rate adaptation algorithms for DASH have been proposed in the literature. For example, Liu et al. [6, 7] proposed a rate adaptation algorithm for DASH which uses segment fetch time (SFT) as metrics to decide switching-up/down of media bitrates. SFT denotes a time period from requesting a segment to receiving the last byte of the segment by a DASH client. SFT is compared with media duration contained in a segment to decide whether the media bitrate is higher than, lower than, or approximately equal to the end-to-end bandwidth. However, the effect of caching on rate adaptation for DASH was not studied in [6, 7].

It is common that DASH is operated in networks that include proxy caches capable of caching streamed content. A segment will be cached when a proxy cache first receives and responds to a request for the segment. Such a caching is denoted as passive caching to distinguish with the prefetching. The content provider provides multiple representations for a media clip, and the client may dynamically request different segments from different representations as DASH supports rate adaptation. Hence, segments from multiple representations may be cached by a caching proxy, and the cached segments for each cached representation are likely to form an incomplete representation. This paper considers pull-based strategy as the operating scenario, while content preplacement/push-based strategy is out of the scope of this paper.

A consequence of caching incomplete representations is variation in SFT observed by the client. The reason is that a GET segment requested by a client may be served by a proxy cache or an origin server depending on whether or not the proxy caches (on the path of passing the request towards the origin server) have cached the requested segment. The variation in SFT may further result in a change in buffered media time especially when the caching status of consecutive segments in media presentation order varies, for example, when one segment is cached but the next one is not.

The variations in the SFT and buffered media time caused by the cache misses may be interpreted as congestion or throughput changes in the rate adaptation algorithm. A rate adaptation algorithm can use SFT as in [6, 7] or buffered media time as in [8] to determine switch-up/down to a higher/lower bitrate representation. However, a consequence of caching in DASH is that the representation level may change frequently due to variations in SFT and buffered media time. Frequent changes in the media quality, such as encoded media bitrate and frame rate, may be annoying to users. Furthermore, requesting a high-bitrate encoded segment upon observing a short SFT for fetching cached segments may result in buffer draining.

In addition to the previously discussed impacts of incompletely cached representations on rate adaptation, dynamically varying network throughput can also cause changes in buffered media time. Paper [9] presented bitrate and video quality planning algorithms for mobile streaming to reduce number of buffer underruns and frequency of quality changes. The method presented in [9] uses a GPS-based bandwidth-lookup service to enable client to predict bandwidth using combination of geographical location and past network conditions. In a certain trip, the receiver uses the predicted bandwidth in the potential future route to plan future quality so that it consumes the buffer completely while at the same time avoids buffer underruns during outages and reduces the number of quality changes.

To cope with the problems in the traditional rate adaptation methods for DASH operating over proxy caches, this paper presents a novel joint client-driven prefetching and cache-aware rate adaptation algorithm for DASH. The proposed joint client-driven prefetching and rate adaptation algorithm determines the representation for the next requested media segments and also for the subsequent segments which the client will most probably request subsequently. Then, as part of a regular HTTP GET request, the client also indicates the segments expected to be requested subsequently (hereafter referred to as anticipated segments) so that the proxy cache can prefetch the segments to respond to the future requests of the client. Another important contribution of this paper is a new algorithm of predicting buffered media times which can be used in rate adaptation for DASH operating in networks including proxy caches. The predicted buffered media time is derived from the following two factors. The first factor is the caching status of the requested segment and the anticipated segments. The second factor is the separately measured SFTs from the proxy cache to the client and from the origin server to the proxy cache.

The rest of the paper is organized as follows. Section 2 presents related works and highlights the drawbacks of current proxy-driven prefetching techniques when applied in DASH. A brief overview of the terminology and the architecture of DASH operating in networks including proxy caches is described in Section 3. The proposed signaling method between a DASH client and a proxy cache is presented in Section 4. The proposed joint client-driven prefetching and rate adaptation (CLICRA) method are presented in Section 5. Simulation results are presented in Section 6, while Section 7 concludes the paper.

2. Related Work

Prefetching segments at proxy caches for DASH mainly involves two issues, namely, specifying the time of issuing prefetching requests and selecting segments to be prefetched. To deal with these issues, this paper proposes a novel client-driven proxy prefetching method which moves the intelligence from the proxy cache to the DASH clients. To our knowledge, no prior work in the literature uses client-driven proxy prefetching methods. On the other hand, proxy-driven cache has been proposed, for example, by Chen et al. [10]. The authors developed a proxy-driven active prefetching method to decide when to prefetch uncached segment to overcome the shortcomings of passive caching. In the same work, proxy cache is used to prefetch segments based on the media bitrates and the estimated bandwidth between the "origin" server and the proxy cache to reduce congestion between them and reduce the transmission delay jitter perceived by the proxy cache. The prefetching method in [10] was developed under the assumption that the bandwidth between the proxy cache and the streaming client is large enough to provide smooth streaming. However, such an assumption may not always be true, for example, in mobile media streaming over wireless networks, which are characterized with a limited and varying bandwidth.

In general, proxy-driven prefetching methods have limitations to be used in DASH because of the following reasons. The proxy-driven prefetching and client-driven rate adaptation for DASH cannot operate well together, since intelligence of prefetching and rate adaptations are located in two different entities, that is, proxy cache and client, respectively. Proxy-driven prefetching methods typically prefetch future segments of a specific media bitrate in a certain window without being aware of whether or not a switch-up/down will occur at a DASH client, or a proxy cache has to estimate clients' rate adaptation behavior. However, such estimation is very difficult as DASH clients do not use a uniform rate adaptation algorithm. When switching-up/down representation occurs in a DASH client, prefetched segments of the previously cached representation may become useless for the DASH client, and the segments of new representations have to be prefetched. Moreover, proxy-driven prefetching method causes a dramatic increase of the computational and memory demands for deciding when and which segments needed to be prefetched. A general philosophy in DASH is to solve similar scalability issues by locating the intelligence functionality, such as rate adaptation and scheduling of requesting media segments, at the DASH client. For segment fetching, either a serial or a parallel segment fetching method can be used in DASH, by requesting and receiving media segments in sequential [6] and in parallel fashion [11], respectively. The parallel segment fetching method also prefetches future segments. This, however, differs from the client-driven prefetching method as follows. In the parallel segment fetching method, subsequent segments are prefetched to the client regardless of whether or not the subsequent segments are cached by a proxy cache. In the proposed method, segments which are not cached by proxy caches are fetched and cached but not sent immediately to the streaming client. The client-driven prefetching method is superior to parallel segment prefetching method in two aspects. First, unnecessary congestion between a proxy cache and DASH clients can be avoided by prefetching and caching in proxy caches instead of the client. Second, the client-driven prefetching method prefetches and caches segments which are not cached by the proxy cache.

3. Terminology and Architecture of DASH

In DASH, Media Presentation Description (MPD) provides the necessary information for a client to establish an adaptive dynamic streaming over HTTP. MPD contains information describing media presentation, such as an HTTP-URL of each segment to facilitate HTTP GET requests for segments. DASH introduced concept of representation, which is one of the alternative choices of the media content or a subset thereof typically differing by the encoding choice, for example, by bitrate, resolution, language, codec, and so forth. A representation is identified by a representation ID.

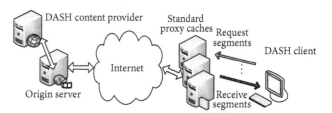

Figure 1: Typical DASH system [11].

A segment contains certain duration of media data starting from a specific presentation time and metadata to decode and present the included media content. Such duration is referred to as media segment duration or segment duration, while the staring presentation time of a segment is denoted as segment start time. A segment number is used to specify the start time and the segment duration for a segment. A segment is identified by a URI and can be requested by a HTTP GET request.

Figure 1 shows a typical media distribution architecture using DASH. The depicted end-to-end DASH system consists of a DASH content provider, an origin server, standard proxy caches, and a number of DASH clients. DASH enables rate adaptation by dynamically requesting media segments from different representations to match a varying network bandwidth. A representation level is used to specify the level of media bitrate, wherein a higher bitrate is associated with a higher representation level, and vice versa. When a DASH client switches up/down the representation level, coding dependencies within the representation have to be taken into account. In DASH, a general concept named Stream Access Point (SAP) is introduced to provide a codec-independent solution for accessing or switching representations. As SAP is specified as a position in a representation that enables playback of a media stream to be started using only the information contained in a representation data starting from that position onwards (preceded by the initialization segment, if any).

A DASH client first accesses an MPD to obtain information of available representations and the URI or URI template for each segment. The client continuously requests and receives segments from a server. DASH clients request media segments from different representations for reacting to varying network resources. Rate adaptation decisions typically take place each time before requesting a segment. If DASH operates in a network including a cache or many caches, a client's GET segment request is first redirected to a cache. If the cache has the requested segment, the request will be served by the cache and the segment fetching time is reduced. Otherwise, the request will be forwarded to the origin server.

4. Signaling Method for Joint Client-Driven Prefetching and Rate Adaptation

Figure 2 shows parts of DASH system architecture, which includes a DASH client and proxy caches. DASH system architecture is shown in Figure 1. The proxy cache can be

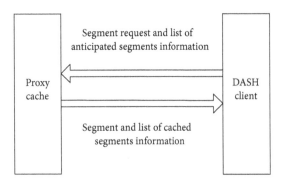

Figure 2: System architecture for DASH assisted with CLICRA-aware cache.

a conventional proxy cache or a proxy cache with segment prefetching functionality as proposed in this paper, which is capable of processing the signaling sent from the DASH client and optionally creating signaling to the DASH client.

The signaling method includes two signaling directions from a DASH client to a proxy cache and signaling from a proxy cache to a DASH client as presented in Sections 4.1 and 4.2, respectively. The signaling method is specific for DASH operating in networks including proxy caches. It should be noted that the signaling presented in Section 4.1 provides the main functionality of the proposed client-driven joint rate adaptation and prefetching. To achieve an enhanced performance of rate adaptation, the signaling presented in Section 4.2 can be further deployed.

4.1. Signaling of Anticipated Segment Information. In the client to proxy cache signaling, the DASH client informs the proxy cache that the DASH client is likely to request one or multiple subsequent segments from a specific representation in the future, referred subsequently to as anticipated segments. For example, the anticipated segment information may be conveyed to the proxy cache by using a new HTTP header named anticipated segment header, when the client sends segment request. The signaling could be received by a CLICRA-aware proxy cache or a conventional proxy cache. If the proxy cache is aware of the signaling and wishes to deploy the conveyed anticipated segment information to improve its efficiency, then it may take advantage of the anticipated segment information to prefetch the anticipated segments, if they have not already been cached by the proxy cache. Otherwise, if the proxy cache is aware of the signaling and does not wish to use the information, or if the proxy cache is not aware of the signaling, then it should ignore the information carried in the header and can operate conventionally, that is, as if the proxy cache did not receive the additional header. Consequently, the anticipated segment informational signaling does not bring any negative effect to proxy caches and could improve proxy cache performance in case it is aware of the signaling.

Note that the signaling is expected to be received by the proxy cache which is closest to the client. To achieve this goal, the anticipated segment header could be included in the connection header of HTTP; hence, the anticipated segment

signaling will be only received by the closest proxy cache and will not be received by any other proxy caches nor the origin server.

When compared to proxy-driven prefetching mechanisms, the signaling method releases the processing load at the proxy cache and avoids the problem of scalability when the number of clients connected to the proxy cache increases.

4.2. Signaling of Caching Information. In addition, the DASH client indicates to the proxy cache that caching information of one or multiple subsequent segments of one or multiple representations is requested by the DASH client for the purpose of rate adaptation. The caching information includes the caching status, the time instant of starting to fetch a segment, and the segment fetch time for fetching a segment from the origin server to the proxy cache if the segment is cached. The previous information can be obtained by the proxy cache without intensive computational processing. Hence, the proposed signaling does not affect the efficiency of the proxy cache.

In the proxy cache to client signaling, the proxy cache may inform the DASH client about the caching information of the specified subsequent segments of the representations.

Similar to Section 4.1, the caching information request and the caching information itself can be signaled between the client and the proxy cache using two new headers, called caching request and caching, respectively. The caching request signaling may also be received by the proxy cache, which may or may not be aware of the signaling. In the former case, the proxy cache may inform the client about the caching information together with the responding segment. In the later case, the proxy cache ignores the header as discussed in Section 4.1.

5. Joint Client-Driven Prefetching and Rate Adaptation

This section proposes a novel joint client-driven prefetching and rate adaptation (CLICRA), which moves the processing intelligence from a proxy cache to DASH clients unlike the traditional proxy-driven prefetching methods.

The proposed CLICRA method selects the media bitrate for the current segment to be requested and the anticipated segments. By indicating the anticipated segments to the proxy cache, it can prefetch the anticipated segments which are neither cached nor being fetched, which are hereafter referred to as uncached anticipated segments. Hence, the client-driven joint rate adaptation and proxy cache prefetching are realized by using the anticipated segment information signaling presented in Section 4.1 for DASH operating in networks including proxy caches.

To specify the representation of the segment to be requested and of the anticipated segments, we propose a method of predicting buffered media time for DASH operating in networks including proxy caches. Our method takes into account incompletely cached representations and its impact on the buffered media time changing trend. The proposed buffered media time prediction method uses the signaling method presented in Section 4.2.

The following sections are organized as follows. A buffered media time prediction method for DASH operating in networks including proxy caches is proposed in Section 5.1. Section 5.2 presents the proposed rate adaptation method, which switches up/down to higher/lower bitrate encoded representation based on the predicted buffered media times.

5.1. Buffered Media Time Prediction Method for Enhanced Rate Adaptation. The DASH client estimates the future trend of the buffered media time by taking into account the fact that the SFTs for fetching a segment from the proxy cache and fetching from the origin server are different. As presented in [6], SFT refers to the time duration from requesting a segment to receiving the last byte of the segment at a DASH client. Hence, the differentiated SFTs can be estimated according to the caching status of selected subsequent segments determined by the client. The proposed buffered media time prediction method enables the rate adaptation algorithm to adapt media bitrate in advance and to avoid unnecessary switch-up/down representation level when DASH operates in networks including proxy caches. The main symbols appearing in rest of the paper are summarized in Table 1 for ease of reference.

Buffered media time can be predicted by adding the differences of the media segment duration and SFTs of the subsequent segments to the current buffered media time. In several candidate representations with rid in the range of $[\mathrm{rid}_c - \gamma, \mathrm{rid}_c + \gamma]$, subsequent segments with segment numbers in the range of $[\mathrm{snum}_c, \mathrm{snum}_c + w]$ can be predicted as

$$\overline{B}_{t_{\mathrm{rec}}(\mathrm{rid},\mathrm{snum})} = \overline{B}_{t_{\mathrm{rec}}(\mathrm{rep},\mathrm{snum}-1)} + \mathrm{MSD} - \overline{\mathrm{SFT}}\,(\mathrm{rid},\mathrm{snum}), \tag{1}$$

where $\overline{B}_{t_{\mathrm{rec}}(\mathrm{rid},\mathrm{snum})}$ denotes the predicted buffered media time when the snum-th segment is to be received by the client, and MSD and $\overline{\mathrm{SFT}}\,(\mathrm{rid},\mathrm{snum})$ denote the predefined media segment duration and the predicted SFT for fetching the segment, respectively.

In addition to the predicted buffered media times, variation of predicted buffered media time ($\overline{BV}$) is estimated after receiving the $(\mathrm{snum}_c + w)$th segment compared to the current buffered media time. $\overline{BV}$ with representation identifier rid and subsequent segments window size w is calculated as

$$\overline{BV}\,(\mathrm{rid}, w) = \sum_{\mathrm{sid}=\mathrm{snum}_c}^{\mathrm{snum}_c+w} \left(\mathrm{MSD}\,(\mathrm{rid},\mathrm{sid}) - \overline{\mathrm{SFT}}\,(\mathrm{rid},\mathrm{sid}) \right). \tag{2}$$

To solve (1) and (2), the SFTs of subsequent segments within a sliding window are predicted according to the caching status of subsequent segments at the corresponding time to issue the requests.

5.1.1. Segment Fetch Time Prediction. SFT is predicted using one of the following three equations depending on the

TABLE 1: Definition of the main symbols.

$\overline{B}$	Predicted buffered media time
$\overline{B}_{t_{\mathrm{rec}}(\mathrm{rid}_c,\mathrm{snum})}$	$\overline{B}$ at time instants $t_{\mathrm{rec}}\,(\mathrm{rid}_c,\mathrm{snum})$
$\overline{BV}$	Variation of predicted buffered media time
br	Media bitrate
CS	Caching status
MSD	Predefined media segment duration
(rid, snum)	Representation ID and segment number to identify a segment
t_{cache}	Time to cache a segment
t_{rec}	Time to receive a segment
t_{req}	Time to request a segment
$\theta_B^\uparrow, \theta_B^\downarrow$	Upper threshold, lower threshold of predicted buffered media time
$\theta_{BV}^\uparrow, \theta_{BV}^\downarrow$	Upper threshold, lower threshold of variation of predicted buffered media time
$\mathrm{snum}, \mathrm{snum}_c$	Segment number, current segment number to be requested by client
SFT	Segment fetch time
$\overline{\mathrm{SFT}}$	Estimated SFT for a subsequent segment
$\widetilde{\mathrm{SFT}}^c$	SFT measured by client
$\widetilde{\mathrm{SFT}}^p$	SFT measured by proxy cache
$\widetilde{\mathrm{SFT}}_{p2c}$	SFT measurement from proxy cache to client
$\widetilde{\mathrm{SFT}}_{s2p}$	SFT measurement from the origin server to proxy cache
$\widetilde{\mathrm{SFT}}'_{p2c}$	The recent sample of $\widetilde{\mathrm{SFT}}_{p2c}$
$\widetilde{\mathrm{SFT}}'_{s2p}$	The recent sample of $\widetilde{\mathrm{SFT}}_{s2p}$
$p2c$	Proxy cache to the client
$s2p$	Origin sever to the proxy cache
$\mathrm{rid}, \mathrm{rid}_c, \mathrm{rid}_p$	Representation ID, The current representation ID, the previous representation ID
$w, w_f,$ and w_p	Window size of the subsequent, prefetching and previous segments
γ	Window size of the representation ID

caching status of the segment. The predicted SFT is denoted as $\overline{\mathrm{SFT}}\,(\mathrm{rid},\mathrm{snum})$, which is represented as representation ID, that is, rid, since the SFT is proportional to the encoded bitrate of representation.

Case 1. A segment is cached by a proxy cache, and $\overline{\mathrm{SFT}}\,(\mathrm{rid},\mathrm{snum})$ can be set to measured SFT from the proxy cache to DASH client $\widetilde{\mathrm{SFT}}_{p2c}$, see (Appendix C.1) as

$$\overline{\mathrm{SFT}}\,(\mathrm{rid},\mathrm{snum}) = \widetilde{\mathrm{SFT}}_{p2c}\,(\mathrm{rid}). \tag{3}$$

Case 2. A segment is being fetched by a proxy cache, and SFT is predicted as the sum of the time spent to fetch remaining part of the segment and the time required to receive the segment from the cache to the client. The time spent to fetch remaining part of the segment is the time span between the time of caching by the proxy cache (t_{cache} discussed in

Section 6.2) and requesting by the client (t_{req} discussed in Section 6.2). Consider

$$\overline{\text{SFT}} \, (\text{rid}, \text{snum}) = t_{\text{cache}} \, (\text{rid}, \text{snum}) - t_{\text{req}} \, (\text{rid}, \text{snum}) \\ + \widehat{\text{SFT}}_{p2c} \, (\text{rid}) \,. \tag{4}$$

To be compliant with the response cacheability of the cache operation as specified in HTTP/1.1 [12], only a fully cached segment is sent to a DASH client responding to HTTP GET segment request.

Case 3. A segment is neither cached nor being fetched by the proxy cache, and SFT is predicted as the sum of the estimated SFTs from the origin server to the proxy cache $\widehat{\text{SFT}}_{s2p}$, see (Appendix C.2) and $\widehat{\text{SFT}}_{p2c}$, as

$$\overline{\text{SFT}} \, (\text{rid}, \text{snum}) \\ = \widehat{\text{SFT}}_{s2p} \, (\text{rid}) + \widehat{\text{SFT}}_{p2c} \, (\text{rid}) \,. \tag{5}$$

From (1)-(2) and (3)–(5), $\overline{B}_{t_{\text{rec}}(\text{rid},\text{snum})}$ and $\overline{BV}$ (rid, w) can be predicted. Since $\overline{\text{SFT}}(\text{rid}, \text{snum})$ depends on the caching status, the next section presents a method of updating and predicting the caching status of a segment when the segment is to be requested.

5.1.2. Caching Status Update and Prediction.

5.1.2. Caching Status Update and Prediction. This section presents a method of updating the caching status to the caching status conveyed from the proxy cache and predicting future caching status of a segment when the segment is to be requested. In Section 4.2, the proposed signaling method signals the caching status (CS) of subsequent segments at the time instant when the proxy cache responds to the client request for the current requested segment. Hence, the predicted caching status of each segment in a certain sliding window is estimated consecutively by the DASH client based on the informed caching information as described later.

Figure 3 shows an example of consecutively estimating the caching status of segments from #n to #n + 2 when the DASH client issues the requests for the corresponding segments. Specifically, the figure depicts one initial signaled caching status and three sets of caching status at time instants $t\_\text{req}(n)$, $t\_\text{req}(n + 1)$, and $t\_\text{req}(n + 2)$, that is, times to issue the requests for segment #n, #n + 1, and #n + 2, respectively. In Figure 3, the cached segments, being fetched segment and uncached segment, are represented with light blue, green, and orange blocks, respectively.

As shown in Figure 3, steps 1, 2, and 3 are used to determine the segment caching statuses at $t\_\text{req}(n)$, $t\_\text{req}(n + 1)$, and $t\_\text{req}(n+2)$, respectively. Each step includes processes of requesting a segment, identifying the earliest uncached anticipated segments and updating the caching status in a sliding window. The client indicates the earliest uncached segment information to the proxy cache which can prefetch them. In turn, the client can update the caching status, for example, updating the earliest uncached segments to "being fetched" segment according to the receiving caching information. This example sets the sliding window to 2.

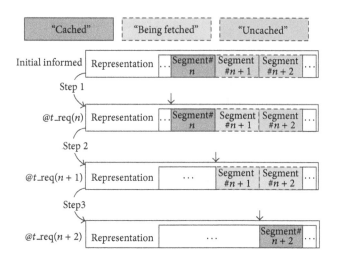

FIGURE 3: Example of estimating each segment caching status when the segment is to be requested.

The following steps describe the processes of updating and predicting for this example.

Step 1. Updating of the CS at the time to issue the request for the segment #n, that is, @$t_{\text{req}}(n)$ based on the initial caching status signaled from the proxy cache. As the segment #n + 1 is the earliest uncached anticipated segment, its CS is updated from "uncached" to "being fetched" @$t_{\text{req}}(n)$. And the CSs of other segments are same as the initial CSs.

Step 2. Updating of the CS@$t_{\text{req}}(n + 1)$ based on CS@ $t_{\text{req}}(n)$. Let us assume that segment #n + 1 is not fully fetched to the proxy cache when segment #n is received by the DASH client. So, CS of segments #n+1 is "being fetched." The CS of segment #n+2 is updated from "uncached" to "being fetched" @$t_{\text{req}}(n+1)$ as similar to updating the CS of segments #n + 1 in step 1.

Step 3. Updating of the CS@$t_{\text{req}}(n + 2)$, that is, time instant to issue the request for segment #n + 2. Assume that segment #n + 2 is cached when segment #n + 1 is received by the DASH client. Thus, segments #n + 2 caching status changes to "cached" from "being fetched".

For the detailed procedure of updating and predicting caching status and equations of determining t_{cache} and t_{req}, please refer Appendix B.

5.2. Joint Rate Adaptation Algorithm for Requested Segment and Anticipated Segments.

5.2. Joint Rate Adaptation Algorithm for Requested Segment and Anticipated Segments. The main objectives of rate adaptation for DASH consist of the following three aspects. First, the rate adaptation aims to provide the maximum possible media bitrate. Second, it tries to avoid playback interruptions. And third, it should reduce the bitrate adaptation frequency and the average magnitude of the bitrate change for each adaptation to provide a stable playback quality. The first two targets require the rate adaptation to adapt media bitrates quickly to the varying network resources, but the last target requires it to react conservatively to the long-term network resource variations.

To achieve the aforementioned objectives, this paper proposes a novel technique which selects an identical encoded media bitrate of a representation for the current requested segment and the anticipated segments. The proposed CLICRA examines the predicted buffered media times at several future time instants in the adjacent representations and selects the encoded media bitrates of the representation so that the predicted buffered media times are in a safety level.

The predicted buffered media times based rate adaptation method can ignore short-term SFT variations similarly to the current buffered media time-based method by using a conservative threshold to invoke a rate adaptation. With the knowledge of predicted buffered media times, the DASH client no longer needs to wait until the buffered media time reaches a certain threshold which will invoke a rate adaptation.

Rate adaption consists of switching-up, switching-down, or keeping a representation unchanged.

Switching-down (switching-up) representation occurs when the network capacity is lower (larger) than the threshold required to deliver the current bitrate encoded representation and enables the delivery of one of the lower (higher) bitrate encoded representations. If the network capacity is lower (larger) than the media bitrate, then the buffer filling rate is lower (higher) than the buffer consumption rate. So, a lower (higher) network capacity can be detected by checking if one (multiple) predicted buffered media time(s) in the current representation is (are) lower (higher) than the predefined threshold (and in a higher bitrate encoded representations are higher than a defined switch-up threshold). Here, the predicted buffered media times consist of multiple predictions in future times when the segment is to be received by the client and denoted as $\overline{B}_{t_{rec}(rid,snum)}$. An identical lower (higher) bitrate encoded representation, also denoted as lower (higher) representation level, is selected as the representation for the requested segment and for the anticipated segments so that the predicted buffered media times in the selected lower (higher) representation level are higher than the switching-down (switching-up) threshold.

In all other cases, the representation is kept unchanged.

6. Simulation Results

In the performed simulations, the CLICRA method was operated at the DASH client, and only the signaling functionality was operated at the proxy cache. The proposed CLICRA method for DASH was implemented in ns2 [13]. Two combinations of rate adaptation and proxy cache were also implemented in ns2 to compare it with the proposed method. In the first combination, called TraRA in this paper, a traditional rate adaptation algorithm for DASH similar to [6] was operated with a conventional proxy cache without prefetching. In the second combination, called TraCaMaRA in this paper, the same traditional rate adaptation was operated with a proxy-driven prefetching method similar to the active prefetching method [10].

In many DASH services, it is expected that a large number of DASH clients are streaming at the same time and therefore compete for a limited bandwidth. A network simulator, such as ns2, can be considered a good choice for evaluating prefetching and rate adaptation methods for a large number of clients.

6.1. Network Topology and Settings. The network topology used in the simulation is shown in Figure 4. One origin server, two cascaded proxy caches, a network element, and n DASH clients were included in the topology. The two layers of proxy caches were equipped with the caching functionality, but the network element, which could be for example be a router collecting multiple digital subscriber line (DSL) connections, does not provide caching functionality. The same media segments will be sequentially delivered from the origin server to proxy caches #1 and #2, where they were cached to serve future requests. The same media segment may be delivered from proxy cache #2 to the network element and to DASH clients multiple times. Therefore, in case many clients start streaming at the same time, the bandwidth consumption from proxy cache #2 to the network element is expected to be large. Bandwidths from the network element to clients, that is, links #4, were different for different clients as described later.

In our simulation, a group of five DASH clients were simulated wherein the bandwidths of link #4 were set to 0.4 Mbits/s, 0.7 Mbits/s, 1.0 Mbits/s, 1.3 Mbits/s, and 1.6 Mbits/s, respectively. To evaluate DASH performance under dynamically changing shared network resources and varying caching ratios at proxy caches, DASH clients were set to start media streaming progressively at intervals of 200 s from 0 s to 800 s. The simulated DASH client numbers for each group assigned to a certain bandwidth were set to 2, 4, 6, 4, and 2 at [0s, 50s], [200s, 250s], [400s, 450s], [600s, 650s], and [800s, 850s], respectively. So, the total number of simulated DASH clients was 90. All clients requested the same media clip, and the playback duration of the media clip was 600 s.

To achieve adaptive HTTP streaming, the streaming server provides ten sets of representations for clients to adapt the media bitrates wherein the media bitrates include 64, 128, 192, 256, 384, 512, 640, 896, 1152, and 1408 Kbits/s for representation levels 0 to 9, respectively. The bitrate difference between adjacent representations increases as a function of the bitrate for observing a roughly equivalent quality improvement. In the simulations, segment duration, the initial buffering time, and ε were set to 5 s, 10 s, and 30 s, respectively. w, w_p, and w_f were set to 10, 6, and 5, respectively. $\theta_B^{\uparrow}$, $\theta_B^{\downarrow}$, $\theta_{BV}^{\uparrow}$, and $\theta_{BV}^{\downarrow}$ were set to 60 s, 20 s, -30, and -50, respectively.

To simulate the dynamic nature of the Internet, two exponential (Exp) traffic senders were connected each to one proxy cache. The Exp traffic senders #2 and #3 generate on/off traffic. During the "on" periods, packets were generated at constant burst rates of 5 Mbits/s and 10 Mbits/s by the Exp senders #2 and #3, respectively. During the "off" periods, no traffic is generated. Burst times and idle times were taken from exponential distributions. In the simulation, the average on- and off-times were set to 2 s. Exp receiver #2 is connected to the second proxy cache, while receiver #3 is connected to the network element. The origin server also includes an internal exponential traffic generator, which generates

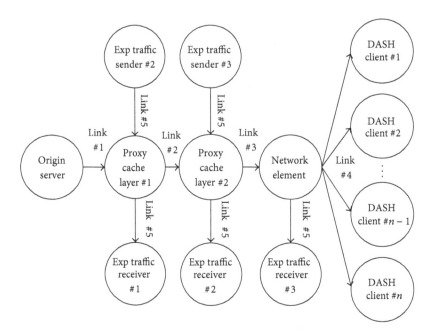

FIGURE 4: Network topology.

TABLE 2: Two sets of simulation settings.

Setup	Receive window size	Link parameters	Links #1 and #2			Link #3			Link #5
			Setting #1	Setting #2	Setting #3	Setting #1	Setting #2	Setting #3	Setting #1, #2, #3
Setup 1	1000 Kbytes	Bandwidth (Mbits/s)	10	10	20	20	40	40	10
		Link delay (ms)	100	100	100	10	10	10	10
Setup 2	60 Kbytes	Bandwidth (Mbits/s)	20	20	20	40	40	40	10
		Link delay (ms)	50	100	150	10	10	10	10

packets with a burst rate of 5 Mbits/s during the "on" periods and sends the packets to the Exp traffic receiver #1. The internal exponential traffic generator is used to simulate a scenario where the origin server not only serves DASH clients but also serves other clients such as web browser clients.

The maximum receive window size a receiver can advertise is 65535 bytes in the 16-bit TCP header. In such a case, the achievable maximum TCP throughput is limited to the ratio of the receive window size and RTT. For larger window sizes to accommodate high speed transmission paths, RFC 1323 [14] specifies the window scaling that allows a receiver to advertise a window size larger than 65535 bytes. To evaluate the proposed method in different receive window sizes and RTTs, two different receive window sizes of 60 KBytes and 1000 Kbytes were tested.

For both window sizes, three different sets of link bandwidths and delays were tested as shown in Table 2. A recent measurement on the Internet reported in [15] was considered to set the link delays. The bandwidths were set according to the number of DASH clients and the media bitrates of provided representations. With the set bandwidth, the clients undergo different levels of network congestion and experience different media bitrates. For each setting in Table 2 simulations were run three times to smooth out the impacts of random starting times of different clients.

6.2. Simulation Results and Analysis. The proposed method was evaluated with respect to the perceived streaming experience at the DASH clients and the network resource usage from the origin server to the proxy cache. The perceived streaming experience at the DASH client was evaluated with respect to the convergence in the representation level indicating the media bitrates, the achievable media bitrate, and the playback interruption frequency. The network resource usage was measured in terms of the amount of media traffic from the origin server to the proxy cache layer #2, and the cache hit ratio at the proxy cache layer #2.

6.2.1. Simulation Results for Setup 1. Simulation results were reported for the three different bandwidth combinations with the given delays in the links #1, #2, and #3. The receive window size was set to 1000 Kbytes; hence, the throughput is mainly controlled by the bandwidth of the links.

Table 3 shows the buffer underflow counts for the proposed CLICRA method and the traditional methods Tra-CaMaRA and TraRA, with bandwidth settings #1, #2, and #3. In the bandwidth settings #1 and #3, buffer underflow occurred at most 7 times for the proposed CLICRA method in all 90 clients, each of which streamed 600 s duration of a media clip. In the bandwidth setting #2, buffer underflow

TABLE 3: Buffer underflow count.

Bandwidth	CLICRA	TraCaMaRA	TraRA
Setting #1	4	86	77
Setting #2	10	279	345
Setting #3	7	95	181

occurred 10 times for the proposed CLICRA. However, for the TraCaMaRA and TraRA, buffer underflow occurred 77–345 times in all three bandwidth settings.

To evaluate convergence in the representation levels, Figure 5 shows points indicating switching frequency and amplitude with bandwidth setting #1, wherein the x axis denotes the mean of the absolute difference in the representation levels between adjacent segments, called switching amplitude, and the y axis denotes the ratio of the count of representation level switches divided by the count of all received segments. Thus, a point in the bottom-left corner of the figure indicates a superior convergence compared to a point in the top-right corner. Figure 5 also shows the average values of each method as specifically labeled points. Average values of switching frequency and amplitude of each method were reported in Table 4. It shows that the average switching frequency and amplitude were lower than 0.1 and 0.1 for the proposed method but were in the range of 0.2–0.5 and 0.2–0.8, respectively, for the traditional methods.

Simulation results show that the proposed CLICRA method not only provides significantly lower switching frequencies but also lower switching amplitudes compared to the traditional TraCaMaRA and TraRA methods as its corresponding points were clustered in the bottom-left corner for the proposed method; however, those of the competing methods were widely spread and appear at the top-right corner.

The reasons of relatively high buffer underflow count and high switching representation frequency and amplitude in TraCaMaRA can be described as follows. The traditional proxy-driven proxy segments prefetching method prefetches subsequent segments without being aware of the representations of the subsequent segments at DASH clients. The prefetched segments will become useless in case clients switch to a new representation level. Therefore, unnecessary segments may be prefetched, which may result in congestion between the origin server and DASH clients and further result in buffer underflow in a large number of clients. TraRA and TraCaMaRA employ an SFT-based rate adaptation method, which compares the ratio of media segment duration divided by SFT with a rate adaptation threshold to decide whether or not to switch-up representation levels. The incompletely cached representations in proxy caches caused a large variation in terms of SFT measured at a DASH client in fetching cached segments from proxy caches and fetching uncached segments from the origin server. TraRA may switch-up a representation level after observing a smaller SFT for fetching the cached segments from proxy cache and without checking if the subsequent segments in a higher representation were cached by a proxy cache or not. Hence, after switching-up the representation level, a DASH client took larger SFT to fetch

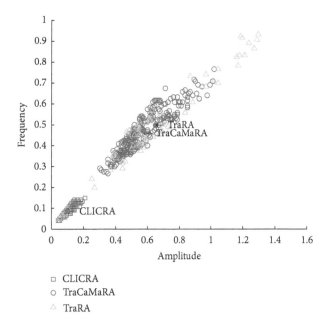

FIGURE 5: Switch frequency and amplitude.

subsequent segments of a higher representation level if such segments were not cached by proxy caches. In case a large number of DASH clients make such incorrect switching-up decisions, the network between the origin server and the proxy cache may suffer from congestion which further results in buffer draining and switching-down representation levels at a large number of DASH clients. Such a repetitive cycle of switching-up/down representation levels resulted in high switching frequencies and amplitudes.

In contrast, the proposed method predicts the SFT for subsequent segments based on the caching statuses of subsequent segments in a certain sliding window and the separately measured SFTs from the origin server to the proxy cache and from the proxy cache to DASH clients. Thus, incorrect switching up/down representation levels can be reduced. Furthermore, the proposed client-driven prefetching method specifies the anticipated segments at DASH clients and indicates the earliest uncached anticipated segments to the proxy cache so that it can prefetch the indicated anticipated segment, hence, reducing prefetching of unnecessary segments as well as decreasing congestion and buffer underflow counts.

Figure 6 shows the average received media bitrates over time, where the x and y axes denote the simulation time t_0 (s) and the average received media bitrate for each client in the interval $[(t_0 - 200), t_0]$, respectively. The proposed CLICRA method shows higher achievable media bitrates compared to the traditional TraRA method. Furthermore, Table 5 shows the number of transmitted bytes from the origin server to the proxy cache. In most of the cases, CLICRA consumed less bandwidth from the origin server to the proxy cache compared to TraCaMaRA. It can be observed that more traffic was delivered from the origin server to the proxy cache by CLICRA compared to TraCaMaRA with bandwidth setting #3. The possible reason is that CLICRA clients quickly

TABLE 4: Switch frequency and amplitude for receive window 1000 Kbytes.

Bandwidth	Frequency			Amplitude		
	CLICRA	TraCaMaRA	TraRA	CLICRA	TraCaMaRA	TraRA
Setting #1	0.0867	0.4695	0.4984	0.0978	0.5736	0.6491
Setting #2	0.0743	0.2201	0.4959	0.0825	0.3142	0.7176
Setting #3	0.0734	0.2060	0.4611	0.0805	0.2832	0.6653

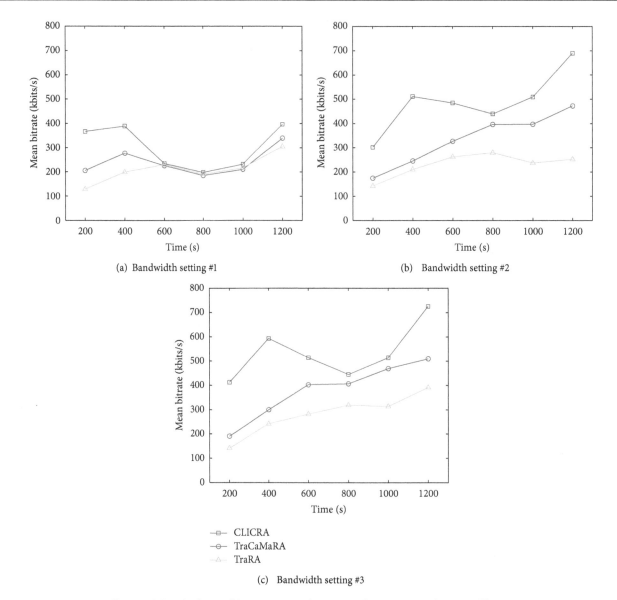

(a) Bandwidth setting #1

(b) Bandwidth setting #2

—□— CLICRA
—○— TraCaMaRA
—△— TraRA

(c) Bandwidth setting #3

FIGURE 6: Received mean bitrate over simulation time for receive window 1000 Kbytes.

switch-up to higher bitrates encoded representations and the TraCaMaRA remains at relatively lower bitrates encoded representations, which causes the results of delivered traffics in CLICRA and TraCaMaRA. Such a result shows that the proposed CLICRA method outperforms TraCaMaRA in terms of fully utilizing the available bandwidth to provide a higher playback quality to the clients.

Figure 7 shows the average cache hit ratio at the proxy cache #2 for clients' requests over time, where the x and y axes denote the simulation time t_0 and the average hit ratio for each client in the interval $[(t_0 - 200), t_0]$, respectively. The cache hit ratios of CLICRA were much larger than those of TraRA. In the beginning, CLICRA outperforms TraCaMaRA. Since 600 s, TraCaMaRA shows similar cache hit ratio with the proposed CLICRA method, but the high cache hit ratio of TraCaMaRA does not demonstrate its superiority due to the high buffer underflow count, the high switching frequency,

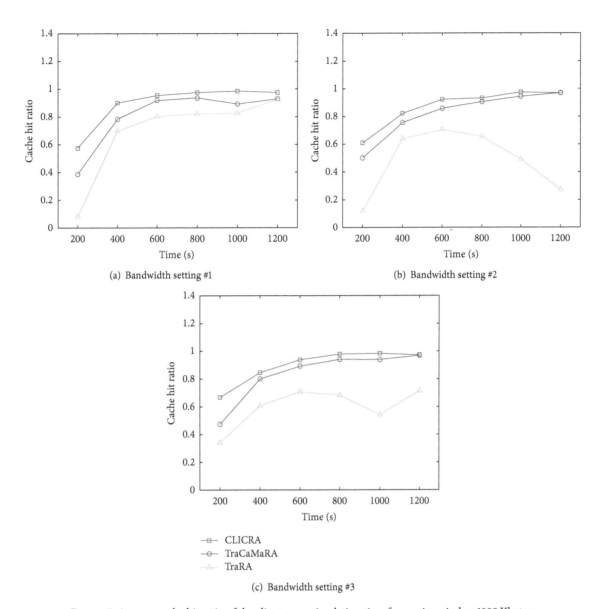

(a) Bandwidth setting #1

(b) Bandwidth setting #2

-□- CLICRA
-○- TraCaMaRA
-△- TraRA

(c) Bandwidth setting #3

FIGURE 7: Average cache hit ratio of the clients over simulation time for receive window 1000 Kbytes.

TABLE 5: Transmitted bytes (Gbytes) from the origin server to the proxy cache.

Bandwidth	CLICRA	TraCaMaRA	TraRA
Setting #1	132.0	159.3	118.6
Setting #2	216.4	287.1	169.1
Setting #3	251.7	234.9	199.9

and the large bandwidth consumption caused by TraCa-MaRA.

6.2.2. Simulation Results for Setup 2. Simulation results were reported for the three different delay combinations with the given bandwidth in the links #1, #2, and #3. The receive window size was set to 60 Kbytes; hence, the throughput is affected by delays of the links in addition to bandwidths. The results were reported in a similar fashion as in the previous section. Tables 6, 7, and 8 show the buffer underflow count, the number of transmitted bytes from the origin server to the proxy cache layer #2, and switching frequency and amplitude with the three different link delays. Figures 8 and 9 show the average received media bitrates over the simulation time and the average cache hit ratio at proxy cache #2 for clients' requests, respectively. The simulation results show that the proposed method is significantly superior to the traditional methods, similarly to the results of the first simulation setup. The reasons were the same as discussed in the simulation results for the first setup.

7. Conclusions

This paper showed that when streaming management in a proxy cache and rate adaptation in streaming clients

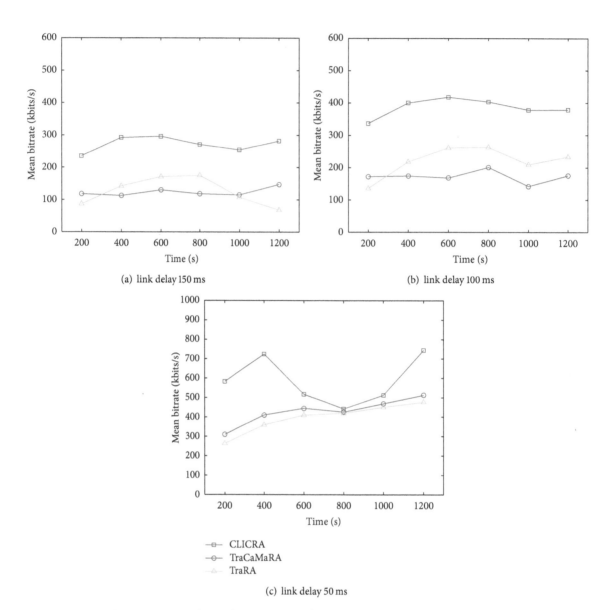

(a) link delay 150 ms

(b) link delay 100 ms

— □ — CLICRA

— ○ — TraCaMaRA

— △ — TraRA

(c) link delay 50 ms

FIGURE 8: Received mean bitrate over simulation time for receive window 60 Kbytes.

TABLE 6: Buffer under flow count for receive window 60 Kbytes.

Link delay	CLICRA	TraCaMaRA	TraRA
150 ms	91	872	668
100 ms	44	741	371
50 ms	4	219	22

TABLE 7: Transmitted bytes (Gbytes) from the origin server to proxy cache.

Link delay	CLICRA	TraCaMaRA	TraRA
150 ms	118.9	121.0	102.2
100 ms	180.3	180.5	162.0
50 ms	271.6	353.8	219.7

using dynamic adaptive streaming over HTTP (DASH) are performed independently, network resources are not used efficiently and the streaming experience at DASH clients is degraded. To address these problems, this paper proposed a signaling method from a streaming client to a proxy cache to manage prefetching and caching of segments and from the proxy cache to the streaming client to feedback the caching status and the segment fetch time from the origin server to the proxy cache. Based on the signaling, the proposed client-driven joint proxy cache management and rate adaptation (CLICRA) method estimated the deliverable media bitrate between the origin server and the proxy cache and separately between the proxy cache and the streaming client. Hence, the fetching time and the buffered media duration can be predicted for subsequent segments according to the caching status and the estimated deliverable media bitrates. The proposed CLICRA method not only specifies the media bitrate of the representation level for the requested segments but also for the anticipated segments, which the client will most probably request shortly. The information

TABLE 8: Switch frequency and amplitude for receive window 60 Kbytes.

Link delay	Frequency			Amplitude		
	CLICRA	TraCaMaRA	TraRA	CLICRA	TraCaMaRA	TraRA
150 ms	0.1117	0.4712	0.4548	0.1388	0.6982	0.6502
100 ms	0.0906	0.3902	0.4892	0.1040	0.5810	0.6892
50 ms	0.0700	0.1596	0.2273	0.0744	0.2092	0.3024

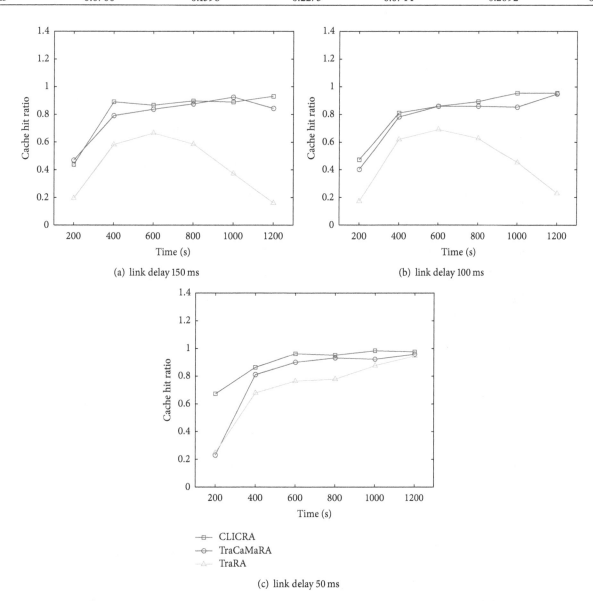

(a) link delay 150 ms

(b) link delay 100 ms

(c) link delay 50 ms

FIGURE 9: Average cache hit ratio of the clients over simulation time for receive window 60 Kbytes.

of the anticipated segments is passed on to the proxy cache so that it can prefetch the anticipated segments. Therefore, the proposed CLICRA method efficiently uses the limited network resources between the origin server and the proxy cache and avoids congestion. CLICRA shows improved performance with respect to buffer underflow count, switching frequency, and achievable media bitrate at the clients and bandwidth consumption from the origin server to the proxy cache and cache hit ratio at the proxy cache compared to competing techniques.

Appendices

The Appendix is organized as follows. The detailed rate adaptation algorithm is presented in Appendix A, which describes the detailed realization of determining joint media bitrates for the requested segment and the anticipated segment presented in Section 5.2. Appendix B presents the caching status update and prediction which is summarized in Section 5.1.2. Finally, Appendix C proposes a method of separately measuring SFT which is used in Section 5.1.1.

A. Rate Adaptation

Rate adaptation actions (summarized in Section 5.2) consist of switching-up or down the representation level and keeping the representation level unchanged.

A.1. Switching-Up Representation Level. Two conditions are used to decide whether or not to switch-up to a higher bitrate encoded representation.

The first condition is to check whether or not the network capacity is large enough to deliver the *current* level of representation in time so that the buffered media time will remain in a safety level against playback interruption. The condition is that all predicted buffered media times at time instants t_{rec} $(\text{rid}_c, \text{snum})$, denoted as $\overline{B}_{t_{\text{rec}}(\text{rid}_c, \text{snum})}$, are higher than a certain threshold $\theta_B^{\uparrow}$ under the assumption that the DASH client sets rid to current representation ID rid_c; that is, the following inequality must hold:

$$\forall \text{snum} \in [\text{snum}_c, \text{snum}_c + w] :$$
$$\overline{B}_{t_{\text{rec}}(\text{rid}_c, \text{snum})} > \theta_B^{\uparrow}. \tag{A.1}$$

The second condition is to check if the network capacity is large enough so that the *higher* level of representation is delivered in time and the buffered media time will remain in a safety level. This condition is to measure if network capacity is large enough so that the variation of the buffered media time is higher than a certain threshold compared to the current buffered media time. It is that all $\overline{B}_{t_{\text{rec}}(\text{rid}, \text{snum})}$ must be higher than a certain threshold and variation of predicted buffer media time $\overline{BV}$ $(\text{rid}, \text{snum}_c + w)$ must be higher than a certain threshold under the assumption that the DASH client switches-up to a higher bitrate encoded representation. In other words, if there is a higher level of rid within $[\text{rid}_c + 1, \text{rid}_c + \gamma]$, the following two inequalities must hold:

$$\exists \, \text{rid} \in [\text{rid}_c + 1, \text{rid}_c + \gamma] :$$
$$\left\{ \forall \text{snum} \in [\text{snum}_c, \text{snum}_c + w] : \overline{B}_{t_{\text{rec}}(\text{rid}, \text{snum})} > \theta_B^{\uparrow} \right\},$$
$$\left\{ \overline{BV} \, (\text{rep}, \text{seg}_{\text{rec}} + w) > \theta_{BV}^{\uparrow} \right\}, \tag{A.2}$$

where γ is window size of rid as defined in Table 1. rid is a variable instead of constant, which is different to the first condition where rid is constantly set to rid_c.

The proposed decision of switch-up to a higher bitrate encoded representation is made conservatively but quickly to provide stable and high playback quality as much as possible. The conservative decision is made by using multiple conditions as described earlier, and the quick decision is made by using predicted buffered media times for DASH operating in networks including proxy caches.

A.2. Switching-Down Representation Level. The decision of switching-down to a low bitrate encoded representation is made when the network capacity is decreased, and the *current* level of representation cannot be delivered in time. The late

delivery results in that buffered media time will decrease to an unsafe level causing playback interruption. Late delivery may lead to variation of buffered media time compared to the current buffered media time which is lower than a certain threshold. The following condition must hold to switch down to a low bitrate encoded representation:

$$\forall \text{snum} \in [\text{snum}_c, \text{snum}_c + w] :$$
$$\overline{B}_{t_{\text{rec}}(\text{rid}_c, \text{snum})} < \theta_B^{\downarrow} \text{ or } \overline{BV} \, (\text{rid}_c, \text{snum}_c + w) < \theta_{BV}^{\downarrow}. \tag{A.3}$$

The new representation level is set as the highest rid value within the range of $[\text{rid}_c - 1, \text{rid}_c - \gamma]$ if the following holds:

$$\text{rid} = \underset{\text{rid} \in [\text{rid}_c - \gamma, \text{rid}_c - 1]}{\arg \max} \left\{ \overline{B}_{t_{\text{rec}}(\text{rid}, \text{snum})} \geq \theta_B^{\downarrow} \right\}. \tag{A.4}$$

Otherwise, rid of the requesting segment is decided as

$$\text{rid} = \underset{\text{rid} \in [0, \text{rid}_c - \gamma - 1]}{\arg \max} \left\{ br_{\text{rid}} < br_{\text{rid}_c} \frac{\text{MSD}}{\text{SFT}} \right\}, \tag{A.5}$$

where br_{rid} and br_{rid_c} denote the media bitrates with representation ID equals to rid and rid_c.

B. Caching Status Update and Prediction Process

The caching status update and consecutive prediction method (summarized in Section 5.1.2) includes the following processes.

Process 1. Caching statuses of subsequent segments is updated as those signaled from the proxy cache. rid is set to $\text{rid}_c - \gamma$, snum is set to snum_c, and t_{req} (rid, snum) is set to the current time.

Process 2. Emulate issuing a request for snum(th) segment at t_{req} (rid, snum) and the time to receive the segment, that is, t_{rec} (rid, snum), which can be predicted as

$$t_{\text{rec}} \, (\text{rid}, \text{snum})$$
$$= t_{\text{req}} \, (\text{rid}, \text{snum}) + \overline{\text{SFT}} \, (\text{rid}, \text{snum}). \tag{B.1}$$

Then, t_{req} (rid, snum + 1) is set to t_{rec} (rid, snum). The scheduling method presented in [6] is deployed to request and receive segment sequentially. But, the idling period between two consecutive requests is set as in [11].

Process 3. Emulate signaling the earliest uncached "anticipated segment" information to the proxy cache if there is an uncached segment in several "anticipated segments" in a certain sliding window (w_f). The earliest one is conveyed to the proxy cache so that the latter can prefetch it. Therefore, if an earliest uncached "anticipated segment" information is conveyed to the proxy cache, then the client updates the caching status of the uncached "anticipated segment" as "being fetched" and estimates the time instant of caching the "being fetched" segments, that is, t_{cache}, which is predicted as

$$t_{\text{cache}} \, (\text{rid}, \text{snum})$$
$$= t_{\text{req}} \, (\text{rid}, \text{snum}) + \widetilde{\text{SFT}}_{s2p} \, (\text{rid}). \tag{B.2}$$

Process 4. Update the caching status of the "anticipated segments" from "being fetched" to "cached" if the time to request the next segment, that is, t_{req} (rid, snum + 1), is larger than t_{cache} (rid, snum).

Process 5. Increase snum and go to step 2 if snum $\leq$ snum$_c$ + w.

Process 6. Increase rid and go to step 1 if rid $\leq$ rid$_c$ + γ.

Processes 5 and 6 are used to consecutively check subsequent segments specified by snum and rid which are in the range of [snum$_c$, snum$_c$ + w] and [rid$_c$ - γ, rid$_c$ + γ], respectively.

C. Measured SFTs

The measured SFTs from the origin server to the proxy cache and from the proxy cache to the DASH client, that is, $\widetilde{SFT}_{s2p}$ (rid) and $\widetilde{SFT}_{p2c}$ (rid), are used in the consecutive SFT prediction in Section 5.1.1. This appendix explains how $\widetilde{SFT}_{s2p}$ (rid) and $\widetilde{SFT}_{p2c}$ (rid) are measured by the DASH client.

C.1. SFT Measurement from the Proxy Cache to the DASH Client. The $\widetilde{SFT}_{p2c}$ (rid) can be specified as SFT measured by the DASH client minus SFT from the origin server to the proxy cache, which depends on the caching status of the segment.

Each time after receiving a new segment, the recent sample of measured SFT from the proxy cache to the DASH client ($\widetilde{SFT}'_{p2c}$) is specified as follows.

Case 1. The received segment is a cached segment by the proxy cache, and the measured SFT by the DASH client ($\widetilde{SFT}^c$) is $\widetilde{SFT}'_{p2c}$; hence, $\widetilde{SFT}'_{p2c}$ can be set as

$$\widetilde{SFT}'_{p2c} (\text{rid}_c) = \widetilde{SFT}^c, \tag{C.1}$$

where $\widetilde{SFT}^c$ can be measured by the DASH client.

Case 2. The received segment is a being fetched segment by the proxy cache, and $\widetilde{SFT}'_{p2c}$ is determined as

$$\widetilde{SFT}'_{p2c} (\text{rid}_c) = \widetilde{SFT}^c - \left(t_{cache} - t_{req} \right), \tag{C.2}$$

where t_{req} and $\widetilde{SFT}^c$ can be measured by the DASH client, and t_{cache} is measured at the proxy cache and informed to the DASH client.

Case 3. The received segment is uncached, and $\widetilde{SFT}'_{p2c}$ can be specified as

$$\widetilde{SFT}'_{p2c} (\text{rid}_c) = \widetilde{SFT}^c - \widetilde{SFT}^p, \tag{C.3}$$

where $\widetilde{SFT}^p$ is measured at the proxy cache and informed to the DASH client.

Each time after receiving a new segment, $\widetilde{SFT}_{p2c}$ (rid) is updated from the previous $\widetilde{SFT}_{p2c}$ (rid) and the recent sample of $\widetilde{SFT}_{p2c}$ (rid$_c$), that is, $\widetilde{SFT}'_{p2c}$ (rid$_c$), as

$$\widetilde{SFT}_{p2c} (\text{rid})$$
$$= \alpha\widetilde{SFT}_{p2c} (\text{rid}) + \beta\widetilde{SFT}'_{p2c} (\text{rid}_c) \left(\frac{br_{\text{rid}}}{br_{\text{rid}_c}} \right), \tag{C.4}$$

where α and β are weighting factors of the previous estimate and the recent measurement sample, and br_{rid} and br_{rid_c} denote the media bitrates of representation with representation ID equals to rid and rid$_c$, respectively. Since the SFT is proportional to the encoded media bitrates, the scaling factor, that is, ($br_{\text{rid}}/br_{\text{rid}_c}$), is multiplied to represent $\widetilde{SFT}'_{p2c}$ in terms of rid. A segment typically contains several seconds of media duration (five seconds are used in this paper). This is already long in terms of providing an effective rate adaptation method to promptly react to bandwidth changes. So, α and β are both set to 0.5.

C.2. SFT Measurement from the Origin Server to the Proxy Cache. The idea of specifying $\widetilde{SFT}_{s2p}$ (rid) is to use $\widetilde{SFT}^p$, which is measured at the proxy cache and informed from the proxy cache to the DASH client.

Each time after receiving a new segment, a recent sample of measured SFT from the origin server to the proxy cache ($\widetilde{SFT}'_{s2p}$) is specified as

$$\widetilde{SFT}'_{s2p} (\text{rid}) = \widetilde{SFT}^p \cdot \left(\frac{br_{\text{rid}}}{br_{\text{rid}_r}} \right), \tag{C.5}$$

where $\widetilde{SFT}^p$ denotes the measured SFT from the origin server to the proxy cache for the recently cached segment, and br_{rid_r} denotes the bitrate of the recently cached segment. The cached segment is considered as recently cached segment if the duration from start time to fetch a segment to the current time is less than or equal to a certain threshold (ε). The candidates consist of a list of segments having segment numbers in the range of [snum$_c$ - w_p, snum$_c$ + w] and rid in the range of [rid$_c$-γ, rid$_c$+γ]. Then, $\widetilde{SFT}_{s2p}$ (rid$_c$), is estimated as

$$\widetilde{SFT}_{s2p} (\text{rid}) = \alpha\widetilde{SFT}_{s2p} (\text{rid}) + \beta\widetilde{SFT}'_{s2p} (\text{rid}), \tag{C.6}$$

where both α and β are also set to 0.5.

It may occur that $\widetilde{SFT}_{s2p}$ or $\widetilde{SFT}'_{s2p}$ in (C.6) does not exist when updating $\widetilde{SFT}_{s2p}$. For example, α (β) can be set as 1 if $\widetilde{SFT}'_{s2p}$(or $\widetilde{SFT}_{s2p}$) does not exist. In case both do not exist, $\widetilde{SFT}_{s2p}$ is estimated as a predefined value such as half of MSD. Similar process is applied to update $\widetilde{SFT}_{s2p}$ in (C.4).

If a segment which has not been fully received by the proxy cache but the scaled spent time for fetching the part of the segment as in (C.5) was already larger than $\widetilde{SFT}_{s2p}$, then

$\widetilde{\text{SFT}}_{s2p}$ (rid) is updated according to (C.6) by considering the scaled spent time as $\widetilde{\text{SFT}}'_{s2p}$.

In case there is no $\widetilde{\text{SFT}}'_{s2p}$ for a certain period of time, for example, 60s as used in our simulation, the client estimates that the segments are continuously cached in a relatively long period of time at the current representation. The client indicates to the proxy cache the adjacent higher representation as the representation for the anticipated segments so that the proxy cache can prefetch the segment from the higher representation. So, $\widetilde{\text{SFT}}_{s2p}$ (rid) can be updated even in case the current representation is fully cached.

References

[1] R. Fielding, J. Gettys, J. C. Mogul et al., "Hypertext Transfer Protocol-HTTP/1.1," RFC 2616, June 1999.

[2] T. Kim and M. H. Ammar, "Receiver buffer requirement for video streaming over TCP," in *Visual Communications and Image Processing (VCIP '06)*, Proceedings of SPIE, San Jose, Calif, USA, January 2006.

[3] "3GPP TS 26.234 Release 9: Transparent end-to-end packet-switched streaming service (PSS); protocols and codecs".

[4] "ISO/IEC 23009-1: Dynamic adaptive streaming over HTTP (DASH)-Part 1: Media presentation description and segment formats," Draft International Standard, August 30, 2011.

[5] "3GPP TS 26.247 Release 10: Transparent end-to-end packet-switched streaming Service (PSS); Progressive download and dynamic adaptive Streaming over HTTP (3GP-DASH)," http://www.3gpp.org/ftp/Specs/html-info/26247.htm.

[6] C. Liu, I. Bouazizi, and M. Gabbouj, "Rate adaptation for adaptive HTTP streaming," in *Proceedings of the 2nd Annual ACM Multimedia Systems Conference (MMSys'11)*, pp. 169–174, San Jose, Calif, USA, February 2011.

[7] C. Liu, I. Bouazizi, M. M. Hannuksela, and M. Gabbouj, "Rate adaptation for dynamic adaptive streaming over HTTP in content distribution network," *Signal Processing*, vol. 27, no. 4, pp. 288–311, 2012.

[8] N. Färber, S. Döhla, and J. Issing, "Adaptive progressive download based on the MPEG-4 file format," *Journal of Zhejiang University Science A*, vol. 7, supplement 1, pp. 106–111, 2006.

[9] H. Riiser, P. Vigmostad, C. Griwodz, and P. Halvorsen, "Bitrate and video quality planning for mobile streaming scenarios using a GPS-based bandwidth lookup service," in *Proceedings of the IEEE International Conference on Multimedia and Expo (ICME '11)*, Barcelona, Spain, July 2011.

[10] S. Chen, B. Shen, S. Wee, and X. Zhang, "Designs of high quality streaming proxy systems," in *Proceedings of the 23 Annual Joint Conference of the IEEE Computer and Communications Societies (INFOCOM '04)*, pp. 1512–1521, Hong Kong, China, March 2004.

[11] C. Liu, I. Bouazizi, and M. Gabbouj, "Parallel adaptive HTTP media streaming," in *Proceedings of the International Conference on Computer Communications and Networks (ICCCN '11)*, Maui, Hawaii, August 2011.

[12] R. Fielding, J. Gettys, J. Mogul et al., Eds., "HTTP/1.1, part 6: Caching," draft-ietf-httpbis-p6-cache-17 (work in progress), October 2011.

[13] "The network simulator Ns-2," http://www.isi.edu/nsnam/ns/.

[14] V. Jacobson, R. Braden, and D. Borman, "TCP extensions for high performance," RFC1323, May 1992.

[15] H. Zhang, Y. Zhang, and Y. Liu, "Modeling internet link delay based on measurement," in *Proceedings of the International Conference on Electronic Computer Technology (ICECT '09)*, Macau, China, February 2009.

10

Bandwidth Management in Wireless Home Networks for IPTV Solutions

Tamás Jursonovics[1] and Sándor Imre[2]

[1] *Deutsche Telekom AG—Products & Innovation, T-Online-Allee 1, 64295 Darmstadt, Germany*
[2] *Department of Telecommunications, Budapest University of Technology, Budapest, Hungary*

Correspondence should be addressed to Tamás Jursonovics; jursonovicst@gmail.com

Academic Editor: Massimiliano Laddomada

The optimal allocation of the retransmission bandwidth is essential for IPTV service providers to ensure maximal service quality. This paper highlights the relevance of the wireless transport in today's IPTV solution and discusses how this new media affects the existing broadcast technologies. A new Markovian channel model is developed to address the optimization issues of the retransmission throughput, and a new method is presented which is evaluated by empirical measurements followed by mathematical analysis.

1. Preface

The terminology of Open IPTV Forum (OIPF) specification release 2 [1] has been chosen to describe the internet protocol television IPTV features in this paper because we experience a wide diversity of terms in several journals which may confuse the reader. We believe that the OIPF terms are straightforward, and they can be easily interpreted on any IPTV solutions although our work is independent from the standard itself.

2. Motivation

The telecommunication industry is tardily changing. The emerging market of the new generation over-the-top (OTT) services from Google, Microsoft, Apple, or Amazon had put a big pressure on operators to move away from the traditional telecom model and assess threats and opportunities from OTT players. There is a big race for the customers today, and legacy industry has to extend its portfolio with various value adding services like triple-play, rich communication, or mobile payment. This paper evaluates one specific topic of this competition, the video broadcasting services.

We have observed the rapid evolution of the IPTV services in the last decade. The high-definition broadcast got popular since its introduction in 2004, and the accessibility of 3D content is growing year by year. The consumer electronic devices become integrated part of our life, customers access digital content from set-top boxes (STBs) to tablets and mobile devices. From the IPTV service provider point of view, the demand of high-quality services emerged; however, the infrastructure of the access network remained the same. The main technology of telecommunication operators providing internet remained the 20–30 years old twisted copper pairs.

On one hand, the IPTV Service Providers are motivated by the maximization of their customer reach, but in many cases digital subscriber line xDSL offers inadequate bandwidth for high quality services [1]. access network providers need to find a solution which enables them to utilize their current infrastructure. The answers may include the implementation of a more advanced encoding algorithm (H.264, H.265) which results in having the same quality on smaller throughput [2] or the introduction of a hybrid service which replaces the most bandwidth consuming scheduled content transport with digital video broadcasting DVB-X technology [3], the usage of progressive download, or, as we point out in our work, the implementation of a more effective bandwidth allocation in the access network which would ensure a more efficient transport.

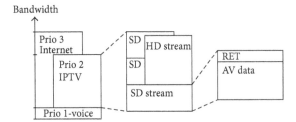

FIGURE 1: Bandwidth allocation in the access network.

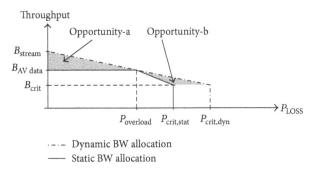

FIGURE 2: Static versus dynamic bandwidth allocation.

On the other hand, the service portability allows consumers to access the content not only on STBs, but also from various hand-held devices. Today the prime wireless access technology within the consumer domain is the wireless local area network WLAN connection, therefore service platform providers have to adapt their IPTV solution to support the specific requirements of this wireless communication channel.

Most of the current research papers [4–6] take only one of the above mentioned two aspects into consideration. The effect of the wireless channel is usually addressed on the media access control layer, and the research of the IPTV distribution focuses only on the quality of the fixed network infrastructure. Our research does address the above described overlap of the IPTV delivery over WLAN in a limited resource environment of xDSL technology. We present the concept and main problems of bandwidth allocation in Section 3. Our new theoretical model is introduced by Section 4. We develop a more effective bandwidth allocation algorithm in Section 5, which we evaluate and validate. Finally, Section 6 concludes our work and shows some potential further application areas.

3. Bandwidth Allocation

Let us begin the discussion of bandwidth management by introducing a typical triple-play bandwidth allocation scheme on Figure 1. Access network providers usually dedicate a reserved bandwidth in the access network for voice communication and share the remaining throughput between IPTV and internet services with a priority for the former one.

The actual throughput of IPTV service depends on the user's configuration. In most of the cases, a token-based stream management allows the customers to simultaneously receive multiple streams for live viewing or recording purposes (1SD+1HD or 3SD+0HD).

One token allocates bandwidth for the AV (audio-video) data transport and reserves a dedicated bandwidth for the retransmission RET service. We discuss the problem and tradeoff of this bandwidth allocation, therefore, in the following paragraphs, we are going to describe it in details.

The balance between the assigned bandwidth for AV data and the reserved bandwidth for RET service is crucial for achieving the maximal quality in IPTV solutions. On one hand the stream bandwidth as constant in time (because of the widely applied is considered constant bitrate CBR video

encoding) the more throughput is assigned for the AV data and the better stream quality can be achieved by the increase of the encoding bitrate but the less opportunity is given for error correction. A smooth sharp stream may be disturbed by blocking or full frame outages due to the insufficient RET throughput. On the other hands reserving high bandwidth for error correction degrades the overall stream quality due to the low encoding bitrate. Based on different network installations, the ratio of RET bandwidth to AV data is usually tuned between 10 and 25%, but a suboptimal value may significantly reduce the throughput and, quality of an IPTV Solution.

4. Proposed Model for Bandwidth Allocation IPTV Solutions in WLAN Home Networks

The main concept and benefits of our research are showed by Figure 2. The solid line represents the theoretical throughput of the AV data stream at various packet loss probabilities in case of static bandwidth allocation. The function is constant till $P_{overload}$ loss probability, where the loss rate is so high that the retransmission traffic fully occupies its reserved bandwidth. Above this, rate retransmission does not have enough bandwidth to recover all the packet losses; therefore, the actual throughput of AV data stream is decreasing (not transmitted packets), and customers experience quality deterioration. We also declare a critical bandwidth value (B_{crit}) for AV data transmission. [Below this value, it does not make sense to provide IPTV service due to the massive losses.

A dynamic bandwidth allocation (dash-dot line on Figure 2) increases the throughput of the AV stream at low packet loss rates to achieve a better quality for the IPTV service (opportunity-a). Secondly, at higher loss rates, the throughput of AV stream decreased to avoid double packet delivery (opportunity-b) which enables the operator to expand the value of the critical packet loss rate ($P_{crit,dyn}$) and provides a lower quality but error-free IPTV service in a worst environment.

In this paper we present only one part of our overall research, the optimal selection of the retransmission throughput. Our method—introduced by the upcoming sections—predicts the loss attributes of the wireless transmission and defines the optimal value of the RET throughput considering the overall loss parameters with the aim of

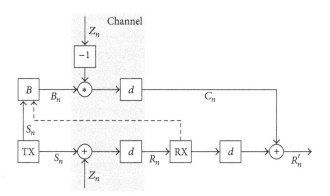

FIGURE 3: Channel model.

minimizing packet losses. First, we describe the channel and the bandwidth models.

4.1. The Channel Model.

Considering the requirements above and the attributes of a WLAN transport, we decided to introduce a discrete-time channel and a Markov model for the mathematical description of the UNIT-17 interface (AV data streams in the Access and residential Networks). We consider not only the packet arrival, but also the retransmission traffic as a discrete-time stochastic process, and we prove that it is a homogeneous Markov chain.

Let $S_n = \{0,\ \text{for all } n\}$ represent the number of sent packets at the time n on Figure 3, TX the multicast content delivery function, $Z_n = \{0; 1, \text{for all } n\}$ an additive white noise in the wireless communication channel, d the transmission delay, and RX the open IPTV terminal function (OITF). The received packets are expressed with $R_n = \{0,\ \text{for successful packet transmission}; 1,\ \text{for packet loss}\}$. We assume that the receiver detects a packet loss (by checking the sequence numbers of packets) and requests the retransmission $B_n = \{1,\ \text{for a packet retransmission}; 0\ \text{otherwise}\}$ of every lost packets only once from the B Fast Channel Change/Retransmission server. We also assume that the retransmission request communication is protected by an error-free protocol, like TCP. By this definition, we obtain

$$B_n = R_n = Z_{n-d}. \qquad (1)$$

The B_n signal travels through the same wireless channel; therefore, it is also effected by the same Z_n noise, and it may be also lost. We model this effect by expressing the received correction signal $C_n = \{0, 1\}$ with three operators, an inverter (-1), a multiplier $(^*)$, and a channel transmission delay (d). These functions enable us to assign the value of 1 for C_n only in the case when the retransmission signal is not effected by the channel noise (not lost), and the value of 0 otherwise.

The final received and corrected signal $R'_n = \{0,\ \text{for successful packet transmission}, 1\ \text{for packet loss (unsuccessful retransmission), and } 2\ \text{for successful packet retransmission}\}$ is

$$R'_n = R_{n-d} + C_n = S_{n-2d} + Z_{n-2d} + B_{n-d} * Z_{n-d}^{-1}$$
$$= S_{n-2d} + Z_{n-2d} + Z_{n-2d} * Z_{n-d}^{-1}. \qquad (2)$$

Let us observe that the first term of the addition equals to 0 by definition and the last term equals to the sampling of the Z_n white noise with its own delayed signal. The autocorrelation of the white noise is zero for all nonzero time shifts [7]; therefore, R'_n can be described as a sequence of an independent random variable which satisfies the Markov property. $X_n \overset{\text{def}}{=} R'_n$ is a homogeneous Markov chain.

Let $X_n = 0$ if the nth packet is received correctly; $X_n = 1$ if the nth packet is lost and has not been retransmitted; finally $X_n = 2$ if the nth packet is successfully retransmitted after loss. We analyzed and described a three-state Markov model in our previous publication; therefore, we simply list most important properties. For a detailed discussion including the resolution of (3)–(6) and for the meaning of the probabilities, please refer to our former paper [8].

The transition matrix

$$\begin{bmatrix} 1 - p_{01} - p_{02} & p_{01} & p_{02} \\ p_{10} & 1 - p_{10} - p_{12} & p_{12} \\ p_{20} & p_{21} & 1 - p_{20} - p_{21} \end{bmatrix}. \qquad (3)$$

The steady-state packet loss rate

$$P_{\text{LOSS,steady}} = (p_{02}p_{21} + p_{01}p_{20} + p_{01}p_{21})$$
$$\times (p_{01}p_{20} + p_{01}p_{21} + p_{02}p_{21} + p_{10}p_{02} + p_{12}p_{01}$$
$$+ p_{12}p_{02} + p_{21}p_{10} + p_{20}p_{10} + p_{20}p_{12})^{-1}. \qquad (4)$$

The steady-state packet retransmission rate

$$P_{\text{RET,steady}} = (p_{10}p_{02} + p_{12}p_{01} + p_{12}p_{02})$$
$$\times (p_{01}p_{20} + p_{01}p_{21} + p_{02}p_{21} + p_{10}p_{02} + p_{12}p_{01}$$
$$+ p_{12}p_{02} + p_{21}p_{10} + p_{20}p_{10} + p_{20}p_{12})^{-1}. \qquad (5)$$

And the probability of loss burst with length l

$$P_{\text{RET,burst}}(l) = (1 - p_{20} - p_{21})^{l-1}(p_{20} + p_{21}). \qquad (6)$$

4.2. The Model of Bandwidth Limitation.

The previous section introduced how the wireless channel affects the packet transmission, and now we are going to analyze the the bandwidth allocation in IPTV solutions.

We introduce three planes of the IPTV packet transmission. The *transmitter* plane represents the provider's network, *receiver* plane represents the OITF, and *playout* plan represents the content presentation within the OITF. The events of the packet loss usually show a burstiness in wireless communication [9–11]. Therefore, we investigate an intraburst loss on Figure 4 after the first k consecutive packet losses (b) the receiver requests them for retransmission (c) which packets are delivered within the allocated bandwidth for packet transmission (d) to the presentation device (e). For a successful retransmission, all retransmitted packet should

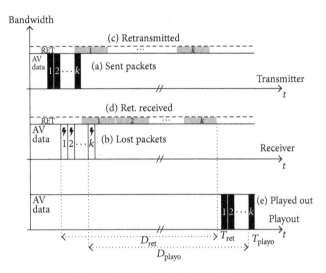

FIGURE 4: Intraburst retransmission.

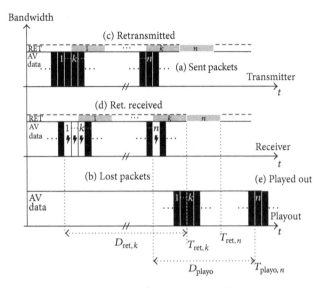

FIGURE 5: Interburst retransmission.

arrive earlier than their presentation time ($T_{\text{ret}} \leq T_{\text{playo}}$). Expressing this condition with the durations

$$D_{\text{pkg}} + \text{RTT} + k\frac{B_{\text{AV}}}{B_{\text{RET}}}D_{\text{pkg}} < (k-1)D_{\text{pkg}} + D_{\text{playo}}, \quad (7)$$

where D_{pkg} is the average transmission time for a packet, RTT is the round-trip time, B_{AV} and B_{RET} are the allocated bandwidths on the communication channel, and D_{playo} is the packet playout buffer in the OITF. The formula of the maximal number of consecutive packets which can be successfully retransmitted is defined as

$$k_{\text{RET,intra,max}}\left(\frac{B_{\text{RET}}}{B_{\text{AV}}}\right) = \frac{D_{\text{playo}} - 2D_{\text{pkg}} - \text{RTT}}{D_{\text{pkg}}\left((1/(B_{\text{RET}}/B_{\text{AV}})) - 1\right)}. \quad (8)$$

The actual throughput of the AV stream may vary by installations; therefore, we expressed this value as a ratio of B_{RET} and B_{AV}.

Second, we highlight the barrier of interburst behavior on Figure 5. After a loss of long burst, the retransmission bandwidth is occupied by the traffic of the retransmitted packets even if there is no other packet loss at the time in the video stream. This means that a loss event *blocks* the retransmission channel. We are interested in the following question: assuming a $k < k_{\text{RET,intra,max}}$ long burst of loss, after how many packets (n) can a new loss burst occur which would be also successfully retransmitted (e.g., what is the minimal distance ($n - k$) between two loss bursts if the first burst lasts for k packets?). Now, $T_{\text{ret},k} \stackrel{\text{def}}{=} T_{\text{playo},k}$, and $T_{\text{ret},n} \leq T_{\text{playo},n}$. Figure 5 shows that

$$D_{\text{pkg}} + \text{RTT} + (k+1)\frac{B_{\text{AV}}}{B_{\text{RET}}}D_{\text{pkg}} < (n-1)D_{\text{pkg}} + D_{\text{playo}},$$

$$(9)$$

where $n > k$. Expressing n

$$n_{\text{RET,inter,min}}\left(k, \frac{B_{\text{AV}}}{B_{\text{RET}}}\right) = (k+1)\frac{B_{\text{AV}}}{B_{\text{RET}}} + \frac{\text{RTT} - D_{\text{playo}}}{D_{\text{pkg}}} + 2.$$

$$(10)$$

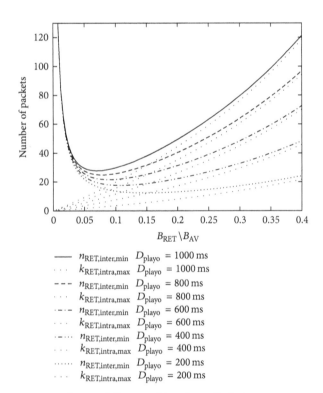

——	$n_{\text{RET,inter,min}}$	$D_{\text{playo}} = 1000$ ms
$\cdots$	$k_{\text{RET,intra,max}}$	$D_{\text{playo}} = 1000$ ms
– – –	$n_{\text{RET,inter,min}}$	$D_{\text{playo}} = 800$ ms
$\cdots$	$k_{\text{RET,intra,max}}$	$D_{\text{playo}} = 800$ ms
–·–·–	$n_{\text{RET,inter,min}}$	$D_{\text{playo}} = 600$ ms
$\cdots$	$k_{\text{RET,intra,max}}$	$D_{\text{playo}} = 600$ ms
–··–··–	$n_{\text{RET,inter,min}}$	$D_{\text{playo}} = 400$ ms
$\cdots$	$k_{\text{RET,intra,max}}$	$D_{\text{playo}} = 400$ ms
$\cdots\cdots$	$n_{\text{RET,inter,min}}$	$D_{\text{playo}} = 200$ ms
$\cdots$	$k_{\text{RET,intra,max}}$	$D_{\text{playo}} = 200$ ms

FIGURE 6: Intra- and interburst limitation.

We present the above declared functions (8)–(10) on Figure 6. This graph shows that at small values of $B_{\text{AV}}/B_{\text{RET}}$ (0%–15%), the effect of the inter-burst blocking is greater. For example, at 5% the maximal consecutive burst length is 10 packets, and the retransmission channel is blocked by this traffic for 30 packets. Above 20%, this effect becomes insignificant.

We also state that with grater playout buffer (D_{playo}), RET is able to correct larger loss bursts at the price of a greater end-to-end delay.

5. The Optimal Retransmission

In this section, we introduce a new method for retransmission bandwidth allocation based on our models with the aim of achieving a better video quality. The method is realized in a test environment, and our hypothesis is measured and proved.

Traditional RET algorithms request all lost packets; therefore, they have to implement a network layer traffic shaping to fit the actual retransmission throughput into the allocated bandwidth. This is usually done by packet queuing which increases the overall packet retransmission time; therefore, the probability of a retransmission packet arrives late (after its playout time) is great. Several papers addressed this problem [12], introducing a selective retransmission protocol by evaluating the traffic on the application level, and assigning priority and importance for each packet retransmissions.

The main advantages of our method are the minimal additional delay, the low resource needs, and the consideration of the wireless channel. Our method assess the RET mechanism on the network layer, skips (forbids) the retransmission requests of a lost packet according to the above described intra- and interburst channel blocking, and takes the special properties of the wireless channel into consideration. Our algorithm consists of three steps.

(1) The packet arrival process is continuously monitored for packet loss.

(2) $k_{RET,intra,max}$ and $n_{RET,inter,min}$ are calculated.

(3) A lost packet is requested retransmission only if the intra- and inter-burst channel blocking do not forbid the retransmission; otherwise, the retransmission request is skipped.

5.1. Empirical Evaluation. To evaluate our model and methods, we followed the OIPF system architecture [13] and implemented the following OIPF functions in a test environment (source codes are available on [14]).

(1) Multicast content delivery function, *ser*, c++ application generates UDP/RTP multicast traffic and implements a simple control protocol hosted by an x86 Linux server connected to the core network of Deutsche Telekom (DT).

(2) RET server, *ret*, c++ application stores the multicast traffic in a circular buffer and implements a simple retransmission request protocol hosted by the same x86 Linux server.

(3) Unit-17 interface, part a was realized by the ADSL2+ access network of DT and was provided by a DLink ADSL modem.

(4) Unit-17 interface, part b was realized by a 802.11 b WLAN network and was provided by a Cisco 1200 series wireless access point (AP) connected to the ADSL modem.

(5) OITF: *cli*, c++ application implements a simple multicast receiver and controls functions of the multicast

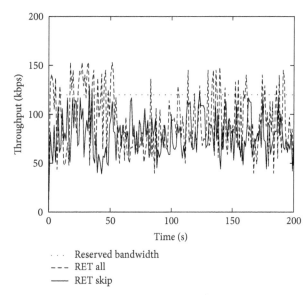

FIGURE 7: Retransmission throughput.

content delivery function and RET server. Hosted on a x86 Linux laptop connected to the Cisco AP.

Figure 7 shows the throughput of the retransmission stream in two cases: traditional retransmission (*RET all*: all lost packets were requested for retransmission) and our new retransmission method (*RET skip*: retransmission requests may be skipped based on the actual parameters of the channel). It can be clearly seen that our algorithm kept the retransmission throughput under its dedicated bandwidth which ensured the in-time delivery of the retransmission packets however we intentionally skipped those retransmission requests which in time delivery would not be ensured due to the channel blocking (intra- and inter-burst effect).

The main benefit of our method is showed by Figure 8. We compared the total packet loss rate in the above mentioned two cases, and we found that with the smart skipping of packet retransmission requests, we were able to achieve a better (smaller) loss rate then retransmitting all of the packets. Our method avoided the effect of late retransmission. IF a packet is requested for retransmission without ensuring the necessary transport bandwidth, then it may delay further retransmission requests which may arrive to late after their playout time. This causes an inefficient retransmission bandwidth utilization which increases the overall packet loss rate (on the *playout* plane).

5.2. The Effect of the Intraburst Limitation. Let us analyze our results theoretically as well. In this and in the upcoming section, we characterize the Unit-17 interface with the transition matrix of our Markov model and the design attributes of the access network. Applying the intra- and inter-burst limitations on our model, we derive the probability of the retransmission skip caused by our algorithm. Finally, we express the overall packet loss rate which is a key indicator for the quality of the video transmission.

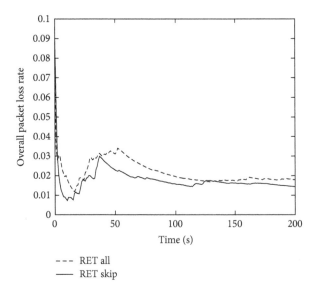

FIGURE 8: Overall packet loss rate.

The intra-burst limitations have a significant short-time effect if the distance of the burst losses is great ($p_{00} \rightarrow 1$). Our question is about the probability of retransmission packet skip. First, we calculate the maximal number of consecutive retransmission requests

$$k_{\text{RET,intra,max}} = \frac{D_{\text{playo}} - 2D_{\text{pkg}} - \text{RTT}}{D_{\text{pkg}} \left((B_{\text{AV}}/B_{\text{RET}}) - 1 \right)}. \quad (11)$$

The probability of l long retransmission request is given by the Markov model (6). We calculate the probability of m packet skips if the retransmission burst is greater than $k_{\text{R,burst,max}}$, which is

$$P_{\text{skip}}(m) = (p_{20} + p_{21}) \left(1 - p_{20} - p_{21} \right)^{k_{\text{RET,intra,max}} - 1 + m}. \quad (12)$$

The overall probability of a packet skip is given by

$$P_{\text{skip,intra}} = \lim_{i \to \infty} \sum_{i=1}^{\infty} \frac{P_{\text{skip}}(i)}{i}$$

$$= \lim_{i \to \infty} \sum_{i=1}^{\infty} \frac{(p_{20} + p_{21}) \left(1 - p_{20} - p_{21} \right)^{k_{\text{RET,intra,max}} - 1 + i}}{i}$$

$$= (p_{20} + p_{21}) \left(1 - p_{20} - p_{21} \right)^{k_{\text{RET,intra,max}} - 1}$$

$$\times \lim_{i \to \infty} \sum_{i=1}^{\infty} \frac{(1 - p_{20} - p_{21})^{i}}{i}. \quad (13)$$

Let us observe that the last sum can be expressed as a special form of the polylogarithm (also known as Jonquière's function)

$$Li_s(z)|_{s=1} = \sum_{k=1}^{\infty} \frac{z^k}{k^s} \bigg|_{s=1} = \sum_{k=1}^{\infty} \frac{z^k}{k}, \quad (14)$$

for every $-1 \le z < 1$. ($1 - p_{20} - P_{21}$ satisfies this criteria. Therefore using the well-known formula of $Li_1(z) = -\ln(1 - z)$), the equation can be expressed in a closed form

$$
\begin{aligned}
P_{\text{skip,intra}} &= (p_{20} + p_{21}) \left(1 - p_{20} - p_{21} \right)^{k_{\text{RET,intra,max}} - 1} \\
&\quad \times (-1) \ln \left(1 - (1 - p_{20} - p_{21}) \right) \\
&= (p_{20} + p_{21}) \left(1 - p_{20} - p_{21} \right)^{k_{\text{RET,intra,max}} - 1} \\
&\quad \times (-1) \ln \left(p_{20} + p_{21} \right).
\end{aligned} \quad (15)
$$

The overall packet loss can be expressed as a sum of the probability of packet skip (15) and the steady state probability of packet loss (4).

5.3. The Effect of the Interburst Limitation. We ask the same question as in the previous section, what is the probability of packet skip? Let us assume that the first burst is small enough to be retransmitted ($k < k_{\text{RET,intra,max}}$). The probability of retransmission burst is of l size is given by our Markov model (6). The probability of k retransmission burst followed by $n-k$ good transmission burst and a second retransmission

$$
\begin{aligned}
f(k, n) &= (p_{20} + p_{21}) \left(1 - p_{20} - p_{21} \right)^{k-1} p_{20} \\
&\quad \times (p_{01} + p_{02}) \\
&\quad \times (1 - p_{01} - p_{02})^{n-k-1} p_{02}.
\end{aligned} \quad (16)
$$

The first packet of the second retransmission burst is skipped if $n < n_{\text{RET,inter,min}}(k)$. From this, we can calculate the probability of one packet skip for k

$$P_{\text{skip,inter,k}} = \sum_{i=k}^{n_{\text{RET,inter,min}}(k)} f(k, i). \quad (17)$$

For the overal packet skip probability, we have to summarize (17) for every $k < k_{\text{R,burst,max}}$

$$P_{\text{skip,inter}} = \sum_{j=1}^{k_{\text{RET,intra,max}}} \sum_{i=j}^{n_{\text{RET,inter,min}}(j)} f(j, i). \quad (18)$$

The overall packet loss can be expressed as a sum of the probability of packet skip (18) and the steady-state probability of packet loss (4).

6. Conclusion

In this paper, we highlighted the relevance of the wireless transport in today's IPTV solutions, and we pointed out that it's and the access network's combined effect on the bandwidth management is not discussed deeply by publications. Our general research project targets this specific area by introducing several optimization methods from which we presented one, the optimization of the packet retransmission on the previous pages.

We created a new discrete-time channel model to describe the effect of the burst losses on the IPTV service quality and the role of the packet retransmission. We proved that it is a Markov Chain, and as part of our results, we expressed and evaluated its most important quantitative parameters. Using our model, we also introduced an algorithm for retransmission optimization in IPTV solutions over WLAN home networks.

As a further evaluation of our results, we created a testbed in alignment with the OPIF system architecture, and we performed the empirical analysis of our channel model and methods. We showed that our concept improved the overall packet loss characteristics. Furthermore, we enclosed a mathematical analysis of our algorithm, and we derived the theoretical packet loss probabilities to support our measurements.

In the next research phases, we are going to investigate, introduce, and leverage our theoretical results of throughput management in the adaptive bitrate streaming technologies for IPTV solutions, and we are going to evaluate our channel model in the media access control layer of the wireless access technologies.

References

[1] Open IPTV Forum, "Release 2 Specifications," http://www.oipf.tv/specifications.html.

[2] A. Abramowski, "Towards H. 265 video coding standard," in *Proceedings of the Photonics Applications in Astronomy, Communications, Industry, and High-Energy Physics Experiments*, vol. 8008 of *Proceedings of the SPIE*, 2011.

[3] H. Benot, *Digital Television: Satellite, Cable, Terrestrial, Iptv, Mobile Tv in the Dvb Framework*, Focal Press, 2008.

[4] M. M. Hassani, S. V. Jalali, and A. Akbari, "Evaluating TCP flows behavior by a mathematical model in WLAN," *Journal of Basic and Applied Scientific Research*, vol. 2, no. 3, pp. 2809–2814, 2012.

[5] A. C. Begen, "Error control for IPTV over xDSL networks," in *Proceedings of the 5th IEEE Consumer Communications and Networking Conference (CCNC '08)*, pp. 632–637, January 2008.

[6] H. Bobarshad, M. Van Der Schaar, and M. R. Shikh-Bahaei, "A low-complexity analytical modeling for cross-layer adaptive error protection in video over WLAN," *IEEE Transactions on Multimedia*, vol. 12, no. 5, pp. 427–438, 2010.

[7] A. Papoulis, *Probability, Random Variables and Stohastic Processes*, McGraw-Hill, 1965.

[8] T. Jursonovics and S. Imre, "Analysis of a new Markov model for packet loss characterization in IPTV Solutions," *Infocommunications Journal*, vol. 2, pp. 28–33, 2011.

[9] T. Jursonovics and Zs. Butyka, "The implementation and analysis of interactive multimedia mobile services," in *Proceedings of the 11th Microcoll Conference,*, pp. 149–152, Budapest, Hungary, 2003.

[10] T. Jursonovics, Zs. Butyka, and S. Imre, "Multimedia transmission over mobile networks," in *International Conference on Software, Telecommunications and Computer Networks (SoftCOM '04)*, pp. 453–457, Dubrovnik, Croatia, Ancona, Italy, 2004.

[11] A. Nafaa, T. Taleb, and L. Murphy, "Forward error correction strategies for media streaming over wireless networks," *IEEE Communications Magazine*, vol. 46, no. 1, pp. 72–79, 2008.

[12] Á. Huszák and S. Imre, "Source controlled semi-reliable multimedia streaming using selective retransmission in DCCP/IP networks," *Computer Communications*, vol. 31, no. 11, pp. 2676–2684, 2008.

[13] Open IPTV Forum, Functional Architecture [V2. 1] [2011-03-15], http://www.oipf.tv/specifications.html.

[14] http://www.mcl.hu/~jursonovics/.

11

A Secure and Stable Multicast Overlay Network with Load Balancing for Scalable IPTV Services

Tsao-Ta Wei,[1,2] Chia-Hui Wang,[1] Yu-Hsien Chu,[2,3] and Ray-I Chang[3]

[1] Department of Computer Science and Information Engineering, Ming Chuan University, No. 5, Deming Road., Guishan Township, Taoyuan County 333, Taiwan
[2] Technical Division, Develop Department, YES Information Incorporated, Xinyi District, Taipei 110, Taiwan
[3] Department of Engineering Science and Ocean Engineering, National Taiwan University, Taipei 106, Taiwan

Correspondence should be addressed to Chia-Hui Wang, wangch@mail.mcu.edu.tw

Academic Editor: Pin-Han Ho

The emerging multimedia Internet application IPTV over P2P network preserves significant advantages in scalability. IPTV media content delivered in P2P networks over public Internet still preserves the issues of privacy and intellectual property rights. In this paper, we use SIP protocol to construct a secure application-layer multicast overlay network for IPTV, called SIPTVMON. SIPTVMON can secure all the IPTV media delivery paths against eavesdroppers via elliptic-curve Diffie-Hellman (ECDH) key exchange on SIP signaling and AES encryption. Its load-balancing overlay tree is also optimized from peer heterogeneity and churn of peer joining and leaving to minimize both service degradation and latency. The performance results from large-scale simulations and experiments on different optimization criteria demonstrate SIPTVMON's cost effectiveness in quality of privacy protection, stability from user churn, and good perceptual quality of objective PSNR values for scalable IPTV services over Internet.

1. Introduction

Due to the prevalent broadband Internet access and advanced video compression techniques, the Internet Protocol Television (IPTV) has been emerging as one of the most popular Internet applications. IPTV can further benefit Internet users by entertainment, social, and business values, but IPTV faces more challenges of scalability, privacy, and service quality over the public Internet due to the conventional client-server architecture applied.

The success of well-known P2P video-streaming systems such as PPStream [1], PPLive [2], Sopcast [3], and TVants [4] has proven that P2P paradigm is a feasible solution to deliver bandwidth-hunger IPTV media content in large scale over the pervasive Internet. However, the above-mentioned proprietary P2P video-streaming systems still suffer the issues of long startup delays, significant video-switching delays, large peer playback lags, and security due to the peer heterogeneity and churn [5–7].

Therefore, the P2P overlay networks for future multimedia Internet should overcome the previous shortcomings to further promise quality of service, security, and experience to the IPTV end users. Moreover, the P2P overlay architecture for promising IPTV services should be not only easily convergent in heterogeneous networks, but also feasibly integrated with other Internet applications.

In this paper, we apply SIP protocol [8] to construct an application-layer multicast (ALM) overlay network, which is called SIPTVMON, with privacy protection, load balancing, and stability for IPTV to overcome the disadvantages previously mentioned in P2P video-streaming systems. Our contributions in proposed SIPTVMON for IPTV service are summarized as follows.

(i) Stability for Peer Heterogeneity and Churn. Since the peers (i.e., users) with ever-changing Internet access bandwidth may join and leave the IPTV service anytime as they wish, we continue to optimize SIPTVMON overlay tree with minimum SIP signaling overhead to achieve stable IPTV service by the product of average link bandwidth and service life time in peers.

(ii) Security Provision. Most of the IPTV content preserves intellectual property rights, so the content delivery paths in SIPTVMON tree are secured against Internet eavesdroppers via elliptic-curve Diffie-Hellman (ECDH) [9] key exchange algorithm and AES [10] encryption.

(iii) Shorter Service Delays. Users may enjoy rapidly switching different IPTV channels over P2P networks and suffer the significant video-switching delay and larger playback lag, so our proposed SIPTVMON provides not only the peer's graceful leaving procedures realized by SIP protocols, but also the above-mentioned stability optimization for peers' joining and leaving to minimize average service delay from the user churn.

(iv) Interoperability with Other Internet Applications. The applied SIP protocol in SIPTVMON has been widely and successfully deployed in Voice over IP (VoIP) applications. Moreover, the core of IP Multimedia Subsystem (IMS) [11] in 3G telecommunication is also constructed by SIP protocol. We believe that the proposed SIPTVMON framework not only can cooperate with SIP-enabled Internet applications like prevalent VoIP applications, but also is feasible to help IMS in 3G mobile networks to achieve scalable IPTV service provision in more cost-effective way.

The remainder of this paper is organized as follows. In Section 2, we describe the related works of ALM overlay network, privacy protection for IPTV media streaming, and SIP-signaling protocol. The details of proposed SIPTVMON architecture with security, load balancing, and stability are presented in Section 3. Section 4 describes simulation experiments for SIPTVMON and their performance results for P2P IPTV. Finally, we conclude the paper and future work.

2. Related Work

As shown in Figure 1, the logical topology applied in current P2P video-streaming technologies is roughly classified into tree, mesh (i.e., multiple trees), and hybrid of tree and mesh [12]. Though tree-based P2P structure preserves simplicity, it is vulnerable to peers' dynamics of heterogeneity and churn. Mesh-based P2P structure improves the resilience to the dynamics from peers, but it preserves more complex peer partnership relations. In this paper, we adopt tree-based, rather than mesh-based, P2P architecture in proposed SIPTVMON to cost-effectively achieve low service latency, security provision, and stability for IPTV users churn over Internet.

We briefly review the related works in proposed solutions to construct an application-layer multicast overlay network with privacy protection, load sharing, and stability for scalable IPTV service.

2.1. Application Layer Multicast (ALM). ALM is an application-level traversal method for IP multicast packets without the help from routers through unicast tunneling. ALM is also known as a cost-effective tool to construct overlay networks for large-scale Internet multimedia applications. ALM has the advantages of less overhead of maintenance than routers, provision of much larger multicast groups than IP multicast, less compatibility issues than IP multicast and, easier extension to new features like security, error control, stability, and so forth.

Because routers usually disable forwarding IP multicast packets to prevent the flooding of multicast data, self-organization algorithms for effective transmissions in logical topology of multicast overlay network become the essential of ALM mechanism.

As shown in Figure 1(a), a single-tree ALM aims to provide best-effort single-source data streaming with the optimization of reduced latency and loss rates. For example in [13, 14], to join an ALM tree for streaming data, a new member (i.e., multicast agent, MA, USA) must first connect to a directory server, a rendezvous point to which every member MA must connect at the first time. Then, it will be able to obtain a member list to find the lowest round trip time (RTT), loss rate, or bandwidth among existing members for the better quality of multimedia-streaming service from source ALM.

The mesh topology illustrated in Figure 1(b) is applied to provide bandwidth-consuming peer-to-peer video streaming with the advantages of avoiding replicating group management across multiple (per-source) trees, and resilience of member failure [15]. ALM mesh can be regarded as the superposed overlay of multiple spanning trees. Compared with the single-tree approach, the multiple-tree approach is more complicated.

In [16], a low-delay high-bandwidth mesh called Fast-Mesh for peer-to-peer live streaming is proposed. In this work, the authors propose a centralized heuristic with complete mesh knowledge to minimize the maximum delay of all peers in the mesh. They demonstrate via simulations that their solution can reach a small average delay of 50 ms to 100 ms for hundreds peers in the mesh with a source data rate of 10 kbps. In their experimental test bed over the Internet across several countries, the implemented Fast-Mesh still shows low delay, ranging from tens to 500 ms with a small data source rate of 30 kbps.

In our proposed SIPTVMON, a single-source ALM tree scheme is applied for its simplicity in not only the applied privacy protection, but also the tree adjustment in optimization of both scalability and stability for IPTV services. Moreover, the tree-based SIPTVMON can also lessen average service delays for large-scale peers and reduce the flow of control messages.

2.2. Privacy Protection for IPTV. The privacy protection for Internet video streaming is usually done by symmetric encryption for less time consuming. There are two kinds of symmetric encryption mechanisms. One is the full encryption approach; the other is selective encryption. Generally speaking, the main disadvantages of selective encryption are insufficient security and video content dependent. On the contrary, full encryption is often criticized for the longer calculation delay which is not suitable for real-time video

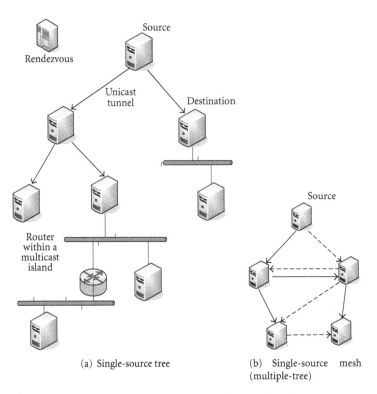

(a) Single-source tree

(b) Single-source mesh (multiple-tree)

FIGURE 1: P2P IPTV structure of tree and mesh.

streaming. However, based on the results of a processing speed experiment [17] on full encryption in 2007, the criticism of longer delays is not an issue. In this test, which involved a computer with Intel dual core 1.83 GHz, the encryption bit rate for triple DES, DES, and AES can attain to 104 Mbps, 272 Mbps, and 792 Mbps, respectively. The bit rate of video-streaming service on Internet is very rarely higher than 10 Mbps, thus showing that full encryption has the potential to support real-time video transmission like IPTV.

For the cost-effective privacy protection of real-time video streaming in IPTV, advanced encryption standard (AES), which is a symmetric-key encryption standard adopted by the US government, is most applicable to protect voice data from eavesdropper over Internet. The standard comprises three block ciphers, AES-128, AES-192, and AES-256, adopted from a larger collection originally published as Rijndael. Each of these ciphers has a 128-bit block size, with encryption key sizes of 128, 192, and 256 bits, respectively.

Since AES is a symmetric crypto system, it needs a key management infrastructure to issue a common secret key (i.e., session key) for later video encryption/decryption between sender and receiver in IPTV.

As summarized in [18], three different methods of the session key distribution are preshared key, public-key encryption, and the Diffie-Hellman (DH) key exchange [19]. There is only a very small amount of data that has to be exchanged in the preshared key method. But, it will incur the scalability issue in large group of communication peers. The public-key encryption can be used to create a scalable privacy-protection IPTV system and usually requires

public key infrastructure (PKI) to distribute public key. Its disadvantage is consuming much more resource than the preshared key.

Generally, the third method of DH also has the scalability to protect large-scale IPTV services without the need of PKI. To prevent DH from man-in-the-middle (MITM) attack, authentication [20] between sender and receiver is needed further. Thus, applying DH session key negotiation to protect IPTV services will consume more resource of bandwidth and computation than the previous ones but without the need of centralized PKI.

In SIPTVMON, we use the popular modified DH called elliptic curve DH (i.e., ECDH [9]) key exchange via SIP-signaling protocol, since ECDH preserves much less computation overhead to construct the secure multicast overlay tree for IPTV's privacy protection.

2.3. SIP Signaling for P2P IPTV. As illustrated in Figure 2, SIP [8] is the currently widely used signaling standards for VoIP call setup and management (e.g., registration, resource administration, status, and capability exchange). Session description protocol (SDP) [21] is SIP's companion protocol to explicitly present parameters of functions applied in call setup and session management, such as the key exchange information for negotiating secret key for DH signaling. real-time transport protocol (RTP) [22] is the well-known application-layer protocol for delivering real-time media data like IPTV video packets.

As shown in Figure 3, the option k in SDP within SIP can carry the public keys for DH signaling to negotiate a common secret key for encrypting the IPTV video in RTP

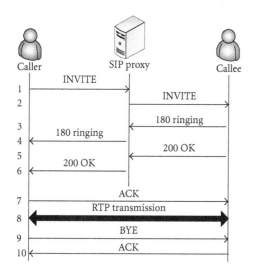

FIGURE 2: Basic operations of VoIP session via SIP signaling.

payload from source MA (sMA) to destination MA (dMA). Then, dMA can use this common secrete key to decrypt the encrypted RTP payload.

Since SIP with companion SDP not only can handle the setup, modification, and teardown of multimedia session, but also supports many extensions, enhancements, resource management, and interworking with other heterogeneous systems, such as privacy protection mentioned above, transferring information during ongoing session, instant messaging, and so forth, SIP is the best signaling protocol over Internet for the control messages applied to furnish the proposed solutions of security, load balancing, and stability in SIPTVMON for scalable IPTV services.

3. SIPTVMON: Secure ALM Overlay with Load-Balance and Stability for IPTV Using SIP

SIPTVMON is an overlay network composed of a super agent (SA, i.e., rendezvous) and different MAs on different multicast islands over Internet to effectively provide IPTV service for a dedicated media source from content server. SIPTVMON's MAs are dedicated computer systems or software applications to receive content data from sMA, then multicast it to their local subscribers, or unicast it again to one or more other dMAs over different multicast islands as illustrated in Figure 4. Besides, SA [23] will not only take the responsibilities to keep locations of MA and the detailed topology information of SIPTVMON but also help to forward the video from one source MA to destination MA, which is located in a private multicast island to furnish the ubiquitous IPTV service over the pervasive Internet.

However, the topology of SIPTVMON will change from time to time because the Internet users can subscribe or unsubscribe the IPTV service at any time, and the corresponding MA may join or leave the SIPTVMON while either its local users subscribe or no user subscribes the IPTV service. Meanwhile, every dMA in its multicast island may preserve different capabilities of system resources and outbound network bandwidth to forward the media content,

so we propose a load-sharing scheme for SIPTVMON to prevent overloading sMA from jeopardizing perceptual quality of IPTV service for end users.

3.1. MA Joins/Leaves SIPTVMON with Security Provision. According to the long tail theory of customer demographic [24], usually most of the customers, like newly joined MAs of SIPTVMON, will not stay with SIPTVMON for a long period. To further reduce the processing overhead of reconnecting disjoint trees in SIPTVMON while a nonleaf node of MA occasionally leaves SIPTVMON, the new dMA should be joined to the leaf node of MA in SIPTVMON.

The procedures of a new MA-joining SIPTVMON are illustrated in Figure 5 and described as follows.

(J1) New MA denoted as MA_{new} sends a SIP "REGISTER" request with specified content identifier and registration identifier to SA to ask SA for the connection address of a leaf MA, to which the MA_{new} can be connected and join the SIPTVMON tree.

(J2) SA plays a role of SIP proxy and oracle of SIPTVMON topology information to send back the SIP "OK" response with SDP body of corresponding connection address of a leaf node MA_{leaf}, in which the new MA_{new} can be connected to SIPTVMON. Therefore, the SA must maintain all up-to-date SIPTVMON topology information to effectively and correctly reply the access request with a capable leaf node of handling the forwarding requested video to the new subscriber MA_{new}. That is the reason why SA is called the super agent.

(J3) After successful registration, MA_{new} needs to prepare the public parameters and key for the peer by ECDH key exchange algorithm. Elliptic curve [9] function's parameter $Eq_1(a_1, b_1)$, base point $G_1 = (x_1, y_1)$, and a random private key k_{new} are generated by MA_{new}. Then, a public key P_{new} can be calculated by k_{new}, Eq_1 and G_1.

(J4) MA_{new} sends a SIP "INVITE" request message to remote MA_{leaf} via SA proxy. The SDP body in the SIP message includes the ECDH public data of Eq_1, G_1, and P_{new}.

(J5) While MA_{leaf} receives the MA_{new}'s "INVITE" message and MA_{new} is authorized to join the SIPTVMON, it will randomly generate a private key k_{new} and then calculate a public key P_{leaf} according to k_{new} and receive Eq_1 and G_1. Besides, the common private key K_c for encrypting video content can be computed by k_{leaf}, received P_{new}, Eq_1 and G_1.

(J6) Then MA_{leaf} responses a SIP "OK" message with SDP body including the public key P_{leaf} back to MA_{new}.

(J7) While MA_{new} receives the public key P_{leaf} from MA_{leaf}'s SIP "OK" message, MA_{new} can use P_{leaf}, private key k_{new}, Eq_1 and G_1 to compute the common private key K_c for later decrypting the encrypted video.

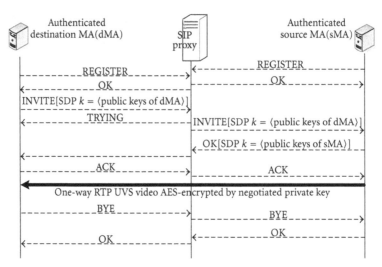

FIGURE 3: DH key negotiation via SIP/SDP signaling.

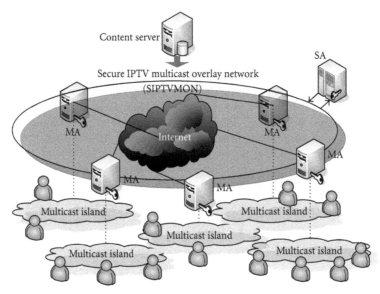

FIGURE 4: Primary SIPTVMON architecture.

(*J8*) Then, MA_{new} will send to MA_{leaf} a SIP "ACK" message via SA to confirm the completion of ECDH key exchange and the successful member join in SIPTVMON. Meanwhile, SA can also update its SIPTVMON tree topology information of new member join accordingly.

While a nonleaf MA needs to leave SIPTVMON after its local users in multicast island sequentially unsubscribe the IPTV service and it has no obligation to forward video for other MAs (i.e., child nodes of the leaving MA), the child nodes must reconnect to other MAs in SIPTVMON to continue the IPTV service.

As shown in the example of Figure 6, procedures of a nonleaf node MA_l leaving SIPTVMON without breaking IPTV service of its child nodes are illustrated, and the details are described as follows.

(*L1*) The MA_l will first send leaving requests of SIP "BYE" with SDP body of the video content identifier and its registration identifier to acknowledge not only its parent node to cease forwarding video later, but also its child nodes (i.e., MA_{c1} and MA_{c2}) to seek other new parent nodes of MA to replace their old parent MA_l for continuing IPTV video streaming.

(*L2*) The acknowledged child nodes (i.e., MA_{c1} and MA_{c2}) will send reregistration requests of SIP "REGISTER" with SDP body of the same video content identifier, their registration identifiers, and the reason of reregistration to the oracle SA to ask for the connection information of new parent nodes, respectively.

(*L3*) SA will send back response messages of SIP "OK" with SDP body of the connection information of new parents (i.e., MA_{s1} and MA_{s2}) to the leaving-acknowledged child nodes (i.e., MA_{c1} and MA_{c2}).

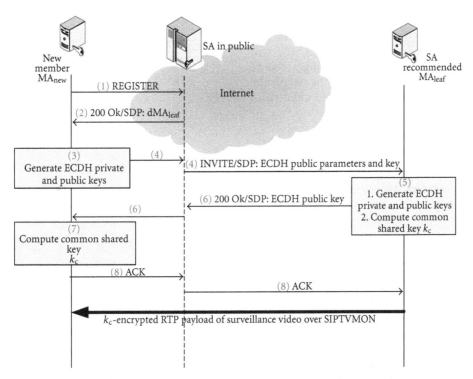

FIGURE 5: SIPTVMON's join procedures for a new MA (i.e., MA$_{new}$).

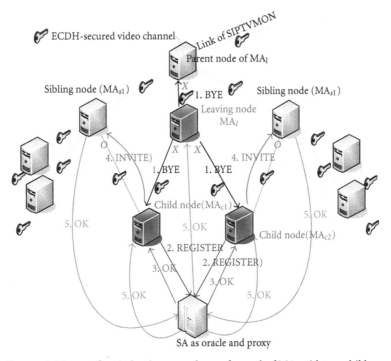

FIGURE 6: Message flow in leaving procedures of a nonleaf MA$_l$ with two children.

(L4) The acknowledged child nodes for parent node's leaving will be able to directly send reconnect requests of SIP "INVITE" message with SDP body of the video content identifiers, their registration identifiers and the ECDH public information like previous step (J4) in new MA's join procedures to their new parent nodes (i.e., MA$_{s1}$ and MA$_{s2}$) respectively.

(L5) The new IPTV connections will be immediately established from new parents to the leaving-acknowledged child nodes, right after new parents (i.e., MA$_{s1}$ and MA$_{s2}$) respond the positive SIP "OK" message via the oracle SA to acknowledged child nodes and leaving MA with SDP body of the corresponding video content identifier, corresponding registration identifier, and the ECDH public information like previous step (*J6*) in new MA's join procedures. Meanwhile, the sibling nodes MA_{s1} and MA_{s2} will start, respectively, forwarding video to children of MA_{c1} and MA_{c2}, and simultaneously the leaving MA_l stops forwarding video to children of MA_{c1} and MA_{c2}.

Such gracefully leaving procedures for a nonleaf MA_l leaving SIPTVMON can minimize the IPTV service disruption from subsequent video packets loss for the descendant nodes below the leaving node MA_l to maintain the overall quality of IPTV services for users.

Since all the SIP messages including request and response in the previous procedures in new MA's join and old MA's leaving will be forwarded via the so-called SIP proxy (i.e., oracle SA), these messages can easily help SA updating its SIPTVMON topology information to cost-effectively provide correct information upon later requests from SIPTVMON members.

3.2. Optimizations for SIPTVMON of Load Sharing and Stability.
IPTV is a near real-time application service, and the delay constraint is not as strict as video conferencing and voice over IP. Therefore, IPTV service stability is more important than service latency. As the SIPTVMON's member MAs, which preserve different capabilities of system resources and network bandwidth, may join, leave, or fail in the overlay network of SIPTVMON during IPTV service session, the avoidance of IPTV service disruption must be considered in proposed SIPTVMON architecture.

The larger outbound link bandwidth of MAs in SIPTVMON not only supports higher bit rate of IPTV video, but also more connections to remote dMA with good quality of IPTV service. In previous researches [25, 26], the ALM tree's node with more outdegree (i.e., higher bandwidth) should be moved to the top of the tree to perform the optimization of load sharing in overlay network to pursue better quality of service.

Furthermore, another important factor of optimization, which will affect stability of SIPTVMON, is user lifetime, because Internet users may join and leave IPTV services in different timing. In the paper [27], authors presented that Internet user's lifetime in video-streaming systems will follow the long-tailed distribution [24]. It means that just a few users will stay in the system for a long time and most users will stay in the system for a short period of time.

To apply both factors mentioned above, which may affect stability of overlay network, [26] uses the product of bandwidth and life time (i.e., Bandwidth and life-Time Product, BTP) for load-sharing optimization of overlay network. The BTP value function, as shown in (1), is used as a criterion to optimize the overlay network service with low service latency and disruption. However, this BTP function is too sensitive to the variation of bandwidth on Internet to frequently reconstruct the overlay network. We have

$$BTP = \text{bandwidth} \times \text{lifetime}. \qquad (1)$$

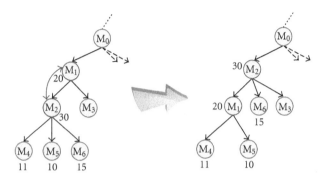

Figure 7: Example of ABTP optimization for a SIPTVMON tree.

Therefore, we further propose an improved criterion called averaging bandwidth life-time product (ABTP) to effectively minimize service disruption during optimization for SIPTVMON. The improved value function of ABTP is defined as follows:

$$ABTP = \frac{\sum_{i=1}^{n} \text{Bandwidth}_i}{n} \times \text{lifetime}. \qquad (2)$$

As shown in (2), ABTP is evaluated as a criterion of load-sharing optimization for SIPTVMON by averaging the latest n measured bandwidth values of a node (i.e., MA) and then multiplying by the value of this node's life-time in SIPTVMON. According to the ABTP value of each node in SIPTVMON, we can reconstruct the SIPTVMON as the examples illustrated in Figure 7. At the left hand side of Figure 7, node M_2 preserves higher ABTP value than node M_1, and node M_2 should be moved to higher level than node M_1. But, node M_1 preserves one less degree than node M_2, and then two child nodes of M_2 with less ABTP values will link to the child nodes of M_1 for leaving them in the same level. Meanwhile, the original child node of M_2 with largest ABTP value will be moved with node M_2 to upper layer. Then, this optimization can keep the degrees of nodes M_1 and M_2 unchanged. The example of optimized SIPTVMON tree is illustrated at the right hand side of Figure 7.

Because the oracle SA also plays the role of SIP proxy, not only the running topology of SIPTVMON tree, but also both of MAs' bandwidth and life-time can be recorded by all the forwarded SIP messages in SA. Consequently, optimization score like ABTP can be calculated by SA. Then, SA can recommend the optimization procedures via SIP "UPDATE" request messages to corresponding SIPTVMON's MAs participated in the ongoing IPTV session to initiate the optimization. In SIP protocol, the request message "UPDATE" is designed to enable the modification of session information.

The SIP message flow shown in Figure 8 illustrates to the optimization of the example from Figure 7, and the procedures are described in details as follows.

(*O1*) While oracle SA detects that the optimization score of M_2 at lower level is larger than the M_1 at higher level in SIPTVMON tree, SA sends M_2 the SIP "UPDATE" with the SDP body of M_2's video content identifier, registration identifier (for authentication),

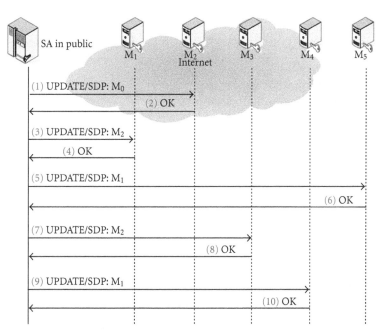

FIGURE 8: SIP message flow for SIPTVMON optimization in Figure 7.

and the recommended new parent M_0's connection information.

(O2) After M_2 receives the recommendation of new parent from SA, it will first start the similar leaving procedures mentioned above but without acknowledging its children to rejoin other parents, and then M_2 and its children start the join procedure with ECDH scheme mentioned above to connect to new parent M_0. When the join procedure is completed, M_2 sends the SIP "OK" response message to SA.

(O3) SA then sends M_1, which preserves low optimization score, by the SIP "UPDATE" message with the SDP body of authentication identifiers and the recommended new parent M_2's connection information.

(O4) After M_1 receives the recommendation of new parent from SA, it will first start the similar leaving procedures mentioned above but without acknowledging its current children to rejoin other parents, and then M_1 with its current children starts the join procedure with ECDH scheme mentioned above to connect to new parent M_2. When the join procedure is completed, M_2 sends the SIP "OK" response message to SA.

(O5) Because M_1's child M_3 has been moved to lower level of SIPTVMON than M_2's children M_4, M_5, and M_6, M_3 with higher optimization score must first exchange position with M_2's child M_5 with the lowest score. Therefore, SA sends M_5 the SIP "UPDATE" message with similar SDP body to ask M_5 to reconnect to new parent M_1.

(O6) After M_5 rejoins M_1 like previous steps, M_5 sends the SIP "OK" response message to SA.

(O7) Then M_1's child M_3 has to move to the same level as M_2's children. SA sends M_3 the SIP "UPDATE" message with similar SDP body to ask M_3 to reconnect to new parent M_2.

(O8) After M_3 rejoins M_2 like previous steps, M_3 sends the SIP "OK" response message to SA.

(O9) Since current out degree of M_2 is higher than before, the child M_4 with lowest score should move to the lower level of M_1 with one available degree. Therefore, SA sends M_4 the SIP "UPDATE" message with similar SDP body to ask M_4 to reconnect to new parent M_1.

(O10) After M_4 rejoins M_1 like previous steps, M_4 sends the SIP "OK" response message to SA to finish the procedures of optimization.

The adjustment of SIPTVMON tree for optimization of load-sharing and stability may incur the service disruption, but ABTP can smooth the variation of bandwidth on Internet to avoid unnecessary adjustment of SIPTVMON and then further effectively reduce the service disruption. ABTP optimization has two major advantages to the load-sharing and stability for proposed SIPTVMON.

(i) ABTP optimization follows the long-tailed distribution: The one who stays longer in the system can have larger ABTP value easily. Even if a node has large bandwidth, it may not have larger ABTP value because his lifetime is short. As time goes by, a node in SIPTVMON with large bandwidth can have an extremely large ABTP value, and ABTP optimization will move this node to a very high level of the SIPTVMON tree to achieve stable SIPTVMON.

(ii) ABTP value can avoid the unnecessary optimizations: Since the Internet bandwidth varies from

TABLE 1: Simulation parameters for SIPTVMON.

Parameter	Values
MA quantity	2000, 4000, 6000, 8000, 10000
Degree of MA	2 to 5 outdegree (uniform distribution)
Link bandwidth	Mean: 400 kbits, Std: 10, normal distribution
Link delay	Mean: 0.08 s, Std: 0.05, normal distribution
Optimization (Opt.)	Bandwidth only (B), life time only (T), BTP, Averaging bandwidth only (ABO), ABTP
Simulation time	20000 seconds
Opt. cycle	40 seconds

time to time, the averaging bandwidth value can cost-effectively reduce the unnecessary optimization overhead and possible service disruptions.

In following section, we will present the simulations and performance results of the optimization for load-sharing and stability via ABTP criterion for the proposed SIPTVMON.

4. Experiments and Performance of SIPTVMON

To demonstrate our proposed optimization scheme via ABTP criteria for SIPTVMON, we use the well-known simulation tool OMNeT++4.0 [28] to construct a vital SIPTVMON with new MAs joining, old MAs leaving and timely SIPTVMON adjustment for optimization at load-sharing and stability (i.e., criteria of bandwidth only, life time only, BTP [26], averaging bandwidth only, and ABTP). The optimization criterion of averaging bandwidth only is abbreviated as ABO, and it considers only the averaging bandwidth part of ABTP. The video source's average bit rate is 280 Kbps from the popular MPEG-4-coding data. The detailed simulation parameters and corresponding test values are listed in Table 1.

During the simulation for SIPTVMON, we recorded the count of control messages and service disruptions, tree depths, service latency, average packet loss rate, count of MA with packet loss, and average perceptual PSNR values for different optimization criteria. We will perform each test case five times to find out the mean and standard deviation of these simulation results.

As shown in Figure 9, ABTP criterion outperforms other four optimization criteria in less overhead of control messages. Those criteria (i.e., B and ABO) without considering life time preserve more control messages. It is because the possibility of high-level nodes leaving from SIPTVMON tree will be higher. It also indicated that more control messages are needed to repair the SIPTVMON for continuing IPTV service if MA's life time is not considered in optimization for load sharing.

While an old MA leaving SIPTVMON or SIPTVMON's adjustment for load sharing, service disruption may occur to degrade the quality of IPTV video-streaming service for those dMAs under detached parent in SIPTVMON. According to the results from Figure 10, ABTP also preserves less average count of service disruption to help SIPTVMON to achieve better quality of service.

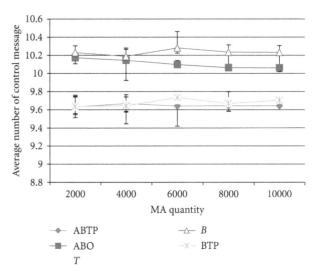

FIGURE 9: Average number of control messages on different MA quantity and optimization criteria.

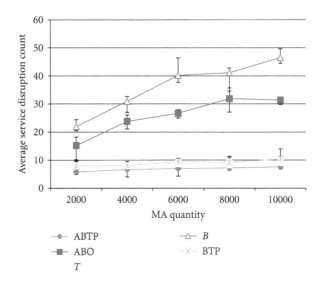

FIGURE 10: Average count of service disruption on different MA quantity and optimization criteria.

As shown in Figure 11, ABTP optimization criterion keeps lower depths of SIPTVMON tree than other criteria, except the test case of small MA quantity of 2000 nodes. Those optimization criteria considering both bandwidth and life time usually keep less depth than others in most test cases.

While the depth of SIPTVMON tree getting larger, the IPTV service latency of bottom dMAs is also getting longer. However, as shown in Figure 12 for the test case of MA quantity 6000, the value of service latency will keep growing after simulation starts. It is because the tree is growing and the increasing depth indicates increasing service latency. While the member of MA in SIPTVMON tree reaches 6000 and some of these MA may start to leave SIPTVMON tree, the service latency will stop increasing due to the adjustment of SIPTVMON tree through different optimization criteria. The optimization criterion T preserves much more service latency during simulation time than other criteria since the

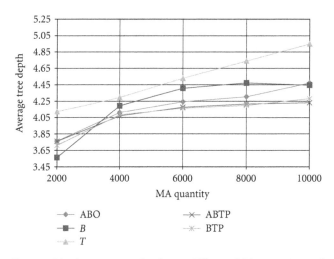

FIGURE 11: Average tree depth on different MA quantity and optimization criteria.

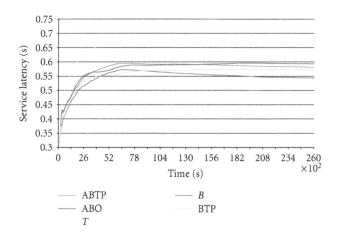

FIGURE 12: Service latency from different optimization criteria on MA quantity of 6000.

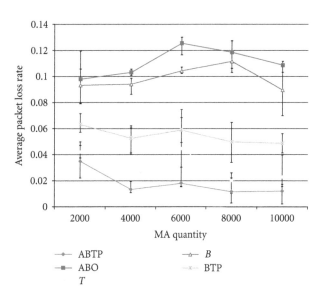

FIGURE 13: Average packet loss rates on different MA quantity and optimization criteria.

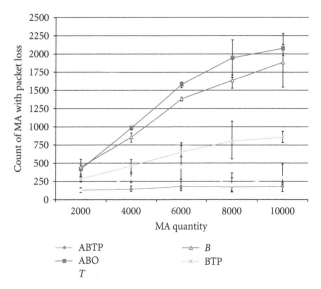

FIGURE 14: Count of MA with packet loss on different MA quantity and optimization criteria.

bandwidth criterion was not considered to effectively reduce both the depth of SIPTVMON tree and corresponding service latency.

ABO considers same criteria of bandwidth only with criterion B, but ABO preserves larger service latency than criterion B. This is because the averaging bandwidth from ABO will not decrease the tree depth of SIPTVMON in the same large scale as B.

As shown in Figure 12, the reason why optimization criterion ABTP cannot achieve best results in service latency is because it considers both of the averaging bandwidth and life time. It is not very possible for criterion ABTP to outperform less service latency than criterion B.

Due to the possible service disruption from the SIPTV-MON's optimization procedures, we count the packet loss for every MA during the service disruptions within simulation to calculate the average packet loss rate for the whole SIPTVMON tree. The calculation of average packet loss rate l_{avg} is shown in (3). In (3), l_i indicates the packet loss rate of MA$_i$ on the SIPTVMON, and it is derived from the ratio of

the count packet loss in MA$_i$ to the total packets of original video source. Then, n is the MA quantity in Table 1. One has

$$l_{\text{avg}} = \frac{\sum_{i=1}^{n} l_i}{n}. \tag{3}$$

As shown in Figure 13, proposed ABTP optimization criterion for SIPTVMON outperforms other criteria in less average packet loss rates. While we count the number of SIPTVMON's MA preserving packet loss, as illustrated in Figure 14, the ABTP optimization criterion further demonstrates much more scalability for SIPTVMON than other criteria applied.

Moreover, the packet loss may jeopardize the playback quality of the IPTV video, so we derive the average perceptual PSNR values from the packet loss rates previously recorded

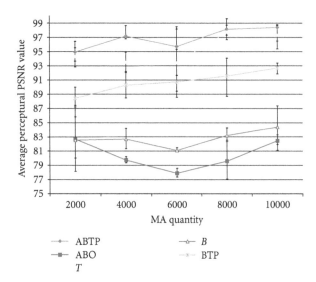

FIGURE 15: Average perceptual PSNR values on different MA quantity and optimization criteria.

for all MAs on SIPTVMON. The calculation of average perceptual PSNR value p_{avg} is shown in (4). As the same definition in (3), l_i indicates the packet loss rate of MA_i on the SIPTVMON and n is the MA quantity. Then, the PSNR function in (4) provides an estimated PSNR value for the input loss rate of l_i. One has

$$p_{avg} = \frac{\sum_{i=1}^{n} PSNR(l_i)}{n}. \tag{4}$$

As shown in Figure 15, similar with most of previous experimental results, the proposed ABTP optimization criterion applied in SIPTVMON outperforms much better perceptual quality for end users than other criteria applied. In our simulation results, the average perceptual PSNR value still reaches the best even at the largest scale of MA quantity to 10000 in SIPTVMON for IPTV service.

5. Conclusion and Future Work

In this paper, we propose a secure overlay network-called SIPTVMON using application-layer multicast with load-sharing and stability schemes to cost-effectively provide scalable IPTV services for users churn such as frequent joining and leaving. The proposed SIPTVMON constructed by SIP signaling can provide Internet users with scalable and stable IPTV video streaming with privacy protection, and the simulations and results demonstrate that our SIPTVMON's proposed optimization criterion (i.e., ABTP) considering the product of averaging bandwidth and life time in peers not only has the better performance in overhead of control message, service disruption, and service latency from tree depth than other optimization criteria but also preserves very acceptable perceptual quality in objective PSNR values with privacy provision.

In near future, we plan to deploy SIPTVMON over the global Internet test-bed (e.g., PlanetLab [29]) for further demonstration. We also like to investigate SIPTVMON's

reliability features of open-loop and close-loop error controls such as peer's packet cache for retransmission and adaptive forward error correction (FEC) to further improve P2P IPTV's quality of service over Internet.

Acknowledgment

The work was partially supported by National Science Council, Project Numbers NSC 100-2221-E-130-009, NSC 100-2628-H-002-003-MY2, and NSC 100-2218-E-002-007, Taiwan.

References

[1] PPStream, http://www.ppstream.com.

[2] PPLive, http://www.pptv.com.

[3] SopCast, http://www.sopcast.org.

[4] TvAnts, http://tvants.en.softonic.com.

[5] X. Hei, C. Liang, J. Liang, Y. Liu, and K. W. Ross, "A measurement study of a large-scale P2P IPTV system," *IEEE Transactions on Multimedia*, vol. 9, no. 8, pp. 1672–1687, 2007.

[6] X. Hei, Y. Liu, and K. W. Ross, "IPTV over P2P streaming networks: the mesh pull approache," *IEEE Communications Magazine*, vol. 46, no. 2, pp. 86–92, 2008.

[7] D. Ciullo, M. A. Garcia, A. Horvath et al., "Network awareness of P2P live streaming applications: a measurement study," *IEEE Transactions on Multimedia*, vol. 12, no. 1, pp. 54–63, 2010.

[8] H. Schulzrinne and J. Rosenberg, "The IETF internet telephony architecture and protocols," *IEEE Network*, vol. 13, no. 3, pp. 18–23, 1999.

[9] K. Malhotra, S. Gardner, and R. Patz, "Implementation of elliptic-curve cryptography on mobile healthcare devices," in *Proceedings of the IEEE International Conference on Networking, Sensing and Control (ICNSC '07)*, pp. 239–244, London, UK, April 2007.

[10] C. H. Wang, Y. H. Chu, and T. T. Wei, "SIPTVMON: a secure multicast overlay network for load-balancing and stable IPTV service using SIP," in *Proceedings of the 30th IEEE Conference on Computer Communications Workshops (INFOCOM WKSHPS '11)*, pp. 97–102, Shanghai, China, April 2011.

[11] G. Camarillo and M. A. Garcia-Martin, *The 3G IP Multimedia Subsystem-Merging the Internet and the Cellular Worlds*, John Wiley & Sons, New York, NY, USA, 2004.

[12] F. Wang, Y. Xiong, and J. Liu, "MTreebone: a collaborative tree-mesh overlay network for multicast video streaming," *IEEE Transactions on Parallel and Distributed Systems*, vol. 21, no. 3, pp. 379–392, 2010.

[13] Y. Chu, S. G. Rao, S. Seshan, and H. Zhang, "Enabling conferencing applications on the internet using an overlay multicast architecture," in *Proceedings of the ACM Applications, Technologies, Architectures, and Protocols for Computers Communications (SIGCOMM '01)*, pp. 55–67, August 2001.

[14] C. K. Yeo, B. S. Lee, and M. H. Er, "Application layer multicast architecture for media streaming," in *Proceedings of the 7th IASTED International Conference on Internet and Multimedia Systems and Applications*, pp. 455–460, Honolulu, Hawaii, USA, August 2003.

[15] C. K. Yeo, B. S. Lee, and M. H. Er, "A survey of application level multicast techniques," *Computer Communications*, vol. 27, no. 15, pp. 1547–1568, 2004.

[16] D. Ren, Y.-T. H. Li, and S.-H. G. Chan, "Fast-mesh: a low-delay high-bandwidth mesh for peer-to-peer live streaming," *IEEE Transactions on Multimedia*, vol. 11, no. 8, pp. 1446–1456, 2009.

[17] http://www.cryptopp.com/benchmarks.html.

[18] J. Arkko, E. Carrara, F. Lindholm, M. Naslund, and K. Norrman, "Multimedia Internet KEYing (MIKEY)," IETF, RFC 3830, August 2004.

[19] M. E. Hellman, "An overview of public key cryptography," *IEEE Communications Magazine*, pp. 42–49, 2002.

[20] C. C. Yang, R. C. Wang, and W. T. Liu, "Secure authentication scheme for session initiation protocol," *Computers & Security*, vol. 24, no. 5, pp. 381–386, 2005.

[21] M. Handley and V. Jacobson, "Session Description Protocol (SDP)," IETF, RFC4566, July 2006.

[22] H. Schulzrinne et al., "RTP: A Transport Protocol for Real-Time Applications," IETF RFC 3550, July 2003.

[23] Y. Chu, S. G. Rao, S. Seshan, and H. Zhang, "A case for end system multicast," *IEEE Journal on Selected Areas in Communications*, vol. 20, no. 8, pp. 1456–1471, 2002.

[24] C. Anderson, "The long tail," in *Wired*, 2004.

[25] D. Andersen, "Resilient overlay networks," *SIGOPS*, vol. 35, pp. 131–145, 2001.

[26] G. Tan and S. A. Jarvis, "Improving the fault resilience of overlay multicast for media streaming," *IEEE Transactions on Parallel and Distributed Systems*, vol. 18, no. 6, pp. 721–734, 2007.

[27] K. Sripanidkulchai, A. Ganjam, B. Maggs, and H. Zhang, "The feasibility of supporting large-scale live streaming applications with dynamic application end-points," in *Proceedings of the ACM Conference on Computer Communications (SIGCOMM '04)*, pp. 107–120, Portland, Ore, USA, September 2004.

[28] OMNet++, http://www.omnetpp.org/.

[29] PlanetLab, an open platform for developing, deploying and accessing planetary-scale serviceshttp://www.planet-lab.org/.

12

A Low-Complexity Resource Allocation Algorithm for MIMO-OFDMA Multicast Systems with Spectrum-Guarantee Provisioning

Ioannis G. Fraimis and Stavros A. Kotsopoulos

Wireless Telecommunications Laboratory (WTL), Department of Electrical and Computer Engineering, University of Patras, 26500 Rio, Greece

Correspondence should be addressed to Stavros A. Kotsopoulos, kotsop@ece.upatras.gr

Academic Editor: Floriano De Rango

We study the important problem of resource allocation for the downlink of Multiple-Input Multiple output (MIMO) Multicast Wireless Systems operating over frequency-selective channels and we propose a low-complexity but efficient resource allocation algorithm for MIMO-enabled OFDMA systems. The proposed solution guarantees a minimum spectrum share for each user while also takes advantage of the multicast transmission mode. The presence of multiple antennas in both transmitter and receiver offers spatial diversity to the system along with the frequency diversity added by the OFDMA access scheme. The computational complexity is reduced from exponential to linear and validation of the proposed solution is achieved through various simulation scenarios in comparison with other multicast and unicast reference schemes used in MIMO-OFDMA systems. Numerical results and complexity analysis demonstrate the feasibility of the proposed algorithm.

1. Introduction

Future wireless systems along with voice are envisioned to provide plethora of rich multimedia services like mobile TV, video conferencing, and so forth, with various bandwidth requirements [1–5]. The introduction of new applications such as streaming video and up-to-date information distribution services (e.g., news, stock market, weather forecasting, etc.) has brought about the need for communication between one sender and many receivers. Communication between one transmitter and multiple receivers can be achieved by either the unicast or the multicast transmission mode [1–8].

Works [1–4] study Multimedia Broadcast Multimedia Service (MBMS) delivery to large group of users. Particularly, in [1, 2] authors conclude that a hybrid unicast-multicast delivery offers the best system resource utilization, while in [3], the case of reserved resources for multicast services is investigated and in [4] the use of multiple transmit and receive antennas is considered for multicasting, in order to achieve higher data rates. However, the aforementioned studies refer to Wideband Code Division Multiple Access (WCDMA) mobile networks and Orthogonal Frequency Division Multiple Access (OFDMA) scheme is the modulation and multiple access scheme adopted for next-generation wireless systems [5–17].

OFDMA is based on Orthogonal Frequency Modulation (OFDM) scheme and helps exploit multiuser diversity in frequency-selective channels, since it is very likely that some subcarriers that are in deep fade for some users are in good channel state for at least one of the other users [9, 12, 14]. Because of its superior performance over frequency-selective channels, OFDMA is embedded in multicast technologies for the efficient transmission of multimedia streams to mobile devices using TV [5], and it is the preferred technology in the Broadband Wireless Access (BWA) standards [10]. Finally, authors in [11, 12] show that the optimal policy in order to eliminate intracell interference is the exclusive assignment of each subcarrier to only one user.

Dynamic resource allocation algorithms have been developed in order to exploit the multiuser diversity that OFDMA

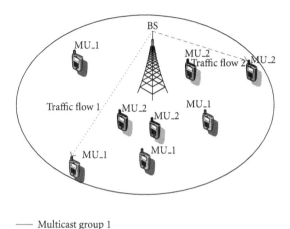

— Multicast group 1
— Multicast group 2

FIGURE 1: Multiple users demand the same data content.

offers and improve system capacity. More specifically, in [13] the available subcarriers are divided into a number of partitions and each user acts in parallel and attempts to select the partition with the highest average channel gain while in [14], capacity enhancement is achieved along with fairness criteria imposed to users. Similarly, authors in [15] introduced an iterative scheme so that quality-of-service (QoS) requirements of users are fulfilled with the objective to minimize the total transmit power.

On the other hand, when multiple users demand the same multimedia content (Figure 1), we can overcome the policy of exclusive subcarrier assignment to each user and allow many users to share the same subcarrier [6, 8]. In this case, the transmitter establishes one link with a group of users which demand the same multimedia content. This kind of transmission is called multicast transmission in contrast to unicast transmission mode, wherein data has to be transmitted to each user separately. This is a great advantage of multicast mechanism which enhances significantly the system capacity.

To that end, authors in [6] propose a low-complexity algorithm which aims at improving the system data rate. The algorithm assigns each subcarrier to the group with the best channel conditions and the biggest number of member multicast users, and in [7] a heuristic algorithm for allocating resources is proposed in order to minimize power consumption. However, the aforementioned schemes focus on Single-Input Single-Output (SISO) systems and cannot be applied to MIMO systems directly [8], which are going to play a key role in future BWA communications [18, 19].

In fading environments, MIMO technology offers significant increase in link range and improvement in spectrum efficiency without additional spectrum and power requirements. Due to these properties, MIMO systems have received much attention by researchers and manufacturers. The block diagram of a MIMO system is given in Figure 2, wherein we can see the spatial diversity added to the system by the presence of multiple antennas. Spatial diversity in combination with the fading diversity of the OFDMA

technology, can improve significantly the overall system performance.

The high computational complexity of optimally allocating subcarriers in MIMO systems [18] has driven many studies to propose exclusive allocation of each subcarrier to only one user despite the presence of multiple antennas in both transmitter and receiver [19–26]. In [17] we apply this approach, and more particularly we use the suboptimal subcarrier allocation criteria introduced in [19]. Similarly, authors in [8] apply a greedy suboptimal approach and allocate each subcarrier to the multicast group which offers the highest capacity gain without considering fair spectrum accessibility for users.

In this paper, motivated by works in [6, 8], we extend our work in [17] by addressing the resource allocation problem in an MIMO-aided wireless system, wherein multiple groups of users demand the same content with bandwidth access guarantees, contrary to schemes in [6, 8] which apply greedy policy and the only target is the maximization of the aggregate data rate. Moreover, the proposed scheme gives much better data rates compared to static Time Division Multiple Access (TDMA) scheme [27] and reduced complexity implementation.

The rest of the paper is organized as follows. Section 2 introduces the multiple antenna OFDMA multicast system model and formulates the optimization problem. The proposed suboptimal algorithm is analyzed in Section 3, while algorithm complexity issues are investigated in Section 4. Section 5 gives the simulation parameters and Section 6 presents the numerical results. Finally, Section 7 contains concluding remarks.

2. System Model and Problem Formulation

The block diagram of the considered MIMO-OFDM-based wireless multicast system is given in Figure 2, wherein the spatial multiplexing mode of MIMO is assumed as in [8, 17, 19]. We consider a base station (BS) which serves K wireless users over N subcarriers. Let N_t be the number of antennas at the BS and N_r the number of antennas at each wireless user. Thus, the channel matrix of user k on subcarrier m is an $N_r \times N_t$ matrix denoted by

$$\mathbf{H}_{k,n} = \begin{pmatrix} h_{1,1}^{k,n} & h_{1,2}^{k,n} & \cdots & h_{1,N_t}^{k,n} \\ h_{2,1}^{k,n} & h_{2,2}^{k,n} & \cdots & h_{2,N_t}^{k,n} \\ \vdots & \vdots & \ddots & \vdots \\ h_{N_r,1}^{k,n} & h_{N_r,2}^{k,n} & \cdots & h_{N_r,N_t}^{k,n} \end{pmatrix}, \tag{1}$$

where $h_{r,t}^{k,n}$ is the channel gain from the tth transmit antenna to the rth receive antenna of user k on the mth subcarrier. It is also assumed that the eigenvalues of $\mathbf{H}_{k,n}\mathbf{H}_{k,n}^{T}$ are $\{\lambda_{k,m}^{(i)}\}_{i=1}^{M}$, where $M = \min(N_r, N_t)$. Hence, for certain values of k, n, a group of eigenchannels exists denoted by the above eigenvalues, according to SVD decomposition. Also, denoting the $N_t \times 1$ transmitted signal $\mathbf{X}_{k,n} = [x_{k,n}^1, x_{k,n}^2, \ldots, x_{k,n}^{N_t}]$

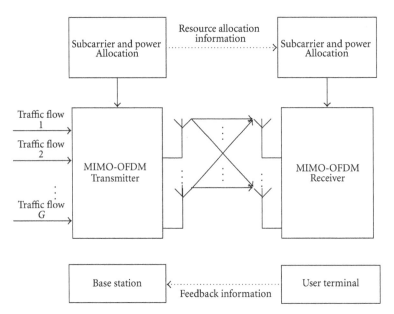

FIGURE 2: Block diagram of MIMO-OFDM multicast system.

and the $N_r \times 1$ received signal $\mathbf{Y}_{k,n} = [y^1_{k,n}, y^2_{k,n}, \ldots, y^{N_r}_{k,n}]$ is then

$$\mathbf{Y}_{k,n} = \mathbf{H}_{k,n} \left(\sum_{k=1}^{K} \mathbf{X}_{k,n} p_{k,n} \right) \mathbf{N}_{k,n}, \tag{2}$$

where $\sum_{k=1}^{K} \mathbf{X}_{k,n} p_{k,n}$ is the overall transmitted signal on subcarrier n and $p_{k,n}$ represents the power of subcarrier n when assigned to user k. $\mathbf{N}_{k,n}$ is the $N_r \times 1$ noise vector.

Each user's bits are modulated into N M-level Quadrature Amplitude Modulation (QAM) symbols, which are subsequently combined using the IFFT into an OFDMA symbol. For a square M-level QAM using Gray bit mapping, the Bit Error Rate (BER) can be approximated to within 1 dB for $r^i_{k,n} \geq 4$ and $\mathrm{BER}^i_{k,n} \leq 10^{-3}$ as in [28], being

$$\mathrm{BER}^i_{k,n} \approx \frac{1}{5} \exp\left[\frac{-1.5 p_{k,n} \lambda^i_{k,n}}{N_0 \left(2^{r^i_{k,n}} - 1 \right)} \right],$$

$$r^i_{k,n} = \log_2\left(1 + \frac{p_{k,n} \lambda^i_{k,n}}{N_0 \Gamma^i_{k,n}} \right), \tag{3}$$

where $\Gamma^i_{k,n} = -\ln(5\,\mathrm{BER}^i_{k,n})/1.5$. For simplicity, it is assumed $\mathrm{BER}^i_{k,n} = \mathrm{BER}$ and $\Gamma^i_{k,n} = \Gamma$.

The great advantage of the multicast transmission is that data can be delivered to multiple receivers through a single transmission. However, each member user (MU) of a multicast group (MG) experiences a different Signal-to-Noise Ratio (SNR) on a specific subcarrier from other users in the same group. In other words, achievable data rates by individual users in a group are not equal on a particular subcarrier, and a widely adopted approach is to transmit at the data rate determined by the MU with the worst channel condition in an MG [6, 8]. This approach assures that a multicast service can be provided to all users within an MG.

Therefore, the BS transmits data to the jth group through subcarrier n with rate

$$r_{j,n} = \arg \min_{k \in \mathcal{K}_j} \frac{W}{N} \sum_{i=1}^{M} \log_2\left(1 + \frac{\lambda^i_{k,n} p_{k,n}}{N_0 \Gamma} \right), \tag{4}$$

where $\mathcal{K}_j$ denotes the user set of multicast group j and W refers to the total system bandwidth. Hence, the aggregate data rate of group j, with the help of (4), is

$$R_{j,n} = \sum_{k \in K_j} r_{j,n} = \left| \mathcal{K}_j \right| \cdot r_{j,n}, \tag{5}$$

where $| \cdot |$ denotes the cardinality of the set.

In this paper, the following assumptions are used.

(i) The BS has perfect knowledge of channel state information (CSI) of all users in the system via dedicated feedback channels, and it is able to determine the maximum rate a user can receive data, as well as on which subcarrier the transmission takes place.

(ii) The transmitted signals experience slowly time varying fading, so the channel coefficients can be regarded as constants during the resource allocation process.

(iii) The transmission power is equally distributed among subcarriers; that is, $p_{k,n} = p_n = P_t/N$, $k = 1 \cdots K$, $n = 1 \cdots N$. Water-filling power allocation brings marginal performance enhancement over fixed power allocation combined with Adaptive Coding and Modulation (ACM), as authors in [11] have proven.

(iv) We assume the subcarrier allocation matrix $X_{G \times N} = [x_{j,n}]$, whereby $x_{j,n} = 1$ if MG j is assigned subcarrier n and $x_{j,n} = 0$ if not. A subcarrier can be shared by multiple users but only by users of the same MG. Each subcarrier can be assigned to only one MG.

(v) K wireless users are divided into G MGs which demand G different multicast services.

Considering the assumptions previous, the optimization problem in order to maximize the aggregate data rate while a minimum spectrum share is ensured for each MG is formulated as follows:

$$\max_{x_{j,n},p_{j,n}} \sum_{j=1}^{G} \sum_{n=1}^{N} x_{j,n} R_{j,n} \qquad (6)$$

subject to

$$x_{j,n} \in \{0,1\}, \quad \forall j,n, \qquad (7)$$

$$\sum_{j=1}^{G} x_{j,n} = 1, \quad \forall n, \qquad (8)$$

$$\sum_{n=1}^{N} x_{j,n} \geq C_j, \quad \forall j, \qquad (9)$$

$$\sum_{j=1}^{G} C_j \leq N, \quad C_j \in Z_+, \qquad (10)$$

$$\sum_{j=1}^{G} \sum_{n=1}^{N} x_{j,n} p_{j,n} \leq P_t, \qquad (11)$$

$$p_{j,n} \geq 0, \quad \forall j,n. \qquad (12)$$

In the problem formulation, the binary variable $x_{j,n}$ represents the assignment of subcarrier n to the multicast group j and constrains (8) and (7) ensure that intracell interference is avoided since one subcarrier can only be allocated to at most one MG. Constraint (9) guarantees a portion of the available resources to each MG. The concept of minimum bandwidth assurance has also been studied in [16] for relay-enhanced systems, and it is also considered in our approach in [17] for MIMO systems, while (10) express that the subcarriers guaranteed for all groups cannot exceed the total number of available subcarriers in the system. Finally, constraints (11) and (12) express the BS power limitation, whereby P_t denotes the total BS transmission power.

It is very hard to determine the optimal solution of the problem (6)–(12) within a designated time, since the problem in (6)–(12) is NP hard and has exponential complexity of $\mathcal{O}(G^N)$ (Section 4). It also involves both continuous and binary variables, and the nonlinear constraints increase the difficulty in finding the optimal solution. Hence, we resort to suboptimal heuristic algorithms which are more suitable for practical implementations.

3. The Proposed Resource Allocation Algorithm

This section provides and analyzes the proposed low complexity resource allocation (LCRA) algorithm. The pseudocode of the LCRA algorithm is given in Algorithm 1. For the sake of clarity, the pseudocode is divided into steps which are described as follows:

Inputs:

$\mathcal{N} = \{1, 2, \ldots, N\}$,

$\mathcal{G} = \{1, 2, \ldots, G\}$,

$\mathcal{C} = \{C_1, C_2, \ldots, C_G\}$ such that (10) is fulfilled,

$R_{G \times N} = [R_{j,n}]$ % computed by (5).

Outputs: $X_{G \times N} = [x_{j,n}]$.

(1) **Initialization:**

$x_{j,n} = 0$, for $j = 1 \cdots G$ and $n = 1 \cdots N$.

Inputs of the LCRA algorithm are the sets of the total available subcarriers $\mathcal{N}$, the set $\mathcal{G}$ of MGs, the set $\mathcal{C}$ which represents the spectrum access guarantee of each MG, and the rate matrix $R_{G \times N}$ which denotes the attainable data rates of MGs on each one of the available subcarriers. Output is the subcarrier allocation matrix, and in step 1 subcarrier indicators $x_{j,n}$ are set to zero for all MGs and all subcarriers.

(2) **While** $\mathcal{C} \neq \{\}$:

    (i) Find $\tilde{j} \in \mathcal{G}$ an $\tilde{n} \in \mathcal{N}$ with $R_{\tilde{j},\tilde{n}} \geq R_{j,n} \forall j,n$

    (ii) **If** $\sum_{n=1}^{N} x_{\tilde{j},n} \geq C_{\tilde{j}}$ % examines (9)

        (a) $\mathcal{C} \leftarrow \mathcal{C} \setminus \{C_{\tilde{j}}\}$

        (b) $\mathcal{G} \leftarrow \mathcal{G} \setminus \{\tilde{j}\}$

    (iii) **Else**

        (a) Set $x_{\tilde{j},\tilde{n}} = 1$

        (b) $\mathcal{N} \leftarrow \mathcal{N} \setminus \{\tilde{n}\}$ % satisfies (8).

In step 2, the BS seeks the matching of MG j^* and subcarrier n^* which contributes the most to the total capacity. In the following, the algorithm examines if the selected MG has already its minimum spectrum portion (9). If that is true, the minimum spectrum index C_{j^*} the particular MG is excluded from the set $\mathcal{C}$ and consequently MG j^* is excluded from subsequent iterations of this part of the LCRA algorithm. In case the MG has not been allocated its minimum number of channels, the subcarrier n^* is allocated to MG j^* and then the subcarrier n^* is excluded from the set of available subcarriers $\mathcal{N}$ in order to fulfill (8). The procedure is repeated until the set $\mathcal{C}$ is empty or, in other words, each MG has got its minimum subcarrier allotment. The procedure could also stop if there were no more available subcarriers, despite the fact that some MGs may have lower number of subcarriers than C_j, $j = 1 \cdots G$. However, this situation is excluded because of (10).

(3) **While** $\mathcal{N} \neq \{\}$:

    (i) Find j^*, n^* such that $R_{j^*,n^*} \geq R_{j,n} \forall j,n$

    (ii) Set $x_{j^*,n^*} = 1$, $\mathcal{N} \leftarrow \mathcal{N} \setminus \{n^*\}$ % satisfies (8)

    (iii) Update (6).

In step 3, if unallocated subcarriers exist, those are allocated according to the criterion of maximizing the aggregate data rate by allocating a subcarrier to the group with the best channel condition among all MGs. Then the selected subcarrier is excluded from the set $\mathcal{N}$ (satisfaction of (8)). This part enhances the system capacity.

Inputs:
$\mathcal{N} = \{1, 2, \ldots, N\}$
$\mathcal{G} = \{1, 2, \ldots, G\}$
$\mathcal{C} = \{C_1, C_2, \ldots, C_G\}$ such that (10) is fulfilled.
$R_{G \times N} = [R_{j,n}]$ % computed by(5)
Outputs:
$X_{G \times N} = [x_{j,n}]$
Initialization:
$x_{j,n} = 0$, for $j = 1 \cdots G$ and $n = 1 \cdots N$
While$\mathcal{C} \neq \{\}$:
  Find $\tilde{j} \in \mathcal{G}$ an $\tilde{n} \in \mathcal{N}$ with $R_{\tilde{j},\tilde{n}} \geq R_{j,n} \forall j, n$
If$\sum_{n=1}^{N} x_{\tilde{j},n} \geq C_{\tilde{j}}$ % examines(9)
    $\mathcal{C} \leftarrow \mathcal{C} \setminus \{C_{\tilde{j}}\}$
    $\mathcal{G} \leftarrow \mathcal{G} \setminus \{\tilde{j}\}$
Else
    Set $x_{\tilde{j},\tilde{n}} = 1$
    $\mathcal{N} \leftarrow \mathcal{N} \setminus \{\tilde{n}\}$ % satisfies(8)
While$\mathcal{N} \neq \{\}$:
    Find j^*, n^* such that $R_{j^*,n^*} \geq R_{j,n} \forall j, n$
    Set $x_{j^*,n^*} = 1$
    $\mathcal{N} \leftarrow \mathcal{N} \setminus \{n^*\}$ % satisfies(8)
    Update (6).

ALGORITHM 1:

TABLE 1: Algorithm complexity.

Exhaustive search	LCRA	[17]	Optimal user selection [18]	Subcarrier allocation in [8]
$\mathcal{O}(G^N)$	$\mathcal{O}(G \times N)$	$\mathcal{O}(K \times N)$	$\mathcal{O}(K^{\lfloor N_T/N_R \rfloor N})$	$\mathcal{O}(G \times N)$

4. Complexity Analysis

The problem described by (6)–(12) is a binary integer programming problem with nonlinear constraints and finding the optimal solution requires G^N possible subcarrier assignments. As a result the exhaustive search has an exponential complexity $\mathcal{O}(G^N)$ with respect to the number of subcarriers.

In step 1, the algorithm requires constant time in order to form the involved sets and the power portion for each subcarrier.

In the second step, the pair of group and subcarrier which gives the highest $R_{j,n}$ among G MGs is found. In case an MG has been assigned its minimum channel portion, it is excluded from subsequent operations. In the worst case G comparisons are required for each one of the available subcarriers. For N subcarriers, we need $G \times N$ operations. Therefore, the complexity of this step reaches $\mathcal{O}(G \times N)$.

Step 3 searches for the best MG j^* among G MGs for the remaining $N - \sum_{j=1}^{G} C_j$ unallocated subcarriers. This step demands $G \times (N - \sum_{j=1}^{G} C_j)$ comparisons at most and therefore the $\mathcal{O}(G \times (N - \sum_{j=1}^{G} C_j))$ complexity.

The overall LCRA complexity is upper bounded by $\mathcal{O}(G \times N)$ order of complexity, whereby the complexity of [17] is $\mathcal{O}(K \times N)$ and always $G \leq K$. The computational complexity of the LCRA has a form of $\mathcal{O}(L^\delta)$, with $L = G \times N$ and $\delta = 1$ which is a linear [29], and the proposed LCRA scheme is a linear-time algorithm which is very efficient

compared to the number of operations G^N for the exhaustive search.

It is worth mentioning that the design assumptions that only users of the same MG are capable of sharing a subcarrier and the spatial multiplexing MIMO mode we adopted, reduce significantly the system complexity. Exhaustive search for the optimal user selection for MIMO systems requires $\mathcal{O}(K^{\lfloor N_T/N_R \rfloor N})$, assuming that, for every subcarrier, we select a subset of users and every selected user will use the full dimension of its receive signal space. Hence, finding optimal solution is prohibitive even for moderate values of K and N [18]. In our problem formulation, the complexity is also independent of the number of receive and transmit antennas and this is a feature of great importance since the computation complexity of MIMO-OFDMA systems increases significantly by the presence of multiple antennas [18]. Table 1 summarizes computational complexities of the proposed LCRA algorithm and other reference schemes.

5. Simulation Models and Parameters

We consider an OFDMA system with $N = 128$ subcarriers, wherein a BS serves G MGs and each one has equal number of users. Both BS and users are equipped with multiple antennas, and we consider $N_r = N_t = 2$ for our simulations. The available spectrum is $W = 1 \, \text{MHz}$ and the Additive White Gaussian Noise (AWGN) is $N_0 = -80 \, \text{dBW/Hz}$

TABLE 2: Simulation parameters.

Parameters	Values
Bandwidth	1 MHz
Number of subcarriers	128
Number of transmit antennas	2
Number of receive antennas	2
Fast fading	Jakes Model
Number of multipath components (taps)	6
AWGN spectral density (single-sided)	-80 dBW/Hz
Number of users	16
Maximum doppler shift	30 Hz

(single-sided PSD). In all simulations presented in this section, we consider frequency-selective channel which consists of six independent Rayleigh multipath components (taps) for every downlink transmission path between any of the N_t transmit antennas and N_r receive antennas of each multicast user. As in [9, 14, 30], an exponentially decaying power profile is considered, whereby the ratio of the energy of the lth tap to the first tap is equal to e^{-2l}. We also assume a maximum delay spread of $5\,\mu s$ and maximum doppler of 30 Hz. In all simulation scenarios the number of channel realizations is equal to 1000 and 10 time samples for each realization are used. The main simulation parameters are summarized in Table 2.

In all scenarios, the proposed LCRA algorithm is compared for different values of C_j, with the subcarrier allocation method proposed in [8] and static TDMA allocation proposed in [27] for multiple MGs. According to TDMA algorithm, each user is given a fair share of the channel resource regardless of the channel state. In our case, we apply the TDMA methodology for each MG according to (4) and (5). We find the user that determines the data rate of each group, otherwise the user with worst channel conditions on a subcarrier and we apply TDMA based on each MG. In order to distinguish the TDMA applied in multicast mode and unicast mode, we denote TDMA-MC the multicast TDMA algorithm and TDMA-UC the unicast TDMA algorithm. Both in the algorithm in [8] and in static TDMA algorithm, uniform power distribution is used. In addition, in our simulations we include popular unicast schemes like max-SNR scheduler and unicast schedulers with minimum bandwidth assurance for each user. For the unicast scheme with minimum bandwidth assurance, we use our proposed algorithm in [17], which fits for MIMO systems. For max-SNR scheduler, fairness is not a design priority and assigns any subcarrier to the user with the highest SNR. Finally, in all simulations, different variants of the LCRA scheme are considered.

Each variant is determined by the value of C_j which is equal for all MGs in each variant. In the simulations scenarios described in the next section, for each variant $C_j = \lfloor N/(m \cdot G) \rfloor$, where $m \in Z_+$. In case of unicast transmissions, m is substituted by w. The relationship between these two variables for users in each MG is $w = K_j \cdot m$, $j = 1, \dots G$.

Hence, for unicast transmissions, there is $c_k = \lfloor N/(w \cdot G) \rfloor$ and we can see that as m increases, the number of guaranteed resources for each MG decreases.

It is important to highlight that as the number of MUs in an MG tends to infinity, the ergodic system capacity becomes independent of the MG size [31].

We validate the proposed scheme based on: (1) The spectral efficiency and (2) the fairness pointer. Spectral efficiency is defined by (13). S_E is the total system data rate averaged by the system bandwidth:

$$S_E = \frac{\sum_{j=1}^{G} \sum_{n=1}^{N} x_{j,n} R_{j,n}}{W}, \tag{13}$$

Fairness pointer is given in (14), where F_p is in the range of 0 and 1. If resources are equally partitioned to all MGs, then the pointer achieves 1 [14, 30]:

$$F = \frac{\left(\sum_{j=1}^{G} \sum_{n=1}^{N} R_{j,n} \right)^2}{G \cdot \sum_{j=1}^{G} \left(\sum_{n=1}^{N} R_{j,n} \right)^2}. \tag{14}$$

In case of unicast transmission, (14) is formed as follows:

$$\mathcal{F} = \frac{\left(\sum_{k=1}^{K} \sum_{n=1}^{N} b_{k,n} \right)^2}{K \cdot \sum_{k=1}^{K} \left(\sum_{n=1}^{N} b_{k,n} \right)^2}, \tag{15}$$

where, $b_{k,n}$ denotes the achieved bit rate of user k on subcarrier n.

6. Numerical Results

In this section, we give the performance of the LCRA in comparison with the reference multicast and unicast schemes described in the previous section. We launch simulations for various scenarios and those are outlined in the following.

6.1. LCRA Scheme versus SNR. In Figures 3 and 4, we have set target BER $= 10^{-6}$ and the SNR varies from 0 to 40 in increment of 5. The number of multicast groups is $G = 4$ for with $|\mathcal{K}_1| = |\mathcal{K}_2| = |\mathcal{K}_3| = |\mathcal{K}_4| = 4$ each one. Figure 3 shows the total system data rate versus the average SNR for the proposed LCRA scheme in comparison with the reference multicast and unicast schemes described in the beginning of the section, while Figure 4 gives the fairness pointer against the average SNR.

From Figure 3, we see that multicast transmissions enjoy higher spectral efficiency than the reference unicast schemes and all LCRA variants achieve lower spectral efficiency than the algorithm in [8], wherein fairness is not considered. On the other hand, in Figure 4 LCRA variants show more fairness than the algorithm in [8] which is an objective goal of the proposed approach.

6.2. Proposed LCRA Algorithm versus BER. This simulation scenario investigates spectral efficiency and fairness of the LCRA algorithm along with the other reference schemes against the average BER. Average BER varies from 10^{-7}

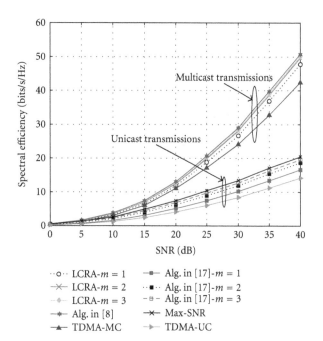

FIGURE 3: System data rate versus average SNR.

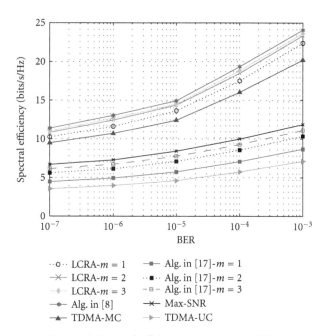

FIGURE 5: Spectral efficiency versus average BER.

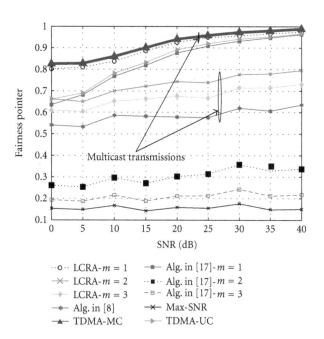

FIGURE 4: Fairness versus average SNR.

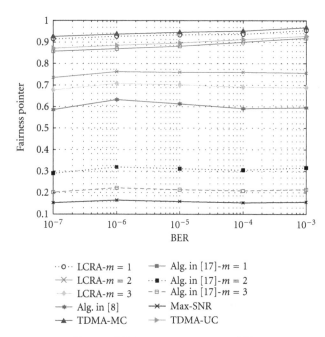

FIGURE 6: Fairness versus average BER.

to 10^{-3} with average SNR being set to 20 dB. Figure 5 plots the spectral efficiency for various values of BER and shows that as the average BER grows the same happens with the achieved spectral efficiency. However, multicast schemes provide superior performance over unicast schemes. Specifically, the algorithm in [8] and max-SNR scheme give better results than the other schemes. On the other hand, from Figure 6 we see that fairness seems to be unaffected by the average BER.

6.3. LCRA Algorithm versus Multiple MGs.

In this simulation case, various numbers of multicast groups are considered from 2 to 8, whereby SNR = 20 dB and BER = 10^{-6}. Figure 7 depicts the spectral efficiency against the number of groups for all the aforementioned multicast schemes, while Figure 8 shows the fairness pointer against the number of MGs served by the BS.

From Figure 7, we can see the tradeoff between the guaranteed number of resources for each MG and the achieved system spectral efficiency and as the number of MGs increases, the system data rate increases too, because of

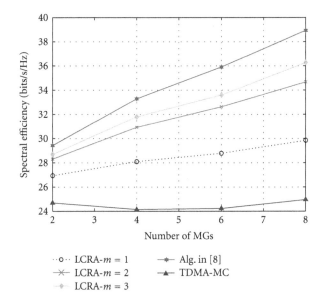

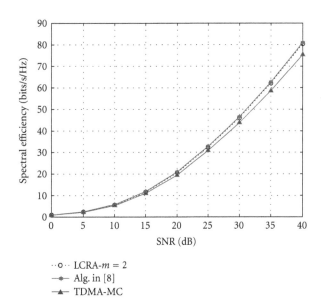

FIGURE 7: Spectral efficiency versus number of MGs.

FIGURE 9: Spectral efficiency versus SNR-no pathloss difference between MGs.

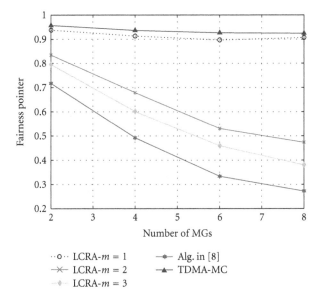

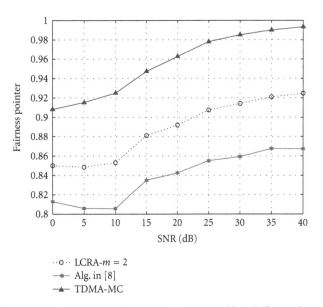

FIGURE 8: Fairness pointer versus number of MGs.

FIGURE 10: Fairness pointer versus SNR—no pathloss difference between MGs.

the additional multiuser diversity. In parallel with achieved spectral efficiency, the same happens with fairness pointer but in a different way. The difference is that fairness decreases as the number of MGs increases (Figure 8). According to conclusions in [31], even if the number of MGs tends to infinity, the performance of all schemes will reach a bound.

6.4. LCRA and Bandwidth Distribution. We consider two different multicast services which are provided to the available users. Thus, users are divided into two MGs, namely, MG-1 and MG-2 and we also consider that we have $|\mathcal{K}_1| = |\mathcal{K}_2| = 8$ users in each group. Figures 9 and 10 plot the total spectral efficiency as well as the total fairness obtained

when there is no pathloss difference between the two MGs. Similar plots are shown in Figures 11 and 12 when there is 5 dB pathloss difference between the two MGs. Individual group transmission rates (bits/s/Hz) when pathloss does not exist and when pathloss exists are given in Figures 13 and 14, respctively, while bandwidth distributions are shown in Figures 15 and 16 for the cases we study in this section. For ease of presentation, we consider 1 variant of the proposed LCRA algorithm with $m = 2$ which means that, for each MG, we guarantee $C_j = \lfloor N/(2 \cdot 2) \rfloor = 32$ subcarriers, where $j = 1, \ldots, G$.

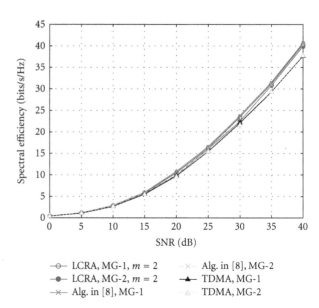

FIGURE 11: Spectral efficiency versus SNR—pathloss difference between MGs.

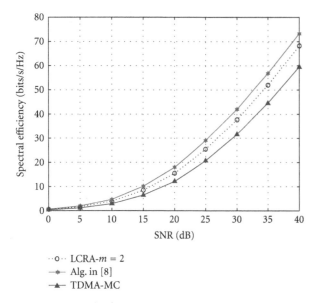

FIGURE 13: Individual MG spectral efficiency versus SNR—no pathloss difference between MGs.

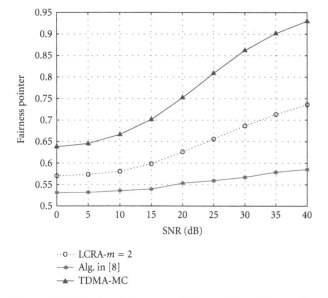

FIGURE 12: Fairness pointer versus SNR—pathloss difference between MGs.

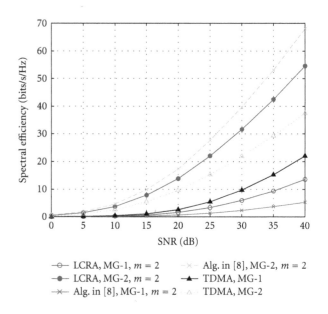

FIGURE 14: Individual MG spectral efficiency versus SNR—pathloss difference between MGs.

From Figures 9 and 11, we see the negative impact of pathloss on the overall spectral efficiency as it is expected, for all schemes. Moreover, all schemes show similar performance in case there is no pathloss. On the other hand, when pathloss exists, LCRA gives lower system throughput from the algorithm in [8] and better results than TDMA (Figure 11). Figures 10 and 12 show the decrease in the fairness pointer for all schemes and the slight increase in fairness differences among all schemes (Figure 12) which pathloss brings about.

When there is no pathloss difference between the groups, individual MG rates seem to be very close as well as their assigned spectrum. More specifically, the average channel distribution is 64.6 and 63.4 subcarriers for MG-1 and MG-2, respectively. The proposed LCRA gives 64.4 subcarriers to MG-1 and 63.6 to MG-2 on average, while with TDMA, strict fairness exists with 64 subcarriers to each group.

On the other hand, when pathloss is considered in simulations, we see that the group with less pathloss (MG-2) gives better performance than multicast group MG-1 in all schemes. The gap between the achievable bit rates of MG-1 and MG-2 is wider with the scheme in [8] and smaller with TDMA than in LCRA as we see from plots in Figure 14. Moreover, Figure 16 shows that MG-1 in LCRA has

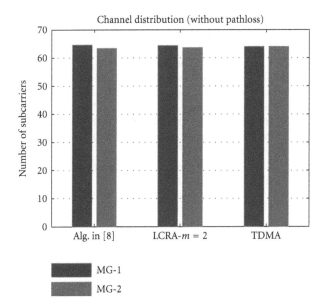

FIGURE 15: Channel distribution—no pathloss difference between MGs.

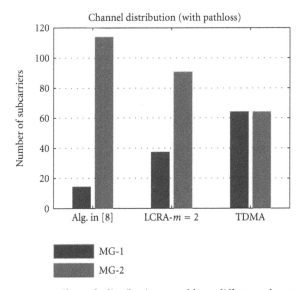

FIGURE 16: Channel distribution—pathloss difference between MGs.

a bigger share of bandwidth with 37.3 subcarriers on average than with the scheme in [8], which gives 14.3 subcarriers on average. In this case, when pathlosses exist, the proposed LCRA contributes more to system fairness. Note that, according to the parameter m, we can regulate system fairness as well as the bandwidth share of each multicast group.

7. Conclusion

In this paper, a resource allocation algorithm for the MIMO multicast systems over frequency-selective channels has been introduced. Multicasting enables multiple users to share a subcarrier and results have shown that this enhances

significantly the total throughput. The capacity can become even higher by the presence of multiple MGs which bring more diversity into the system.

The proposed algorithm proved also to be very useful in systems wherein multiple MGs coexist, particularly in case their wireless link conditions are very different. LCRA is capable of providing bandwidth access guarantees to MGs in a flexible and controllable way that other reference schemes are unable to provide.

In parallel the proposed solution achieves low-complexity implementation by reducing the computational complexity from exponential to linear. Additionally, its computational complexity is independent of the presence of multiple antennas in both BS and users and as it is analyzed proved to be comparable with other low-complexity schemes.

References

[1] F. Hartung, U. Horn, J. Huschke, M. Kampmann, T. Lohmar, and M. Lundevall, "Delivery of broadcast services in 3G networks," IEEE Transactions on Broadcasting, vol. 53, no. 1, pp. 188–198, 2007.

[2] A. Alexiou, C. Bouras, V. Kokkinos, and E. Rekkas, "An improved mechanism for multiple MBMS sessions assignment in B3G cellular networks," Wireless Networks, vol. 16, no. 3, pp. 671–686, 2010.

[3] Y.-C. Lai, P. Lin, Y. Fang, and W.-H. Chen, "Channel allocation for UMTS multimedia broadcasting and multicasting," IEEE Transactions on Wireless Communications, vol. 7, no. 11, pp. 4375–4383, 2008.

[4] A. M. C. Correia, J. C. M. Silva, N. M. B. Souto, L. A. C. Silva, A. B. Boal, and A. B. Soares, "Multi-resolution broadcast/multicast systems for MBMS," IEEE Transactions on Broadcasting, vol. 53, no. 1, pp. 224–233, 2007.

[5] M. R. Chari, F. Ling, A. Mantravadi et al., "FLO physical layer: an overview," IEEE Transactions on Broadcasting, vol. 53, no. 1, pp. 145–159, 2007.

[6] J. Liu, W. Chen, Z. Cao, and K. B. Letaief, "Dynamic power and subcarrier allocation for OFDMA-based wireless multicast systems," in Proceedings of the IEEE International Conference on Communications (ICC '08), Beijing, China, May 2008.

[7] J. Y. Kim, T. Kwon, and D. H. Cho, "Resource allocation scheme for minimizing power consumption in OFDM multicast systems," IEEE Communications Letters, vol. 11, no. 6, pp. 486–488, 2007.

[8] J. Xu, S. J. Lee, W. S. Kang, and J. S. Seo, "Adaptive resource allocation for mimo-ofdm based wireless multicast systems," IEEE Transactions on Broadcasting, vol. 56, no. 1, pp. 98–102, 2010.

[9] I. G. Fraimis, V. D. Papoutsis, and S. A. Kotsopoulos, "A decentralized subchannel allocation scheme with Inter-cell Interference Coordination (ICIC) for multi-cell OFDMA systems," in Proceedings of the 53rd IEEE Global Communications Conference (GLOBECOM '10), December 2010.

[10] Y. Ben-Shimol, I. Kitroser, and Y. Dinitz, "Two-dimensional mapping for wireless OFDMA systems," IEEE Transactions on Broadcasting, vol. 52, no. 3, pp. 388–396, 2006.

[11] J. Jang and K. B. Lee, "Transmit power adaptation for multiuser OFDM systems," IEEE Journal on Selected Areas in Communications, vol. 21, no. 2, pp. 171–178, 2003.

[12] G. Li and H. Liu, "On the optimality of the OFDMA network," IEEE Communications Letters, vol. 9, no. 5, pp. 438–440, 2005.

[13] T. C. H. Alen, A. S. Madhukumar, and F. Chin, "Capacity enhancement of a multi-user OFDM system using dynamic frequency allocation," *IEEE Transactions on Broadcasting*, vol. 49, no. 4, pp. 344–353, 2003.

[14] V. D. Papoutsis, I. G. Fraimis, and S. A. Kotsopoulos, "Fairness-aware resource allocation for the SISO downlink over frequency-selective channels," in *Proceedings of the IEEE Wireless Communications and Networking Conference (WCNC '10)*, April 2010.

[15] M. Ergen, S. Coleri, and P. Varaiya, "Qos aware adaptive eesource allocation techniques for fair scheduling in OFDMA based broadband wireless access systems," *IEEE Transactions on Broadcasting*, vol. 49, no. 4, pp. 362–370, 2003.

[16] C. S. Bae and D. H. Cho, "Fairness-aware adaptive resource allocation scheme in multihop OFDMA systems," *IEEE Communications Letters*, vol. 11, no. 2, pp. 134–136, 2007.

[17] V. D. Papoutsis, I. G. Fraimis, and S. A. Kotsopoulos, "Resource allocation algorithm for MIMO-OFDMA systems with minimum resources guarantee," in *Proceedings of the IEEE International Conference on Electronics, Cicuits and Systems (ICECS '10)*, Athens, Greece, December 2010.

[18] P. W. C. Chan and R. S. Cheng, "Capacity maximization for zero-forcing MIMO-OFDMA downlink systems with multiuser diversity," *IEEE Transactions on Wireless Communications*, vol. 6, no. 5, pp. 1880–1889, 2007.

[19] G. Li and H. Liu, "On the optimality of downlink OFDMA MIMO systems," in *Proceedings of the 38th IEEE Asilomar Conference on Signals, Systems and Computers*, pp. 324–328, California, Calif, USA, November 2004.

[20] Z. J. Guan, H. Li, C. Q. Xu, X. L. Zhou, and W. J. Zhang, "Adaptive subcarrier allocation for MIMO-OFDMA wireless systems using Hungarian method," *Journal of Shanghai University*, vol. 13, no. 2, pp. 146–149, 2009.

[21] J. Xu, J. Kim, W. Paik, and J. S. Seo, "Adaptive resource allocation algorithm with fairness for MIMO-OFDMA system," in *Proceedings of the IEEE Vehicle Technology Conference (VTC '06)*, Melbourne, Australia, May 2006.

[22] A. N. Zaki and A. O. Fapojuwo, "A graph-based resource allocation algorithm for downlink MIMO-OFDMA networks," in *Proceedings of the IEEE Global Telecommunications Conference (GLOBECOM '09)*, December 2009.

[23] M. S. Maw and I. Sasase, "Resource allocation scheme in MIMO-OFDMA system for user's different data throughput requirements," *IEICE Transactions on Communications*, vol. E91-B, no. 2, pp. 494–504, 2008.

[24] B. Da and C. C. Ko, "Resource allocation in downlink MIMO-OFDMA with proportional fairness," *Journal of Communications*, vol. 4, no. 1, pp. 8–13, 2009.

[25] S. Xiao, X. Xiao, B. Li, and Z. Hu, "Adaptive subcarrier allocation for multiuser MIMO OFDM systems in frequency selective fading channel," in *Proceedings of the IEEE International Wireless Communications, Networking & Mobile Computing Conference*, Wuhan, China, 2005.

[26] X. Lu and Z. Li, "An adaptive resource allocation algorithm based on spatial subchannel in multiuser MIMO/OFDM systems," in *Proceedings of the IEEE International Conference on Communications (ICC '08)*, J. Cai and X. Chen, Eds., Beijing, China, May 2008.

[27] H. Rohling and R. Grunheid, "Performance comparison of different multiple access schemes for the downlink of an OFDM communication system," in *Proceedings of the IEEE Vehicle Technology Conference (VTC '97)*, May 1997.

[28] S. T. Chung and A. J. Goldsmith, "Degrees of freedom in adaptive modulation: a unified view," *IEEE Transactions on Communications*, vol. 49, no. 9, pp. 1561–1571, 2001.

[29] G. Li and H. Liu, "Downlink radio resource allocation for multi-cell OFDMA system," *IEEE Transactions on Wireless Communications*, vol. 5, no. 12, pp. 3451–3459, 2006.

[30] Z. Shen, J. G. Andrews, and B. L. Evans, "Adaptive resource allocation in multiuser OFDM systems with proportional rate constraints," *IEEE Transactions on Wireless Communications*, vol. 4, no. 6, pp. 2726–2737, 2005.

[31] C. Suh and J. Mo, "Resource allocation for multicast services in multicarrier wireless communications," *IEEE Transactions on Wireless Communications*, vol. 7, no. 1, pp. 27–31, 2008.

13

Multi-Objective Genetic Algorithm for Task Assignment on Heterogeneous Nodes

Carolina Blanch Perez del Notario, Rogier Baert, and Maja D'Hondt

SSET Department of IMEC, Kapeldreef 75, 3001 Leuven, Belgium

Correspondence should be addressed to Carolina Blanch Perez del Notario, blanch@imec.be

Academic Editor: Yifeng He

Task assignment in grid computing, where both processing and bandwidth constraints at multiple heterogeneous devices need to be considered, is a challenging problem. Moreover, targeting the optimization of multiple objectives makes it even more challenging. This paper presents a task assignment strategy based on genetic algorithms in which multiple and conflicting objectives are simultaneously optimized. Specifically, we maximize task execution quality while minimizing energy and bandwidth consumption. Moreover, in our video processing scenario; we consider transcoding to lower spatial/temporal resolutions to tradeoff between video quality; processing, and bandwidth demands. The task execution quality is then determined by the number of successfully processed streams and the spatial-temporal resolution at which they are processed. The results show that the proposed algorithm offers a range of Pareto optimal solutions that outperforms all other reference strategies.

1. Introduction

Nowadays multimedia applications such as multicamera surveillance or multipoint videoconferencing, are increasingly demanding both in processing power, and bandwidth requirements. In addition, there is a tendency towards thin client applications where the processing capacities of the client device are reduced and the tasks are migrated to more powerful devices in the network.

In this respect, grid computing can integrate and make use of these heterogeneous computing resources which are connected through networks, overcoming the limited processing capabilities at a client's device.

In the context of distributed media processing we can think of scenarios such as video control rooms where multiple video streams are processed and simultaneously displayed. One way to downscale the processing and bandwidth requirements at the displaying device is by transcoding the video streams at the servers to lower temporal or spatial resolutions. This is done, however, at the cost of a degraded perceived video quality and an increased processing cost at the server. Therefore, in grid computing we may need to optimize and trade off multiple objectives, targeting for instance

quality maximization of the stream execution and minimization of the energy consumption on the client/servers simultaneously. In this respect, implementing a suitable strategy for task assignment/scheduling becomes crucial for achieving a good performance in grid computing. This subject has been thoroughly studied in literature, and various heuristic approaches have been widely used for scheduling. In particular, Genetic Algorithms (GAs) have received much attention as robust stochastic search algorithms for various optimization problems. In this context, works such as [1–3] have used Genetic Algorithms to approach task scheduling within a device. In [1, 2], genetic algorithms are combined with heuristics such as "Earliest Deadline First" to assign tasks onto multiple processors. The work in [3] extends the analysis to heterogeneous processors where the algorithm can also determine the optimal number of processors, given a number of tasks. In [4, 5], the work is extended to multiple processing nodes in the network. This way, in [4], a thorough study is done on the performance of different GA operators on a scheduling problem on grid computing systems. Heterogeneous processors are considered with the target to minimize the makespan and flow time of the tasks.

The authors in [5] use also GA to address a similar objective in grid computing. As in [4] neither data transmission nor resource cost is considered.

In [6], a combination between GA and ACO algorithms is presented for task scheduling among multiple nodes but no bandwidth considerations are made. In [7], the authors use evolutionary fuzzy systems to solve job scheduling in decentralized computational grids where jobs between grid clusters are exchanged. The average response time per job is minimized but again the overhead of data transfers is not considered. The work in [8] also uses a genetic-based algorithm to assign multiple tasks in grid computing and minimize the make-span in the task execution but unlike previous works, the transmission time to the processing node is considered. Similar considerations are taken in [9] where the authors propose a strategy based on the Ant Colony Optimization algorithm (ACO) to effectively assign tasks to computing resources, given the current load conditions of each computing resource and network status.

Note that the presented works only consider single objective optimization. It is in works such as [10–16] where GAs are used to address multiple objectives in the resolution of scheduling problems. This way, in [10], the authors address the Job Shop scheduling problem while targeting multiple objectives, namely, minimal make-span and minimal machine workload. However, the case study addressed is very simple and only homogeneous processors are considered. The work in [11] addresses the flow-shop scheduling problem with an adaptive genetic algorithm. Pareto fronts are used to guide a multiple-objective search: the total completion time and total tardiness. As in our work, multiple objectives are addressed, however, task assignments at system level and bandwidth limitations are not considered. The authors in [12] consider heterogeneous processors and a multiobjective GA targets in this case the minimization of the make-span, flow-time, and reliability. The work in [13] is an early work on applying GA for multiobjective optimization, in this case to minimize both task execution and power during cosynthesis of distributed embedded systems. In [14], the performance of a NSGA-II-based evolutionary algorithm is compared to the true Pareto front of solutions found with the Branch and Bound method. The objectives targeted are the make-span and the task completion time. Finally, in [15] the method of particle swarm optimization is combined with evolutionary method outperforming typical genetic algorithms.

However, in none of these works [12–15], there is any consideration made over bandwidth constraints. Only in [16] the network resources in terms of bandwidth and latency are considered. In this case, an Ant Colony Optimization algorithm is developed to address grid scheduling.

In our approach, we use GAs to target multiple objectives for task assignment in grid computing and we consider bandwidth availability between nodes. Moreover, in comparison with all related work presented, in our analysis, we introduce an extra dimension on the task assignment problem by considering the downscaling of the video streams to lower spatial/temporal resolution. This offers a tradeoff between bandwidth and processing constraints on one hand and perceived video quality on the other hand. By doing this the effective system capacity to process tasks is increased while a graceful degradation of the video stream quality is allowed. Additionally, we target multiple objectives such as task quality maximization, client's energy minimization, and minimization of the bandwidth usage.

The rest of the paper is structured as follows. Section 2 describes the scenarios for distributed media processing considered. Section 3 describes the basic strategies for task assignment as well as the strategy for quality maximization while Section 4 introduces the strategy based on genetic algorithms. We present the results and compare the performance of the different strategies in Section 5. Finally, Section 6 concludes this work.

2. Scenario of Distributed Media Processing

In the context of distributed video processing, we are considering a scenario such as the one of a video control room. Several video contents are streamed towards the client device, where the content is visualized, while the required video processing can be distributed between the client and other processing nodes such as servers.

We assume all processing nodes to be heterogeneous with a different amount of processing resources, such as CPUs and GPUs. In addition, we assume that the client's device has more limited processing capacities than the server nodes. Concretely, we consider 4CPUs and 1GPU at each server node, while only 2CPUs at the client node. We assume moreover that multiple codec implementations for these different processor types are available. To overcome the limited processing at the client node, we perform distributed processing over other nodes in the network. In this case, the decoding task is executed at a server, and the resulting output (raw video) is transmitted to the client's device. Note that this highly increases the bandwidth requirements, which should fit in the maximum available bandwidth towards the client that we assume of 1 Gbps and shared from any server node to the client node. Therefore, to fit both processing and bandwidth requirements, one possibility is to trans-code (decode and reencode at a lower temporal or spatial resolution) the video streams at the server's side. This lowers both its bandwidth and decoding processing requirements at the end device at the cost of a reduced perceived quality and increased server processing.

The following section describes the task assignment strategies used in the scenario described.

3. Single Objective Assignment Strategies

An efficient task assignment strategy is a key element in the context of distributed grid computing. In this section, we describe the assignment strategies that we implement for comparison with our evolutionary-based approach.

Round-Robin Strategy (RR). The stream processing tasks are assigned in turns on the different available processing elements, that is, client device and server nodes.

Max-Min Heuristic (MM). This is a well-known heuristic [17] that assigns the most demanding stream processing tasks first on the processor that is going to finish them the earliest.

TransCode-All Strategy (TA). We assign all video streams to be spatially trans-coded at the server nodes. This lowers the processing requirements for decoding at the client devices while it also reduces the bandwidth usage. However, this happens at the cost of a reduced quality of the video streams. As trans-coding is an intensive task (decoding plus encoding) the trans-coding of the streams is evenly distributed among the available servers (by means of round robin) to avoid processing overload of a server.

Strategy Maximum Quality (MaxQ). In addition to the presented strategies, we implement a strategy that targets the maximization of the quality of the stream assignment. We describe this strategy next for the case of 1 server and 1 client node, where P_{client} and P_{server} are the total processing cost at client and server for the current task assignment, and P_{client}^{max} and P_{server}^{max} are the maximum processing capacity at the client node and server respectively. In a similar way, BW is the bandwidth required by the current task assignment while BW^{max} corresponds to the maximum available bandwidth.

We consider that the assignment and execution, t_i, of video stream "i" can take one of the following values:

   c: stream assigned to be decoded at the client at original temporal and spatial resolution.

   s: stream assigned to be decoded at the server at original temporal and spatial resolution.

   temp: stream transcoded to lower temporal resolution at the server.

   spat: stream transcoded to lower spatial resolution at the server.

   comb: stream transcoded to both lower temporal and spatial resolution at the server.

This way, our task assignment consists of a set of $t_i \in \{c, s, temp, spat, comb\}$ for every $i \in \{1, \dots, N\}$ where N is the total number of video streams to be processed.

We want to find a task assignment solution whose bandwidth and processing demands at client and server fit within the bandwidth and processing constraints:

$$BW = \sum_i BW_i \leq BW^{max},$$

$$P_{client} = \sum_i P_{i,client} \leq P_{client}^{max}, \tag{1}$$

$$P_{server} = \sum_i P_{i,server} \leq P_{server}^{max},$$

$$\forall i \mid t_i \in \{c, s, temp, spat, comb\}.$$

Algorithm 1 is described in the following paragraphs and table.

In Step 1, the algorithm assigns as many stream decoding tasks as possible to execute on the client device; this number of tasks is constrained by the processing power at the device.

Step 1: Maximize $\{k \mid t_i = c \ \nabla i = \{1, \dots, k\}, P_{client} \leq P_{client}^{max}\}$
Step 2: Set $t_i = s \ \nabla i = \{(k+1) \cdots N\}$
WHILE ($P_{client} \geq P_{client}^{max}$ or $P_{server} \geq P_{server}^{max}$ or $BW \geq BW^{max}$)
   Step 3: IF $\exists i = max_i\{BW_i \mid t_i = s\}$
         THEN $t_i = temp$
      ELSE IF $\exists i = max_i\{BW_i \mid t_i = temp\}$
           THEN $t_i = spat$
        ELSE IF $\exists i = max_i\{BW_i \mid t_i = spat\}$
             THEN $t_i = comb$
   END
  Repeat Step 3 until $BW \leq BW^{max}$
  Step 4: IF ($P_{server} \geq P_{server}^{max}$ *and* $t_i = comb \ \nabla i = \{1, \dots, N\}$
          *THEN **STOP***
      ELSEIF $P_{client} \geq P_{client}^{max}$ *THEN*
         IF $\exists i \mid t_i = c$ *THEN*
            Set $t_i = s$
        *ELSE **STOP***
  END
END

ALGORITHM 1

In Step 2, the remaining tasks, exceeding the processing power at the client device, are assigned for processing at the server.

Then, we check if the current assignment meets bandwidth and processing constraints. While either bandwidth or processing constraints at client or server are not met, the algorithm will gradually transcode video tasks to lower temporal or spatial resolution at the server (done in Step 3) or will migrate some of the decoding tasks from the client device to the server (done in Step 4). This process continues till the assignment fits the system bandwidth and processing constraints.

In Step 3 we proceed as follows.

(i) Find those stream which are currently assigned at original temporal and spatial resolution to the server ($t_i = s$). From those, pick the stream with the biggest BW demand and transcode it to lower temporal resolution ($t_i = temp$).

(ii) If there are no streams available at full temporal resolution, then we take a stream at lowered temporal resolution ($t_i = temp$) with the highest bandwidth demand and transcode it to a lower spatial resolution ($t_i = spat$).

(iii) If all streams have been spatially transcoded, then we pick one of them (at highest bandwidth) and transcode it both temporally and spatially ($t_i = comb$).

Note that at this point (Step 3), we are trying to find those stream tasks (t_i) that demand the maximum bandwidth (generally also the highest processing) in order to reduce the bandwidth demands by trans-coding the minimum amount of streams.

This procedure is repeated till the bandwidth constraint is met.

Finally, in Step 4, if the processing constraints at the client are exceeded we migrate one client task to the server side. If at the server's side the processing constraints are not met and all streams have been spatially and temporally transcoded, the assignment loop is stopped. It is not possible to downscale the stream tasks further, and therefore we cannot find an assignment that satisfies all constraints while processing all streams.

3.1. Evaluation of Stream Assignment Cost.

If the task assignment exceeds any of the system constraints in (1), then the execution of some tasks will fail. This way, an individual stream processing task fails when it does not fit within the available processing or bandwidth resources. For instance, the node where the stream is assigned may not have sufficient processing resources, or even if the processing is completed at the server, the available bandwidth could be insufficient to deliver the server's output to the client causing the stream processing to fail.

Related to this, we can attach to each assignment solution a corresponding cost in terms of end video quality, bandwidth usage, and energy consumption. This cost is determined by how many stream tasks are successfully completed and how (on which device and at what spatial-temporal resolution) they are executed.

Therefore, for a specific stream assignment solution we first need to estimate which stream processing tasks can be successfully completed and which will fail due to not meeting current processing and bandwidth constraints. Then, depending on the specific execution of each individual stream processing, we can attach a cost, in terms of quality, consumed bandwidth, and energy at the client's side, as defined in Table 1.

Note that the data in Table 1 corresponds to streams of Standard Definition (SD, 720 × 480 pixels). We also consider streams of Common Intermediate Format (CIF, 352 × 288 pixels) and High Definition (HD, 1920 × 1080 pixels) where bandwidth and energy costs are scaled accordingly with respect to SD resolution.

A stream processing fails when it does not fit within the available processing, or bandwidth resources. For instance, the node where the stream is assigned may not have sufficient processing resources or even if the processing is completed at the server, the available bandwidth could be insufficient to deliver the server's output to the client causing the stream processing to fail.

We attach successfully processed streams a quality value of 1 when the content is displayed at the client at its original temporal and spatial resolution. If the video stream is downscaled to a lower temporal/spatial resolution in order to fit bandwidth or processing constraints, the perceived video quality will be slightly degraded, and therefore, we attach a lower quality value. This favors that to maximize the streams quality, assignment solutions where the original spatial and temporal resolution of the streams are kept are preferred. Note that the quality value of any stream at its original resolution (CIF, SD, or HD) is identical; only in transcoding, we consider the quality degraded; that is, an HD-streamed spatially transcoded (to SD) is attached a 0.8 quality

TABLE 1: Definition of task execution costs (SD resolution).

Stream Execution	Quality TQ$_i$	Bandwidth TBW$_i$	Energy TE$_i$
Failed execution	0	0 Mbps	0
Decoding at client	1	20 Mbps	1
Decoding at server	1	146 Mbps	0
Temporal transcoding	0.9	10 Mbps	0.5
Spatial transcoding	0.8	7 Mbps	0.25
Temporal and Spatial transcoding	0.7	3.5 Mbps	0.12

(distortion of 0.2) while a stream at original SD resolution is attached the maximum quality of 1 (0 distortion).

The bandwidth cost per stream is also dependent on how the stream processing is performed. This way, if decoding is performed at the server's side, the stream is transmitted raw to the client, which highly increases the bandwidth requirements. On the contrary, if the stream is transcoded at a server to a lower spatial or temporal resolution, the bandwidth requirements are reduced. For the sake of simplicity, we assume the same bandwidth cost for all video streams with the same spatial-temporal resolution. In addition, we consider that reducing the temporal resolution from 30 frames per second to 15 approximately reduces the bandwidth by half. Similarly, we assume that reducing the spatial resolution to the immediate lower resolution roughly reduces the bandwidth to approximately one-third of the original resolution.

Finally, in terms of energy/processing cost at the client's device, we assume that the energy cost is negligible when the video decoding task is executed on a server, and the raw output video stream is merely transmitted to the client device for display. When the decoding task is executed at the client, the corresponding energy cost is dependent on the temporal and spatial resolution of the decoded stream. We assume that decoding a video sequence at 15 fps requires approximately half of the processing/energy than decoding the same sequence at 30 fps. In a similar way, when the spatial resolution is lowered, for example from SD to CIF, we can roughly assume 1/4 of the decoding energy costs. Finally, the combination of lowering temporal and spatial resolution corresponds to a decoding cost of 18 of the original resolution. In case of a failed task execution, we assume no processing effort at the client's side and therefore no energy consumption. Note that the values in Table 1 are taken as approximate and reference values and have no impact on the relative performance of the assignment strategies.

To obtain the total quality TQ, bandwidth TBW, or energy cost TE for the complete assignment, we simply need to sum all individual stream processing costs as follows:

$$\text{Quality TQ} = \sum_{i=1}^{N} \text{TQ}_i \qquad (2)$$

or equivalently

$$\text{Distortion TDist} = \sum_{i=1}^{N} \text{Max Quality} - \sum_{i=1}^{N} \text{TQ}_i, \qquad (3)$$

$$\text{Bandwidth TBW} = \sum_{i=1}^{N} \text{TBW}_i, \qquad (4)$$

$$\text{Energy TE} = \sum_{i=1}^{N} \text{TE}_i, \qquad (5)$$

where N is the total number of streams considered in the assignment.

4. Multiobjective Genetic Algorithm

The heuristic and strategies presented in the previous section target at most one single objective optimization. However in practice we may want to optimize multiple objectives simultaneously. For instance, we may need to maximize the video streams quality while minimizing the bandwidth usage and the energy cost at the client. This multiobjective optimization is challenging, especially when multiple heterogeneous nodes and multiple ways of processing the streams (decoding, trans-coding) are considered. To achieve this, we base ourselves on genetic algorithms and use the concept of Pareto fronts of solutions. This allows us to obtain a set of Pareto optimal assignment solutions from which we can choose the solution that best meets the constraints or our preferences towards a certain objective. In addition, a genetic algorithm is a flexible tool where the target objective can be easily modified. The remainder of this section describes how the genetic algorithm is implemented.

4.1. Genetic Algorithm Structure. A genetic algorithm (GA) is a search heuristic that mimics the process of natural evolution. In a genetic algorithm, a population of strings (called chromosomes), which encode candidate solutions (called individuals of the population) to an optimization problem, evolves toward better solutions. The evolution usually starts from a population of randomly generated individuals and happens in generations. In each generation, the fitness of every individual in the population is evaluated, multiple individuals are selected from the current population (based on their fitness), and modified (recombined and possibly randomly mutated) to form a new population. The new population is then used in the next iteration of the algorithm. Generally, each generation of solutions improves the quality of its individuals. The algorithm terminates when either a maximum number of generations has been produced, or a satisfactory fitness level has been reached. The structure of our genetic algorithm can be summarized as follows.

Step 1. Initialize the population of chromosomes.

Step 2. Evaluate each chromosome with the *fitness* function.

Step 3. Crossover operation: select parents according to fitness and create new children chromosomes.

Step 4. Random *mutation* of chromosomes.

Step 5. Elitist *selection:* retain fittest chromosomes among those of the old generation and the new ones resulting from Steps 3 and 4.

Step 6. Repeat Steps 2 to 5 till termination condition is reached.

4.2. Representation of the Solution Domain. Traditionally, solutions are represented in binary as strings of 0s and 1s, but other encodings are also possible. In our case, we use a decimal representation. Each possible stream assignment solution is represented as a chromosome, which is composed of several gens. In our case, the length of the chromosome is equal to the number of streams that need to be scheduled in the system. Each of the genes in the chromosome represents the node that is going to process the stream and how it is going to be processed. Table 2 gives a description of the meaning of each possible gene value in the chromosome. In this example, the available processing nodes are the client device S0 and two server nodes S1 and S2.

Figure 1 shows an example of chromosome (assignment solution). By looking at the gene description in Table 2, we can see that the corresponding stream task assignment would be as follows: the first two streams ("2") are decoded at server S1, the third and fourth streams ("1") are executed at the client device S0, the next three streams are transcoded at server S2 to a lower spatial resolution ("8"), and the last stream is processed at server S1 where it is transcoded to lower temporal resolution ("3").

We now detail how to compute the cost of the assignment solution in Figure 1. Assuming all streams are of SD resolution, the corresponding cost of this assignment according to Table 1 would be the following.

For streams 1 and 2 decoded at the server at full resolution and transmitted raw to the client:

$$\begin{aligned} \text{BW}_1 = \text{BW}_2 &= 146\,\text{Mbps}, \\ \text{TQ}_1 = \text{TQ}_2 &= 1, \qquad (6) \\ \text{TE}_1 = \text{TE}_2 &= 0. \end{aligned}$$

For streams 3 and 4 decoded at the client device at full resolution:

$$\begin{aligned} \text{BW}_3 = \text{BW}_4 &= 20\,\text{Mbps}, \\ \text{TQ}_3 = \text{TQ}_4 &= 1, \qquad (7) \\ \text{TE}_3 = \text{TE}_4 &= 1. \end{aligned}$$

For streams 5, 6, and 7 spatially transcoded at a server:

$$\begin{aligned} \text{BW}_5 = \text{BW}_6 = \text{BW}_7 &= 7\,\text{Mbps}, \\ \text{TQ}_5 = \text{TQ}_6 = \text{TQ}_7 &= 0.8, \qquad (8) \\ \text{TE}_5 = \text{TE}_6 = \text{TE}_7 &= 0.25 \end{aligned}$$

For stream 8 that is temporally transcoded at a server before being sent to the client:

$$\text{BW}_8 = 10\,\text{Mbps}, \qquad \text{TQ}_8 = 0.9, \qquad \text{TE}_8 = 0.5. \qquad (9)$$

Therefore, the total value of the assignment in the three-dimension space is

$$\sum_i \text{BW}_i = 363\,\text{Mbps}, \qquad \sum_i \text{TQ}_i = 7.3, \qquad \sum_i \text{TE}_i = 3.25. \qquad (10)$$

TABLE 2: Description of genes.

Gene value	Meaning on task execution
"1"	Decoded at client device S0
"2"	Decoded at S1 and transmitted to S0
"3"	Transcoded at S1 to lower temporal resolution
"4"	Transcoded at S1 to lower spatial resolution
"5"	Transcoded at S1 to lower spatial-temporal resolution
"6"	Decoded at S2 and transmitted to S0
"7"	Transcoded at S2 to lower temporal resolution
"8"	Transcoded at S2 to lower spatial resolution
"9"	Transcoded at S2 to lower spatial-temporal resolution

2	2	1	1	8	8	8	3

FIGURE 1: Example of chromosome.

4.3. Initialization of GA Population. In general terms we initialize the population of assignment solutions by random generation. We also include in the initial population solutions that contribute to distribute the tasks processing evenly among the existing processing elements as well as solutions that imply transcoding of all processing tasks (as this may facilitate convergence to suitable assignments in high load scenarios). By doing so, we are making sure that certain potentially useful features are present in the population.

With respect to the population size, its optimal value is highly dependent on the scenario dimensions. In our case, we experimented with populations of size 10 to 40 and determined experimentally that a population of size 30 was suitable for the considered scenarios.

In addition, in a dynamic scenario where the number of tasks to be processed may be varying over time, we can improve convergence by reusing previously found solutions as part of the initial population for a new scenario. For instance, if the stream tasks to be processed increase from N to $N + 1$, then we can use the assignment solutions found for N streams as initial population for the assignment of $N + 1$ streams, while a random assignment is added for the extra $N + 1$th stream. This helps the algorithm converge and finds an optimal solution. Moreover, it helps preserve the previous assignment solution as it minimizes the change of tasks assignments in the system.

4.4. Fitness Function. The goal of the fitness function is to evaluate how good an assignment solution is with respect to the defined target objectives. If we consider the optimization of a single objective, for instance, maximization of the video quality, we can define the fitness function as the quality value of every assignment:

$$\text{Fitness} = \text{Quality} = \sum_{i=1}^{N} TQ_i \qquad (11)$$

N = total number of streams.

This way, the fittest assignments are those with the highest video stream quality.

If we are considering multiple objectives such as video quality, bandwidth usage, and energy consumption at the client device, a particular assignment solution will result in a certain value in these three axes. In other words, each assignment solution can be represented as a point in the multiobjective space with the objective values (TDist, TBW, and TE).

Each of these values is obtained as the sum of distortion, bandwidth and energy for all N stream tasks considered:

$$\text{TDist} = \sum_{i=1}^{N} \text{TDist}_i, \quad \text{TBW} = \sum_{i=1}^{N} \text{TBW}_i, \quad \text{TE} = \sum_{i=1}^{N} \text{TE}_i. \qquad (12)$$

With the task distortion related to the task quality as

$$\text{TDist}_i = \text{Max } Q_i - TQ_i. \qquad (13)$$

To minimize multiple objectives, we would like then to minimize the following function where $w1$, $w2$, and $w3$ are the weights for the different objectives:

$$f(\text{dist}, \text{BW}, E) = w1 * \text{TDist} + w2 * \text{TBW} + w3 * \text{TE}. \qquad (14)$$

Minimizing (14) is then equivalent to maximizing the following fitness function in our GA:

$$\text{Fitness} = \frac{1}{f(\text{dist}, \text{BW}, E)}. \qquad (15)$$

To avoid the need of weighting factors in the fitness function, we use the concept of Pareto points for the multiobjective optimization. Pareto points are optimal tradeoffs in the multiobjective space and obtaining the set of Pareto points from all assignment solutions is equivalent to exploring a range of weights in (14)-(15).

We are therefore interested in obtaining a range of Pareto optimal solutions in said multiobjective space. In addition, we evaluate the fitness of an assignment solution according to how close the solution is to a Pareto point or to the actual Pareto envelope.

In Figure 2, we can see that this favors that non-Pareto solutions like A, which lie close to the Pareto front, are selected to breed and mutate hopefully generating Pareto points within new areas of the Pareto front. This helps newer generations of Pareto front spread over the bidimensional space without losing diversity and concentrating around the specific area of the initial Pareto points.

To evaluate the fitness of each solution point, we compute the Euclidean distance from each point to the closest point in the hypothetical Pareto front. In a three-dimensional objective space, this is expressed as

$$\text{Fitness}(i) = \frac{1}{\text{min}} \left(\text{Euclid}(i, j) \right)$$

$$= \frac{1}{\text{min}} \left(\sqrt{(i_1 - j_1)^2 + (i_2 - j_2)^2 + (i_3 - j_3)^2} \right)$$

$$\nabla j \in \text{Pareto front}, \qquad (16)$$

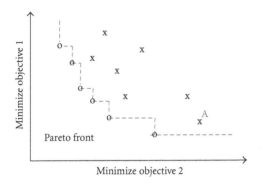

FIGURE 2: Pareto front of solutions.

o Pareto
x Non-Pareto

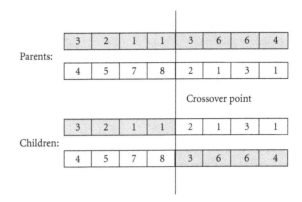

FIGURE 3: Single-point crossover.

where every point has the following representation in the three-dimensional multiobjective space $i = \langle i_1, i_2, i_3 \rangle$. The closer a point is to this Pareto front, the fitter it is considered. Note that Pareto points, already belonging to the Pareto envelope, have the minimum distance to it and therefore are assigned the highest fitness values. This guarantees that they are always kept for the next generation of the GA.

4.5. Selection of Individuals According to Fitness. During each successive generation, a proportion of the existing population of solutions is selected to breed a new generation. Individual solutions can be selected through a fitness-based process, where fitter solutions (as measured by the fitness function) are typically more likely to be selected. In our case, we do not use a probabilistic selection but an elitist selection, that is, the fittest members of the population are used to breed a new population. Moreover, after crossover and generation of new child solutions, we apply again elitist selection and retain in the solution space those solutions that are the fittest among the parents and the newly generated children solutions. We use the fitness function as described in the earlier section. In practice, this means that for the selection of the parent chromosomes during the crossover and mutation steps, we select the Pareto optimal points from the pool of chromosome/solutions (as these are the fittest points in our space) and from the non-Pareto points, we take the fittest ones.

The elitism we apply in the selection is similar to the one applied in the Nondominated sorting GA or NSGA [18] in the sense that the Pareto or nondominated solution points are identified and given the highest fitness value. Our approach differs however in the treatment of the non-Pareto solutions, in our case, the fitness of these points is computed based on the distance to the Pareto front, more similar to the Strength Pareto Evolutionary Algorithm (SPEA). With respect to SPEA [19], we apply a similar elitist selection, after both crossover and mutation as the Pareto solutions are always kept for the next generation. However, unlike SPEA, we do not maintain a fixed size for the Pareto population, and to avoid a too early convergence of the algorithm, we allow

a high degree of mutation among the solutions in the Pareto front.

4.6. Evolution: Crossover and Mutation. The *crossover* step consists in creating a second generation of solutions from an initial population of solutions. For each new solution to be produced, a pair of "parent" solutions is selected for breeding from the current population. By producing a "child" solution using the crossover, a new solution is created which typically shares many of the characteristics of its "parents". In our algorithm, crossover is implemented as single-point crossover. This is, a random point is selected in the parent chromosome, and the information before and after that point is exchanged and recombined between the two parents creating in this way two child solutions that share the parent's characteristics. The single-point crossover is represented in Figure 3.

Crossover is applied on a percentage of the population given by the *crossover rate*. Out of the new population of "parents" and "child" chromosomes, we apply an elitist selection and keep a population with size of the initial population with the fittest individuals. Generally, the average fitness of the new population will have increased, since only the best individuals from the first generation are selected for breeding. After crossover, the *mutation* step is implemented. The purpose of mutation in GAs is preserving and introducing diversity. Mutation should allow the algorithm to avoid local minima by preventing the population of chromosomes from becoming too similar to each other, thus slowing or even stopping evolution. Mutation is implemented by randomly changing some of the genes in the chromosome with a probability given by the *mutation rate*.

We use a high mutation rate in our approach, as this helps the algorithm avoid local minima. Nevertheless, we do not risk losing good features of the solution space, thanks to the elitist selection applied after crossover or mutation, that is, the fittest solutions are always kept; therefore, if the mutated solutions are less fit than the original solutions, the original solutions are retained.

4.7. Parameter Selection for Genetic Algorithm. The way the Genetic Algorithm evolves towards fitter solutions is highly dependent on the parameter selection. In this respect, the percentage of the population on which the crossover and

Table 3: Assignment quality versus population size.

Nos. of tasks/population	10	20	30	40
10	10	19.7	28	35.9
20	10	19.9	28.4	36.8
30	10	19.9	28.7	36.5
40	10	19.9	28.4	36.6

Table 4: GA parameters.

Crossover rate	0.7
Mutation rate	0.3
Population size	30
Max generations	30

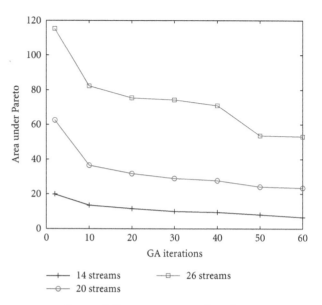

Figure 4: Convergence versus iterations.

mutation steps are implemented is given by the crossover and mutation rate parameters, respectively. As explained in the previous section, a high mutation rate is selected to prevent the algorithm from a too early convergence and falling in local minima. A similar approach is taken in [14, 20]. Moreover, in [14], a similar crossover rate is also selected. Unlike [14] however, we require a lower population size and lower number of generations. This is possibly due to the fact that the elitist selection we implement helps speed up the convergence.

Table 3 shows the impact of the population size on the quality of the assignment solution found (with task quality as single objective) for a different number of tasks considered. We can first see that when the number of tasks increases it becomes more difficult to find an optimal assignment with high quality; this is due to the limited bandwidth and processing constraints in the system. This way, for 10 the tasks considered the assignment found guarantees perfect quality (equal to the number of tasks) while as the task increases the maximum quality attained differs from the perfect quality value.

In addition, we observed that to reach a high-quality solution, it is advisable to use a population with at least the same size than the number of tasks considered. Therefore, for the number of tasks considered in our scenarios, a population size of 30 individuals proves to be suitable. In this respect, we observed that bigger populations cause slow convergence and increased execution cost while small ones tend to evolve to less fit solutions.

In terms of number of iterations, we let the algorithm evolve during 30 generations. This value is experimentally found to be a good tradeoff in terms of achieving a good convergence while still having a reduced execution time.

Table 4 summarizes the parameter selection for the evolution of the Genetic Algorithm. The parameter values selected are also close to the suggested ones in [21].

4.8. Convergence of Genetic Algorithm. One way to analyze the convergence of our multiobjective GA is by measuring the area/volume under the Pareto front of solutions in the multiobjective space. The reason is that the minimization of several objectives in our GA translates to Pareto fronts

becoming closer to all objective axes, in other words, Pareto fronts with lower areas/volumes underneath.

Figure 4 shows the evolution of the area under the Pareto front versus the number of iterations for a different number of tasks in the system. In this case, the GA evolves with the objective to minimize both distortion and energy at the client. As we can see with an increasing number of iterations, the area below the Pareto front decreases. This indicates that the Pareto fronts obtained gradually improve and achieve lower values of distortion and energy.

As explained earlier, tenths of iterations are sufficient in our scenario to find good assignment solutions that outperform the reference methods.

4.9. Execution Cost of Genetic Algorithm. Our genetic algorithm is an in-house-developed Matlab code and does not form part of the Matlab Optimization toolbox. The code has not been optimized for speed and its average execution time for 10 iterations of the algorithm is in the order of a couple of seconds. In this respect, the computational cost of the reference methods such as MaxQ and Min-Max is almost negligible with respect to GA. However, these methods achieve suboptimal results and are not able to tackle a multiobjective optimization.

Note that genetic algorithms are subject to parallelization, which can speed up its execution considerably. Therefore, a more dedicated and optimized implementation of the algorithm exploiting parallelism would highly reduce its execution time. However, developing such algorithm is out of the scope of this paper. In previous work such as [14], we can observe similar execution times for the GA algorithm and a similar amount of tasks considered. In [22], an optimized implementation of a GA on a SUN 4/490 only requires 1 to 2 s to perform 1000 iterations showing that a dedicated implementation can reduce the execution time considerably. In this respect in our approach, the number of iterations needed

TABLE 5: Relative execution cost.

Nos. of tasks/population	10	20	30	40
10	8	9	8.5	8
20	14	15	18	19
30	20	20	30	32
40	27	29	40	41

is in the order of tenths of iterations, which would further reduce the execution time.

In addition, the computational load of the GA is marginal when compared to the high-computational load of any transcoding, decoding operation that takes place in the servers in our scenario. Therefore, the execution of the GA can be placed on such a server with high processing power elements such as a GPU.

Last but not least, in our cloud computing scenario we could expect that new stream processing tasks enter or leave the system not faster than every couple of minutes. Therefore, global or partial recomputations of the stream assignments are not frequently needed.

To give an indication of how the complexity of our algorithm scales, Table 5 shows the relative execution cost versus the number of tasks, and the size of GA population considered. We can see how, as expected, the execution cost increases almost proportionally with the size of the population. The increase with the number of tasks considered is much less noticeable. This has the advantage that scaling up the scenario to a higher number of tasks does not have a big impact on the GA algorithm complexity.

Note also that for large-scale problems, we could address the task scheduling problem in a hierarchical way, that is, tasks can be initially distributed locally among clusters of processing devices and within each cluster; GA can be applied to obtain the optimal assignment. This would limit the complexity increase of the GA optimization.

5. Experimental Results

In this section, we compare the performance of the different assignment strategies considered. We first focus on a single objective optimization, namely, quality, where we use the fitness definition in (11). Figure 5 shows the performance of each assignment strategy with respect to the system load (given by an increasing number of SD streams to be displayed at the client's device). We can see that from 4 video streams up to 10, both GA and MaxQ strategies outperform all others while achieving the maximum quality. In this respect, note that the maximum quality equals N, the total number of streams, as the maximum quality per stream is 1 (see Table 1). From 10 streams on, it is only the GA that achieves a close to optimal quality. This shows that the higher the load in the system is, the more advanced strategy we need to find a suitable assignment. Moreover, at high load transcoding with slight degradation of the stream quality becomes necessary in order to fit all streams into the available constraints.

We then focus on multiple objectives optimization for a specific system load. We consider the processing of 20 video

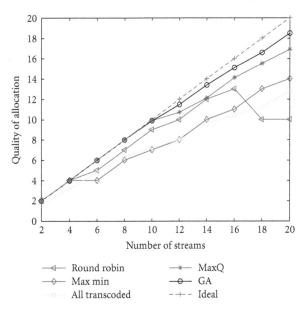

FIGURE 5: Performance of strategies versus system load.

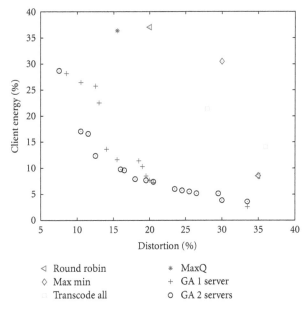

FIGURE 6: Energy-distortion tradeoffs.

streams of mixed spatial resolutions: CIF, SD, and HD at 30 fps. We compare the different strategies as well as the availability of one single server node with respect to two server nodes where tasks can be migrated to.

Figure 6 shows how the GA clearly outperforms all other strategies when targeting both quality maximization (equivalently distortion minimization) and minimization of energy at the client device. This way, the assignment solutions found by GA incur in lower energy at the client and lower distortion than the solutions found by the other strategies. We can see that in the GA Pareto front, some assignment solutions reach 7% of distortion while the MaxQ Strategy reaches around 15% distortion. Similarly, for the same

TABLE 6: Assignment strategies for HD/SD/CIF streams.

	Failed tasks	Decode @client	Decode @server	Temp trans	Spat trans	Temp & spat trans	Dist (%)	Energy (%)
RR	0/0/4	4/3/2	3/4/0	−/−/−	−/−/−	−/−/−	20	37
MM	0/0/6	7/6/0	0/1/0	−/−/−	−/−/−	−/−/−	30	30.4
TA	0/0/4	−/−/−	−/−/−	−/−/−	−/−/−	7/7/2	36	14
MaxQ	−/−/−	2/6/0	0/0/1	0/0/1	0/0/0	5/1/4	15.5	36.3
GA_1	−/−/−	4/0/1	2/5/0	1/2/0	0/0/1	0/0/4	8.5	28
GA_2	−/−/−	0/0/1	3/5/0	0/1/0	4/0/1	0/1/4	13	22.5
GA_3	−/−/1	0/1/0	5/5/0	1/0/0	1/0/0	0/1/5	15.5	11.6

distortion than MaxQ, the GA points lower the energy from 35% to roughly 10%.

Two sets of Pareto solutions are shown for the GA, one corresponding to the use of 1 server and another to the use of 2 servers. Naturally, having two servers available to process, the tasks allow the GA find better assignment solutions. Similarly, for the reference strategies, we show two points (assignment solution) for each strategy displayed. The two points correspond to the use of 1 server and 2 servers respectively, where generally the use of 2 servers achieves lower distortion but also higher energy consumption (as more streams can be processed).

Note that both distortion and energy values are given as percentages from the maximum possible distortion or energy. This way, the maximum energy cost at the client is defined as the cost of processing the decoding tasks of all streams at full spatial and temporal resolution, while the maximum distortion (100%) corresponds to a failed execution for all streams. In general, the relative distortion is defined as

$$\text{Distortion (\%)} = 100\% - \text{Quality (\%)}. \tag{17}$$

This way, from Table 1, successfully processing all N streams at its original spatial-temporal resolution would result in a maximum quality value of N (equivalent to 100% quality or 0% distortion). In a similar way, transcoding the temporal resolution of all N streams would correspond to a total quality of $0.9 * N$ (equivalent to a quality of 90% or distortion of 10%).

We can further analyze the assignment solutions found by the different strategies in Table 6. This table shows some of the assignment solutions of 1 server in Figure 6.

In this table, for the different kind of stream processing assignment, a distinction is made between the different original stream resolutions (HD/SD/CIF). This way, for example, in the assignment of the round robin (RR) strategy 4 CIF streams fail, while 4 HD streams, 3 SD, and 2 CIF are successfully decoded at the client, and 3 HD and 4 SD streams are decoded at the server. Finally, no streams are transcoded in this strategy. By analyzing Figure 6 and Table 6, we can see that strategies such as round-robin (RR) and max-min (MM) cannot find an assignment with a good tradeoff in terms of quality and energy cost. The reason is that none of these strategies considers either bandwidth constraints or transcoding. In this example, both round-robin and max-min succeed in distributing the load evenly among nodes and

meet the processing constraints. However, decoding streams at the server nodes generates high bandwidth demands towards the client. This exceeds the bandwidth availability and causes failed processed streams (in particular the high bandwidth HD streams). Therefore in this case the use of 2 servers further degrades the performance as more streams are processed at the server's side, and this aggravates the bandwidth demand. This way, under high load some stream transcoding would be required to fit into both available processing and bandwidth constraints.

However, transcoding all streams at the server nodes (TA strategy) is neither an optimal assignment as we enforce the quality degradation of all streams. Moreover, transcoding tasks are processing intensive and exceed the processing capacity at the servers resulting in some failed stream processing. In this case, the use of 2 servers increases the overall processing capacity but the assignment remains quite suboptimal in terms of distortion and energy.

In contrast, the MaxQ strategy succeeds in finding an assignment with low distortion value (15%). However, its energy cost is relatively high (36%). In Table 6, we can see that all 20 streams are successfully processed, out of which 10 are transcoded temporally and spatially while 8 are decoded at the client device at full resolution. In this example, the processing capacities with one server are enough for the amount of transcoding involved, while the main limiting factor remains the bandwidth.

It is finally the GA that outperforms all strategies by addressing both objectives and finding a set of assignment solutions, that is, Pareto optimal in both senses. Moreover, having 2 server nodes available for processing allows the GA to find even better tradeoffs (lower Pareto curve) in terms of quality and energy. Note also that the set of GA solutions offers an energy range from 30% to 10% for low distortion values. This way, we can reduce the energy at the client by factor 3 by trading off some stream quality. This offers the flexibility to choose between different operating points at grid level according to how scarce the processing power and energy at the client is.

In Table 6, we only show a few of the set of Pareto optimal solutions found by the GA. We can see how GA_1 assignment solution reaches the lowest distortion (8.5%) at 20% lower energy cost than MaxQ strategy. This assignment distributes more evenly the streams between client and server and chooses to transcode temporally and spatially only 4 streams of HD resolution. The GA_2 assignment provides a tradeoff

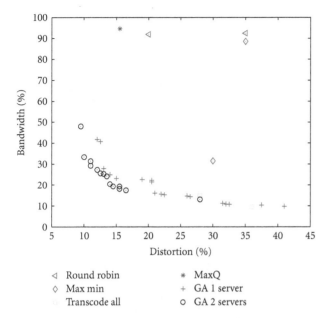

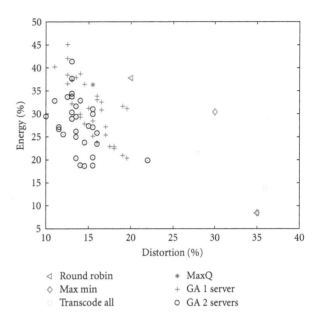

FIGURE 7: Bandwidth-distortion tradeoffs.

FIGURE 9: Projection onto energy-distortion space.

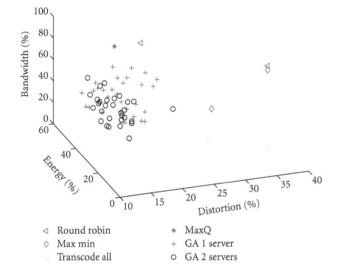

FIGURE 8: Pareto points in 3D space.

of slightly higher distortion (13%) but an energy cost 40% lower than that provided by MaxQ. Finally, GA_3 assignment provides similar distortion than MaxQ (15.5%) but it further reduces the energy consumption, demanding almost 70% less energy than MaxQ.

Figure 7 shows a similar comparison with respect to the bandwidth usage and distortion incurred by the different assignment solutions. In this case, the GA targets optimization of both distortion and bandwidth objectives and clearly outperforms all other strategies as shown by the lower distortion and bandwidth values obtained in the GA Pareto front. We can see in this respect how the MaxQ solution has a high bandwidth cost (close to 100%) while the GA solutions in the Pareto front require for the same distortion barely 20% of the maximum bandwidth. In addition, considering two

servers further allows a distortion and bandwidth reduction, possibly due to the fact that more processing power is available for transcoding the highly demanding HD streams.

Finally, Figure 8 shows the optimality of the different assignments in the three-dimensional space of distortion, bandwidth usage, and client's energy cost. The GA targets the minimization of these three objectives and the Pareto front becomes a Pareto surface.

As in the previous figures, the assignments found for 1 and 2 servers are displayed. Once again, we can see that the assignments found by the GA outperform all other strategies in terms of distortion, energy and bandwidth while at the same time, it provides a good tradeoff for all three objectives. Indeed, we can see that the GA solution points concentrate around lower distortion values (especially those corresponding to use of 2 servers), lower bandwidth, and lower energy values. For the sake of clarity, in Figure 9, we show the projection of Figure 8 on the two-dimensional space of energy and distortion where the better results of GA can be seen clearly.

In practice, both processing and bandwidth constraints may vary over time. Therefore, we may require a new stream assignment to fit the new constraints. One possible way to tackle this is by simply rerunning the assignment strategy. However, as the GA strategy already produces a set of assignment solutions with different energy-distortion-bandwidth tradeoffs, another possibility is to simply choose from the set of solutions a different operating point (assignment solution) that satisfies the new constraints. This way, if the current assignment solution requires a processing of 50% at the client's side, switching to a new assignment with 30% processing may be suitable for a more overloaded client device. We can also cope with variations in bandwidth or processing constraints by targeting more limiting constraints, for instance, 80% of the maximum bandwidth and maximum processing power. By doing so, the assignment is slightly overdimensioned and can cope with variations of up to 20–25% above the current constraints. This would also help avoid too frequent task migrations in the system.

6. Conclusion

We have presented an evolutionary-based strategy for stream processing assignment in a client-cloud multimedia system where multiple heterogeneous devices are considered. In this context, we not only decide on which node each stream is assigned but we also consider the possibility of stream transcoding to a lower temporal or spatial resolution. This extends the system capacity at the cost of smooth quality degradation in the task execution.

Moreover, both processing capacities in the nodes and bandwidth availability are taken into consideration. The proposed strategy is highly flexible and can target multiple objectives simultaneously. It outperforms all other considered strategies while providing a wide range of tradeoffs in the assignment solutions.

Acknowledgment

The authors would like to thank Yiannis Iosifidis for his insights on genetic algorithms.

References

[1] Y.-W. Zhong and J.-G. Yang, "A hybrid genetic algorithm with Lamarckian individual learning for tasks scheduling," in *Proceedings of the IEEE International Conference on Systems, Man and Cybernetics (SMC '04)*, pp. 3343–3348, October 2004.

[2] K. Dahal, A. Hossain, B. Varghese, A. Abraham, F. Xhafa, and A. Daradoumis, "Scheduling in multiprocessor system using genetic algorithms," in *Proceedings of the 7th IEEE Computer Information Systems and Industrial Management Applications (CISIM '08)*, pp. 281–286, June 2008.

[3] M. R. Miryani and M. Naghibzadeh, "Hard real-time multi-objective scheduling in heterogeneous systems using genetic algorithms," in *Proceedings of the 14th International CSI Computer Conference (CSICC '09)*, pp. 437–445, October 2009.

[4] J. Carretero, F. Xhafa, and A. Abraham, "Genetic algorithm based schedulers for grid computing systems," *International Journal of Innovative Computing, Information and Control*, vol. 3, no. 6, pp. 1053–1071, 2007.

[5] R. Entezari-Maleki and A. Movaghar, "A genetic algorithm to increase the throughput of the computational grids," *International Journal of Grid and Distributed Computing*, vol. 4, no. 2, 2011.

[6] J. Liu, L. Chen, Y. Dun, L. Liu, and G. Dong, "The research of ant colony and genetic algorithm in grid Task scheduling," in *Proceedings of the International Conference on MultiMedia and Information Technology, (MMIT '08)*, pp. 47–49, December 2008.

[7] A. Folling, C. Grimme, J. Lepping, and A. Papaspyrou, "Robust load delegation in service grid environments," *IEEE Transactions on Parallel and Distributed Systems*, vol. 21, no. 9, pp. 1304–1316, 2010.

[8] K.-M. Yu and C.-K. Chen, "An evolution-based dynamic scheduling algorithm in grid computing environment," in *Proceedings of the 8th International Conference on Intelligent Systems Design and Applications (ISDA '08)*, pp. 450–455, November 2008.

[9] A. Michalas and M. Louta, "Adaptive task scheduling in grid computing environments," in *Proceedings of the 4th International Workshop on Semantic Media Adaptation and Personalization (SMAP '09)*, pp. 115–120, December 2009.

[10] X. Yang, J. Zeng, and J. Liang, "Apply MGA to multi-objective flexible job shop scheduling problem," in *Proceedings of the International Conference on Information Management, Innovation Management and Industrial Engineering (ICIII '09)*, pp. 436–439, December 2009.

[11] M. Basseur, F. Seynhaeve, and E.-G. Talbi, "Path relinking in Pareto multi-objective genetic algorithms," in *Proceedings of the 3rd International Conference on Evolutionary Multi-Criterion Optimization (EMO '05)*, pp. 120–134, March 2005.

[12] P. Chitra, S. Revathi, P. Venkatesh, and R. Rajaram, "Evolutionary algorithmic approaches for solving three objectives task scheduling problem on heterogeneous systems," in *Proceedings of the IEEE 2nd International Advance Computing Conference (IACC '10)*, pp. 38–43, February 2010.

[13] R. P. Dick and N. K. Jha, "MOGAC: a multiobjective genetic algorithm for hardware-software cosynthesis of distributed embedded systems," *IEEE Transactions on Computer-Aided Design of Integrated Circuits and Systems*, vol. 17, no. 10, pp. 920–935, 1998.

[14] M. Camelo, Y. Donoso, and H. Castro, "MAGS—an approach using multi-objective evolutionary algorithms for grid task scheduling," *International Journal of Applied Mathematics and Informatics*, vol. 5, no. 2, 2011.

[15] F. S. Kazemi and R. Tavakkoli-Moghaddam, "Soving a multi-objective multi-mode resource-constrained project scheduling problem with particle swarm optimization," *International Journal of Academic Research*, vol. 3, no. 1, 2011.

[16] Y. Hu and B. Gong, "Multi-objective optimization approaches using a CE-ACO inspired strategy to improve grid jobs scheduling," in *Proceedings of the 4th ChinaGrid Annual Conference (ChinaGrid '09)*, pp. 53–58, August 2009.

[17] M. Maheswaran, S. Ali, H. J. Siegel, D. Hensgen, and R. Freund, "Dynamic mapping of a class of independent tasks onto heterogeneous computing systems," in *Proceedings of the 8th IEEE Heterogeneous Computing Workshop (HCW '99)*, pp. 30–44, San Juan, Puerto Rico, April 1999.

[18] N. Srinivas and K. Deb, "Multi-objective optimization using non-dominated sorting in genetic algorithms," *Evolution Computing*, vol. 2, no. 3, pp. 221–248, 1994.

[19] E. Zitzler and L. Thiele, "Multiobjective evolutionary algorithms: A comparative case study and the strength Pareto approach," *IEEE Transactions on Evolutionary Computation*, vol. 3, no. 4, pp. 257–271, 1999.

[20] Y. Iosifidis, A. Mallik, S. Mamagkakis et al., "A framework for automatic parallelization, static and dynamic memory optimization in MPSoC platforms," in *Proceedings of the 47th Design Automation Conference, (DAC '10)*, pp. 549–554, June 2010.

[21] A. Y. Zomaya, C. Ward, and B. Macey, "Genetic scheduling for parallel processor systems: Comparative studies and performance issues," *IEEE Transactions on Parallel and Distributed Systems*, vol. 10, no. 8, pp. 795–812, 1999.

[22] S. H. Hou, N. Ansari, and H. Ren, "Genetic algorithm for multiprocessor scheduling," *IEEE Transactions on Parallel and Distributed Systems*, vol. 5, no. 2, pp. 113–120, 1994.

14

An Efficient Periodic Broadcasting with Small Latency and Buffer Demand for Near Video on Demand

Ying-Nan Chen and Li-Ming Tseng

Department of Computer Science and Information Engineering, National Central University, Chung-Li 32054, Taiwan

Correspondence should be addressed to Ying-Nan Chen, ynchen@dslab.csie.ncu.edu.tw

Academic Editor: Hsiang-Fu Yu

Broadcasting Protocols can efficiently transmit videos that simultaneously shared by clients with partitioning the videos into segments. Many studies focus on decreasing clients' waiting time, such as the fixed-delay pagoda broadcasting (FDPB) and the harmonic broadcasting schemes. However, limited-capability client devices such as PDAs and set-top boxes (STBs) suffer from storing a significant fraction of each video while it is being watched. How to reduce clients' buffer demands is thus an important issue. Related works include the staircase broadcasting (SB), the reverse fast broadcasting (RFB), and the hybrid broadcasting (HyB) schemes. This work improves FDPB to save client buffering space as well as waiting time. In comparison with SB, RFB, and HyB, the improved FDPB scheme can yield the smallest waiting time under the same buffer requirements.

1. Introduction

How to efficiently maintain the exhausted bandwidth with the growth in the number of clients is an important issue of VOD deployment. Dan et al. [1] presented that 80 percent of the demand is for a few number (10 or 20) of very popular videos. One way to broadcast a popular video is to partition the video into segments, which are transmitted on several channels currently and periodically. The approach (called periodic broadcasting [2]) lets multiple users share channels and thus obtains high bandwidth utilization. One of the channels only broadcasts the first segment in real time. The other channels transmit the remaining segments. When clients want to watch a video, they wait for the beginning of the first segment on the first channel. While clients start watching the video, their set-top boxes (STBs) or computers still download and buffer unreceived segments from the channels to enable them to play the video continuously.

The staggered broadcasting [3] scheme treats a complete video as a single segment and then transmits it on each channel at different start times. The fast broadcasting (FB) scheme [4] improves segment partitioning and arrangement to yield shorter service latency. The harmonic broadcasting

(HB) scheme [5] initially partitions a video into equally sized segments, which are further divided into smaller subsegments according to the harmonic series. HB can yield the minimum waiting time [6]; however, its implementation is difficult due to the multitude of broadcasting channels [7]. The recursive frequency-splitting (RFS) [7] scheme broadcasts a segment as close to its frequency as possible to achieve a near-minimal waiting time. The study [8] focuses on reducing the computation complexity of RFS. Paris [9] proposed a fixed-delay pagoda broadcasting (FDPB) scheme that required clients to wait for a small-fixed delay before watching the selected videos.

The staircase broadcasting (SB) scheme [10] requires a client to buffer only 25% of a playing video. In modifying the FB scheme, the reverse fast broadcasting (RFB) scheme [11] also buffers 25% of video size, merely half of what is required by the FB scheme. By combining RFS and RFB the hybrid broadcasting scheme (HyB) [12] yields small client buffering space and waiting time. The study in [13] proposed a generalized reverse sequence-based model to reduce their client buffer requirements. This work aims at improving FDPB to reduce required playback latency and buffering space. We prove the applicability of the improved FDPB, and compare

Stream 1		
Substream	1	2
First segment	1	2
Last segment	1	3

Stream 2		
Substream	1	2
First segment	4	7
Last segment	6	10

Stream 3				
Substream	1	2	3	4
First segment	11	14	18	23
Last segment	13	17	22	28

(a) The segment allocation on three channels

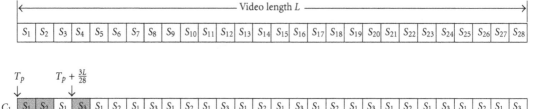

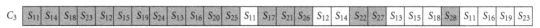

(b) The segment broadcasting on three channels

FIGURE 1: Illustration of channel allocation for the FDPB-3 scheme.

its performance with that of several existing approaches. Given a bandwidth of 5 channels, the new scheme reduces the broadcast latency by as much as 24% when compared to HyB and 34.5% when compared to RFB and SB. The buffer requirements for these schemes are about 25% of video size.

The rest of this paper is organized as follows. Section 2 introduces FDPB and proposes its improvement. Performance analysis and comparison are in Section 3. We make brief conclusions in Section 4.

2. Proposed Scheme

This section briefly reviews FDPB and then presents the improvement.

2.1. Fixed-Delay Pagoda Broadcasting (FDPB) Scheme. To help explain the improved FDPB, we first review the FDPB scheme in the literature [9]. Suppose that a video of duration L is broadcast over k channels. The scheme partitions each video into m equal-size segments of duration $l = L/m$. These segments will be broadcast at different frequencies over the k channels. The FDPB-p scheme requires customers to wait for a fixed time interval $w = pl$, where $p \in$ int, $p \geq 1$. Segment S_i is thus transmitted at least once every $p + i - 1$ slots. The FDPB-p scheme partitions each channel C_j into $c_j = \sqrt{p + i - 1}$ subchannels in such a way that slot j of

channel C_j belongs to its subchannel j. FDPB then maps segments into subchannels in a strict sequential fashion.

Figure 1 illustrates the video partition and segment arrangement of FDPB-3. Channel C_1 is partitioned into two subchannels because $\sqrt{3 + 1 - 1}$ is close to 2. Let S_i be the ith segment. Since $p = 3$, segment S_1 needs to be broadcast at least once every three slots and is assigned to subchannel 1. The first segment of subchannel 2 is segment S_2, which appears at least once every $3 + 2 - 1 = 4$ slots. We thus map two segments into subchannel 2, and channel C_1 transmits three segments (i.e., S_1 to S_3). The first segment of channel C_2 is segment S_4, which is broadcast at least once every $3 + 4 - 1 = 6$ slots. Since 6 is close to $4 = 2^2$, channel C_2 is partitioned into two subchannels. The first subchannel periodically transmits segments S_4 to S_6, and the second subchannel broadcasts segments S_7 to S_{10}. The first segment of channel C_3 is segment S_{11}, which is broadcast at least once every $3 + 11 - 1 = 13$ slots. Similarly, since 13 approaches to $16 = 4^2$, channel C_3 is partitioned into four subchannels. The first subchannel sends segments S_{11} to S_{13}, the second subchannel sends segments S_{14} to S_{17}, the third subchannel sends S_{18} to S_{22}, and the fourth subchannel sends S_{23} to S_{28}. Hence, channel C_3 broadcasts 18 segments. Figure 1(b) demonstrates how to broadcast the segments on three channels and how to download the segments colored gray. Suppose that a client starts receiving the segments at time T_p. This figure shows that the client begins to watch the video at time $T_p + 3L/28$.

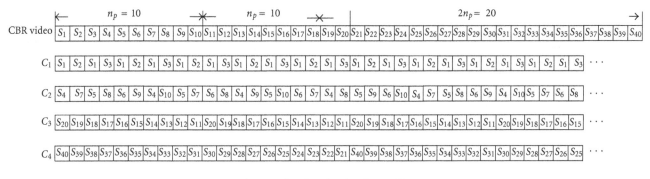

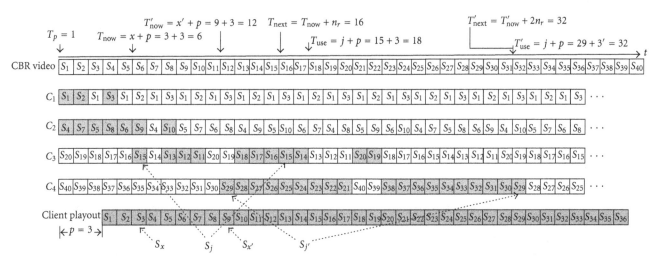

FIGURE 2: Segment transmission by RFDPB-3.

FIGURE 3: An illustration of segment downloading by RFDPB-3, where $k = 4$, $n_p = 10$, and $N = 40$.

2.2. Improvement of FDPB. By integrating the RFB with FDPB, this work designs the RFB-FDPB (RFDPB) scheme, which gains small low buffer requirements as well as waiting time.

2.2.1. Segment Delivery on the Server Side. Let k be the number of allocated channels. The data transmission rate of each channel is assumed to equal the playback rate b. An RFDPB server broadcasts segments according to the following steps.

(1) The largest number of segments that FDPB-p can transmit using $k - 2$ channels is assumed to equal n_p. The RFDPB-p scheme then equally divides a constant-bit-rate (CBR) video into N segments, denoted by $S_1, S_2, \ldots, S_N$ in sequence, where $N = 4n_p$. Let L be the length of the video. The length of a segment, l, thus equals L/N.

(2) Channels C_1 to C_{k-2} periodically send segments S_1 to S_{n_p} according to FDPB-p.

(3) Segments S_{2n_p} to S_{n_p+1} are transmitted on channel C_{k-1}.

(4) Segments S_{4n_p} to S_{2n_p+1} are broadcast on channel C_k.

Figure 2 illustrates the segment delivery by RFDPB-3, where $k = 4$. The server broadcasts segments S_1 to S_{10} on channels C_1 to C_2 by FDPB-3 because FDPB-3 can transmit 10 segments using two channels, as indicated in Figure 1. Due to $n_p = 10$, RFDPB periodically broadcasts segments S_{20} to S_{11} and S_{40} to S_{21} on channels C_3 and C_4.

2.2.2. Segment Reception on the Client Side. Suppose that a client has enough buffers to store portions of a playing video. Let l be a basic time unit during video playing. We also let T_p be the time that the client starts downloading the video and be the origin (i.e., the first time unit) of the time axis throughout the paper. The following steps are involved in playing a video at the client.

(1) The client receives the segments on channels C_1 to C_{k-2} immediately when they are available on networks. Figure 3 further demonstrates the segment downloading, where the segments downloaded by a client are gray.

(2) The segment downloading on channel C_{k-1} is as follows. Suppose that the client first sees segment S_j on channel C_{k-1} at time T_{now} and next segment

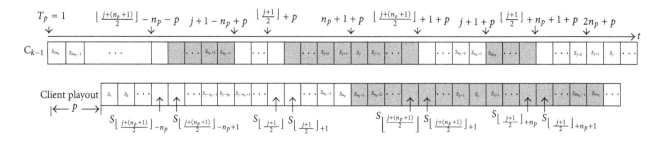

(Not to scale)

FIGURE 4: The segment downloading on channel C_{k-1} under RFDPB-p.

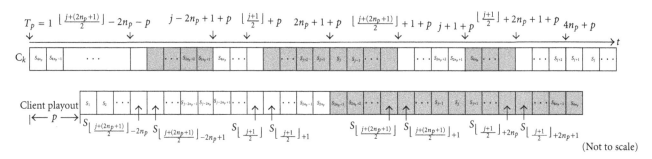

(Not to scale)

FIGURE 5: The segment downloading on channel C_k under RFDPB-p.

S_j at time T_{next}. The client is also assumed to play segments S_x and S_j at time T_{now} and T_{use}, respectively. The work in [11, 12] indicates that if $T_{\text{next}} \leq T_{\text{use}}$, the client does not need to receive segment S_j at time T_{now} and actually performs the downloading at time T_{next}, without causing playing interruption. FDPB further reveals that a client has to wait for a fix time unit p to play received segments. Thus, $T_{\text{use}} = j + p$th time unit, $T_{\text{now}} = x + p$th time unit, and $T_{\text{next}} = T_{\text{now}} + n_p$. Substituting these equations into $T_{\text{next}} \leq T_{\text{use}}$, we obtain

$$x + n_p \leq j. \tag{1}$$

If this inequality holds, a client does not receive segment S_j at time T_{now}; otherwise, it immediately downloads it. Suppose that the client first sees segment S_{15} with only diagonal lines on channel C_3 at the 6th time unit, as indicated in Figure 3. Due to $p = 3$, $x = 3$, $j = 15$, and $n_p = 10$, $T_{\text{now}} = x + p = 6$, $T_{\text{use}} = j + p = 18$, and $T_{\text{next}} = T_{\text{now}} + n_p = 16$. Clearly, it is unnecessary to download segment S_{15} at this time unit because inequality (1), $x + n_p = 13 \leq j = 15$, holds. The result also reflects that the client does not have to receive the segment when $T_{\text{next}} = 16 \leq T_{\text{use}} = 18$. When next segment S_{15} colored gray in Figure 3 arrives at the 16th time unit, the inequality is no more true, $13 + 10 > 15$, and the client thus downloads it.

(3) The segments on channel C_k are received in the similar way, as also indicated in Figure 3. Suppose that the client first sees segment $S_{j'}$ on channel C_k at

time T'_{now}, and next segment $S_{j'}$ at time T'_{next}. The client is also assumed to play segments $S_{x'}$ and $S_{j'}$ at time T'_{now} and T'_{use}. Similarly, if $T'_{\text{next}} \leq T'_{\text{use}}$, the client does not receive segment $S_{j'}$. Substituting $T'_{\text{use}} = j' + p$th time unit, $T'_{\text{now}} = x' + p$th time unit, and $T'_{\text{next}} = T'_{\text{now}} + 2n_p$ into inequality $T'_{\text{next}} \leq T'_{\text{use}}$ obtains

$$x' + 2n_p \leq j'. \tag{2}$$

If the inequality is true, the client skips the downloading of segment $S_{j'}$. Suppose that the client first sees segment S_{29} with only diagonal lines on channel C_4 at the 12th time unit, as indicated in Figure 3. Due to $p = 3$, $x' = 9$, $j' = 29$, and $n_p = 10$, $T'_{\text{now}} = x' + p = 12$, $T'_{\text{use}} = j' + p = 32$, and $T'_{\text{next}} = T'_{\text{now}} + 2n_p = 32$. Clearly, it is unnecessary to download segment S_{29} at this time unit because inequality (2), $x' + 2n_p = 29 \leq j' = 29$, is true. The result also reflects that the client does not have to receive the segment when $T'_{\text{next}} = 32 \leq T'_{\text{use}} = 32$. When next segment S_{29} colored gray in Figure 3 arrives at the 32nd time unit, the inequality is no more true, $29 + 20 > 29$, and the client thus downloads it.

(4) The client plays the video in the order of $S_1, S_2, \ldots, S_N$ at time $T_p + p$.

(5) Stop loading data from networks when all the segments have been received.

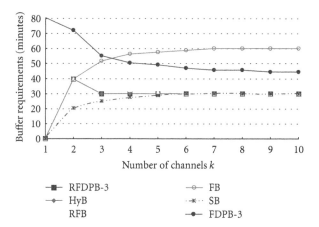

FIGURE 6: Comparison of the maximum buffer requirements in the number of minutes of a 120-minute video.

TABLE 1: The maximum buffering space required by different schemes in the percentage of video size using k channels.

k	1	2	3	4	5	6	7	8	9	10
RFDPB-3	0	33	25	25	25	25	25	25	25	25
HyB	0	33	25	25	25	25	25	25	25	25
RFB	0	33	29	27	26	25	25	25	25	25
FB	0	33	43	47	48	49	50	50	50	50
SB	0	17	21	23	24	25	25	25	25	25
FDPB-3	67	60	46	42	41	39	38	38	37	37

2.2.3. Workable Verification.

This section describes that the RFDPB scheme guarantees continuous playing on the client side. Because the segment broadcasting on channels C_1 to C_{k-2} is based on FDPB [9], RFDPB is workable for these channels. We next prove that the segment arrangements on channels C_{k-1} and C_k also ensure a client to continuously play a video. FDPB further indicates that a video server must broadcast segment S_j at least once in every $j + p - 1$ time units to keep on-time data delivery on the client side. For the RFDPB scheme, a server broadcasts segment S_j on channel C_{k-1} in every n_p time units, where $n_p + 1 \leq j \leq 2n_p$. Because $j + p - 1 > n_p$, an RFDPB client can receive video segments on channel C_{k-1} on time. Similarly, the RFDPB scheme requires a server to transmit segment $S_{j'}$ on channel C_k in every $2n_p$ time units, where $2n_p+1 \leq j' \leq 4n_p$. Because $j' + p - 1 > 2n_p$, the segment delivery on this channel is also on time. Accordingly, RFDPB ensures continuous video playing at the client.

3. Analysis and Comparison

Before investigating entire buffer requirements for RFDPB, this paper analyzes the segment downloading on channel C_{k-1} first. For RFDPB-p, a client plays the segments received from this channel during time units $n_p + 1 + p$ to $2n_p + p$. The possible time to download the segments is during the pth to $2n_p + p$th time units. Suppose that a client sees segment S_j at the $n_p + 1 + p$th time unit. Inequality (1) makes a

TABLE 2: The maximum numbers of segments, N, offered by different schemes.

k	1	2	3	4	5	6	7	8	9	10
FDPB-6	7	25	71	186	485	1286	3425	9195	24790	67054
RFDPB-6	1	3	28	100	284	744	1940	5144	13700	36780
HyB	1	3	4	12	36	100	292	804	2260	6088
FB (RFB)	1	3	7	15	31	63	127	255	511	1023
SB	1	3	7	15	31	63	127	255	511	1023

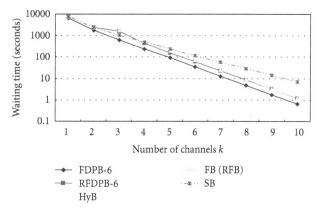

FIGURE 7: The maximum waiting time incurred on new clients at different numbers of channels ($L = 120$ minutes).

complete segment-downloading diagram for channel C_{k-1}, as indicated in Figure 4, where the segments downloaded by the client are colored gray. The figure shows that the client does not continuously download segments, and some segments are skipped. The segments are not downloaded during the first to $\lfloor (j + (n_p + 1))/2 \rfloor - n_p + p$th time units, during the $j + 1 - n_p + p$th to $\lfloor (j + 1)/2 \rfloor + p$th time units, during the $\lfloor (j+(n_p+1))/2 \rfloor +1+p$th to $j+p$th time units, and during the $\lfloor (j + 1)/2 \rfloor + n_p + 1 + p$th to $2n_p + p$th time units, respectively. Such results reflect that the client can delay downloading these segments by n_p time units, due to (1). Similarly, (2) also makes a complete segment-downloading diagram for channel C_k, as indicated in Figure 6, where a client is assumed to see segment S_j at the $2n_p + 1 + p$th time unit.

The RFDPB scheme uses the same methodology as HyB, combining a nonharmonic scheme and the RFB to reduce clients' waiting time and buffering spaces (Figure 5). For segment broadcasting on channels C_1 to C_{k-2} using the nonharmonic scheme, channels C_{k-1} and C_k broadcast the other segments according RFB. Yu's work [12] has proved HyB only buffer 25% of video size for $k \geq 3$, where k is the number of broadcasting channels. The proof of the maximum number of segments buffered by a client for RFDPB is similar to that of HyB, so this paper neglects it. Therefore, let $B(k)$ be the maximum number of segments buffered by a client, where k is the number of broadcasting channels. For RFDPB,

$$B(1) = 0$$
$$B(2) = 1 \tag{3}$$
$$B(k) = n_p, \quad k \geq 3.$$

TABLE 3: The waiting time (seconds), offered by RFDPB-9, RFDPB-6, HyB, and RFDPB-3 schemes.

k	1	2	3	4	5	6	7	8	9	10
RFDPB-9	7200	2400	1350	385.71	139.66	52.6	19.9	7.47	2.79	1.04
RFDPB-6	7200	2400	1542.86	432	152.11	58.06	22.27	8.4	3.15	1.17
HyB	7200	2400	1800	600	200	72	24.66	8.96	3.19	1.18
RFDPB-3	7200	2400	1800	540	192.86	72.97	28.57	11.07	4.19	1.58

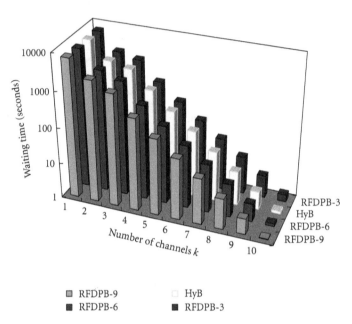

FIGURE 8: The maximum waiting time (RFDPB and HyB) incurred on new clients at different numbers of channels ($L = 120$ minutes).

The previous analysis indicates that RFDPB buffers at most $n_r/N = 25\%$ of video size. Table 1 lists the comparison of maximum buffering spaces required by RFDPB-3, FB, SB, RFB, FDPB-3, and HyB. RFDPB-3 reduces the buffering space up to 32.4% when compared to FDPB-3 and up to 50% when compared to FB and has the same good result with the other schemes. Given a video of 120 minutes, Figure 6 shows the buffer requirements at different channels. To understand how well the RFDPB scheme performs on clients waiting time, this work calculates the values of N offered by RFDPB-6, SB, FB, RFB, FDPB-6, and HyB given different numbers of server channels, as listed in Table 2. The inverse of N offered by each scheme reflects the waiting time for a new client to start his/her VOD service. Figure 7, which is drawn in a logarithmic scale, shows that RFDPB-6 performs close to FDPB-6 stably. For $k \geq 4$, the RFDPB-6 outperforms all the schemes, except the FDPB-6. To understand the relationship between RFDPB and HyB schemes, this work calculates clients' waiting time of RFDPB-9, RFDPB-6, HyB, and RFDPB-3, as listed in Table 3. Figure 8 shows that, for $p \geq 6$, RFDPB-p outperforms HyB. The previous comparisons clearly indicate that RFDPB exhibits a good tradeoff between client buffering spaces and waiting time.

4. Conclusions

This paper presents an improved version of FDPB for efficient periodic broadcasting of popular videos. The proposed scheme takes advantage of the FDPB and the RFB schemes to obtain small waiting time and low buffer demand. Through mathematical analysis, we prove the applicability of this scheme by demonstrating that client playback continuity is guaranteed. Given a bandwidth of 5 channels, the new scheme reduces the broadcast latency by as much as 24% when compared to HyB and 34.5% when compared to RFB and SB. The buffer requirements for these schemes are about 25% of video size.

References

[1] A. Dan, D. Sitaram, and P. Shahabuddin, "Dynamic batching policies for an on-demand video server," *Multimedia Systems*, vol. 4, no. 3, pp. 112–121, 1996.

[2] D. Saparilla, K. W. Ross, and M. Reisslein, "Periodic broadcasting with VBR-encoded video," in *Proceedings of the 18th Annual Joint Conference of the IEEE Computer and Communications Societie (INFOCOM '99)*, pp. 464–471, March 1999.

[3] K. C. Almeroth and M. H. Ammar, "The use of multicast delivery to provide a scalable and interactive video-on-demand service," *IEEE Journal on Selected Areas in Communications*, vol. 14, no. 6, pp. 1110–1122, 1996.

[4] L-S. Juhn and L. M. Tseng, "Fast data broadcasting and receiving scheme for popular video service," *IEEE Transactions on Broadcasting*, vol. 44, no. 1, pp. 100–105, 1998.

[5] L-S. Juhn and L. M. Tseng, "Harmonic broadcasting for video-on-demand service," *IEEE Transactions on Broadcasting*, vol. 43, no. 3, pp. 268–271, 1997.

[6] Z.-Y. Yang, L. S. Juhn, and L. M. Tseng, "On optimal broadcasting scheme for popular video service," *IEEE Transactions on Broadcasting*, vol. 45, no. 3, pp. 318–322, 1999.

[7] Y.–C. Tseng, M. H. Yang, and C. H. Chang, "A recursive frequency-splitting scheme for broadcasting hot videos in VOD service," *IEEE Transactions on Communications*, vol. 50, no. 8, pp. 1348–1355, 2002.

[8] J.-P. Sheu, H. L. Wang, C. H. Chang, and Y. C. Tseng, "A fast video-on-demand broadcasting scheme for popular videos," *IEEE Transactions on Broadcasting*, vol. 50, no. 2, pp. 120–125, 2004.

[9] J. F. Paris, "A fixed-delay broadcasting protocol for video-on-demand," in *Proceedings of the 10th International Conference on Computer Communications and Networks (ICCCN '01)*, pp. 418–423, Scottsdale, Ariz, USA, October 2001.

[10] L.-S. Juhn and L. M. Tseng, "Staircase data broadcasting and receiving scheme for hot video service," *IEEE Transactions on Consumer Electronics*, vol. 43, no. 4, pp. 1110–1117, 1997.

[11] H.-F. Yu, H. C. Yang, and L. M. Tseng, "Reverse Fast Broadcasting (RFB) for video-on-demand applications," *IEEE Transactions on Broadcasting*, vol. 53, no. 1, pp. 103–110, 2007.

[12] H.-F. Yu, "Hybrid broadcasting with small buffer demand and waiting time for video-on-demand applications," *IEEE Transactions on Broadcasting*, vol. 54, no. 2, Article ID 4433980, pp. 304–311, 2008.

[13] H.-F. Yu, P. H. Ho, and H. C. Yang, "Generalized Sequence-Based and Reverse Sequence-Based Models for Broadcasting Hot Videos," *IEEE Transactions on Multimedia*, 2008.

15

Secure and Reliable IPTV Multimedia Transmission Using Forward Error Correction

Chi-Huang Shih, Yeong-Yuh Xu, and Yao-Tien Wang

Department of Computer Science and Information Engineering, HungKuang University, Taichung 433, Taiwan

Correspondence should be addressed to Yeong-Yuh Xu, yyxu@sunrise.hk.edu.tw

Academic Editor: Hsiang-Fu Yu

With the wide deployment of Internet Protocol (IP) infrastructure and rapid development of digital technologies, Internet Protocol Television (IPTV) has emerged as one of the major multimedia access techniques. A general IPTV transmission system employs both encryption and forward error correction (FEC) to provide the authorized subscriber with a high-quality perceptual experience. This two-layer processing, however, complicates the system design in terms of computational cost and management cost. In this paper, we propose a novel FEC scheme to ensure the secure and reliable transmission for IPTV multimedia content and services. The proposed secure FEC utilizes the characteristics of FEC including the FEC-encoded redundancies and the limitation of error correction capacity to protect the multimedia packets against the malicious attacks and data transmission errors/losses. Experimental results demonstrate that the proposed scheme obtains similar performance compared with the joint encryption and FEC scheme.

1. Introduction

As digital technologies process, Internet Protocol Television (IPTV) has emerged in the past years to deliver high-quality multimedia services to end users over IP broadband networks. Generally, IPTV has multifaceted content such as video/audio/text/graphic/data and needs to provide the user-required quality of experience (QoE), interactivity, security, and reliability in the IP-based networks [1]. The typical IPTV applications include the cable TV-like service and video on demand (VoD). In the cable TV-like service, the service provider can provide the entertainment, news, and sports programs in a regular standard definition (SD) or further high definition (HD) format, while the VoD service supports more personal options to select their favorite multimedia content. Because the IP technology is basically the same for the IPTV and Internet applications, IPTV is likely to integrate the existing and independent services over the home network connection.

Since the content delivered through IPTV is mostly of high economic value and of copyright with user's subscription, secure and reliable transmission becomes an important issue in provisioning IPTV content and services. The basic principle of the service and content protection is to ensure that users are only able to obtain the services they are entitled to access and use the content in accordance with the right they have been granted [2, 3]. For content and service protection, the conditional access system (CAS) and digital right management (DRM) are two primary protection technologies on IPTV [4]. CAS is employed in the conventional TV industry to restrict certain television programs to certain users according to a billing mechanism. On the other hand, DRM is often utilized in the information technology (IT) industry to protect the digital data against illegal copy and redistribution. In both CAS and DRM, data encryption is one common security tool to provide the robust security control on the valued data. An essential requirement for data encryption in IPTV is the need to transmit a single encrypted stream to many users. Since different users can be authorized to receive different packages of services, this requirement is generally met by using multiple layers of encryption. In addition, frequent update of encryption keys is desired to avoid unauthorized data sharing due to illegal key extracting. Although the data encryption is a well-designed technique in protecting sensitive data, its efficacy in IPTV environment can be affected based on the IP delivery characteristics such as packet loss [5, 6]. In order to protect the multimedia stream against transmission errors/losses, forward error correction (FEC) deliberately produces redundant data to enable the reconstruction of any multimedia packets which are lost during transmission. The IPTV standard developed by Digital Video Broadcasting (DVB) project specifies an application-layer FEC to perform packet loss repair for IPTV streaming media [7, 8].

One of the possible solutions to support a secure and reliable transmission is the integration of data encryption and FEC recovery [9–12]. The typical operation of this integration is to first encrypt the source data using a secret key which is available only at the end nodes, and then to generate the redundant FEC data for loss recovery purpose by encoding the encrypted data. Both the encrypted and redundant data are transmitted along the network path and the receiver processes the received data in a reverse order (i.e., FEC decoding and decryption). In [13], an image-coding scheme has been proposed to provide encryption and FEC based on Error Correction Codes (ECCs) over noisy channels. Related works in [14, 15] use turbo-codes-based error control scheme to combine with encryption for secure data transmission. Moreover, the cryptographic encryption scheme based on Advanced Encryption Standard (AES) [16] and the FEC protection scheme using turbo codes have been integrated to ensure a reliable and secure transmission [17]. Although the joint encryption and FEC scheme is effective enough, several performance problems arise in terms of computational cost and management cost. All costs contribute to the delay time, which is critical to the multimedia services, and complicate the IPTV system design. In general, the computational cost largely originates from the processing overhead including FEC encoding/decoding and encryption/decryption, while the management cost derives from the generation of multiple keys, frequent key updates, channel feedback messages carrying network conditions, and so on. In [18, 19], an iterative decoding approach for digital signatures has been developed to perform the error correction, in addition to the authentication capacity provided by the digital signature itself. However, this approach becomes more effective as an FEC scheme is present and most importantly the transmission data remains unsafe to the malicious attacks. It is therefore necessary to design a IPTV transmission system with light performance cost in delivering multimedia content securely and reliably.

In this paper, we propose a security-enhanced FEC scheme which achieves a secure and reliable transmission for valued IPTV content, by means of packet-level Reed-Solomon (RS) codes [20] with a set of security constraints on the FEC coding parameters. The proposed secure FEC focuses on providing the content or service protection to prevent malicious users from acquiring the unauthorized data, while aiming at improving data goodput by recovering the potential transmission errors/losses. Two key features of the secure FEC are (1) to transmit FEC-encoded data only and hence the original content data are prevented from exposing to the malicious users directly and (2) to deliberately control the amount of FEC-encoded data so that the error correction capacity provided by the FEC-encoded data fails to reconstruct source content data. As to the authorized user, the successful data reconstruction relies on an additional data storage between the content server and user. The experimental results show that the proposed secure FEC obtains the same performance as the joint AES encryption scheme with 128-bit key and the packet-level FEC scheme based on Reed-Solomon codes, in the data transmission.

The remainder of this paper is organized as follows. Section 2 reviews the standard packet-level FEC protection scheme using Reed-Solomon codes. Section 3 introduces the proposed secure FEC scheme. Section 4 describes the exposure rate of source data for measuring the security level in this paper and establishes an analytical model associated with the exposure rate. The performance evaluation results are presented and discussed in Section 5. Finally, Section 6 provides some brief concluding remarks and future works.

2. Standard FEC

Without loss of generality, we use systematic Reed-Solomon erasure codes RS (n, k_1) to protect multimedia data from channel losses. The RS encoder chooses k_1 multimedia data items as an FEC block and generates $(n - k_1)$ redundant data items for the block. Every data item has its own sequence number used to indicate the corresponding position within the block. With this position information, the RS decoder can locate the position of the lost items and then correct up to $(n - k_1)$ lost items. Furthermore, a packet-level RS code is applied as FEC since it has a high efficiency over error-prone channels [21]. Figure 1 illustrates the operations of packet-level FEC scheme. Packet-level FEC schemes group the source data packets into blocks of a predetermined size k_1 and then encode $n = k_1 + h_{std}$ packets for network transmission, where $h_{std} \geq 0$ is the number of redundant packets. The coding rate is thus defined as k_1/n. Provided that k_1 or more packets are successfully received, the block can be completely reconstructed. In the standard packet-level FEC, given the target recovery probability R_{std}, the estimated packet loss rate P_B and fixed k_1, the lower bound on n can be computed in the sender using

$$R_{std}(n, k_1, P_B) = \sum_{i=k_1}^{n} \left[\binom{n}{i} (P_B)^{n-i} (1 - P_B)^i \right]. \quad (1)$$

On the other hand, the feedback packets are sent periodically from the receiver to the sender in order to obtain the timely channel information about P_B. Note that packet-level FEC extends the media stream simply by inserting redundant packets into the stream, and, therefore, the method requires only minor modification to the source packets.

3. Secure FEC

The secure FEC scheme aims at supporting reliable and secure transmission for multimedia IPTV flows. To achieve the secure transmission, the proposed FEC scheme is based on the packet-level RS codes and has two features: (1) only the

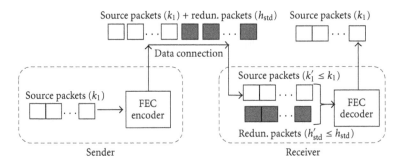

FIGURE 1: Overview of standard packet-level FEC scheme. This figure shows the FEC coding operations at both the sender and receiver. The maximum amount of loss packets that can be recovered is h_{std}.

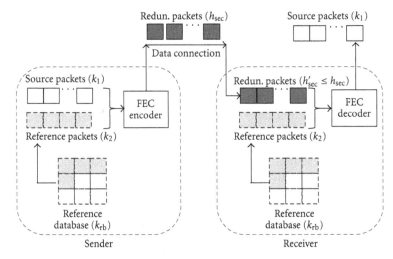

FIGURE 2: Overview of secure FEC scheme. Note that the reference packets k_2 are included in the FEC encoding/decoding, and the sender transmits redundant packets h_{sec}.

redundant data are delivered along the transmission path; in other words, the original source data are used in the encoding stage, and (2) both the data sending side and data receiving side need to maintain a consistent reference database where the reference data are selected to perform the FEC encoding with the source data at the data sending side, and the FEC decoding with the received redundant data at the data receiving side. Transmitting redundant data can avoid that the malicious host directly inspect the content of source data. It is noted that in the standard FEC, the transmission data include source and redundant data. Furthermore, the use of reference data in the FEC encoding/decoding stage causes the FEC decoding failure for the malicious host even if the malicious host attempts to decode the intercepted redundant data. Figure 2 illustrates the operations of secure FEC. The detained procedures can be summarized into five steps.

(1) Both the data sending side and receiving side have the similar k_2 reference packets.

(2) The data sending side generates the FEC redundant packets h_{sec} based on the source packets k_1 and the reference packets k_2.

(3) The data sending side transmits h_{sec} redundant packets through the network to the data receiving side.

(4) The data receiving side receives h'_{sec} packets and $h'_{sec} \leq h_{sec}$.

(5) The data receiving side uses the reference packets k_2 and the received packets h'_{sec} to reconstruct the source packets k_1.

According to the procedures described above, the condition that a block can be successfully recovered is given by

$$h_{sec} + k_2 \geq k_1 + k_2 \longrightarrow h_{sec} \geq k_1. \tag{2}$$

To prevent that the malicious host intercepts the transmitted packets h_{sec} between the data sending side and data receiving side, the value of h_{sec} must not exceed the amount of FEC-encoded source packets. That is

$$h_{sec} < k_1 + k_2. \tag{3}$$

Then the recovery probability in the secure FEC is shown as follows:

$$R_{sec}(h_{sec}, k_1, P_B) = \sum_{i=k_1}^{h_{sec}} \left[\binom{h_{sec}}{i} (P_B)^{h_{sec}-i} (1 - P_B)^i \right], \tag{4}$$

subject to $k_1 \leq h_{sec} < k_1 + k_2$.

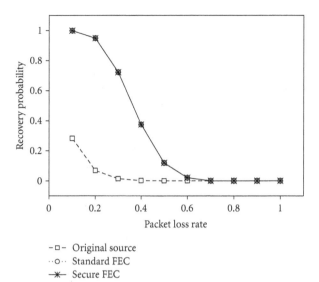

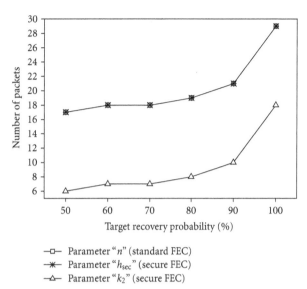

FIGURE 3: Coding rate for both the standard FEC and secure FEC is 2/3 with $k_1 = 12$.

FIGURE 5: Observation on parameter changes with varied target recovery probabilities. The values of k_1 and P_B are 12 and 0.3, respectively.

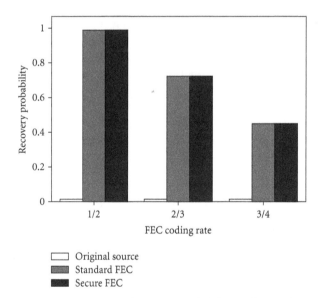

FIGURE 4: Comparison of recovery probability with varied FEC coding rates, when keeping $k_1 = 12$. The packet loss rate is fixed to 0.3.

According to (4), the amount of reference packets k_2 determines the efficiency of the secure FEC scheme since k_1 is typically a predefined value. Larger the value of k_2, higher the FEC recovery rate for a given packet loss rate P_B.

In keeping the consistent reference database between connection ends, the reference data can be initially set up as the secure FEC is installed to start its service and could be updated or expanded by selecting reference data from the reconstructed source data. It is noted that the source data are available only at the connection ends under the decoding constraint on the amount of redundant data (i.e., $k_1 \leq h_{\text{sec}} < (k_1 + k_2)$).

4. Exposure Rate

In this section, we calculate the exposure rate to observe the degree of data inspection for the malicious host. For a data flow transmitting the source packets k_1 along the data path, the exposure rate (ER) can be easily obtained as the malicious host intercepts k_1' packets:

$$\text{ER}_{\text{src}}(k_1', k_1) = \frac{k_1'}{k_1}. \quad (5)$$

Let us assume that the malicious user can intercept the transmission packets in the presence of packet loss rate P_B. Then the value of k_1' can be computed as $k_1' = k_1 \times (1 - P_B)$ and (5) becomes $\text{ER}_{\text{src}}(k_1', k_1) = 1 - P_B$. The exposure rate represents the degree that the source data are exposed to any malicious host with the data interception capacity. As the value of ER approaches to 1, the malicious host can inspect more source content.

In the standard FEC, the delivery blocks inspected by the malicious host fall into one of two different categories: (1) the block is successfully reconstructed and (2) the block is not successfully decoded since the number of received packets is less than the number of source packets. In the first category, all k_1 source packets are completely reconstructed and the expected number of source packets, $E_{\text{FEC}(n,k_1),1}$, can be calculated as

$$E_{\text{FEC}(n,k_1),1} = k_1 \times R_{\text{std}}(n, k_1, P_B). \quad (6)$$

As to the second category, the number of lost packets is greater than $n - k_1$ within n transmitted packets and the expected number of source packets, $E_{FEC(n,k_1),2}$, is derived as follows:

$$E_{FEC(n,k_1),2} = \frac{k_1}{n} \times \sum_{j=n-k_1+1}^{n} \left[\binom{n}{j} \times P_B^j \right.$$

$$\left. \times (1 - P_B)^{n-j} \times (n - j) \right]. \tag{7}$$

Therefore, the total expected number of source packets after decoding an FEC block is given by

$$E_{FEC(n,k_1)} = k_1 \times R_{std}(n, k_1, P_B) + \frac{k_1}{n}$$

$$\times \sum_{j=n-k_1+1}^{n} \left[\binom{n}{j} \times P_B^j \right. \tag{8}$$

$$\left. \times (1 - P_B)^{n-j} \times (n - j) \right].$$

Then, the exposure rate for an FEC block with k_1 source packets and n total transmission packets is given by

$$R_{sec}\left(h_{sec}, k_1, k_2', P_B\right) = \begin{cases} 0, & \text{if } h_{sec}+k_2' < k_1 + k_2, \\ \sum_{i=k_1+k_2-k_2'}^{h_{sec}} \binom{h_{sec}}{i} \times P_B^{h_{sec}-i} \times (1 - P_B)^i, & \text{if } h_{sec}+k_2' \geq k_1 + k_2. \end{cases} \tag{11}$$

Then the exposure rate for the malicious host is given by

$$ER_{sec}\left(h_{sec}, k_1, k_2', P_B\right) = \begin{cases} 0, & \text{if } h_{sec}+k_2' < k_1 + k_2, \\ \left(k_1 \times R_{sec}(h_{sec}, k_2', P_B) + \frac{k_1}{h_{sec}} \right. \\ \left. \times \sum_{j=h_{sec}+k_2'-(k_1+k_2)+1}^{h_{sec}} \left[\binom{h_{sec}}{i} \times P_B^i \right. \right. \\ \left. \left. \times (1 - P_B)^{h_{sec}-i} \times (h_{sec} - i) \right] \right)/k_1, & \text{if } h_{sec}+k_2' \geq k_1 + k_2. \end{cases} \tag{12}$$

$$ER_{std}(n, k_1) = \frac{E_{FEC(n,k_1)}}{k_1}. \tag{9}$$

For our proposed secure FEC scheme, only FEC-encoded redundant packets are injected into the transmission channel, and the amount of injected packets has to be less than the sum of total source packets $(k_1 + k_2)$ for FEC encoding. It is noted that an FEC block can be completely reconstructed at the data receiver only when the amount of received packets is not less than the amount of total source packets. Letting the amount of intercepted packets be h_{sec}' in the secure FEC, we can obtain the following relation

$$h_{sec}' \leq h_{sec} < k_1 + k_2. \tag{10}$$

Based on the relation above, in the secure FEC scheme, the malicious host receives ER = 0 since the malicious host cannot reconstruct the source packets k_1 with the intercepted packets h_{sec}', and all intercepted packets are FEC-encoded redundancies. Considering that the malicious host might have k_2' reference packets and $0 \leq k_2' \leq k_2$, the recovery probability for the malicious host with k_2' is computed as

5. Performance Analysis and Discussions

In this section, the performance of the proposed secure FEC scheme has been evaluated in terms of FEC recovery capacity and data exposure degree. The standard FEC and secure FEC employed packet-level RS codes. In the standard FEC, the values of parameters (k_1, n) were set to $(12, 18)$, and in the secure FEC, the values of k_1 and h_{sec} were 12 and 18, respectively.

5.1. FEC Recovery Capacity. To observe the FEC capacity of the proposed scheme, we compare the secure FEC with the standard FEC and the original source flow. For the original

source flow, the source packets are directly transmitted into the network, while the standard FEC transmits both the source packets and redundant packets. Figure 3 shows the results of the recovery probability as the packet loss rate varies. In Figure 3, all source packets are nearly lost as the packet loss rate is larger than 0.3. For the standard FEC and the secure FEC, both schemes have the decay curve as the packet loss rate increases and their curves are exactly the same for all values of packet loss rates. It is noted that the standard FEC has the loss recovery capacity of $(n-k_1)$ packets while the loss recovery capacity in the secure FEC is given by $(h_{sec} + k_2) - (k_1 + k_2)$ and therefore $(n - k_1)$. As shown in Figure 3, based on the assumption that both schemes require

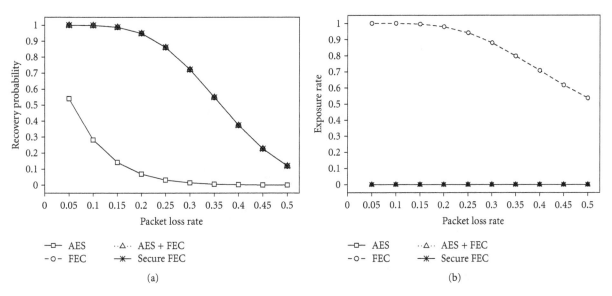

FIGURE 6: System performance comparison with varied packet loss rates. (a) Recovery probability; (b) exposure rate. Noted that label "FEC" represents the standard FEC.

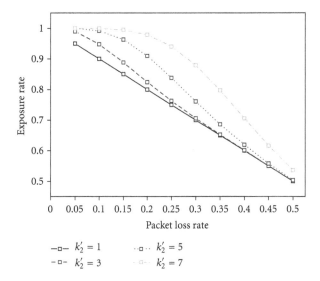

FIGURE 7: Exposure rate performances when different k_2' are applied to the secure FEC. This figure shows the performance impact as the reference packets are leaked to the malicious user.

the same bandwidth consumption (i.e., $h_{sec} = n$), the secure FEC can obtain the similar performance as the standard FEC. The similar observations can also be found in Figure 4. Figure 4 shows the results of the recovery probability for three FEC coding rates of 1/2, 2/3, and 3/4.

To study the operating behavior of the secure FEC, Figure 5 shows the values of parameters (n, h_{sec}, k_2) in packets as the target recovery probability is given. For the secure FEC, the required redundant packets h_{sec} are increased in order to achieve a higher recovery probability. Meanwhile, to ensure the secure transmission, the amount of reference packets k_2 needs to be increased accordingly. It is worth to note that the necessary condition of h_{sec} used in the secure FEC to avoid

the successful FEC decoding by the malicious host is $h_{sec} < (k_1 + k_2)$, and the lower bound of k_2 is hence $k_2 > (h_{sec} - k_1)$. The curve of k_2 presented in Figure 5 is plotted by using its minimum value for a given target recovery probability (i.e., $k_2 = (h_{sec} - k_1) + 1$).

5.2. Data Exposure Degree. We then compare the proposed secure FEC with the encryption scheme, and the joint encryption and FEC scheme. In this study, AES with 128-bit key and packet-level FEC using RS codes are considered. Throughout the evaluation, we assume that a malicious host is located at the receiver side and is capable of performing FEC decoding. Four cases are studied: AES, standard FEC, joint AES and standard FEC, and secure FEC. Figure 6 shows the performance results in terms of recovery probability and exposure rate, from the perspective of a malicious host. From Figure 6, it can be seen that (1) AES has a exposure rate of 0 to guarantee the secure transmission in Figure 6(b) and in Figure 6(a), it has the much lower recovery probability than other three cases; (2) in Figure 6(b), standard FEC obtains the higher values of exposure rates than other cases with secure protection capacities, and as the packet loss rate increases, the exposure rate of FEC is decreased since the recovery probability of FEC is decreased accordingly to receive less source data for the malicious host; and (3) the secure FEC achieves the same performance as the joint AES and FEC scheme in Figures 6(a) and 6(b) to ensure the secure and reliable transmission.

Figure 7 shows the performance impacts when the malicious host is assumed to be capable of acquiring the reference packets. As shown in Figure 7, leaking more reference packets has a higher probability to expose source data to the malicious host. Furthermore, a higher exposure rate is also observed in the presence of lower packet loss rate because the FEC process at the malicious host is easier to reconstruct the source data.

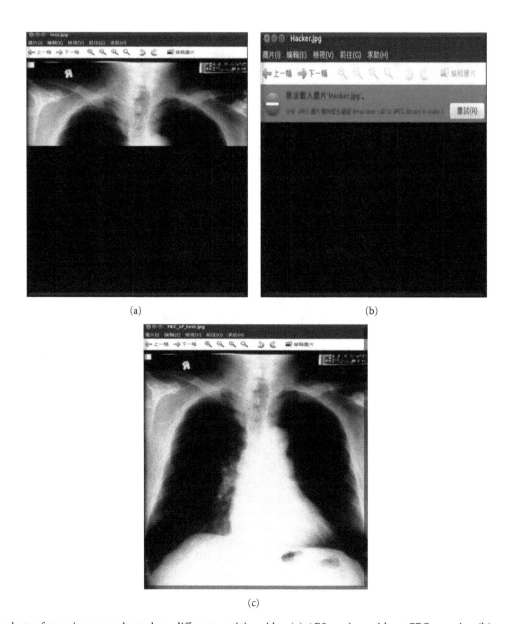

FIGURE 8: Snapshots of experiment results at three different receiving sides. (a) AES receiver without FEC capacity; (b) malicious receiver with FEC capacity; (c) secure FEC receiver.

5.3. Implementation and Experimental Results. To examine the effectiveness of our proposed secure FEC, the secure FEC scheme was implemented on the Linux platform and employed to transmit a sequence of images. In the experimental setup, five machines were connected with a Fast Ethernet LAN. They included an AES sender, an AES receiver, a secure FEC sender, a secure FEC receiver, and a malicious receiver attempting to peak the transmission data. The packet size is 1246 Bytes and all receivers apply the same packet loss traces of $P_B = 0.1$ to the received packet stream.

Figures 8(a)–8(c) presents the snapshots for the AES receiver, malicious receiver, and secure FEC receiver, respectively. From Figure 8, we can observe that (1) the AES receiver can only obtain a part of source packets after decrypting the received data, in the presence of packet loss; (2) the malicious receiver is unable to inspect the content of the transmitted

data for either the AES connection or the secure FEC connection; and (3) the secure FEC receiver can receive the complete source data after the successful FEC reconstruction.

6. Conclusions

In this paper, a novel FEC scheme, which is equipped with both the error correction and security-enhanced capacity, is proposed so as to provide the secure and reliable transmission for valued IPTV content. We have derived the mathematical model to calculate data recovery rate and exposure rate for performance analysis purpose and conducted experiments to demonstrate the validity of the proposed secure FEC. To conclude, the secure FEC can protect the content data against the transmission losses and the unauthorized access. Our future works are (1) to further study the secure FEC applications on the security issues such as authentication and data alteration and (2) to incorporate with encryption and watermarking to achieve robust security promise to end users while the overall performance cost can be minimized.

Acknowledgment

This work was supported by the National Science Council, Taiwan, under Grant no. NSC100-2221-E-241-014.

References

[1] J. Maisonneuve, M. Deschanel, J. Heiles et al., "An Overview of IPTV Standards Development," *IEEE Transactions on Broadcasting*, vol. 55, no. 2, pp. 315–328, 2009.

[2] M. Jeffrey, S. Park, K. Lee, G. Adams, and S. Savage, "Content security for IPTV," *IEEE Communications Magazine*, vol. 46, no. 11, pp. 138–146, 2008.

[3] S. O. Hwang, "Content and service protection for IPTV," *IEEE Transactions on Broadcasting*, vol. 55, no. 2, pp. 425–436, 2009.

[4] H. Zhang, C. Chen, L. Zhao, S. Yang, and L. Zhou, "Content Protection for IPTV-current state of the art and challenges," in *Proceedings of the IMACS Multiconference on Computational Engineering in Systems Applications (CESA '06)*, pp. 1680–1685, Beijing, China, October 2006.

[5] M. Ellis and C. Perkins, "Packet loss characteristics of IPTV-like traffic on residential links," in *Proceedings of the 7th IEEE Consumer Communications and Networking Conference (CCNC '10)*, Las Vegas, Nev, USA, January 2010.

[6] M. Cha, G. Choudhury, J. Yates, A. Shaikh, and S. Moon, "Case study: resilient backbone design for IPTV services," in *Proceedings of the International World Wide Web Conference, IPTV Workshop*, 2006.

[7] Society of Motion Picture and Television Engineers, "Forward error correction for real-time video/audio transport over IP networks," SMPTE specification 2022-1, 2007.

[8] Digital Video Broadcasting (DVB), "IP datacast over DVB-H: content delivery protocols," ETSI TS 102 472.

[9] M. A. Haleem, C. N. Mathur, R. Chandramouli, and K. P. Subbalakshmi, "Opportunistic encryption: a trade-off between security and throughput in wireless networks," *IEEE Transactions on Dependable and Secure Computing*, vol. 4, no. 4, pp. 313–324, 2007.

[10] M. Ruiping, L. Xing, and H. E. Michel, "A new mechanism for achieving secure and reliable data transmission in wireless sensor networks," in *Proceedings of the IEEE Conference on Technologies for Homeland Security: Enhancing Critical Infrastructure Dependability*, pp. 274–279, Woburn, Mass, USA, May 2007.

[11] A. Neri, D. Blasi, L. Gizzi, and P. Campisi, "Joint Security and Channel Coding for Ofdm Communications," in *Proceedings of the European Signal Processing Conference (EUSIPCO'08)*, Lausanne, Switzerland, 2008.

[12] X. Zhu, Q. Sun, Z. Zhang, and C. W. Chen, "A joint ECC based media error and authentication protection scheme," in *Proceedings of the IEEE International Conference on Multimedia and Expo (ICME '08)*, pp. 13–16, Hannover, Germany, June 2008.

[13] C. Nanjunda, M. A. Haleem, and R. Chandramouli, "Robust encryption for secure image transmission over wireless channels," in *Proceedings of the IEEE International Conference on Communications (ICC '05)*, pp. 1287–1291, Seoul, Korea, May 2005.

[14] A. Neri, D. Blasi, P. Campisi, and E. Maiorana, "Joint authentication and forward error correction of still images," in *Proceedings of the European Signal Processing Conference (EUSIPCO'10)*, pp. 2111–2115, Aalborg, Denmark, August 2010.

[15] L. Yao and L. Cao, "Turbo codes-based image transmission for channels with multiple types of distortion," *IEEE Transactions on Image Processing*, vol. 17, no. 11, pp. 2112–2121, 2008.

[16] J. Daemen and V. Rijmen, *The Design of Rijndael: AES—The Advanced Encryption Standard*, Springer, 2002.

[17] H. Cam, V. Ozduran, and O. N. Ucan, "A combined encryption and error correction scheme: AES-turbo," *Journal of Electrical and Electronics Engineering*, vol. 9, no. 1, pp. 891–896, 2009.

[18] N. Zivic, "On using the message digest for error correction in wireless communication networks," in *Proceedings of the International Workshop on Wireless Distributed Networks*, Istanbul, Turkey, September 2010.

[19] N. Zivic and C. Ruland, "Parallel joint channel coding and cryptography," *International Journal of Computer Science and Engineering*, vol. 4, pp. 140–144, 2008.

[20] L. Rizzo, "Effective erasure codes for reliable computer communication protocols," *ACM SIGCOMM Computer Communication Review*, vol. 27, no. 2, pp. 24–36, 1997.

[21] F. Borgonovo and A. Capone, "Efficiency of error-control schemes for real-time wireless applications on the Gilbert channel," *IEEE Transactions on Vehicular Technology*, vol. 54, no. 1, pp. 246–258, 2005.

16

Automatic Story Segmentation for TV News Video Using Multiple Modalities

Émilie Dumont and Georges Quénot

UJF-Grenoble 1/UPMF-Grenoble 2/Grenoble INP, CNRS, LIG UMR 5217, 38041 Grenoble, France

Correspondence should be addressed to Georges Quénot, georges.quenot@imag.fr

Academic Editor: Werner Bailer

While video content is often stored in rather large files or broadcasted in continuous streams, users are often interested in retrieving only a particular passage on a topic of interest to them. It is, therefore, necessary to split video documents or streams into shorter segments corresponding to appropriate retrieval units. We propose here a method for the automatic segmentation of TV news videos into stories. A-multiple-descriptor based segmentation approach is proposed. The selected multimodal features are complementary and give good insights about story boundaries. Once extracted, these features are expanded with a local temporal context and combined by an early fusion process. The story boundaries are then predicted using machine learning techniques. We investigate the system by experiments conducted using TRECVID 2003 data and protocol of the story boundary detection task, and we show that the proposed approach outperforms the state-of-the-art methods while requiring a very small amount of manual annotation.

1. Introduction

Progress in storage and communication technologies has made huge amounts of video contents accessible to users. However, finding a video content corresponding to a particular user's need is not always easy for a variety of reasons, including poor or incomplete content indexing. Also, while video content is often stored in rather large files or broadcasted in continuous streams, users are often interested in retrieving only a particular passage on a topic of interest to them. It is therefore necessary to split video documents or streams into shorter segments corresponding to appropriate retrieval units, for instance, a particular scene in a movie or a particular news in a TV journal. These retrieval units can be defined hierarchically on order to potentially satisfy user needs at different levels of granularity. The retrieval units are not only relevant as search result units but also as units for content-based indexing and for further increasing the content-based video retrieval (CVBR) systems effectiveness.

A video can be analyzed at different levels of granularity. For the image track, the lower level is the individual frame that is generally used for extracting static visual features like color, texture, shape, or interest points. Videos can also be decomposed into shots; a shot is a basic video unit showing a sequence of frames captured by a single camera in a single continuous action in time and space. The shot, however, is not a good retrieval unit as it usually lasts only a few seconds. Higher-level techniques are therefore required to determine a more descriptive segment. We focus in this work on the automatic segmentation of TV journals into individual news or commercial sections if some are present. More specifically, we aim at detecting boundaries between news stories or between a news story and a commercial section. Though this work is conducted in a particular context, it is expected that it could be applied in some other ones with some adaptations, like talk shows for instance. Story segmentation allows better navigation within a video. It can also be used as the starting point for other applications such as video summarization or story search system.

We selected an approach based on multimodal feature extraction. The complementarities of visual and audio information from a video help to develop efficient systems. The story boundary detection is generally more efficient when several and varied features are used. The problem then is to find the best way to use and combine such features. We use a temporal context and machine learning methods to perform the story boundaries detection from multiple features.

2. Related Works

Related works and existing solutions are developed in most cases for broadcast TV and more precisely for broadcast news. It was the case for the task proposed by TRECVID in 2003 and 2004 "Story segmentation" [1, 2] and the more recent ARGOS campaign [3]. Existing techniques for structuring a TV broadcast [4] are classified into three categories: manual approach by skilled workers, metadata-based approach, and content-based approach. We focus on the last category. The approach we explored is to segment at the story level; the video segmentation consists in automatically and accurately determining the boundaries (i.e., the start and the end) of each story.

The authors of [5] presented one of the first works on video segmentation in scenes. Their point of view for scene segmentation is to first locate each camera shot and second combine shots based on content to obtain the start and end points of each scene. They focus on low-level audio properties.

The method proposed by Chaisorn et al. [6, 7] obtained one of the best results at the TRECVID 2003 story boundary detection task as they achieved an $F1$ measure accuracy over 0.75. They first segmented the input video into shots. They then extracted a suitable set of features for modeling the shots contents. They employed a learning-based approach to classify the shots into the set of predefined categories. Finally, they identified story boundaries using a HMM model or inductive rules. However, they selected 13 categories of shots, like Anchor, Sports, Weather, Program logo, Finance, and Speech/Interview. Although effective, their technique required a lot of manually annotated data. The method proposed here requires much less annotated data.

Recently, the authors of [8] segmented videos into stories by detecting anchor person in shots; the text stream is also segmented into stories using a latent-Dirichlet-allocation-(LDA-) based approach. They obtained an $F1$ measure equal to 0.58 on the TRECVID 2003 story boundary detection task. In the paper [9], they presented a scheme for semantic story segmentation based on anchor person detection. The proposed model makes use of a split and merge mechanism to find story boundaries. The approach is based on visual features and text transcripts. The performance of this method is over 0.6 for $F1$ measure also on the TRECVID 2003 story boundary detection task. In the study [10], a set of key events are first detected from multimedia signal sources, including a large-scale concept ontology for images, text generated from automatic speech recognition systems, features extracted from audio track, and high-level video transcriptions. Then, a fusion scheme is investigated using the maximum figure-of-merit learning approach. They obtained an $F1$ measure equal to 0.651 on the TRECVID 2003 story boundary detection task.

In this paper, we propose a more effective method than the actual state of art (evaluated on the same test data). Moreover, our method requires a minimal annotation effort. Though it requires a development set including a number of representative videos with a story segmentation ground truth for training, it does not require or requires very little additional feature annotation like the presence of anchorpersons in shots or of topics like sports, weather, politics, or finance for instance.

3. System Overview

3.1. News Structure. Most news videos have rather similar and well-defined structures. Chaisorn et al. [7] have studied the structure of news videos and noticed:

> "The news video typically begins with several Intro/Highlight video sequences that give a brief introduction of the upcoming news to be reported. The main body of news contains a series of stories organized in terms of different geographical interest, such as international, national, regional and local, and in broad categories of social political, business, sports and entertainment. Each news story normally begins with an anchorperson. Most broadcasts include reports on Sports, Finance or Weather."

There are also, depending on the station, sequences of commercials. Figure 1 illustrates the structure of a typical news video. Although the ordering of news items may differ slightly from broadcast station to station, they all have similar structure and news categories.

3.2. Choice of a Segmentation Unit. Most of the previous works used the shot as a basic segmentation unit for performing story segmentation. However, we noticed that in the TRECVID development set, only 94.1% of the story boundaries match a shot boundary with the 5-second fuzziness allowance of the official evaluation metric. This means that a system working at the shot level cannot find about 6% of the story boundaries. For example, at the end of a story, an anchorperson can appear to give a summary or a conclusion and switch to another topic. In this case, there is no shot transition between the two stories.

On the other hand, the individual frame is a much too small unit not only because of the volume of computations involved by a frame-level evaluation but also because such an accuracy is not required at the application level and because we felt that the segmentation unit should be long enough so that it has a visual meaning when seen by a human being. It was demonstrated during the TRECVID task of Rushes Video Summarization in 2007 that one second is a good duration for a video segment to be meaningful. Two papers showed, in parallel, that one second is enough and sufficient to represent a topic [11, 12].

We finally decided to use a short duration and fixed-length segmentation for the story boundary candidate points and for the segment contents characterization. In preliminary experiments, we also tested segment durations larger

FIGURE 1: The structure of a typical news video.

than one second and the best results were obtained with the smaller ones. We consequently decided to use one second, as the basic unit, which is also consistent with previous works on video summarization [13]. One-second accuracy on story boundary location is also enough from an application point of view.

3.3. Global System Architecture. The idea of our approach is to extract a maximum of relevant information (features or descriptors) and then to fuse it for detecting transitions between the stories. Figure 2 shows the proposed scheme.

Relevant information is extracted on all one-second segments. We use a classification process on the basic units but only in an unsupervised way. Classifying the video segments into different classes (anchorperson, logo presence, weather, speech, silence...) is a fundamental step in recovering structure of a news program. Within a story, we assume that the environment is similar and the discussion focuses on the same topic.

We decided to use the different available modalities. The visual information includes shot detection, the presence of a particular person, and other information such as the presence of channel logo, junk frames, and visual activity. We also use the presence of screen text; we believe that the presence of a text box on a frame on a particular location may have some importance to find story boundaries. For example, in television news the title of a new topic appears in the same place.

We extract audio information like the presence of silence. In fact, when an anchorperson speaks, it happens regularly that a short silence marks the transition between two topics. We also exploit automatic speech recognition (ASR) to extract textual information such as the presence of words that appear frequently near a transition between the stories.

One originality of the proposed approach is that once extracted, the descriptors are expanded with a local temporal context. The main idea of this step is that the value of a descriptor is a possible cue for a story boundary but its temporal evolution in the neighborhood is possibly also very relevant. For example, the appearance or disappearance of a logo is an information more important than only the presence of the logo in the video sequence. Now that we have different sources of information, we need to merge them in order to predict the story boundaries. These sources are merged by early fusion [14].

Once we have different sources of information for each one second segment as well as their local temporal evolution, the challenging task is to segment the broadcast into coherent news stories. Like in major works, we focus on finding the boundaries of every story that succeed in the video stream. In order to perform this detection, we use traditional machine learning methods.

4. Multimodal Features-Based News Stories Segmentation

We present in this section the extraction of the different features. These features are either obtained directly through the application of a third party system that we could not have a chance to improve (e.g., the speech recognizer system (Section 4.2.2)) or built for our purpose (e.g., the anchor person detector (Section 4.1.2)). Application of a text tiling method [15] on the speech transcription was also considered but, surprisingly, it was found that it did not help.

4.1. Visual Features

4.1.1. Shot Detection. We perform a shot boundary detection. As explained previously, in TRECVID development set, 94.1% of the story boundaries appear near a shot boundary. Therefore, this information is very important. Shot boundary detection has been performed by using the system described in [16]. This system detects cut transitions by direct image comparison after motion compensation and dissolve transitions by comparing the norms of the first and second temporal derivatives of the images. It also contains a module for detecting photographic flashes and filtering them out as erroneous cuts and a module for detecting additional cuts via a motion peak detector. This system obtained an overall of recall/precision of 0.819/0.851 at the TRECVID 2003 evaluation campaign. More precisely, it obtained a recall/precision of 0.91/0.92 for cut transitions and of 0.72/0.88 for gradual detection.

Shot boundary detection is performed but it is not directly used as a basis for the candidate story boundaries as this would induce a significant number of missed transitions (at least 6% of story boundaries do not match a shot boundary). Instead it is used as a feature associated to one-second segment units: two binary values are associated with each one-second segment indicating the presence or the absence of a cut or gradual transition within it.

4.1.2. Face and Anchor Person Detector. We use a face detector [17] for which the authors report a face detection rate of 0.903. In order to detect anchor person sequences, we assume that frames with the anchor person are frames that (i) contain a face centered and (ii) are very likely to appear frequently almost "as is" in the video. Consequently, we first select the frames that contain a centered face as candidates to be an anchor person template for a given video. The face being frontal and rather static, in this case the face detector is reliable. For a given video and in order to select an appropriate anchor person template, we expect the average visual similarity of candidates with a prefixed percentage of candidates to be maximal and choose the template frame

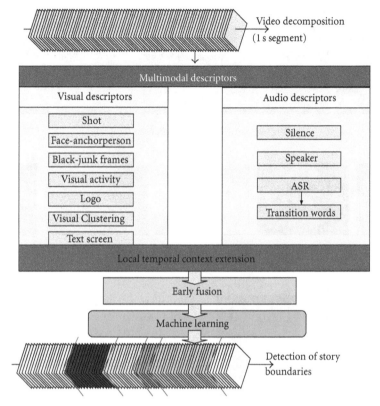

FIGURE 2: Overall system components.

as the frame that exhibits the greatest similarity; Figure 3 shows template samples. The similarity used is based on a Euclidean distance computed between color histogram in the HSV color space (18-3-3 bins). Finally, the similarity between the template and a frame is used like a confidence measure of the presence of an anchor person. Note that preliminary experiments without the face preselection can be used as a plateau detector. This detector has been evaluated on a collection of French TV news videos for anchor person detection on which we obtain an $F1$ measure equal to 0.865 with a recall equal to 0.857 and a precision equal to 0.891.

The anchorperson feature is a single analog (real) value associated with each one-second segment, which is the confidence measure for the segment to contain the anchor person.

4.1.3. Junk Frames. A junk frame is a noninformative frame, typically strong compressions artifacts, transmission errors, or more simply black or single color frames. Figure 4 shows examples of junk frames. A junk sequence may inform us about the possibility of finding a transition around this sequence. Despite its apparent simplicity, the problem of junk detection is quite delicate. We propose a two-step method: detecting black frames and detecting single-color frames. We detect single-color frames by computing the entropy of the distribution of color pixels in gray color space and we remove frames with entropy lower than a predefined threshold. The junk frame feature is a single analog value

associated with each one-second segment indicating the likeliness of the segment to contain one or more junk frames.

4.1.4. Visual Activity. The intensity of motion activity in a video is in fact a measure of "how much" the video content is changing. Considering the high computational complexity caused by existing methods to model the motion feature, we use a more computationally effective color pixel difference-based method to extract the visual activity. The visual activity of a frame can be represented by the percentage of pixels that have changed color between it and the previous frame.

4.1.5. Logo Detection. A TV logo is a graphic representation that is used to identify a channel. A logo is placed in the same place and continuously, except during commercials. Based on this observation, we compute the average frame of the video and the variance of the pixel color in the video, see Figure 5. Pixels with the lowest variance are considered to be part of the logo. Their position will be called the reference position. During the logo detection step, for a given frame, the absolute difference between the colors of the pixels situated at a reference position and their counterpart in the average image is computed. The lower the sum is, the more probable the logo is in the frame. We manually selected the search region for each different channel only to reduce the computational time. However, this method works when applied on the whole image. A temporal filter is applied to the estimated probability of the presence of the logo. This filter outputs a binary value for each one-second segment indicating the presence or the absence of the logo within it.

FIGURE 3: Samples of anchorperson template.

FIGURE 4: Samples of junk frames.

FIGURE 5: Average frames and reference position; CNN images on the right and ABC on the left. The first image represents the average frame (for a selected location), and, on the second image, the pixels with the lowest variance in white are considered to be part of the logo.

4.1.6. Screen Text. The screen text boxes are detected using the method proposed in [18]. Several successive filters are passed on frames: a Sobel filter to determine character edges, then treatment of dilatation and erosion connects the characters together. The connected components that do not hold a mandatory geometry are filtered. Detection is performed on each frame and only the boxes sufficiently stable over time are kept. We only use the presence of a text box information because the quality of many videos is too poor for a good optical character recognition. The text feature is a single analog value associated with each one-second segment indicating the likeliness of the segment to contain one or more text boxes.

4.1.7. Visual Clustering. We perform a clustering in order to group video segments by visual similarity. We represent a video segment by an HSV color histogram, we use the Euclidian distance to compare video segments, and finally we use K-means to perform the clustering. The cluster feature is a discrete integer value associated with each one-second segment indicating the index of the cluster that is closest to the segment contents.

4.2. Audio Features

4.2.1. Silence Detection. The first step of audio segmentation systems is to detect the portions of the input audio stream that exhibit some audio activity or, equivalently, the portions

of silence. The approach for audio activity detection is the bi-Gaussian model of the stream energy profile, where the energy profile is the frame energy or log-energy sequence. The silence feature is a binary value associated with each one-second segment indicating that the segment does contain silence.

4.2.2. Automatic Speech Recognition (ASR). We used here the transcripts proposed during the TRECVID 2003 story segmentation campaign. The speech recognizer makes use of continuous density HMMs with Gaussian mixture for acoustic modeling and 4-gram statistics estimated on large text corpora. Word recognition is performed in multiple passes, where current hypotheses are used for cluster-based acoustic model adaptation prior to the next decoding pass [19]. In our context (i.e., broadcast news), the speech recognizer has a word error rate of 14%. ASR is not directly used for producing a feature. Text tiling was tried on it but it was not able to lead to an overall improvement. However, transitions words extracted from it have been found useful.

4.2.3. Speaker Detection. The speaker detection method is based on [20]. The system used the normalized cross likelihood ratio (NCLR). First, the NCLR is used as a dissimilarity measure between two Gaussian speaker models in the speaker change detection step, and its contribution to the performance of speaker change detection is compared with those of BIC and Hostelling's T2-Statistic measures. Then, the NCLR measure is modified to deal with multi-Gaussian adapted models in the cluster recombination step. This step ends the step-by-step speaker diarization process after the BIC-based hierarchical clustering and the Viterbi resegmentation steps. The speaker diarization error obtained by this method was 7.3%. The speaker feature is a discrete integer value associated with each one-second segment indicating the index of the speaker present in the segment.

4.2.4. Transition Words. Based on the ASR, we extract the most frequent transition words. We first remove all stop

TABLE 1: Transition words and their scores.

Words	$t-3$	$t-2$	$t-1$	t	$t+1$	$t+2$	$t+3$
ABC	0.02	0.03	0.016	0.01	0.12	0.62	0.18
News	0.03	0.16	0.15	0.04	0.29	0.33	0.06
Tonight	0.07	0.23	0.32	0.10	0.14	0.10	0.04
Today	0.18	0.30	0.46	0.02	0.00	0.01	0.02

words from the transcription. Then, we select the most frequent words that appear in a temporal window that overlaps a story transition. Finally, for each selected word w, we determine a score related to the nonuniform probability to find a transition at time $t + i$ sec given that w were pronounced at time t.

Table 1 shows results obtained on ABC videos. If i ranges between -3 and $+3$ seconds, we can notice that the extracted words are ABC, News, Today and Tonight, ABC and News being pronounced one or two seconds after a transition while Today, and Tonight appear a few seconds before a transition. The transition word feature is a single analog value associated with each one-second segment giving the probability of the segment to correspond to a story boundary according to the presence of a possible transition word in its neighborhood.

4.3. Multimodal Features. Multimodal features are the pool of features obtained from single modalities to be used for story boundary detection combined into a global representation. Figure 6 shows a graphical representation of multimodal features. This figure is quite complicated but it is very useful to see the various shapes and the complementarities of the individual features. The multimodal features correspond to a concatenation of all the elements within one column (early fusion) before the local temporal extension.

As it can be seen, silence is well correlated with the ground truth although it lacks precision (it detects a silence between the first two story boundaries). This false alarm can nevertheless be corrected using other features like, for example, anchorperson or shot transition. The combinatorial is very complex, so we rely on an automatic procedure to combine these features and machine learning to analyze them.

The shot detection information is decomposed into two binary values: the first one represents the presence of a cut transition and the second represents the presence of a gradual transition in the one-second segment. The presence of silence and logo are represented by a binary value. Visual cluster and speaker are represented by the cluster index. Finally, other features are numerical values.

5. Multimodal Fusion

Once extracted, the multimodal features can be combined by early fusion in order to detect the transitions between stories. We do this in two steps: we determine the best way to use each feature and then we merge the features using a classifier. The classifier provides a prediction score for story transition. The

fusion is performed with the same basic segmentation unit as the feature extraction: one-second fixed length segments.

5.1. Local Temporal Context. All descriptors are extracted for each one-second segment of a video. Therefore, they do not take into account the temporal information included in a video. Certainly, the information of the presence or absence of a descriptor is important, but the information about the appearance or disappearance can be even more relevant. Based on this observation, we extend the descriptors with a local temporal context, more precisely by the descriptor values in the closest segments.

We use a strategy based on a sliding window: for a one-second segment s coming into sight at time t in the video, we use a sliding window with a fixed length equal to $2l + 1$ and where the current segment is located at the center of the window $W_s = \{s_{t-l}, \ldots, s_t, \ldots, s_{t+l}\}$. For each sliding window, we extract three categories of representations:

(i) the list, V_{all}, of all values contained in the sliding window ($2l + 1$ values);

(ii) the list, V_{diff}, of the differences between each couple of one second segment with an equal distance to s_t plus the central value s_t itself ($l + 1$ values);

(iii) V_{gauss}, the values of the Gaussian distribution, the derivation of Gaussian distribution, and the second derivation of Gaussian distribution (3 values).

The first solution corresponds to feeding the classifier with an input vector that is a concatenation of a number of column vectors around the current one or to use a vertical slice of several columns in the representation given in Figure 6. This is the most complete information that can be passed on and it leaves open to the classifier underlying machine learning method to decide whether it will use for each feature the single central value, the level around it, the variation around it, or any combination of them including how far around it should go. Though this is the most complete, it is also the most costly one and not necessarily the most efficient one. As we can have the intuition that the level, the variation, or a combination of both can be more compact and more synthetic we considered the two other possibilities, the third one being even more compact and synthetic than the second one. We also considered the possibility of optimizing the size of the window and the neighborhood representation type by tuning them using a development set.

5.2. Fusion. Finally, each multimodal vector used as input for the classifier is a concatenation of the best features' representation. We chose to perform an early fusion for avoiding the loss of the correlation information between different features. We have tested several classifiers using WEKA [21] to find the best one for the task. In contrast with a shot transition, a story transition is not necessarily annotated at the same frame for all annotators. In order to take into account the fuzziness of the story transition location in the annotation, we decided to discard five one-second segments on each side of a story transition since

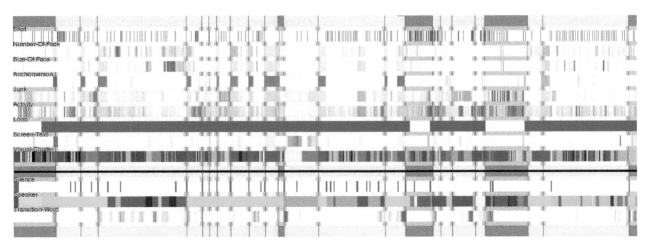

FIGURE 6: Example of multimodal features. Each pixel column corresponds to a one-second segment. The top and bottom thick lines (or stripes) represent the ground truth with transitions in black and stories in light green (news) or dark gray (advertisements/misc). The similar line (or stripe) with a thick black line in the middle shows the same information while also separating the visual features (above) from the audio features (below). Thin lines between the thick ones reproduce the top and bottom thick lines but with lighter colors for the story types and additionally with a 5-second green expansion around the boundaries corresponding to the fuzziness factor associated with the evaluation metric (transitions are counted as correct if found within this extension). These are replicated so that it is easier to see how the feature values or transitions match them. Also, the beginning of the thin lines contains the name of the feature represented in the thick lines immediately below them. Finally, the remaining thick lines represent the feature values with three types of coding. For scalar analog values, the blue intensity corresponds to the real value normalized between 0 and 1. For binary values, this is the same except that only the extreme values are used and that in the case of shot boundaries, blue is used for cuts and red is used for gradual transitions. For cluster index values (clusters and speakers), a random color map is generated and used.

these segments are annotated negatively while they could be positive and since such outliers often lead to a loss of performance. Discarding these segments ensures that all the samples annotated as negative are actually negative while those annotated as positive are chosen as close to the actual transition as possible. This might in turn result into a comparable fuzziness into the location of the detected transitions.

6. Experimental Results

6.1. Experimental Protocol. Our method has been evaluated in the context of the TRECVID 2003 Story Segmentation Task and exactly in the same conditions except, indeed, that it was done later and that it could not be included in the TRECVID 2003 official results. However, the same data, ground truth, protocol, metrics, and evaluation programs have been used. Tuning has been done using only the development data and the tuned system has then been applied only once on the test data. No tuning was done on the test data at all.

The collection contains about 120 hours of ABC World News Tonight and CNN Headline News recorded by the Linguistic Data Consortium from late January through June 1998. We chose this dataset because it is the only one which is available and widely used by the community; it allows us to compare our method with the state of the art.

We developed and tuned the system only within the development set (partitioned itself into a training and a test set by a random process) and then we applied it on the test set. Since story boundaries are rather abrupt changes

of focus, story boundary evaluation is modeled on the evaluation of shot boundaries: to evaluate the story segmentation, an automatic comparison to human-annotated reference is done to extract recall and precision measures. A story boundary is expressed as a time offset with respect to the start of the video file in seconds, accurate to the nearest hundredth of a second. Each reference boundary is expanded with a fuzziness factor of five seconds in each direction, resulting in an evaluation interval of 10 seconds. If a computed boundary does not fall in the evaluation interval of a reference boundary, it is considered a false alarm.

(i) Story boundary recall = number of reference boundaries detected/total number of reference boundaries.

(ii) Story boundary precision = (total number of submitted boundaries minus the total amount of false alarms)/total number of submitted boundaries.

(iii) Story boundary $F1$ measure = 2 × recall × precision/(recall + precision).

6.2. Classifier Selection. We made a selection of the best classifier method for our problem: 48 classifiers from the Weka toolbox have been tested; for more information about these classifiers, see [22]. Figure 7 shows the best results obtained in terms of $F1$ measure within the development set.

Results show that RandomForest is the best classifier for our problem. Results also show that the classifiers in the category of trees are on average the best in our case. This can partially be explained by the non-normalized features that we used. However, this is a complex problem because our descriptors do not have the same scale. For example, it is

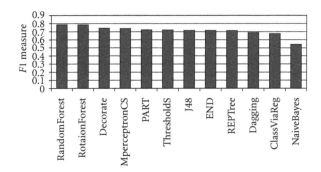

FIGURE 7: Results for the best classifiers.

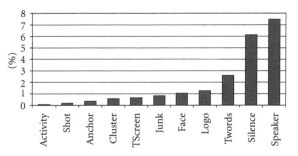

FIGURE 8: Multimodal features lost in terms of F measure.

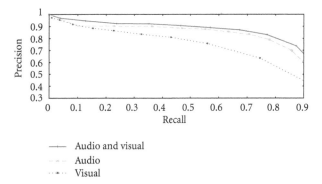

FIGURE 9: Comparison between audio and visual features.

difficult to compare the number of faces in a video segment and a confidence value of visual activity. For our problem, it is also interesting to note that the amount of positive is very low compared to the number of negative. So, classifiers like SVM are not suitable.

6.3. Feature Interest. To prove the relevance of the chosen features, we estimate the performance loss in terms of $F1$ measure when features are individually removed from the pool. We train several classifiers by removing one feature at each time. Finally, we compare their result with those obtained by the method taking into account all features, see Figure 8.

We can see that speaker detection and silence are the most important features for our problem. Features like transition words, logo, face, junk, text screen, and visual cluster are also important. It should be noted that some features are correlated with other ones, and it is logical that the performance loss associated with such a feature is not high. For example, if we remove anchorperson, the performance loss is not very important because this information is partly present in the speaker feature.

We can see that audio features are more interesting than visual features. In order to evaluate this comment, we compare results obtained only using audio features with only visual features, see the recall-precision curve in Figure 9. It is clear that audio features are better; therefore visual features improve results.

6.4. Local Temporal Context Experiments. For each descriptor, we tested different lengths of sliding window (from 1 sec to 31 sec) and different representations (V_{all}, V_{diff}, or V_{gauss}) in order to find the best combination for each descriptor (other descriptors were used without local context information). Figure 10 shows the results for three different descriptors: speaker and face. The curve Base represents results without local temporal extension. It is clear that the local temporal context improves the quality of the predictions. Table 2 shows the best combination for the selected descriptors.

In Figure 11, we compare the performance of the different methods of local temporal context extractions. We can see that the local temporal context improves performance, and the best results are obtained by using the best local

temporal context for each descriptor. This method uses vectors of 231 dimensions. The closest results to this method are obtained using a sliding window equal to 15 and extracting V_{all}, V_{diff}, and V_{gauss} for each descriptor; however, in this case, the dimensions become 650. So the selection of optimal parameter for each descriptor is more interesting.

6.5. Cross-Channel Experiments. In order to assess the robustness of our system, we evaluate it in a cross-channel setting while the domain being the same (namely, TV news programs). The TRECVID 2003 collection contains TV journals from two different channels: CNN and ABC. We evaluated the system while training the system on the full development collection, only the ABC part, or only the CNN part and while testing the system also on these channel combinations. In order to distinguish between the effect of using a smaller training collection and the effect of using only one of the channels, we also trained the system using only half of the full development collection with both channels. We evaluated the following combinations: "ABC to ABC," "CNN to CNN," "all to all," "all/2 to all," "ABC to CNN," and "CNN to ABC". Some features (logo detection and transition words) are always computed separately for each channel.

Figure 12 shows the results of the cross-collection examination. The system has a very stable behavior when the composition of the training and test data is similar. The performance is slightly higher for "ABC to ABC" and slightly lower for "CNN to CNN," possibly indicating that the organization of ABC journals is more stable than that of CNN journals. The size of the training set has no significant effect.

TABLE 2: Best descriptor representation. In this table, we can see for each descriptor the best length l for the sliding window and the selected categories of values.

	Shot	Anchor	Silence	Speaker	Face	TWord	TScreen	Junk	Activity	Logo
Length	1	21	9	15	11	13	5	9	13	21
Values	V_{all}	V_{diff}	V_{diff} V_{gauss}	V_{diff}	V_{all}	V_{all} V_{gauss}	V_{all}	V_{diff}	V_{diff}	V_{diff} V_{gauss}

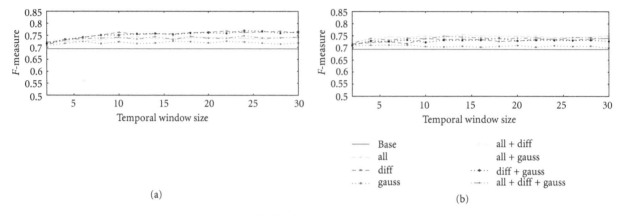

(a)

(b)

FIGURE 10: Results for local temporal context of a descriptor.

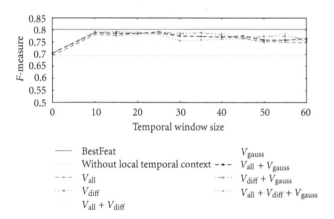

FIGURE 11: Results for local temporal context.

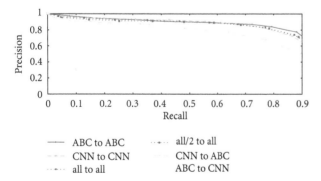

FIGURE 12: Collection results. The comparison of results between a learning on all videos (CNN and ABC) called "all to all," a collection learning "ABC to ABC" and "CNN to CNN," and another generic learning but with the same number of training samples "all/2 to all" as in collection learning.

As expected, we can notice a performance drop for cross-channel experiments. The figure shows that the system performs better for "CNN to ABC" than for "ABC to CNN." However, the quality of the predictions remains good since we get an F measure of 0.696 (recall = 0.642, precision = 0.761). The difference in performance between CNN to ABC and ABC to CNN probably arises from the fact that CNN has the same style of transitions as ABC but CNN also contains specific transitions not observed in ABC.

6.6. *Experiments with Another Corpus.* We have tested our method on another corpus. This corpus consists of 59 videos of France 2 TV News from 1 February to 31 March 2007. The average length of these videos is about 38 minutes, which represents an overall of 37 hours of video. We extracted a subset of multimodal features: junk frames, visual activity, logo, anchorperson, transition words, and speaker detection. We obtained good results: an $F1$ measure equal to 0.870 with a recall equal to 0.897 and a precision equal to 0.844. Our method applies well to another corpus, no adjustment has been made, and the system has been applied as such with the descriptors we had. One reason for this good performance can also come in the quality of videos and probably the story boundaries are easier to predict than on TRECVID 2003 corpus.

6.7. *Results.* We compare our results with the state of the art in Table 3.

(i) The method proposed by Chaisorn et al. [6, 7] obtained one of the best results at the TRECVID 2003 story boundary detection task. They, first, segmented the input video into shots. Then, they extracted a suitable set of features to model the contents of shots.

TABLE 3: Comparison with the state of art.

	Chaisorn et al. 2003 [7]	Misra et al. 2010 [8]	Goyal et al. 2009 [9]	Ma et al. 2009 [10]	Our method	Our method + channel
Recall	0.749	0.54	0.497	0.581	0.878	0.893
Precision	0.802	0.64	0.750	0.739	0.767	0.767
$F1$	0.775	0.58	0.600	0.651	0.819	0.825

They employed a learning-based approach to classify the shots into the set of 13 predefined categories. Finally, they identified story boundaries using an HMM model or inductive rules.

(ii) Misra et al. [8] segmented videos into stories by detecting anchor person in shots; the text stream is also segmented into stories using a latent-Dirichlet-allocation- (LDA-) based approach.

(iii) Goyal et al. [9] presented a scheme for semantic story segmentation based on anchor person detection. The proposed model makes use of a split-and-merge-mechanism to find story boundaries. The approach is based on visual features and text transcripts.

(iv) In Ma et al. [10], a set of key events are first detected from multimedia signal sources, including a large-scale concept ontology for images, text generated from automatic speech recognition systems, features extracted from audio track, and high-level video transcriptions. Then, a fusion scheme is investigated using the maximum figure-of-merit learning approach.

With the proposed method, we have obtained a recall of 0.878 and a precision of 0.767, which gives an $F1$ measure equal to 0.819 with a threshold optimized on the development set. On the same data set, our system is more effective than the actual systems. We have also tested our method using a feature vector expanded with a channel information (ABC or CNN), and the performance of the system was reached up to 0.825.

7. Conclusion

We have presented a method for segmenting TV news videos into stories. This system is based on multimodal features extraction. The originality of the approach is in the use of machine learning techniques for finding the candidate transitions from a large number of heterogeneous low-level features; it is also in the use of a temporal context for the features before their combination by early fusion.

This system has the advantage that it requires no or minimal external annotation. It was evaluated in the context of the TRECVID 2003 story segmentation task and obtained better performance than the current state of the art.

Future work would include other relevant descriptors for this task and an efficient step of normalization. Features of interest could be category topic detection using other sources in a video collection. Regarding the method for predicting the presence of story transition, it could be improved through a process that takes into account the video structure and the temporal information.

Acknowledgment

This work was realized as part of the Quaero Programme funded by OSEO, French state agency for innovation.

References

[1] A. F. Smeaton, P. Over, and W. Kraaij, "TRECVID—an overview," in *Proceedings of TRECVID*, 2003.

[2] T. S. Chua, S. F. Chang, L. Chaisorn, and W. Hsu, "Story boundary detection in large broadcast news video archives - Techniques, experience and trends," in *Proceedings of the 12th ACM International Conference on Multimedia*, pp. 656–659, October 2004.

[3] P. Joly, J. Benois-Pineau, E. Kijak, and G. Quénot, "The ARGOS campaign: evaluation of video analysis and indexing tools," *Signal Processing*, vol. 22, no. 7-8, pp. 705–717, 2007.

[4] A. E. Abduraman, S. A. Berrani, and B. Mérialdo, "TV program structuring techniques: a review," in *TV Content Analysis: Techniques and Applications*, 2011.

[5] J. M. Gauch, S. Gauch, S. Bouix, and X. Zhu, "Real time video scene detection and classification," *Information Processing and Management*, vol. 35, no. 3, pp. 381–400, 1999.

[6] L. Chaisorn and T. S. Chua, "Story boundary detection in news video using global rule induction technique," in *Proceedings of the IEEE International Conference on Multimedia and Expo (ICME '06)*, pp. 2101–2104, July 2006.

[7] L. Chaisorn, T. S. Chua, and C. H. Lee, "A multi-modal approach to story segmentation for news video," *World Wide Web*, vol. 6, no. 2, pp. 187–208, 2003.

[8] H. Misra, F. Hopfgartner, A. Goyal et al., "Tv news story segmentation based on semantic coherence and content similarity," in *Proceedings of the 16th international conference on Advances in Multimedia Modeling*, pp. 347–357, 2010.

[9] A. Goyal, P. Punitha, F. Hopfgartner, and J. M. Jose, "Split and merge based story segmentation in news videos," in *Proceedings of the 31th European Conference on IR Research on Advances in Information Retrieval*, pp. 766–770, 2009.

[10] C. Ma, B. Byun, I. Kim, and C. H. Lee, "A detection-based approach to broadcast news video story segmentation," in *Proceedings of the IEEE International Conference on Acoustics, Speech, and Signal Processing (ICASSP '09)*, pp. 1957–1960, April 2009.

[11] E. Dumont and B. Mérialdo, "Split-screen dynamically accelerated video summaries," in *Proceedings of the 1st TRECVID Video Summarization Workshop (TVS '07)*, pp. 55–59, September 2007.

[12] A. G. Hauptmann, M. G. Christel, W. H. Lin et al., "Clever clustering vs. simple speed-up for summarizing BBC rushes,"

in *Proceedings of the 1st TRECVID Video Summarization Workshop (TVS '07)*, pp. 20–24, September 2007.

[13] E. Dumont and B. Mérialdo, "Automatic evaluation method for rushes summary content," in *Proceedings of the IEEE International Conference on Multimedia and Expo (ICME '09)*, pp. 666–669, July 2009.

[14] C. Snoek, M. Worring, and A. W. M. Smeulders, "Early versus late fusion in semantic video analysis," in *Proceedings of the 13th Annual ACM International Conference on Multimedia*, pp. 399–402, 2005.

[15] M. A. Hearst, "Multi-paragraph segmentation of expository text," in *Proceedings of the 32nd Annual Meeting on Association for Computational Linguistics (ACL '94)*, pp. 9–16, 1994.

[16] G. Quénot, D. Moraru, and L. Besacier, "CLIPS at TRECvid: shot boundary detection and feature detection," in *Proceedings of TRECVID*, 2003.

[17] H. A. Rowley, S. Baluja, and T. Kanade, "Neural network-based face detection," *IEEE Transactions on Pattern Analysis and Machine Intelligence*, vol. 20, no. 1, pp. 23–38, 1998.

[18] J. Poignant, L. Besacier, G. Quénot, and F. Thollard, "From text detection in videos to person identification," in *Proceedings of the IEEE International Conference on Multimedia and Expo*, 2012.

[19] J. L. Gauvain, L. Lamel, and G. Adda, "The LIMSI broadcast news transcription system," *Speech Communication*, vol. 37, no. 1-2, pp. 89–108, 2002.

[20] V. B. Le, O. Mella, and D. Fohr, "Speaker diarization using normalized cross likelihood ratio," in *Proceedings of the 8th Annual Conference of the International Speech Communication Association (Interspeech '07)*, pp. 873–876, August 2007.

[21] M. A. Hall, E. Frank, G. Holmes, B. Pfahringer, P. Reutemann, and I. H. Witten, "The WEKA data mining software: an update," *SIGKDD Explorations Newsletter*, vol. 11, pp. 10–18, 2009.

[22] http://www.cs.waikato.ac.nz/ml/weka/.

17

Background Traffic-Based Retransmission Algorithm for Multimedia Streaming Transfer over Concurrent Multipaths

Yuanlong Cao,[1] Changqiao Xu,[1, 2] Jianfeng Guan,[1] and Hongke Zhang[1, 3]

[1] State Key Laboratory of Networking and Switching Technology, Beijing University of Posts and Telecommunications, Beijing 100876, China
[2] Institute of Sensing Technology and Business, Beijing University of Posts and Telecommunications, Jiangsu, Wuxi 214028, China
[3] National Engineering Laboratory for Next Generation Internet Interconnection Devices, Beijing Jiaotong University, Beijing 100044, China

Correspondence should be addressed to Yuanlong Cao, ylcao@bupt.edu.cn

Academic Editor: János Tapolcai

The content-rich multimedia streaming will be the most attractive services in the next-generation networks. With function of distribute data across multipath end-to-end paths based on SCTP's multihoming feature, concurrent multipath transfer SCTP (CMT-SCTP) has been regarded as the most promising technology for the efficient multimedia streaming transmission. However, the current researches on CMT-SCTP mainly focus on the algorithms related to the data delivery performance while they seldom consider the background traffic factors. Actually, background traffic of realistic network environments has an important impact on the performance of CMT-SCTP. In this paper, we firstly investigate the effect of background traffic on the performance of CMT-SCTP based on a close realistic simulation topology with reasonable background traffic in NS2, and then based on the localness nature of background flow, a further improved retransmission algorithm, named *RTX_CSI*, is proposed to reach more benefits in terms of average throughput and achieve high users' experience of quality for multimedia streaming services.

1. Introduction

The content-rich multimedia streaming, such as video-on-demand (VoD) [1, 2] and Internet Protocol Television (IPTV) will be the most attractive services in the next-generation networks. Most researches have proved the Stream Control Transmission Protocol (SCTP) will be the most promising technology for the large bandwidth consumption of multimedia streaming services [2–4]. Particularly in the future wireless heterogeneous network that the terminals will be equipped with multiple network interfaces and attached multiple heterogeneous access capability at the same time, the SCTP can provide the effective transmission for multimedia streaming services and balance the overhead among multiple access networks.

The SCTP [5] has been proposed and standardized by the Internet Engineering Task Force (IETF) in order to effectively utilize the multihoming environment and support real-time signaling transmission over IP networks, since SS7 has been the only bearer for the signaling traffic in telecommunication networks [6] for many years. SCTP has some important features including: (1) multi-homing. The destination nodes can be reached under the several IP addresses (multi-homed). In SCTP, both sides of the association provide multiple IP addresses combined with a single SCTP port number [7]. (2) Multistreaming which means the parallel transmission of messages over the same association between sender and the receiver. The stream independently carries fragmented messages from one terminal to another, which can achieve a cumulative throughput [8] than other protocols (e.g., TCP). SCTP manages more than one communication path with two major functions: (a) using SACK (selective acknowledgment) to probes primary path connectivity and HEARTBEAT to probe the alternative paths, respectively; (b) fail-over which means once the primary path breaks and selects an alternative path as the primary path.

As an improved version of SCTP, Concurrent Multipath Transfer (CMT) [9] uses the SCTP's multi-homing feature to distribute data across multiple end-to-end paths in a multi-homed SCTP association. CMT is the concurrent transfer of new data from a source to a destination via more than one end-to-end paths, and it is used between multi-homed source and destination hosts to increase the throughputs. Moreover, a CMT sender can maintain more accurate information (such as available bandwidth, loss rate, and RTT) of all the paths, since new data are sent to all destinations concurrently. This feature allows the CMT sender to better decide where to retransmit once data is lost.

There is more and more researches pay attention to multimedia streaming, and CMT-SCTP had been employed as transport protocol as well to study the performance of multimedia streaming services. For example, Stegel et al. [10] proposed solutions on how to provisioning SCTP multi-homing in converged IP-based multimedia environment. Huang and Lin [11] proposed a partially reliable-concurrent multipath transfer (PR-CMT) protocol for multimedia streaming in order to improve the throughput and video quality degrade. In our previous work, we designed a novel Evalvid-CMT platform [3, 4] to investigate and evaluate the performance of CMT for real-time video distribution, and then a meaningful suggestion was pointed out on which strategies for real-time video concurrent multipath transmissions.

Although the advantages of CMT-SCTP has been investigated in variety of attractive services, however, existing evaluation works [1–16] of CMT-SCTP do not consider the impact of background traffic. Actually, Internet measurement studies showed complex behaviors of Internet traffic [17, 18] that are necessary for realistic testing environments. There are several reasons why background traffic is important in performance testing. First, the aggregate behavior of background traffic can induce a rich set of dynamics such as queue fluctuations, patterns of packet losses, and fluctuations of the total link utilization at bottleneck links and can have a significant impact on the performance of CMT-SCTP. Second, network environments without any randomness in packet arrivals and delays are highly susceptible to the phase effect [19], and a good mix of background traffic reduces the likelihood of synchronization [20]. Third, the core of the Internet allows a high degree of statistical multiplexing. Therefore, the performance evaluation of network protocols with little or no background traffic does not fully investigate the CMT-SCTP behaviors that are likely to be observed when it is deployed in the Internet.

On the other hand, there are five retransmission algorithms proposed in [12] to enhance the performance of CMT-SCTP. Previous work [9, 14] take major researching focus on the effects of different retransmission algorithms with different limited receive buffer (*rbuf*) sizes. However, all of the five retransmission algorithms are designed with only one of paths' condition as metric. Liu et al. [16] combines some paths' conditions to select the retransmission path but with an unreasonable metric since loss rate is not be recommended according to RFC4460.

In this paper, taking reasonable background traffic into account, we firstly investigate the effect of background traffic on the performance of CMT-SCTP based on a more realistic simulation topology in NS2 [21]. Considering the nature of background traffic and taking paths' previous states into account, we further propose an improved retransmission algorithm named *RTX_CSI* to achieve more benefits in terms of average throughput and high users' experience of quality for multimedia streaming services.

The rest of paper is organized as follows. Section 2 explains our experimental design for network redundancy in CMT-SCTP. Section 3 presents how effects occurred by designed background traffic. Section 4 addresses the proposed *RTX_CSI* algorithm and its performance evaluation. Section 5 concludes this paper and discusses the future work.

2. Preliminary Work

2.1. Background Traffic Design. In accordance with the Internet survey [22], TCP traffic on the Internet is about 80–83%, and UDP traffic is about 17–20%. Moreover, the content-rich multimedia streaming will be the most attractive services in the future networks, more and more multimedia encoded by VBR will be deployed in Internet. Thus, more reasonable background traffic consists of TCP traffic, CBR traffic, and VBR traffic should be taken into account to evaluate the performance of data delivering.

With the purpose of investigating the effect of background traffic on the performance of CMT-SCTP, our experiments adopt a more realistic simulation scenario for network redundancy in CMT-SCTP, that is, TCP traffic, CBR traffic, and VBR traffic will be employed in our simulation topology designing. Test scenario consists of one path with TCP traffic and UDP/CBR traffic as background traffic (TCP : UDP/CBR is 4 : 1) and another with TCP traffic and UDP/VBR traffic as background traffic (TCP : UDP/VBR is 4 : 1) which is represented by *TCP+UDP/CBR* and *VBR* in below.

2.2. VBR Traffic Generator Loading. Since NS2 still cannot support VBR traffic, in order to enable VBR traffic generator in NS2, we add *PT_VBR* as packet enumeration and then set *VBR* for *PT_VBR*'s value in packet information function [23]. The default values for VBR traffic are set as shown in Table 1.

2.3. Simulation Topology Setup. To investigate the impact of background traffic on the performance of CMT-SCTP completely, a more realistic simulation topology with reasonable background traffic is proposed, which is shown in Figure 1. In the dual dumbbell topology, each router (R1 ~ R4) connects to five edge nodes. The edge nodes are single interfaces and connect to the routes to generate the background traffic. Each edge node attaches with a traffic generator, and four edge nodes generate 80% TCP traffic and one edge node generates 20% UDP traffic (CBR or VBR). According to [24], the propagation delay between the edge nodes and routers is set to 5 ms in order to create the maximum effect occurred by background traffic, and bandwidth is set to 100 Mb. The propagation delay between

TABLE 1: Parameter settings of VBR traffic.

Variable	Value
*Application/traffic/VBR set rate_*	448 Kb
*Application/traffic/VBR set random_*	0
*Application/traffic/VBR set max pkts_*	268435456
*Application/traffic/VBR set max Size_*	200
*Application/traffic/VBR set min Size_*	100
*Application/traffic/VBR set intervaltime_*	200

two routers is set to 45 ms with 10 Mb of bandwidth in accordance with article [25] (CMT-PF addressed in this article is not employed in our experiments for pure study of the impact occurred by background traffic).

The S and R stand for CMT-SCTP sender and receiver, respectively, and connected to the network through two interfaces. CMT-SCTP uses concurrent multipath transfer to send data on both paths with the default parameters recommended by RFC4460. After 0.5 seconds of simulation, the CMT-SCTP sender begins to initiate the association with CMT-SCTP receiver. At 1.0 seconds, edge nodes generate the background traffic, and the total simulation time is 30 seconds.

3. Study of the Impact of Background Traffic

To analyze the impact of the background traffic, this section evaluates the average throughput (delay) of CMT-SCTP with and without background traffic, respectively. To measure the presence of background traffic affecting the performance of CMT-SCTP, we define a metric called *Impact Degree* (denoted as Θ) which can be expressed by

$$\Phi(\Theta_\alpha) = \frac{|\Phi(x_\alpha) - \Phi(y_\alpha)|}{\Phi(x_\alpha)} \times 100\%, \qquad (1)$$

where α stands for *rbuf*; x stands for CMT-SCTP without background traffic condition and y for CMT-SCTP with *TCP + UDP/CBR* and *VBR* traffic condition; $\Phi(x_\alpha)$ is on behalf of average throughput or average delay achieved by CMT-SCTP without background traffic under different α; $\Phi(y_\alpha)$ for average throughput or average delay created by CMT-SCTP with *TCP + UDP/CBR* and *VBR* traffic under different α; $\Phi(\Theta_\alpha)$ stands for impact degree arisen by *TCP + UDP/CBR* and *VBR* traffic. High $\Phi(\Theta_\alpha)$ means that background traffic has high side effects on CMT-SCTP in terms of throughput and delay, that is, low average throughput (high average delay) CMT-SCTP will be reached.

Since default *rbuf* size commonly used in operating systems today is varied from 16 KB to 64 KB and beyond. Herein, we investigate the impact of background traffic on CMT-SCTP under *rbuf* size with 16 KB, 32 KB, 64 KB, 128 KB, and 256 KB. Figures 2, 3, 4, 5, and 6 show throughput reached by CMT-SCTP with or without background under different size of *rbuf*, respectively (the measuring interval is 0.5 s).

As illustrated in Figures 2, 3, 4, 5, and 6, we can point out that: (1) the background traffic presents an impact on throughput clearly; (2) with the increase of the receive buffer, the impact of the background traffic is increased.

Figure 7 shows the comparison on average throughput with and without background traffic under different *rbuf*.

Figure 8 shows the comparison on average delay with and without background traffic under different *rbuf*, respectively.

Based on (1) and above simulation results, Figure 9 shows the corresponding impact degree which occurred by the designed background traffic.

As it shown in Figure 7, when *TCP + UDP/CBR* and *VBR* is employed as the background traffic, the impact degree on average throughput can be calculated as $\Phi(\Theta_{16}) \approx 0.0025$, $\Phi(\Theta_{32}) \approx 0.0047$, $\Phi(\Theta_{64}) \approx 0.0278$, $\Phi(\Theta_{128}) \approx 0.2652$, and $\Phi(\Theta_{256}) \approx 0.5238$. Figure 9 illustrates that larger *rbuf* will lead to larger impact degree, namely, larger side effect will occur by background traffic in terms of average throughput.

As it shown in Figure 8, when *TCP + UDP/CBR* and *VBR* is employed as the background traffic, the impact degree on average delay can be calculated as $\Phi(\Theta_{16}) \approx 0.05019$, $\Phi(\Theta_{32}) \approx 0.0721$, $\Phi(\Theta_{64}) \approx 0.1235$, $\Phi(\Theta_{128}) \approx 0.4941$, and $\Phi(\Theta_{256}) \approx 0.3037$. From Figure 9, we note that larger *rbuf* will lead to larger impact degree. However, when *rbuf* is set more than 256 KB, the impact will be reduced, the reason maybe that data can be received timely as greater receive buffer is used.

From above experiments and analysis, we can conclude that the background traffic can present an obvious impact on CMT-SCTP's performance in terms of throughput and delay, and it will lead to some known problems like congestion. Thus, we need to take background traffic condition into account during designing the retransmission algorithm.

4. RTX_CSI Algorithm

Retransmission algorithms play a more important role in achieving high users' experience of quality for multimedia streaming services. As mentioned in Section 1, there are five retransmission schemes proposed [12] for CMT-SCTP, we call them as *existing retransmission algorithms*. However, all of *exiting retransmission algorithms* do not consider the nature of background traffic. This section will simply introduce the *existing retransmission algorithm* firstly, and then a further improved retransmission algorithm named *RTX_CSI* will be addressed with considering background traffic condition, a necessary performance evaluation will be presented lastly.

4.1. Existing Retransmission Algorithm.

RTX-SAME. Once a new data chunk is scheduled and sent to a destination, all retransmissions of the chunk thereafter are sent to the same destination (until the destination is deemed inactive due to failure).

RTX-ASAP. A retransmission of a data chunk is sent to any destination for which the sender has *cwnd* space available at the time the retransmission needs to be sent. If the sender has available *cwnd* space for multiple destinations, one is chosen randomly.

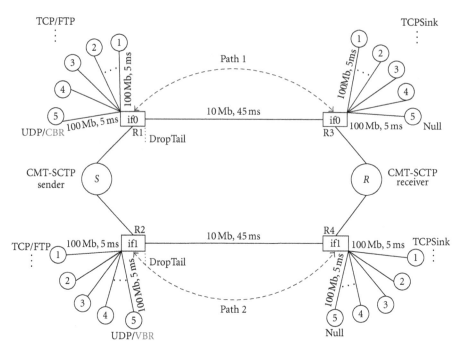

FIGURE 1: Simulation topology for studying the impact of background traffic.

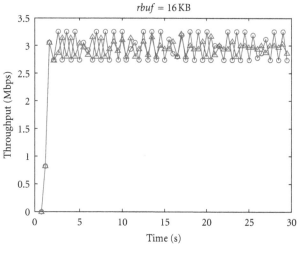

FIGURE 2: Comparison with *rbuf* = 16 KB.

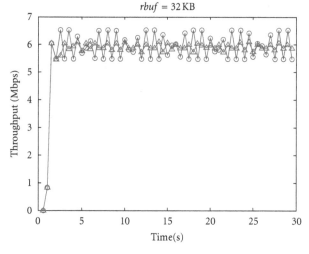

FIGURE 3: Comparison with *rbuf* = 32 KB.

RTX-LOSSRATE. A retransmission of a data chunk is sent to the destination with the lowest loss rate path. If multiple destinations have the same loss rate, one is selected randomly.

RTX-CWND. A retransmission of a data chunk is sent to the destination for which the sender has the largest *cwnd*. A tie is broken randomly.

RTX-SSTHRESH. A retransmission of a data chunk is sent to the destination for which the sender has the largest *ssthresh*. A tie is broken randomly.

However, according to RFC4460, only the *RTX-CWND* and *RTX-SSTHRESH* are recommended retransmission policies, and the others are just for experimental sake. Moreover, the *RTX-CWND* is recommended as the default retransmission strategy since it can present the best performance [12].

4.2. RTX_CSI Description. As mentioned in Section 1, all of *existing retransmission algorithms* do not take the impact of background traffic into account. To fix this issue, we consider

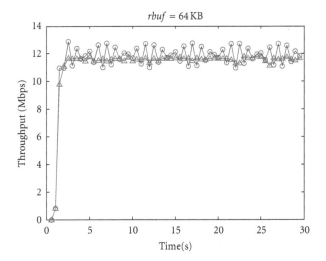

FIGURE 4: Comparison with *rbuf* = 64 KB.

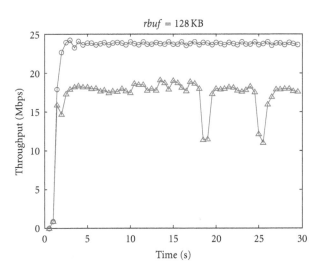

FIGURE 5: Comparison with *rbuf* = 128 KB.

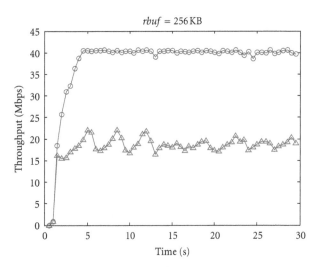

FIGURE 6: Comparison with *rbuf* = 256 KB.

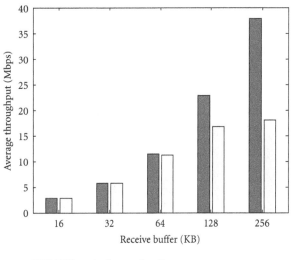

FIGURE 7: Comparison on average throughput.

the localness nature of background flow [19], that is, coming packets will belong to the flow as previously arrived ones in a short period. Correspondingly, the side effect on CMT-SCTP caused by background flow will be the same in short period. As countermeasure of the localness nature of background traffic, paths' previous states should be considered during designing of retransmission algorithm. Therefore, we take paths' previous states into account to design an improved retransmission algorithm named *RTX_CSI* which consists of four more reasonable paths' conditions during selecting retransmission destination. *RTX_CSI* follows the below steps to select candidate path for data retransmission.

(1) A retransmission is sent to the destination that has the largest *cwnd*;

(2) if more than one destination has the largest *cwnd*, then a retransmission is sent to the one that has the largest *ssthresh* value;

(3) if there are more than one destination has the largest *ssthresh* value, then a retransmission is sent to the one that has the lowest *Time Out Records* (*tor*) in specified time span (denoted as τ);

(4) if more than one destination has lowest timeout records in specified timeslot, then a retransmission is sent to the one that has the largest interval $t_{interval}$ ($t_{interval}$ stands for the interval between the last timeout's time and current time);

Definition:

d_i: the i_{th} path in the destination list of core node

d_{list}: the active destination list of core node

d_i^{cwnd}: the *cwnd* value of the i_{th} path

d_i^{ssth}: the *ssthresh* value of the i_{th} path

d_i^{tor}: total timeouts on d_i in timeslot τ

$d_i^{interval}$: the $t_{interval}$ of the i_{th} path

$d_{rtxDest}$: the destination selected to retransmit loss data

Once having packet to resend

1: **for** each destination d_i **do** //scan all paths' condition

2: **if** status of d_i == ACTIVE **then**

3:    put d_i into d_{list}; //ignore the inactive paths

4: **end if**

5: **end for**

6: set $d_s^{cwnd} = d_{list(0)}^{cwnd}$, $d_t^{ssth} = d_{list(0)}^{ssth}$, $d_w^{interval} = d_{list(0)}^{interval}$;

7: **for** ($i = 1$, $i <= $ count(d_{list}), i++) **do**

//select the destination which has largest *cwnd* value in loop

8:    **if** ($d_s^{cwnd} < d_{list(i)}^{cwnd}$) **then**

9:      set $s = i$; set $d_s^{cwnd} = d_{list(i)}^{cwnd}$;

10:    **end if**

//select the destination which has largest *ssthresh* value in loop

11:    **if** ($d_t^{ssth} < d_{list(i)}^{ssth}$) **then**

12:      set $t = i$; set $d_t^{ssth} = d_{list(i)}^{ssth}$;

13:    **end if**

//select the destination which has lowest *tor* value in loop

14:    **if** ($d_t^{tor} > d_{list(i)}^{tor}$) **then**

15:      set $t = i$; set $d_t^{tor} = d_{list(i)}^{tor}$;

16:    **end if**

//select the destination which has largest $t_{interval}$ value in loop

17:    **if** ($d_w^{interval} < d_{list(i)}^{interval}$) **then**

18:      set $w = i$; set $d_w^{interval} = d_{list(i)}^{interval}$;

19:    **end if**

20: **end for**

21: **if** !(($d_j \in d_{list}$)&&($d_j^{cwnd} == d_s^{cwnd}$)&&($j <> s$)) **then**

//path with largest *cwnd* is set as retransmission destination

22:      set $d_{rtxDest} = d_s$;

23: **else if** !(($d_j \in d_{list}$)&&($d_j^{ssth} == d_t^{ssth}$)&&($j <> t$)) **then**

//path with largest *ssthresh* is set as retransmission destination

24:      set $d_{rtxDest} = d_t$; //

25: **else if** !(($d_j \in d_{list}$)&&($d_j^{tor} == d_t^{tor}$)&&($j <> t$)) **then**

//path with lowest tor is set as retransmission destination

26:      set $d_{rtxDest} = d_t$;

27: **else if** !(($d_j \in d_{list}$)&&($d_j^{interval} == d_w^{interval}$)&&($j <> w$)) **then**

//path with largest $t_{interval}$ is set as retransmission destination

28:      set $d_{rtxDest} = d_w$;

//a tie will be broken by random selection

29: **else** set $d_{rtxDest}$ with random d_i ($d_i \in d_{list}$);

30: **end if**

      let loss data be retransmitted on $d_{rtxDest}$

ALGORITHM 1: *RTX_CSI* Algorithm.

(5) if multiple destinations have the largest $t_{interval}$, then a tie will be broken by random selection.

The details of RTX_CSI algorithm are shown in Algorithm 1.

4.3. Simulation Topology Setup. In this section, we adopt the average throughput as the metric in our experiments. Figure 10 shows the simulation topology. Related simulation parameters are set the same as that mentioned in Section 3.

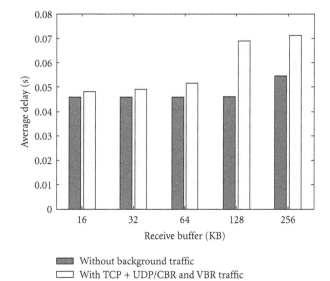

FIGURE 8: Comparison on average delay.

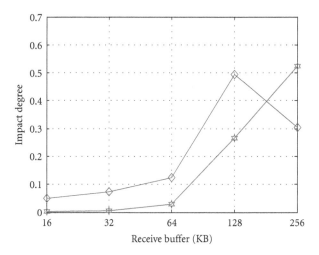

FIGURE 9: Impact degree on average throughput and delay.

We perform two experimental scenarios named Case 1 and Case 2 are examined as follows to study the performance of *RTX_CSI*. In our experiments, the *rbuf* is set to 16 KB, 32 KB, 64 KB, 128 KB, and 256 KB, respectively, and τ is set to 30 s.

Case 1. The loss rate on *TCP + UDP/VBR* traffic path is always kept at 1%, and on *TCP + UDP/CBR* traffic path, it is varied from 1% to 10%;

Case 2. The loss rate on *TCP + UDP/VBR* traffic path is varied from 1% to 10%, and on *TCP + UDP/CBR* traffic path, it is always kept at 1%.

4.4. Performance Evaluation. As mentioned above, according to RFC4460, only the *RTX-CWND* and *RTX-SSTHRESH*

are recommended retransmission policy. So we compare the performance of *RTX_CSI* with the *RTX-CWND* and *RTX-SSTHRESH*.

To compare conveniently, we use (2) illustrated below to express the advantage in terms of average throughput achieved by algorithm *A* (denoted as A_{adv}) over algorithm *B*.

$$A_{\mathrm{adv}} = \frac{A_{\mathrm{aveTh}} - B_{\mathrm{aveTh}}}{B_{\mathrm{aveTh}}} \times 100\%, \qquad (2)$$

where A_{aveTh} and B_{aveTh} are on behalf of average throughput achieved by retransmission algorithm *A* and *B*, respectively.

Firstly, we evaluate the performance of *RTX_CSI*, *RTX_CWND*, and *RTX_SSTHESH* with experimental condition illustrated in Case 1; Figure 11 shows the performance of the three algorithms under different *rbuf*. We can get that the average throughput achieved by the *RTX_CWND*, *RTX_SSTHRESH*, and proposed *RTX_CSI* will rise with the increase of the *rbuf*. But when *rbuf* is set to more than 64 KB, the increments of average throughput are reduced whichever the three algorithms is employed. This phenomenon verifies again that the background traffic presents more serious side effects on performance of CMT-SCTP as larger *rbuf* is used. However, the *RTX_CSI* performs the best performance in the three algorithms, the *RTX_CWND* comes next, and the *RTX_SSTHRESH* presents the worst behavior.

For Case 1, per calculated by (2), detailed comparison on the average throughput can be pointed out as follows.

(1) Comparing to the RTX_SSTHRESH, the RTX_CWND achieves a more advantage about −4.42%, 4.94%, 18.2%, 56.39%, and 55.15% when *rbuf* is 16 KB, 32 KB, 64 KB, 128 KB, and 256 KB, respectively. So, it can be concluded that the RTX_CWND can also present better performance over the RTX_SSTHRESH [12] even under background traffic condition (Case 1).

(2) Comparing to the RTX_CWND, the proposed RTX_CSI achieves more benefits about 1.14%, 0.56%, and 1.62% when rbuf is set to 16 KB, 32 KB, and 64 KB, respectively. Since larger rbuf leads to less packet loss; therefore, when the rbuf is set to 128 KB and 256 KB, the proposed RTX_CSI presents same performance in terms of throughput as the RTX-CWND algorithm.

Secondly, we compare the performance of the *RTX_CWND* and *RTX_SSTHRESH* with the proposed *RTX_CSI* under different *rbuf* with designed experimental scenario addressed in Case 2. As it shown in Figure 12, the average throughput achieved by the three algorithms will rise with the increase of *rbuf*. But with same reason mentioned in Case 1, when *rbuf* is set to more than 64 KB, the increments of average throughput are reduced whichever the three algorithms are employed. In this case, the *RTX_CSI* still performs the best performance. But different from conclusion addressed in [12] and Case 1, only if *rbuf* is larger than 64 KB, the *RTX_CWND* presents a better performance than the *RTX_SSTHRESH*.

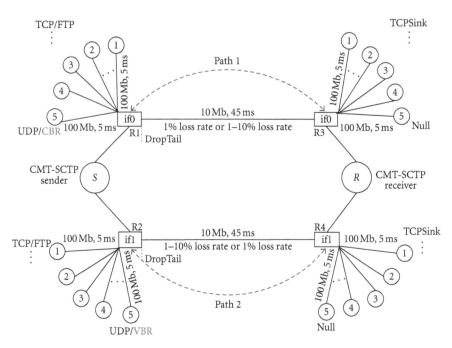

FIGURE 10: Simulation topology for evaluating *RTX_CSI*.

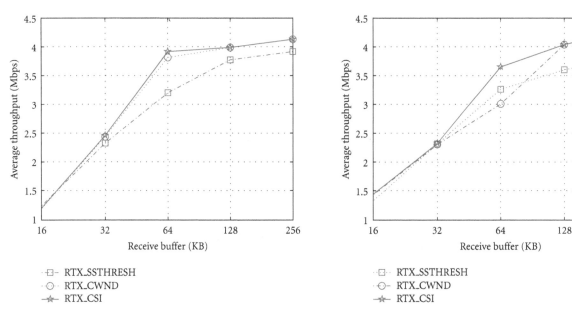

FIGURE 11: Path 1 loss rate is varied from 1–10%, Path 2 is always kept at 1%.

FIGURE 12: Path 2 loss rate is varied from 1–10%, Path 1 is always kept at 1%.

Likewise, for Case 2, detailed comparisons are pointed out per calculated by (2).

(1) Comparing to the *RTX_SSTHRESH*, the *RTX_CWND* achieves a more advantage about 7.26%, −0.15%, −8.02%, 12.05%, and 12.57% when *rbuf* is 16 KB, 32 KB, 64 KB, 128 KB, and 256 KB, respectively. The comparison results are different from the conclusion mentioned in [12], in our experiment (Case 2), comparing to the *RTX_SSTHRESH*, the *RTX_CWDN*

only can achieve obvious more advantages in terms of average throughput when *rbuf* is set to the value which is larger than the default *rbuf* (64 KB). The reason may be that when enormous of variable bite rate packets are lost, their retransmissions not only deteriorate the path's quality but also enlarge the unpredictability of path's condition. Those unexpected conditions make the CMT-SCTP sender cannot tune its congestion window accurately. But when the *rbuf* is set to larger one (more than 64 KB), the sender can correct its congestion window since lots of packets can be received and acknowledged timely thus, the *RTX_CWND* can outperform the *RTX_SSTHRESH*. This phenomenon further verifies the proposed *RTX_CSI* more reasonable with considering the nature of background traffic. Our future work will investigate the reason in detail.

(2) Comparing to the *RTX_CWND*, the proposed *RTX_CSI* achieves more benefits about 0.47%, 0.57%, and 17.56% when rbuf is set to 16 KB, 32 KB, and 64 KB, respectively. As Case 1, when the rbuf is set to 128 KB and 256 KB, the proposed *RTX_CSI* presents same performance in terms of throughput as the *RTX_CWND* with the reason that larger rbuf leads to less packet loss.

From experiments and analysis for Case 1 and Case 2 respectively, we can conclude that the proposed *RTX_CSI* algorithm can achieve a better performance than the *existing retransmission algorithm*, especially for *rbuf* such as 16 KB, 32 KB, and 64 KB which are used commonly. The reason *RTX_CSI* can achieve a more advantage over the two *existing retransmission algorithm* is that the *RTX_CSI* can select a more efficient path as the retransmission destination with considering more reasonable rules such as paths' cwnd, ssthresh value, and historical states to meet some known problems like congestion and packet loss caused by background traffic.

5. Conclusions

In this paper, we designed realistic simulation topologies and examined the performance of CMT-SCTP in terms of throughput, end-to-to packet delay by considering reasonable background traffic. We discussed *how* the presence of background traffic affects the performance of CMT-SCTP in detail, which are generally ignored by most current researchers.

Based on above work, we proposed an improved retransmission algorithm called *RTX_CSI* for CMT-SCTP. *RTX_CSI* takes background traffic into account and considers paths' comprehensive characteristics during selecting retransmission destination to meet the localness nature of background traffic. The simulation results show *RTX_CSI* achieves better efficiency than CMT-SCTP's original retransmission algorithm. So the proposed *RTX_CSI* can be employed to improve the users' experience of quality for multimedia streaming service when CMT-SCTP is used for the multimedia transport protocol.

Acknowledgments

This work is partially supported by the National High-Tech Research and Development Program of China (863) under Grant no. 2011AA010701, in part by the National Natural Science Foundation of China (NSFC) under Grants nos. 61001122 and 61003283 and the Beijing Natural Science Foundation under Grant no. 4102064, in part by the Fundamental Research Funds for the Central Universities under Grants nos. 2012RC0603 and 2011RC0507, and in part by the Natural Science Foundation of Jiangsu Province under Grant no. BK2011171.

References

[1] C. Xu, G. M. Muntean, E. Fallon, and A. Hanley, "Distributed storage-assisted data-driven overlay network for P2P VoD services," *IEEE Transactions on Broadcasting*, vol. 55, no. 1, pp. 1–10, 2009.

[2] Z. Liu, C. Wu, S. Zhao, and B. Li, "UUSee: large-scale operational on-demand streaming with random network coding," in *Proceedings of the IEEE Conference on Computer Communications (INFOCOM '10)*, San Diego, Calif, USA, March 2010.

[3] C. Xu, E. Fallon, Q. Yuansong, Z. Lujie, and M. Gabriel-Miro, "Performance evaluation of multimedia content distribution over multi-homed wireless networks," *IEEE Transactions on Broadcasting*, vol. 57, no. 2, pp. 204–215, 2011.

[4] C. Xu, E. Fallon, M. Gabriel-Miro, X. Li, and A. Hanley, "Performance evaluation of distributing real-time video over concurrent multipath," in *Proceedings of the IEEE Wireless Communications and Networking Conference (WCNC '09)*, Budapest, Hungary, April 2009.

[5] K. Zheng, M. Liu, Z. C. Li, and G. Xu, "SHOP: an integrated scheme for SCTP handover optimization in multihomed environments," in *Proceedings of the IEEE Global Telecommunications Conference*, pp. 1–5, New Orleans, La, USA, December 2008.

[6] R. Stewart, Q. Xie, K. Morneault et al., "Stream control transmission protocol," IETF RFC 2960, October 2000.

[7] P. Natarajan, F. Baker, P. D. Amer, and J. T. Leighton, "SCTP: what, why, and how," *IEEE Internet Computing*, vol. 13, no. 5, pp. 81–85, 2009.

[8] Y. Wang, R. Injong, and H. Sangtae, "Augment SCTP multistreaming with pluggable scheduling," in *Proceedings of the 30th IEEE International Conference on Computer Communications Workshops*, pp. 810–815, Shanghai, China, April 2011.

[9] J. R. Iyengar, P. D. Amer, and R. Stewart, "Concurrent multipath transfer using SCTP multihoming over independent end-to-end paths," *IEEE/ACM Transactions on Networking*, vol. 14, no. 5, pp. 951–964, 2006.

[10] T. Stegel, J. Sterle, U. Sedlar, J. Bešter, and A. Kos, "SCTP multihoming provisioning in converged IP-based multimedia environment," *Computer Communications*, vol. 33, no. 14, pp. 1725–1735, 2010.

[11] C. M. Huang and M. S. Lin, "Multimedia streaming using partially reliable concurrent multipath transfer for multihomed networks," *IET Communications*, vol. 5, no. 5, pp. 587–597, 2011.

[12] J. R. Iyengar, P. D. Amer, and R. Stewart, "Retransmission policies for concurrent multipath transfer using SCTP multihoming," in *Proceedings of the 12th IEEE International Conference on Networks (ICON '04)*, pp. 713–719, Singapore, November 2004.

[13] J. R. Iyengar, P. D. Amer, and R. Stewart, "Performance implications of a bounded receive buffer in concurrent multipath transfer," Tech. Rep., CIS Department, University of Delaware.

[14] J. Liao, J. Wang, and X. Zhu, "cmpSCTP: an extension of SCTP to support concurrent multi-path transfer," in *Proceedings of*

the IEEE International Conference on Communications, pp. 5762–5766, Beijing, China, 2008.

[15] Ł. Budzisz, R. Ferrús, F. Casadevall, and P. Amer, "On concurrent multipath transfer in SCTP-based handover scenarios," in *Proceedings of the IEEE International Conference on Communications*, pp. 1–6, Dresden, Germany, June 2009.

[16] J. M. Liu, H. X. Zou, J. X. Dou, and Y. Gao, "Reducing receive buffer blocking in concurrent multipath transfer," in *Proceedings of the IEEE International Conference on Circuits and Systems for Communications (ICCSC '08)*, Shanghai, China, May 2008.

[17] P. Barford and M. Crovella, "Generating representative web workloads for network and server performance evaluation," in *Proceedings of ACM SIGMETRICS*, pp. 151–160, Madison,Wis, USA, June 1998.

[18] S. Floyd and V. Paxson, "Difficulties in simulating the Internet," *IEEE/ACM Transactions on Networking*, vol. 9, no. 4, pp. 392–403, 2001.

[19] S. Floyd and E. Kohler, "Internet research needs better models," *ACM Computer Communications Review*, vol. 33, no. 1, pp. 29–34, 2003.

[20] S. Ha, L. Le, I. Rhee, and L. Xu, "Impact of background traffic on performance of high-speed TCP variant protocols," *Computer Networks*, vol. 51, no. 7, pp. 1748–1762, 2007.

[21] The Network Simulator—ns-2, http://www.isi.edu/nsnam/ns/.

[22] M. Fomenkov, K. Keys, D. Moore, and K. claffy, "Longitudinal study of Internet traffic in 1998–2003," in *Proceedings of the Winter International Symposium on Information and Communication Technologies (WISICT '04)*, pp. 1–6, Cancun, Mexico, January 2004.

[23] http://www.isi.edu/nsnam/archive/ns-users/webarch/2001/msg05051.html.

[24] A. Caro, P. Amer, and J. Iyengar, "Retransmission policies with transport layer multihoming," in *Proceedings of the 11th IEEE International Conference on Networks*, pp. 255–260, Sydney, Australia, November 2003.

[25] P. Natarajan, J. R. Iyengar, P. D. Amer, and R. Stewart, "Concurrent multipath transfer using transport layer multihoming: performance under network failures," in *Proceedings of the Military Communications Conference (MILCOM '06)*, pp. 1–7, Washington, DC, USA, 2006.

18

Video Classification and Adaptive QoP/QoS Control for Multiresolution Video Applications on IPTV

Huang Shyh-Fang

Department of Information Communication, MingDao University, Changhua 52345, Taiwan

Correspondence should be addressed to Huang Shyh-Fang, hsfncu@gmail.com

Academic Editor: Pin-Han Ho

With the development of heterogeneous networks and video coding standards, multiresolution video applications over networks become important. It is critical to ensure the service quality of the network for time-sensitive video services. Worldwide Interoperability for Microwave Access (WIMAX) is a good candidate for delivering video signals because through WIMAX the delivery quality based on the quality-of-service (QoS) setting can be guaranteed. The selection of suitable QoS parameters is, however, not trivial for service users. Instead, what a video service user really concerns with is the video quality of presentation (QoP) which includes the video resolution, the fidelity, and the frame rate. In this paper, we present a quality control mechanism in multiresolution video coding structures over WIMAX networks and also investigate the relationship between QoP and QoS in end-to-end connections. Consequently, the video presentation quality can be simply mapped to the network requirements by a mapping table, and then the end-to-end QoS is achieved. We performed experiments with multiresolution MPEG coding over WIMAX networks. In addition to the QoP parameters, the video characteristics, such as, the picture activity and the video mobility, also affect the QoS significantly.

1. Introduction

With the development of heterogeneous networks, multiresolution video coding becomes desirable in various applications. It is important to provide a flexible scalable framework for multiresolution video services, where video resolution, quality, and network quality-of-service (QoS) parameters are determined according to the requirements of user equipment and network resources [1–4]. Worldwide Interoperability for Microwave Access (WIMAX) communication is suitable for supporting video delivery because it guarantees the service quality. The network control reserves adequate resources in the network to support video delivery based on QoS parameters, which, in general, includes the peak rate, the mean rate, the mean burst length, the delay, the jitter, the cell loss rate, and so forth [5–7]. A negotiation process may be involved in QoS parameter determination for efficient network resource utilization. As long as the video application requests a suitable set of QoS parameters, the network should be able to deliver the video signals with guaranteed quality [8].

A user could specify a set of QoS parameters satisfying the requirements of video quality before executing an application. The selection of suitable QoS parameters is, however, not trivia for video service users. The QoS must be set based on specific application programming interface (API) and transport mechanism provided by vendors. An ordinary user may not have the knowledge on such network details. Instead, a user may only concern the size of the pictures, that is, the resolution, the video quality, that is, the PSNR, and the frame rate, defined as the quality-of-presentation (QoP) [9]. It is desirable to have a mechanism which shields video applications from the complexity of QoS management and control. It is also much easier to define the QoP parameters than the QoS parameters because QoP directly defines the quality of the user interface to viewers. In multiresolution video services, this approach becomes more important because of the existence of different QoS requirements [10, 11].

2. Multiresolution Video System Architecture

In 1993, the International Standard Organization (ISO) developed MPEG-2, a scalable coding method for moving pictures. The MPEG-2 test model 5 (TM-5) is used in

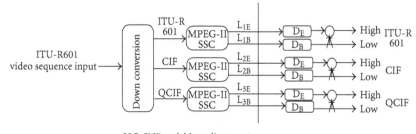

SSC: SNR scalable coding
D$_B$: base layer decoder
D$_E$: enhancement layer decoder

FIGURE 1: Layered coder.

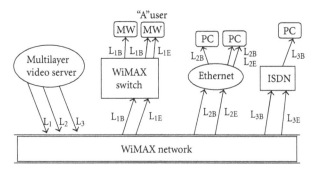

MW: multimedia workstation

FIGURE 2: Scalable multiresolution video services with multilayer transmission.

the course of the research for comparison purposes [1]. The MPEG-2 scalability methods include SNR scalability, spatial scalability, and temporal scalability. Moreover, combinations of the basic scalability are also supported as hybrid scalability. In the case of basic scalability of MPEG-2 TM-5, two layers of video, referred as the lower layer and the enhancement layer, are allowed, whereas in hybrid scalability up to three layers are supported. However, owing to huge variations of video service quality with different network bandwidth and terminal equipment, the two or three layer schemes are still not adequate. A more flexible multiresolution scalable video coding structure may be needed.

The structure of a layered video coder is shown in Figure 1. The input signal is compressed into a number of discrete layers, arranged in a hierarchy that provides different quality for delivering across multiple network connections. In each input format, SNR scalability provides two quality services: basic quality service (lower quality) and enhanced quality service (higher quality). The input video is compressed to produce a set of different resolutions ranging from HDTV to QCIF and different output rates, for example, L1B and L1E. The encoding procedure of the base layer is identical to that of a nonscalable video coding. The input bit stream to the encoder of the enhancement layer is, however, the residual signal which is the quantization error in the base layer. The decoder modules, DB and DE, are capable of decoding base layer and enhancement layer bit strings, respectively. If only the base layer is received, the decoder DB

produces the base quality video signals. If the decoder receives both layers, it combines the decoded signals of both layers to produce improved quality. In general, each additional enhancement layer produces an extra improvement in reconstruction quality.

By combining this layered multiresolution video coding with a QoP-/QoS-controlled WiMAX transmission system, we can easily support multicast over heterogeneous networks. For multiresolution video systems, we focus on SNR scalable schemes with various video formats, such as HDTV, ITU-R 601, CIF, and QCIF. The input video signal is compressed into a number of discrete layers which are arranged in a hierarchy that provides different quality for delivery across multiple network connections. In this QoP/QoS control mechanism, the multicast source produces video streams, each level of which is transmitted on a different network connection with a different set of QoP requirements, shown in Figure 2. For example, the user "A", who is equipped with a multimedia workstation terminal and an QoS connection, receives both base (L1B) and enhanced (L1E) layers of highest resolution, while a PC user with ISDN connection may only receive the base layer of the lowest resolution stream (L3B). With this mechanism, a user is able to receive the best quality signal that the network can deliver.

3. QoP/QoS Control Scheme

We discuss the QoP/QoS control scheme and the negotiation process in a video server-client model. The mulitresolution video server consists of a scalable encoder and a QoP/QoS mapping table. The video client consists of a scalable MPEG decoder, a QoP regenerator, and a call control unit. A video user specifies a set of QoP parameters which satisfies the requirements based on the terminal capability and network connection capacity. The QoP is sent to the server and is translated to a set of QoS parameters by the QoP/QoS mapping table. The QoS is sent back to the client. The call control on the client side performs schedulability test to check if the resources running along the server-network-client path are capable of supporting the tasks. If the schedulability test is passed, the connection is granted. Otherwise, the connection is rejected, and the QoP regenerator produces a degraded QoP set. Then the former negotiation procedure is supposed to be repeated.

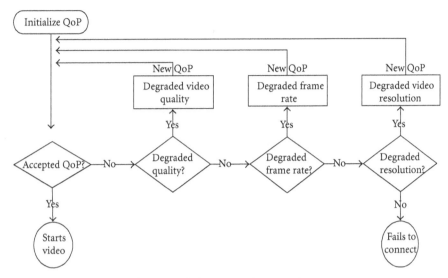

FIGURE 3: QoP regeneration procedure.

3.1. QoP Negotiation. If the original QoP/QoS pair is not affordable, a new QoP is generated with lower quality. The QoP regeneration procedure is shown in Figure 3. A new set of QoP should have lower requirements. However, it is not expected to have large degradation in one change. The degrading of QoP is in the order of the video quality (PSNR), the frame rate, and the resolution. The reason is that we want to make a small change of QoS at the beginning when the original QoP cannot be satisfied. The resolution parameter has the most impact to QoS because in each step of degrading it reduces the image size to 1/4 and changes the rate to roughly 1/4 of the original rate. On the other hand, the PSNR can be changed in a much finer granularity and the impact to the subjective image quality is also the least. Hence, we downgrade the QoP with the order of SNR scalability, temporal scalability, and spatial scalability. Namely, if the image quality can be degraded, we reduce the SNR requirement, because the slight degradation of quality can be accepted by most customers, and it makes the smallest QoS degradation in network. Otherwise, we degrade the frame rate. It can be archived by dropping some of the frames, such as skipping *B*-frames. Dropping some frames only causes slight degradation of the viewing quality and makes less QoS modifications in network rather than reducing the spatial resolution. If the frame rate can be reduced, we downgrade it. Otherwise, we reduce the spatial resolution. If all the QoP parameters are already set to the lowest levels and still cannot match the requirements, the service is denied. It is noteworthy that a QoS parameter may be restored to a higher level in the negotiation procedure. For example, when the spatial resolution is reduced to a lower level, the SNR requirement is restored to the highest level to avoid large change in the bitrates.

4. QoP and QoS Computations

In this section, the definitions and the computations of QoP and QoS used in this work are given and described. Many QoS parameters are generally discussed in technical articles but cannot be simply calculated. Here the QoS parameters in existing WIMAX network products are considered. Based on WIMAX API, the QoS parameters defined by Fore company are used in our experiments. Also the video characteristics affecting the QoP/QoS mapping significantly are discussed.

4.1. QoP Parameters. The QoP parameters represent the requirements of the video quality specified by video users. The QoP is relied on the subjective assessment of viewers and is generally constrained by the terminal equipment and the network capacity. We choose three parameters to represent the QoP: the spatial resolution, the temporal frame rate, and the image fidelity. The spatial resolution ranges from HDTV, ITU-R 601, CIF, to QCIF. The temporal frame rate ranges from 30, 15, to 10 frames/second or even lower. In our experiments, the image fidelity, represented by the PSNR of the reconstructed video, is divided into three grades (high, medium, and low) with 3 dB difference in each adjacent grades.

4.2. Video Characteristics. The purpose of defining the QoP parameters is to estimate the QoS parameters accurately. In addition to the QoP parameters we have defined, however, the video characteristics existing in each video sequence that affect the QoS setting significantly. We define the spatial activity and temporal mobility as two important video characteristics in the QoP/QoS mapping. The QoP is selected by video users while the video characteristics exist along with the video sequences. Both are considered in the QoS calculations.

4.2.1. Spatial Activity (A). The spatial activity represents the degree of variations in image pixel values. Since the removal of the redundancy in the temporal domain is not considered by *I*-frame encoding, we define the spatial activity measure of a video sequence as the average pixel variance of the *I*-frame.

$$A = \frac{1}{K} \sum_{i=1}^{K} \left[\frac{1}{256} \sum_{j}^{256} \left(P_{i,j} - \overline{P}_i \right)^2 \right] \tag{1}$$

$P_{i,j}$: the jth pixel value in ith MicroBlock (MB),

$$\overline{P}_i = \frac{1}{256} \sum_{j=1}^{256} P_j : \text{the mean of pixel values in } i\text{th MB,} \quad (2)$$

K: the number of MBs in a frame.

4.2.2. Temporal Mobility (M).
The temporal mobility reflects the degree of motion in a video sequence. It is more difficult to perform accurate motion estimation for a sequence of higher temporal mobility. Thus, the temporal mobility is defined as the percentage of the intracoded MBs in all P-frames in a sequence

$$M = \frac{1}{N_P} \sum_{i=1}^{N_P} M_P(i),$$
$$M_P(i) = \frac{K_a(i)}{K}, \quad (3)$$

where M_P is the percentage of intra-MBs in ith P-frame, K_a is the number of intra-MBs, and N_P is the total number of P-frames in a sequence.

4.3. QoS Parameters.
QoS parameters that we discuss are related to the video transmission over WIMAX networks. In general, QoS parameters include a broad range of measures, such as, the peak bandwidth, the mean bandwidth, the mean burst length, the end-to-end delay and jitter, and the cell loss rate. Three parameters, the mean bandwidth, the peak bandwidth, and the mean burst length, are computed. A minimum value and a target value for each parameter are requested. The minimum value is chosen as the average value of all tested video sequences, while the target value is chosen as the maximum value of all tested video sequences.

4.3.1. Mean Bandwidth (B).
This is the average bandwidth, expected over the lifetime of the connection and measured in kilobits per second. The mean bandwidth B_k of video sequence k is computed as

$$B_k = \frac{\sum_{i=1}^{n} f_{k,i}}{T_k}, \quad (4)$$

where n is the total number of frames in sequence k, $f_{k,i}$ is the total number of bits of the ith frame in sequence k, and T_k is the total playback time of sequence k.

The total playback time of sequence k is computed as

$$T_k = \sum_{i=1}^{n} t_{k,i}, \quad (5)$$

where $t_{k,i}$ is the playback time of ith frame in sequence k and is supposed to be equal to $1/29.97$. The mean bandwidth is calculated as the total number of bits in a sequence divided by the total playback time. The minimum mean bandwidth $B_{\min}$ is the average value of all tested sequences,

$$B_{\min} = \frac{\sum_{i=1}^{r} B_i}{r}, \quad (6)$$

where r is the total number of video sequences. The target mean bandwidth is the maximum value

$$B_{\text{target}} = \max_{1 \le k \le r} (B_k) \quad (7)$$

among all tested sequences.

4.3.2. Peak Bandwidth (P).
This is the maximum or burst rate at which the transmitter produces data and which is measured in kilobits per second. In MPEG coding, the I-frames usually have the highest rate. Thus the peak bandwidth in sequence k is calculated as the maximum I-frame rate

$$P_k = \max_{1 \le i \le n} \left(\frac{f_{k,i}}{t_{k,i}} \right), \quad (8)$$

in sequence k. In all tested video sequences, the minimum peak bandwidth is set to be the average

$$P_{\min} = \frac{\sum_{i=1}^{r} P_i}{r}, \quad (9)$$

and the target peak bandwidth is set to be the maximum

$$P_{\text{target}} = \max_{1 \le k \le r} (P_k). \quad (10)$$

4.4. The Mapping between QoP and QoS Parameters.
The QoP parameters that directly specify the video quality are friendly to video users. Each QoP set needs to be supported by a particular set of network QoS parameters. In general, higher QoP requires higher QoS. We first determine the mapping for general video services. For a given set of QoP, a corresponding set of QoS is obtained by computing the statistics of the encoded video data. A general QoP/QoS mapping table that consists of many QoP-QoS pairs is then established.

In addition to the QoP parameters, many video characteristics, such as activity and mobility, can also affect the corresponding QoS parameters significantly. In order to make the mapping more accurate, we classify the video sources based on the activity and the mobility. For each class of the video source, a classified QoP/QoS mapping table is then established by the above method. The video characteristics can easily be obtained in a pre-coding application. For real-time video applications, the initial mapping can be obtained from either the general mapping or a realtime analysis based on the first few video frames.

5. Simulation Results

We choose the spatial resolution and the image quality as the set of parameters of QoP. The frame rate is considered fixed in simulations because the current experimental hardware cannot support the full rate (30 fps) video coding. The video sequences include "Garden," "Table Tennis," "Football," "Mobil," "Hockey," "Bus," and "MIT" with ITU-R 601 format (704×480 pels, $4:2:0$ chrominance format). CIF and QCIF formats (352×240 pels, and 176×120 pels) are converted from the ITU-R 601 format. The frame quality is represented by the PSNR with 3 dB difference between two adjacent levels.

TABLE 1: Activity and mobility of video sequences.

Class	Video source	Spatial activity	Temporal mobility
1	Salesman	92.4	2.9%
	Suzie	37.3	3.7%
	Miss American	14.8	0.1%
2	Football	74.8	51.5%
	Hockey	35.8	43.4%
3	Mobil	689.3	2.8%
	MIT	234.1	0.1%
	Tennis	134.0	7.3%
4	Garden	573.2	15.0%
	Bus	509.2	30.9%

TABLE 2: General QoP/QoS mapping table.

QoP parameters		QoS parameters					
Frame Resolu.	Quality	MMB (Kbps)	TMB (Kbps)	MPB (Kbps)	TPB (Kbps)	MMBL (Kbits)	TMBL (Kbits)
QCIF	Low	230	278	250	298	15	18
QCIF	Normal	294	348	281	339	19	22
QCIF	High	373	434	319	350	23	27
CIF	Low	461	863	987	1598	43	87
CIF	Normal	1267	1824	1702	2554	116	186
CIF	High	3786	4983	5021	6385	351	413
ITU-R 601	Low	5132	7013	7552	8977	493	613
ITU-R 601	Normal	7961	9592	10384	12096	740	836
ITU-R 601	High	11324	13866	14231	15731	986	1137

MMB: minimum mean bandwidth. TMB: target mean bandwidth. MPB: minimum peak bandwidth. TPB: target peak bandwidth. MMBL: minimum mean burst length. TMBL: target mean burst Length.

5.1. Analysis of Video Characteristics. For limited number of video sequences available for experiments, we divide the video sequences into four unique classes.

> *Class 1*: low-spatial activity, low-temporal mobility: Salesman, Suzie, Miss American,
>
> *Class 2*: low-spatial activity, high-temporal mobility: Football, Hockey,
>
> *Class 3*: high-spatial activity, low-temporal mobility: MIT, Mobil, Tennis,
>
> *Class 4*: high-spatial activity, high-temporal mobility: Bus, Garden.

Table 1 gives the activity and mobility of video sequence. Accordingly, the video sequences are classified into the four classes. After the classification, a set of mapping relations between video presentation quality (QoP parameters) and throughput/traffic specifications (QoS parameters) can be found. The threshold of classification for the spatial activity is set to 120, and the threshold for the mobility is 20%. These values are acquired by experiments.

The spatial activity represents the pixel variations and also reflects the coding bit rate. Figure 4(a) shows the activity of I-frames in the sequence "Football". Since the peak rate of a video sequence is mainly determined by the I-frame bitrate, the peak bandwidth of QoS is highly correlated to the spatial activity.

Figure 4(b) shows the mobility of P-frames in "Football". The temporal mobility represents the percentage of the intra-coded MBs in P-frames and it directly reflects the coding bitrate of P-frames and B-frames, since both are motion-compensated coding. Because most frames in MPEG are B- or P-frames in general, the temporal mobility is highly related to the mean bandwidth of QoS.

5.2. QoP/QoS Mapping. We establish the QoP/QoS mapping for two cases. One is the general case in which the video characteristics are unknown. The other is the classified case in which the video characteristics are known and the QoS setting can be more precise. Table 2 shows the general QoP/QoS mapping. The low frame quality, represented by PSNR, is set to 30 dB, 30 dB, and 24 dB for QCIF, CIF, and ITU-R 601 format, respectively. Higher frame quality requires 3 dB more for each level. Pictures of smaller size are given higher PSNR because the receiver often upsamples the signals to get larger size pictures. The receiver can adjust their best trade-off between the larger picture size and less mosaics in the picture. The frame resolution is the most important

TABLE 3: Classified QoP/QoS mapping table on CIF.

Class	QoP parameters			QoS parameters					
	Activity	mobility	Frame Quality	MMB (Kbps)	TMB (Kbps)	MPB (Kbps)	TPB (Kbps)	MMBL (Kbits)	TMBL (Kbits)
1	Low	Low	Low	488	587	869	921	53	61
	Low	Low	Normal	547	632	985	1142	58	69
	Low	Low	High	625	829	1145	1378	65	78
2	Low	High	Low	734	902	1302	1639	72	83
	Low	High	Normal	862	1125	1834	2421	87	103
	Low	High	High	1104	1230	2268	2700	109	123
3	High	Low	Low	1207	1430	2588	2958	126	139
	High	Low	Normal	1230	1536	3205	3589	135	158
	High	Low	high	1540	1798	3786	4023	158	172
4	High	High	Low	2198	2388	3906	4366	162	182
	High	High	Normal	3528	3816	5616	6240	234	260
	High	High	High	4503	4792	6901	7658	287	319

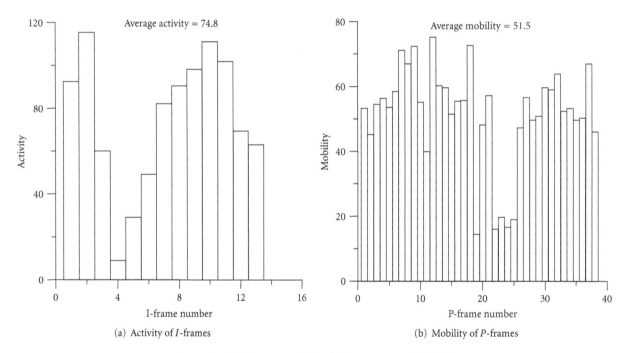

(a) Activity of I-frames

(b) Mobility of P-frames

FIGURE 4: Activity and mobility of video sequence "footfall".

factor affecting the QoS requirements. At the same frame quality level, ITU-R 601 may need 20 times more bandwidth than QCIF. The frame quality also affects the QoS requirements significantly. A 3 dB improvement in PSNR may increase 50% bandwidth requirement. The target values are significantly larger than the minimum values because of the large variations of the video characteristics in all sequences. Thus, before the video characteristics are acquired, the QoS setting for guaranteed service quality may be wasteful in many cases.

Basing on different video classes, we then make QoP/QoS mapping. Table 3 shows the mapping for CIF format. High activities result in high peak bandwidth requirement. Both high activity and high mobility contribute to high mean

bandwidth requirements. It is noteworthy that the differences between the target values and the minimum values are much smaller than that without classifications. Thus the video classification gives more accurate QoS setting than the case with no classifications.

6. Conclusion

We have presented a mechanism of QoP/QoS control in multiresolution MPEG scalable coding structure. The user specifies the video quality represented by a set of QoP parameters. The system maps the QoP setting to the network requirements represented by the QoS parameters by means of mapping tables based on video statistics. The classification of video source improves the accuracy of the QoP/QoS mapping significantly.

References

[1] N. Kamaci, Y. Altunbasak, and R. M. Mersereau, "Frame bit allocation for the H.264/AVC video coder via cauchy-density-based rate and distortion models," *IEEE Transactions on Circuits and Systems for Video Technology*, vol. 15, no. 8, pp. 994–1006, 2005.

[2] "ISO/IEC/JTC1/SC29/WG11 MPEG 93/457," Test Model 5, Draft Vision 1, April 1993.

[3] S. M. Canne, M. Vetterli, and V. Jacobson, "Low-complexity video coding for receiver-driven layered multicast," *IEEE Journal on Selected Areas in Communications*, vol. 15, no. 6, pp. 983–1001, 1997.

[4] H. Doi, Y. Serizawa, H. Tode, and H. Ikeda, "Simulation study of QoS guaranteed ATM transmission for future power system communication," *IEEE Transactions on Power Delivery*, vol. 14, no. 2, pp. 342–348, 1999.

[5] A. Shehu, A. Maraj, and R. M. Mitrushi, "Analysis of QoS requirements for delivering IPTV over WiMAX technology," in *Proceedings of the 18th International Conference on Software, Telecommunications and Computer Networks (SoftCOM '10)*, pp. 380–385, September 2010.

[6] H. Y. Tung, K. F. Tsang, L. T. Lee, and K. T. Ko, "QoS for mobile WiMAX networks: call admission control and bandwidth allocation," in *Proceedings of the 5th IEEE Consumer Communications and Networking Conference (CCNC '08)*, pp. 576–580, Las Vegas, Nev, USA, January 2008.

[7] A. Sayenko, O. Alanen, and J. Karhula, "Ensuring the QoS requirements in 802.16 scheduling," in *Proceedings of the 9th ACM Symposium on Modeling, Analysis and Simulation of Wireless and Mobile Systems (ACM MSWiM '06)*, pp. 108–117, New York, NY, USA, October 2006.

[8] B. Jung, J. Choi, Y. T. Han, M. G. Kim, and M. Kang, "Centralized scheduling mechanism for enhanced end-to-end delay and QoS support in integrated architecture of EPON and WiMAX," *Journal of Lightwave Technology*, vol. 28, no. 16, Article ID 5452987, pp. 2277–2288, 2010.

[9] X. Mei, Z. Fang, Y. Zhang, J. Zhang, and H. Xie, "A WiMax QoS oriented bandwidth allocation scheduling algorithm," in *Proceedings of the 2nd International Conference on Networks Security, Wireless Communications and Trusted Computing (NSWCTC '10)*, pp. 298–301, April 2010.

[10] N. Liao, Y. Shi, J. Chen, and J. Li, "Optimized multicast service management in a mobile WiMAX TV system," in *Proceedings of the 6th IEEE Consumer Communications and Networking Conference (CCNC '09)*, January 2009.

[11] J. F. Huard, I. Inoue, A. A. Lazar, and H. Yamanaka, "Meeting QOS guarantees by end-to-end QOS monitoring and adaptation," in *Proceedings of the 5th IEEE International Symposium on High Performance Distributed Computing*, pp. 348–355, Los Alamitos, Calif, USA, August 1996.

19

Improving Streaming Capacity in Multi-Channel P2P VoD Systems via Intra-Channel and Cross-Channel Resource Allocation

Yifeng He and Ling Guan

Department of Electrical and Computer Engineering, Ryerson University, Toronto, ON, Canada M5B2K3

Correspondence should be addressed to Yifeng He, yhe@ee.ryerson.ca

Academic Editor: Ivan Lee

Multi-channel Peer-to-Peer (P2P) Video-on-Demand (VoD) systems can be categorized into *independent-channel* P2P VoD systems and *correlated-channel* P2P VoD systems. Streaming capacity for a channel is defined as the maximal streaming rate that can be received by every user of the channel. In this paper, we study the streaming capacity problem in multi-channel P2P VoD systems. In an independent-channel P2P VoD system, there is no resource correlation among channels. Therefore, we can find the average streaming capacity for the independent-channel P2P VoD system by finding the streaming capacity for each individual channel, respectively. We propose a distributed algorithm to solve the streaming capacity problem for a single channel in an independent-channel P2P VoD system. The average streaming capacity for a correlated-channel P2P VoD system depends on both the intra-channel and cross-channel resource allocation. To better utilize the cross-channel resources, we first optimize the server upload allocation among channels to maximize the average streaming capacity and then propose cross-channel helpers to enable cross-channel sharing of peer upload bandwidths. We demonstrate in the simulations that the correlated-channel P2P VoD systems with both intra-channel and cross-channel resource allocation can obtain a higher average streaming capacity compared to the independent-channel P2P VoD systems with only intra-channel resource allocation.

1. Introduction

Video-on-demand (VoD) services have been attracting a lot of users because it allows users to watch any video at any time. Traditional client/server architectures for VoD services cannot provide video streams to a large number of concurrent users. To offload the server upload burden, Peer-to-Peer (P2P) technology has been integrated into VoD applications by utilizing the uplink bandwidths of the peers [1–5].

Most of the P2P VoD systems offer many video channels. Users can choose any of the channels that they are interested in at any time. The P2P VoD systems with multiple channels are called *multi-channel* P2P VoD systems. Depending on the resource correlation, multi-channel P2P VoD systems can be categorized into *independent-channel* P2P VoD systems and *correlated-channel* P2P VoD systems. In an independent-channel P2P VoD system, the peers watch the same channel form an independent overlay and share the resources with

each other exclusively within the overlay. In a correlated-channel P2P VoD system, overlay m formed by the peers watching channel m can be correlated with overlay k formed by the peers watching channel k, such that the peers in overlay m can share the resources not only with other peers in overlay m but also with the peers in overlay k. The resources in a correlated-channel P2P VoD system can be utilized in a better way compared to an independent-channel P2P VoD system.

In P2P VoD systems, users would like to watch the video at a high quality. The streaming rate can be used to indicate the video quality. Let $\mathbf{M}$ denote the set of the channels in a P2P VoD system. If channel $m(m \in \mathbf{M})$ is associated with overlay m, *streaming capacity* for channel m, denoted by c_m, is defined as the maximum streaming rate that can be received by every user in overlay m [6, 7]. The *average streaming capacity* c_{avg} for a multi-channel P2P VoD system is defined as $c_{\mathrm{avg}} = \Sigma_{m \in \mathbf{M}} p_m c_m$ where p_m is the priority of channel m, and $\Sigma_{m \in M} p_m = 1$. The priority of a channel can be set by the service provider. For example, the more expensive channel can be assigned a higher priority.

Streaming capacity problem in multi-channel P2P VoD systems is a challenging problem. The average streaming capacity in a multi-channel P2P VoD system is dependent on the number of the peers, the playback time, and the bandwidth of each peer, the server capacity, the overlay construction, and the resource allocation. Optimal resource allocation in a multi-channel P2P VoD system is expected to improve the streaming capacity. However, resource allocation in multi-channel P2P VoD systems is quite challenging due to the following reasons. (1) Peers have heterogeneous upload and download bandwidths and different playback progress. (2) Each channel is heterogeneous in terms of available resources, since the number of the peers in each channel is different. (3) Peers may leave or join a channel dynamically.

In this paper, we improve the average streaming capacity for multi-channel P2P VoD systems by better utilizing both the intra-channel resources and the cross-channel resources. We first investigate the streaming capacity for an independent-channel P2P VoD system, in which we find the streaming capacity for a single channel by optimizing the intra-channel resource allocation in a distributed manner. We then investigate the streaming capacity for a correlated-channel P2P VoD system, in which we find the average streaming capacity for multiple channels by optimizing both intra-channel and cross-channel resource allocation. The proposed cross-channel resource allocation consists of two steps as follows. (1) We optimize the server upload allocation among channels to maximize the average streaming capacity. (2) We introduce *cross-channel helpers* to establish cross-channel links and then utilize cross-channel peer upload bandwidths to improve the average streaming capacity.

The remainder of this paper is organized as follows. Section 2 discusses the related work. Section 3 formulates and solves the streaming capacity problem for an independent-channel P2P VoD System. Section 4 finds the average streaming capacity for a correlated-channel P2P VoD System. The simulation results are provided in Section 5, and the conclusions are drawn in Section 6.

2. Related Work

Streaming capacity in P2P live systems has been examined in the recent literature [6–9]. In [6], the streaming capacity problem is formulated into an optimization problem, which maximizes the streaming rate that can be supported by multitree-based overlay. Sengupta et al. provide a taxonomy of sixteen problem formulations on streaming capacity, depending on whether there is a single P2P session or there are multiple concurrent sessions, whether the given topology is a full mesh graph or an arbitrary graph, whether the number of peers a node can have is bounded or not, and whether there are nonreceiver relay nodes or not [7]. Liu et al. analyze the performance bounds for minimum server load, maximum streaming rate, and minimum tree depth in tree-based P2P live systems, respectively [8]. The streaming capacity under node degree bound is investigated in [9].

Streaming capacity for a single channel in P2P VoD systems has been studied in [10–12]. In [10, 12], the streaming capacity for a single channel is formulated into an optimization problem which maximizes the streaming rate under the peer bandwidth constraints. The throughput maximization problem in a scalable P2P VoD system is studied in [13]. Helpers have been proposed in P2P systems to improve the system performance [11, 14, 15]. In P2P VoD systems, each additional helper increases the system upload capacity, thus offloading the server burden [15]. In [11], the algorithms on helper assignment and rate allocation are proposed to improve the streaming capacity for P2P VoD systems.

Cross-channel resource sharing has been recently studied in multi-channel P2P streaming systems [16–20]. In [16], Wu et al. propose an online server capacity provisioning algorithm to adjust the server capacities available to each of the concurrent channels, taking into account the number of peers, the streaming quality, and the priorities of channels. In [17], a View-Upload Decoupling (VUD) scheme is proposed to decouple what a peer uploads from what it views, bringing stability to multi-channel P2P streaming systems and enabling cross-channel resource sharing. In [18], Wu et al. develop infinite-server queueing network models to analytically study the performance of multi-channel P2P live streaming systems. In [19], the bandwidth satisfaction ratio is used to compare three bandwidth allocation schemes, namely, Naive Bandwidth allocation Approach (NBA), Passive Channel-aware bandwidth allocation Approach (PCA), and Active Channel-aware bandwidth allocation Approach (ACA), in multi-channel P2P streaming systems. In [20], Zhao et al. investigate the streaming capacity in multi-channel P2P live streaming systems when each peer can only connect to a small number of neighbors.

3. Streaming Capacity for an Independent-Channel P2P VoD System

In an independent-channel P2P VoD system, the peers watching the same channel form an overlay. We assume that the server upload bandwidth allocated to channel m, denoted by s_m, is predetermined. An independent-channel P2P VoD system is illustrated in Figure 1. The peers within the same overlay redistribute the video content to each other. A peer belonging to overlay m only caches the video content of channel m, and it does not serve any video content to any peer outside overlay m. In other words, each overlay in an independent-channel P2P VoD System is an isolated subsystem. Therefore, the streaming capacity of a channel is independent of that of another channel. The streaming capacity problem in an independent-channel P2P VoD system is to find the streaming capacity of each individual channel, respectively. We will next focus on the streaming capacity for a single channel.

3.1. Complete Overlay. The streaming capacity for a single channel depends on the constructed overlay. In a P2P VoD system, each peer maintains a buffer to cache the recently received packets in order to smoothen the playback and serve

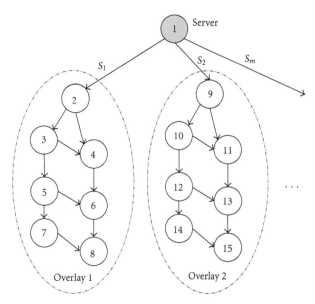

FIGURE 1: Illustration of an independent-channel P2P VoD system.

other peers. There is a *parent-child relationship* between two peers (e.g., peer k and peer j) if the two peers satisfy the following two conditions: (1) peer k (the parent) has an earlier playback progress than peer j (the child), and (2) peer k is buffering the segment(s) which are being requested by peer j. The parent-child relationship is illustrated in Figure 2(a). At the current moment, peer k is playing segment 11, and peer j is playing segment 7. Each peer can hold 5 segments in its buffer. Segment 8, held by peer k, is being requested by peer j. Therefore, peers k and j can establish a parent-child relationship, in which peer k is the parent, and peer j is the child. The server is regarded as a special peer because it contains all the segments of the video. The server has a parent-child relationship with any other peer.

A parent-child relationship is *implemented*, if an overlay link has been established from the parent to the child. A *complete overlay* for a channel is defined as the overlay in which all of the available parent-child relationships have been implemented, and an *incomplete overlay* for a channel is defined as the overlay in which only a part of the available parent-child relationships have been implemented [12]. An example of complete overlay is illustrated in Figure 2(b). Compared to the incomplete overlay, the complete overlay contains more overlay links, thus supporting a higher streaming capacity. Therefore, we will formulate the streaming capacity problem based on the complete overlay. The method for overlay construction is not a study focus of this paper. A complete overlay can be constructed using the existing approaches [2].

3.2. Streaming Capacity Problem for a Single Channel. The set of the overlays (channels) in the independent-channel P2P VoD system is denoted by $\mathbf{M}$. Since each channel is independent in terms of resources, we can just study the streaming capacity of channel m ($\forall m \in \mathbf{M}$).

Overlay m in a P2P VoD system can be modeled as a directed graph $\mathbf{G^{(m)}} = (\mathbf{N^{(m)}}, \mathbf{L^{(m)}})$, where $\mathbf{N^{(m)}}$ is the set of

nodes and $\mathbf{L^{(m)}}$ is the set of directed overlay links. Peer 1 is defined as the server. The relationship between a node and its outgoing links is represented with a matrix $\mathbf{A^{(m)+}}$, whose elements are given by

$$a_{il}^{(m)+} = \begin{cases} 1, & \text{if link } l \text{ is an outgoing link from node } i, \\ 0, & \text{otherwise.} \end{cases}$$
(1)

The relationship between a node and its incoming links is represented with a matrix $\mathbf{A^{(m)-}}$, whose elements are given by

$$a_{il}^{(m)-} = \begin{cases} 1, & \text{if link } l \text{ is an incoming link into node } i, \\ 0, & \text{otherwise.} \end{cases}$$
(2)

The upload capacity of peer i is denoted by $O_i^{(m)}$. The server is denoted as Peer 1. The server upload bandwidth s_m for channel m is actually the upload capacity of Peer 1, which is given by $O_1^{(m)} = s_m$. Upload capacity is typically the bottleneck in P2P systems. We consider *upload constraint* at peer i ($\forall i \in \mathbf{N^{(m)}}$), which is given by $\sum_{l \in \mathbf{L^{(m)}}} a_{il}^{(m)+} x_l^{(m)} \leq O_i^{(m)}$ where $x_l^{(m)}$ is the link rate at link l of overlay m. The upload constraint represents that the total outgoing rate from peer i is no larger than its upload capacity $O_i^{(m)}$. The streaming rate for channel m is denoted by $r^{(m)}$. Each peer except the server (e.g., Peer 1) receives the streaming rate $r^{(m)}$, which can be expressed by $\sum_{l \in \mathbf{L}} a_{il}^{(m)-} x_l^{(m)} = f_i^{(m)} r^{(m)}$, for all $i \in \mathbf{N^{(m)}}$, where $f_i^{(m)} = 0$ if $i = 1$, or $f_i^{(m)} = 1$ otherwise. The *download constraint* is given by $r^{(m)} \leq \min_{i \in \mathbf{N^{(m)}}} I_i^{(m)}$ where $I_i^{(m)}$ is the download capacity of peer i. From the download constraint, we can see that the maximal streaming rate is limited by the minimal download capacity among the peers. Therefore, the users with a very low download bandwidth should not be admitted into the P2P VoD system in order for maintaining a high streaming capacity.

The streaming capacity for channel m is stated as to maximize the streaming rate $r^{(m)}$ that can be received by every user in channel m by optimizing the streaming rate $r^{(m)}$ and the link rate $x_l^{(m)}$ ($\forall l \in \mathbf{L^{(m)}}$) under the upload constraint at each peer. Mathematically, the problem can be formulated as follows:

$$\begin{aligned} \text{maximize} \quad & r^{(m)} \\ \text{subject to} \quad & \sum_{l \in \mathbf{L^{(m)}}} a_{il}^{(m)-} x_l^{(m)} = f_i^{(m)} r^{(m)}, \quad \forall i \in \mathbf{N^{(m)}}, \\ & \sum_{l \in \mathbf{L^{(m)}}} a_{il}^{(m)+} x_l^{(m)} \leq O_i^{(m)}, \quad \forall i \in \mathbf{N^{(m)}}, \\ & x_l^{(m)} \geq 0, \quad \forall l \in \mathbf{L^{(m)}}, \\ & 0 \leq r^{(m)} \leq \min_{i \in \mathbf{N^{(m)}}} I_i^{(m)}. \end{aligned}$$
(3)

The optimization problem in (3) is a Linear Programming (**LP**). It can be solved in a centralized way using

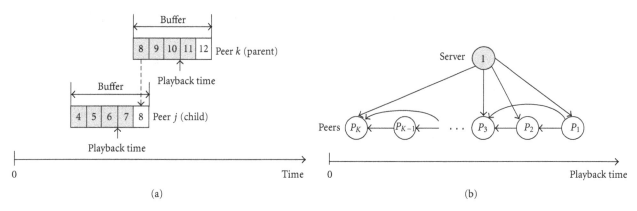

FIGURE 2: Overlay construction for a single channel in an independent-channel P2P VoD system: (a) the parent-child relationship between peer k and peer j, and (b) the complete overlay.

the interior point method [21]. However, the centralized solution is not scalable. Therefore, we will develop a distributed algorithm using the primal-dual method to solve the streaming capacity problem.

3.3. Distributed Algorithm. We will use primal-dual method [22] to develop a distributed algorithm for the optimization problem (3). However, the objective function in problem (3) is not strictly convex with respect to the optimization variables $r^{(m)}$ and $x_l^{(m)}$ ($\forall l \in \mathbf{L}^{(m)}$). Therefore, the corresponding dual function is nondifferentiable, and the optimal values of $r^{(m)}$ and $x_l^{(m)}$ ($\forall l \in \mathbf{L}^{(m)}$) are not immediately available. We first convert the the original optimization problem (3) to an equivalent minimization problem by changing the objective from maximizing $r^{(m)}$ to minimizing $-r^{(m)}$. We then add a quadratic regularization term for the streaming rate $r^{(m)}$ and each link rate $x_l^{(m)}$ ($\forall l \in \mathbf{L}^{(m)}$) to make the objective function strictly convex. Finally, the optimization problem (3) is approximated to the following:

$$\text{minimize} \quad -r^{(m)} + \varepsilon\left(r^{(m)}\right)^2 + \varepsilon \sum_{l \in \mathbf{L}^{(m)}} \left(x_l^{(m)}\right)^2$$

$$\text{subject to} \quad \sum_{l \in \mathbf{L}^{(m)}} a_{il}^{(m)-} x_l^{(m)} = f_i^{(m)} r^{(m)}, \quad \forall i \in \mathbf{N}^{(m)},$$

$$\sum_{l \in \mathbf{L}^{(m)}} a_{il}^{(m)+} x_l^{(m)} \leq O_i^{(m)}, \quad \forall i \in \mathbf{N}^{(m)},$$

$$x_l^{(m)} \geq 0, \quad \forall l \in \mathbf{L}^{(m)},$$

$$0 \leq r^{(m)} \leq \min_{i \in \mathbf{N}^{(m)}} I_i^{(m)},$$

$$(4)$$

where $(\varepsilon(r^{(m)})^2 + \varepsilon \sum_{l \in \mathbf{L}^{(m)}} (x_l^{(m)})^2)$ is the sum of the regularization terms, and $\varepsilon(\varepsilon > 0)$ is called the *regularization factor*. When ε is small enough, the solution for the problem in (4) is arbitrarily close to the solution for the original streaming capacity problem (3).

Let us denote by $(r^{(m)*}, x_l^{(m)*}$ ($\forall l \in \mathbf{L}^{(m)}$)) the optimal solution to the original optimization problem (3), and $(r^{(m)\$}, x_l^{(m)\$}$ ($\forall l \in \mathbf{L}^{(m)}$)) the optimal solution to the approximated optimization problem (4). Based on the original optimization problem (3), we have $r^{(m)*} \geq r^{(m)\$}$. Based

on the approximated optimization problem (4), we have $-r^{(m)\$} + \varepsilon(r^{(m)\$})^2 + \varepsilon \sum_{l \in \mathbf{L}^{(m)}} (x_l^{(m)\$})^2 \leq -r^{(m)*} + \varepsilon(r^{(m)*})^2 + \varepsilon \sum_{l \in \mathbf{L}^{(m)}} (x_l^{(m)*})^2$. Therefore, we can get $0 \leq r^{(m)*} - r^{(m)\$} \leq \varepsilon((r^{(m)*})^2 - (r^{(m)\$})^2 + \sum_{l \in \mathbf{L}^{(m)}} (x_l^{(m)*})^2 - \sum_{l \in \mathbf{L}^{(m)}} (x_l^{(m)\$})^2)$, from which we show that the streaming capacity obtained from the approximated optimization problem (4) with a small regularization factor can approach closely to the truly maximal streaming rate obtained from the original optimization problem (3).

The optimization problem (4) is a convex optimization problem with a strictly convex objective function and the linear constraints [23]. We introduce dual variables $(u_i, v_i, \forall i \in \mathbf{N}^{(m)})$ to formulate the Lagrangian corresponding to the primal problem (4) as below:

$$L\left(\mathbf{x}^{(m)}, r^{(m)}, \mathbf{u}, \mathbf{v}\right)$$

$$= -r^{(m)} + \varepsilon\left(r^{(m)}\right)^2 + \varepsilon \sum_{l \in \mathbf{L}^{(m)}} \left(x_l^{(m)}\right)^2$$

$$+ \sum_{i \in \mathbf{N}^{(m)}} u_i \left(\sum_{l \in \mathbf{L}^{(m)}} a_{il}^{(m)-} x_l^{(m)} - f_i^{(m)} r^{(m)}\right)$$

$$+ \sum_{i \in \mathbf{N}^{(m)}} v_i \left(\sum_{l \in \mathbf{L}^{(m)}} a_{il}^{(m)+} x_l^{(m)} - O_i^{(m)}\right)$$

$$= \varepsilon\left(r^{(m)}\right)^2 - r^{(m)} - r^{(m)} \sum_{i \in \mathbf{N}^{(m)}} u_i f_i^{(m)}$$

$$+ \sum_{l \in \mathbf{L}^{(m)}} \left(\varepsilon\left(x_l^{(m)}\right)^2 + x_l^{(m)} \sum_{i \in \mathbf{N}^{(m)}} \left(u_i a_{il}^{(m)-} + v_i a_{il}^{(m)+}\right)\right)$$

$$- \sum_{i \in \mathbf{N}^{(m)}} v_i O_i^{(m)}.$$

$$(5)$$

Let $I_{\min}^{(m)} = \min_{i \in \mathbf{N}^{(m)}} I_i^{(m)}$. The Lagrange dual function $G(\mathbf{u}, \mathbf{v})$ is the minimum value of the Lagrangian over the vector of link rates $\mathbf{x}^{(m)}$ and the streaming rate $r^{(m)}$:

$$G(\mathbf{u}, \mathbf{v}) = \min_{\left(\mathbf{x}^{(m)} \geq 0, 0 \leq r^{(m)} \leq I_{\min}^{(m)}\right)} \left\{L\left(\mathbf{x}^{(m)}, r^{(m)}, \mathbf{u}, \mathbf{v}\right)\right\}. \quad (6)$$

The Lagrange dual problem is to maximize the Lagrange dual function. That is,

$$\text{maximize} \quad G(\mathbf{u}, \mathbf{v})$$
$$\text{subject to} \quad v_i \geq 0, \qquad \forall i \in \mathbf{N}^{(\mathbf{m})}. \tag{7}$$

We use subgradient method [24] to solve the Lagrange dual problem (7). The dual variables $u_i^{(k+1)}$ and $v_i^{(k+1)}$ at the $(k+1)$th iteration are updated, respectively, by

$$u_i^{(k+1)} = u_i^{(k)} - \theta^{(k)} \left(f_i^{(m)} \left(r^{(m)} \right)^{(k)} - \sum_{l \in \mathbf{L}^{(\mathbf{m})}} a_{il}^{(m)-} \left(x_l^{(m)} \right)^{(k)} \right),$$

$$v_i^{(k+1)} = \max \left\{ 0, v_i^{(k)} - \theta^{(k)} \left(O^{(m)} - \sum_{l \in \mathbf{L}^{(\mathbf{m})}} a_{il}^{(m)+} \left(x_l^{(m)} \right)^{(k)} \right) \right\}, \tag{8}$$

where $\theta^{(k)} > 0$ is the step size at the kth iteration. The algorithm is guaranteed to converge to the optimal value for a step-size sequence satisfying the nonsummable diminishing rule [24]:

$$\lim_{k \to \infty} \theta^{(k)} = 0, \qquad \sum_{k=1}^{\infty} \theta^{(k)} = \infty. \tag{9}$$

The update of the streaming rate $(r^{(m)})^{(k)}$ at the kth iteration is given by

$$\left(r^{(m)} \right)^{(k)} = \min \left\{ \max \left\{ 0, \frac{1 + \sum_{i \in \mathbf{N}^{(\mathbf{m})}} u_i^{(k)} f_i^{(m)}}{2\varepsilon} \right\}, I_{\min}^{(m)} \right\}. \tag{10}$$

At the kth iteration, the link rate $(x_l^{(m)})^{(k)}$ at link l can be calculated from the dual variables:

$$\left(x_l^{(m)} \right)^{(k)} = \max \left\{ 0, \frac{-\sum_{i \in \mathbf{N}^{(\mathbf{m})}} \left(u_i^{(k)} a_{il}^{(m)-} + v_i^{(k)} a_{il}^{(m)+} \right)}{2\varepsilon} \right\}. \tag{11}$$

As shown in (10) and (11), the optimization variables are decomposed. The optimization of the streaming rate is executed at the server as follows. At the kth iteration, the server collects the dual variable $u_i^{(k)}$ from peer i ($\forall i \in \mathbf{N}^{(\mathbf{m})}$), respectively, and then computes the streaming rate $(r^{(m)})^{(k)}$. The optimization of each link rate is executed at each peer as follows. At the kth iteration, each peer only collects the dual variable $u_j^{(k)}$ from each of its children, and then computes the link rate for each of the outgoing links.

A P2P system is inherently dynamic. Peers may join or leave the system at any time. Therefore, the streaming capacity for a single channel varies with time. To handle the time-varying streaming capacity, the server can encode the video using a scalable coding scheme and then adjust the output video rate adaptive to the current streaming capacity.

4. Streaming Capacity for a Correlated-Channel P2P VoD System

In a correlated-channel P2P VoD system, the resources among different channels can be shared with each other. The average streaming capacity in a correlated-channel P2P VoD system can be obtained by optimizing both the intra-channel resource allocation and the cross-channel resource allocation. The optimization of intra-channel resource allocation for a single channel has been presented in Section 3. In this section, we will focus on the cross-channel resource allocation. We will first optimize the server upload allocation among channels to maximize the average streaming capacity in Section 4.1, and then further utilize cross-channel peer upload bandwidth to improve the average streaming capacity in Section 4.2.

4.1. Optimization of Server Upload Allocation among Channels. The server upload allocated for channel m is denoted by s_m. In an independent-channel P2P VoD system, the server upload allocation for each channel is predetermined. Therefore, the server upload bandwidth is not utilized in an optimal way. In this subsection, we treat $\{s_m, \forall m \in \mathbf{M}\}$ as variables and optimize them to maximize the average streaming capacity for a correlated-channel P2P VoD system.

The optimization of server upload allocation for a correlated-channel P2P VoD system is stated as to maximize the average streaming rate by optimizing the server upload allocation, the link rates, and the streaming rate, for each channel, subject to the upload constraint at each peer. Since maximizing the average streaming rate is equivalent to minimizing the negative average streaming rate, we formulate the problem into a minimization problem as follows:

$$\text{minimize} \quad -\sum_{m \in \mathbf{M}} p_m r^{(m)}$$
$$\text{subject to} \quad \sum_{l \in \mathbf{L}^{(\mathbf{m})}} a_{il}^{(m)-} x_l^{(m)} = f_i^{(m)} r^{(m)},$$
$$\forall i \in \mathbf{N}^{(\mathbf{m})}, \forall m \in \mathbf{M},$$
$$\sum_{l \in \mathbf{L}^{(\mathbf{m})}} a_{il}^{(m)+} x_l^{(m)} \leq O_i^{(m)},$$
$$\forall i \in \mathbf{N}^{(\mathbf{m})}, \forall m \in \mathbf{M},$$
$$x_l^{(m)} \geq 0, \qquad \forall l \in \mathbf{L}^{(\mathbf{m})},$$
$$\sum_{m \in \mathbf{M}} s_m \leq s_T,$$
$$s_m \geq 0, \qquad \forall m \in \mathbf{M},$$
$$0 \leq r^{(m)} \leq \min_{i \in \mathbf{N}^{(\mathbf{m})}} I_i^{(m)}, \qquad \forall m \in \mathbf{M}, \tag{12}$$

where p_m is the priority for channel m, and s_T is the server upload capacity. The optimization problem in (12) is an LP. The optimization variables in the optimization problem (12) are the server upload allocation s_m, the link rate vector $\mathbf{x}^{(\mathbf{m})}$, and the streaming rate $r^{(m)}$, for channel m, for all $m \in \mathbf{M}$. The number of the optimization variables is increased with the number of the channels and the number of the links in each overlay. In order to solve the optimization efficiently, we use dual decomposition [22] to decompose the optimization problem (12) into multiple subproblems, each of which is associated with a channel.

We introduce a dual variable λ for the inequality constraint $\sum_{m \in \mathbf{M}} s_m \leq s_T$. The Lagrangian corresponding to the primal problem (12) is given by $L(\mathbf{s}, \mathbf{x}, \mathbf{r}, \lambda) = -\sum_{m \in \mathbf{M}} p_m r^{(m)} + \lambda(\sum_{m \in \mathbf{M}} s_m - s_T)$. Then, the Lagrange dual function [23] is given by $G(\lambda) = \min L(\mathbf{s}, \mathbf{x}, \mathbf{r}, \lambda) = \sum_{m \in \mathbf{M}} \min(-p_m r^{(m)} + \lambda s_m) - \lambda s_T$.

The Lagrange dual problem is to maximize the Lagrange dual function [23]. That is,

$$\begin{aligned} \text{maximize} \quad & G(\lambda) \\ \text{subject to} \quad & \lambda \geq 0. \end{aligned} \tag{13}$$

Subgradient method [24] is used to solve the Lagrange dual problem (13). The dual variable λ is updated at the $(k+1)$th iteration by $\lambda^{(k+1)} = \max\{0, \lambda^{(k)} - \theta^{(k)}(s_T - \sum_{m \in \mathbf{M}} s_m^{(k)})$ where $\theta^{(k)}$ is the step size at the kth iteration. In order to guarantee the convergence, the sequence of the step sizes is required to satisfy the nonsummable diminishing rule in (9).

At the kth iteration, the primal variables $(s_m, \mathbf{x}^{(m)}, r^{(m)})$ for channel m are obtained by solving the following optimization problem:

$$\begin{aligned} \text{minimize} \quad & - p_m r^{(m)} + \lambda s_m \\ \text{subject to} \quad & \sum_{l \in \mathbf{L}^{(m)}} a_{il}^{(m)-} x_l^{(m)} = f_i^{(m)} r^{(m)}, \quad \forall i \in \mathbf{N}^{(m)}, \\ & \sum_{l \in \mathbf{L}^{(m)}} a_{il}^{(m)+} x_l^{(m)} \leq O_i^{(m)}, \quad \forall i \in \mathbf{N}^{(m)}, \\ & x_l^{(m)} \geq 0, \quad \forall l \in \mathbf{L}^{(m)}, \\ & 0 \leq r^{(m)} \leq \min_{i \in \mathbf{N}^{(m)}} I_i^{(m)}, \quad s_m \geq 0. \end{aligned}$$

$$\tag{14}$$

The optimization problem (12) is decomposed into $|M|$ subproblems where $|M|$ is the number of the channels. Subproblem m, represented in (14), is associated with channel m. Subproblem m, for all $m \in \mathbf{M}$, can be solved with a distributed algorithm.

4.2. Cross-Channel Sharing of Peer Upload Bandwidth.

Though the server upload allocation among channels is optimized, the cross-channel resources have not yet been fully utilized. In each channel, there are a number of underutilized peers, which can be utilized by the other channels. For example, the leaf nodes of overlay m contribute zero upload bandwidth to the channel because they have no outgoing links. We can utilize the upload bandwidth of the leaf nodes in overlay m to serve the peers in another channel (e.g., channel k), thus improving the streaming capacity of channel k. However, it is challenging to establish the cross-channel links to enable the cross-channel sharing of peer upload bandwidth.

In this paper, we propose a scheme for cross-channel peer upload sharing. We introduce the concept of *cross-channel helpers*. A *cross-channel helper* is the peer who uses its remaining upload bandwidth to help other peers in another channel.

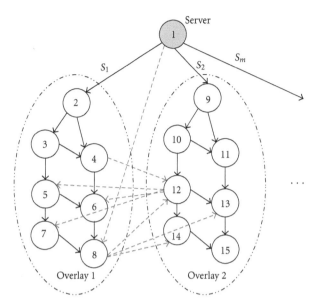

FIGURE 3: Illustration of a correlated-channel P2P VoD system.

Cross-channel helpers are chosen from the peers who have a remaining upload bandwidth greater than a threshold.

Suppose that peer i in channel m is a cross-channel helper serving segment j of channel k, and it has a remaining upload bandwidth b_i. We denote the set of peers watching segment j in channel k by $\mathbf{H}_j^{(k)}$. Peer i can download segment j of channel k from the server or the peers who are buffering segment j, at a rate R_i^{IN}, and then output it to peer h, for all $h \in \mathbf{H}_j^{(k)}$, at a rate R_i^h, respectively. The *bandwidth gain* for peer i is defined as $g_i = (\sum_{h \in \mathbf{H}_j^{(k)}} R_i^h)/R_i^{\text{IN}}$. In order to maximize the bandwidth gain g_i under the flow constraint $R_i^h \leq R_i^{\text{IN}}$, for all $h \in \mathbf{H}_j^{(k)}$, and the bandwidth constraint $\sum_{h \in \mathbf{H}_j^{(k)}} R_i^h \leq b_i$, the optimal download rate at peer i is $R_i^{\text{IN}*} = b_i/|\mathbf{H}_j^{(k)}|$ where $|\mathbf{H}_j^{(k)}|$ is the number of peers watching segment j of channel k, and the optimal outgoing rate to peer h, for all $h \in \mathbf{H}_j^{(k)}$, is $R_i^{h*} = R_i^{\text{IN}*}$. The bandwidth gain should be larger than 1, otherwise, the cross-channel helper consumes a larger bandwidth than it contributes. Figure 3 illustrates a correlated-channel P2P VoD system. As shown in Figure 3, peer 8 in overlay 1 is a cross-channel helper, who downloads a segment from the server and then forwards it to peers 12–14 in overlay 2; peer 12 in overlay 2 is also a cross-channel helper, who downloads a segment from peer 4 in overlay 1 and then forwards it to peers 5–7 in overlay 1.

The proposed scheme for cross-channel peer upload sharing is described as follows.

(1) Channel m ($\forall m \in \mathbf{M}$) finds a partner, channel k ($k \neq m$, $k \in \mathbf{M}$), to help each other, by using a *resource-balancing scheme*, which is described as follows. (i) Calculate B_m^{re}, the amount of the total remaining bandwidth, for channel m ($\forall m \in \mathbf{M}$), the average amount of the total remaining bandwidth is given by $B_{\text{avg}}^{\text{re}} = (\sum_{m \in \mathbf{M}} B_m^{\text{re}})/|\mathbf{M}|$ where $|\mathbf{M}|$

represents the number of channels. (ii) Given the set of unchosen channels $\mathbf{M}^{\mathrm{un}}$, the partner of channel m is determined by $k = \arg_{j \in \mathbf{M}^{\mathrm{un}}} \min((1/2)(B_j^{\mathrm{re}} + B_m^{\mathrm{re}}) - B_{\mathrm{avg}}^{\mathrm{re}})^2$.

(2) Determine the set of cross-channel helpers in channel m, denoted by $\mathbf{Y}^{(m)}$, by choosing the peers who have a remaining upload bandwidth greater than a threshold bth. Sort $\mathbf{Y}^{(m)}$ in a descending order based on the remaining upload bandwidth.

(3) Determine the *demanding segment set* in channel k, denoted by $\mathbf{W}^{(k)}$, by choosing $|\mathbf{Y}^{(m)}|$ segments which are watched by the largest number of peers. Sort $\mathbf{W}^{(k)}$ in a descending order based on the number of watching peers.

(4) Assign the ith cross-channel helper in $\mathbf{Y}^{(m)}$ to serve the peers watching the ith segment in $\mathbf{W}^{(k)}$. Determine the incoming rate and outgoing rates at the ith cross-channel helper to maximize the bandwidth gain.

(5) After allocating the rate for each of the cross-channel links as in Step (4), revise the optimization problem (12) by integrating the cross-channel link rates and then solve it to obtain the optimal server upload allocation for each channel and the optimal link rates within each overlay.

Peer dynamics have an impact on the streaming capacity in correlated-channel P2P VoD systems. First, the peers may leave or join a channel dynamically. Second, the cross-channel helpers may leave the channel, which causes the disconnection of the cross-channel links. To handle the dynamic conditions, the optimizations of intra-channel resource allocation and cross-channel resource allocation need to be performed in a discrete-time manner, in which the peers and the overlay are assumed to remain unchanged during a time slot, and the algorithms for resource allocation are performed at the beginning of each time slot.

5. Simulations

In the simulations, we use two classes of peers: cable/DSL peers and Ethernet peers. Cable/DSL peers take 85% of the total peer population with download capacity uniformly distributed between 0.9 Mbps and 1.5 Mbps and upload capacity uniformly distributed between 0.3 Mbps and 0.6 Mbps. Ethernet peers take the remaining 15% of the total peer population with both upload and download capacities uniformly distributed between 1.5 Mbps and 3.0 Mbps. The length of the video is 60 minutes, which is evenly divided into 60 segments. Each peer maintains a buffer with a capacity of 5 segments. The playback time of each peer is randomly distributed between 0 and 60 minutes. The priorities for all channels are equal.

Figure 4 compares the average streaming capacity between the *equal server upload* scheme and the *optimized server upload* scheme. In the *equal server upload* scheme, each channel is allocated an equal server upload, the link

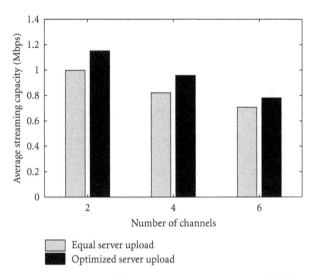

FIGURE 4: Comparison of average streaming capacity with different number of channels.

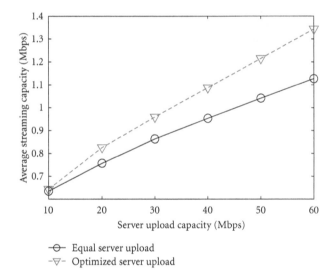

FIGURE 5: Impact of server upload capacity to the average streaming capacity.

rates within each channel are optimized by solving the optimization problem (3). In the *optimized server upload* scheme, the server upload for each channel and the link rates within each channel are jointly optimized by solving the optimization problem (12). The *equal server upload* scheme considers only intra-channel resource allocation [10], while the *optimized server upload* scheme considers both intra-channel and cross-channel resource allocation. The number of the peers in a channel is uniformly distributed between 10 and 150. The server upload capacity is 45.0 Mbps. The optimized server upload scheme improves the average streaming capacity by 14.1% in average compared to the equal server upload scheme.

We show in Figure 5 the impact of server upload capacity to the average streaming capacity for a P2P VoD system with 2 channels. The first channel has 40 peers, and the

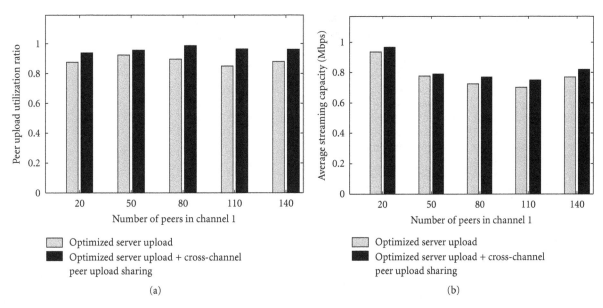

FIGURE 6: Performance improvement brought by cross-channel peer upload sharing: (a) peer upload utilization ratio, and (b) average streaming capacity.

second one has 120 peers. As shown in Figure 5, the average streaming capacity is increased with the server upload capacity. The improvement brought by the optimized server upload scheme is larger when the server upload capacity is larger.

Joint consideration of server upload optimization and cross-channel peer upload sharing can improve the performance in a correlated P2P VoD system, as shown in Figure 6. There are two channels with total 200 peers in the P2P VoD system. The server upload capacity is 20.0 Mbps. We vary the number of the peers in channel 1 from 20 to 140 and evaluate two metrics: peer upload utilization ratio and average streaming capacity. *Peer upload utilization ratio* is defined by $\beta = \Sigma_{i \in \mathbf{N}, i \neq 1} v_i / \Sigma_{i \in \mathbf{N}, i \neq 1} O_i$ where $\Sigma_{i \in \mathbf{N}, i \neq 1} v_i$ represents the sum of the outgoing rates from all peers except the server, and $\Sigma_{i \in \mathbf{N}, i \neq 1} O_i$ represents the sum of the upload capacities of all peers except the server. Due to a better utilization of cross-channel resources, joint consideration of server upload optimization and cross-channel peer upload sharing improves the peer upload utilization ratio by 7.7% in average, as shown in Figure 6(a), and improves the average streaming capacity by 0.04 Mbps in average, as shown in Figure 6(b), compared to *optimized server upload scheme*.

6. Conclusion

In this paper, we studied the streaming capacity problem for multi-channel P2P VoD systems. Depending on the resource correlation, multi-channel P2P VoD systems can be categorized into independent-channel P2P VoD systems and correlated-channel P2P VoD systems. Since there is no resource correlation among channels in an independent-channel P2P VoD system, we just need to find the streaming capacity for each individual channel, respectively. We formulated the streaming capacity problem for a single channel into

an LP problem and solved it with a distributed algorithm. In a correlated-channel P2P VoD system, we optimized both the intra-channel resource allocation and cross-channel resource allocation to improve the streaming capacity. In order to better utilize the cross-channel resource, we first optimized the server upload allocation among channels to maximize the average streaming capacity and then introduced cross-channel helpers to enable cross-channel sharing of peer upload bandwidth. We demonstrated in the simulations that the correlated-channel P2P VoD systems with both intra-channel and cross-channel resource allocation can achieve a higher average streaming capacity compared to the independent-channel P2P VoD systems with only intra-channel resource allocation.

References

[1] J. Li, "PeerStreaming: an on-demand peer-to-peer media streaming solution based on a receiver-driven streaming protocol," in *Proceedings of the IEEE 7th Workshop on Multimedia Signal Processing (MMSP '05)*, pp. 1–4, November 2005.

[2] H. Chi, Q. Zhang, J. Jia, and X. Shen, "Efficient search and scheduling in P2P-based media-on-demand streaming service," *IEEE Journal on Selected Areas in Communications*, vol. 25, no. 1, pp. 119–130, 2007.

[3] S. Annapureddy, C. Gkantsidis, and P. Rodriguez, "Providing video-on-demand using peer-to-peer networks," in *Proceedings of the International Conference on World Wide Web*, 2006.

[4] C. Huang, J. Li, and K. W. Ross, "Peer-assisted VoD: making Internet video distribution cheap," in *Proceedings of the of IPTPS*, 2007.

[5] Y. Huang, T. Z. J. Fu, D. M. Chiu, J. C. S. Lui, and C. Huang, "Challenges, design and analysis of a large-scale p2p-vod system," in *Proceedings of the ACM SIGCOMM Conference on Data Communication (SIGCOMM '08)*, pp. 375–388, August 2008.

[6] S. Sengupta, S. Liu, M. Chen, M. Chiang, J. Li, and P. A. Chou, "Streaming capacity in peer-to-peer networks with topology constraints," Microsoft Research Technical Report, 2008.

[7] S. Sengupta, S. Liu, M. Chen, M. Chiang, J. Li, and P. A. Chou, "Peer-to-peer streaming capacity," *IEEE Transactions on Information Theory*, vol. 57, no. 8, pp. 5072–5087, 2011.

[8] S. Liu, R. Zhang-Shen, W. Jiang, J. Rexford, and M. Chiang, "Performance bounds for Peer-assisted live streaming," in *Proceedings of the ACM SIGMETRICS International Conference on Measurement and Modeling of Computer Systems (SIGMETRICS '08)*, pp. 313–324, June 2008.

[9] S. Liu, M. Chen, S. Sengupta, M. Chiang, J. Li, and P. A. Chou, "P2P streaming capacity under node degree bound," in *Proceedings of the 30th IEEE International Conference on Distributed Computing Systems (ICDCS '10)*, pp. 587–598, June 2010.

[10] Y. He and L. Guan, "Streaming capacity in P2P VoD systems," in *Proceedings of the IEEE International Symposium on Circuits and Systems (ISCAS '09)*, pp. 742–745, May 2009.

[11] Y. He and L. Guan, "Improving the streaming capacity in P2P VoD systems with helpers," in *Proceedings of the IEEE International Conference on Multimedia and Expo (ICME '09)*, pp. 790–793, July 2009.

[12] Y. He and L. Guan, "Solving streaming capacity problems in P2P VoD systems," *IEEE Transactions on Circuits and Systems for Video Technology*, vol. 20, no. 11, pp. 1638–1642, 2010.

[13] Y. He, I. Lee, and L. Guan, "Distributed throughput maximization in P2P VoD applications," *IEEE Transactions on Multimedia*, vol. 11, no. 3, pp. 509–522, 2009.

[14] J. Wang, C. Yeo, V. Prabhakaran, and K. Ramchandran, "On the role of helpers in peer-to-peer file download systems: design, analysis and simulation," in *Proceedings of the IPTPS*, 2007.

[15] P. Garbacki, D. Epema, J. Pouwelse, and M. van Steen, "Offloading servers with collaborative video on demand," in *Proceedings of the IPTPS*, 2008.

[16] C. Wu, B. Li, and S. Zhao, "Multi-channel live P2P streaming: refocusing on servers," in *Proceedings of the 27th IEEE Communications Society Conference on Computer Communications (INFOCOM '08)*, pp. 2029–2037, April 2008.

[17] D. Wu, C. Liang, Y. Liu, and K. Ross, "View-upload decoupling: a redesign of multi-channel P2P video systems," in *Proceedings of the IEEE 28th Conference on Computer Communications (INFOCOM '09)*, pp. 2726–2730, April 2009.

[18] D. Wu, Y. Liu, and K. W. Ross, "Queuing network models for multi-channel P2P live streaming systems," in *Proceedings of the IEEE 28th Conference on Computer Communications (INFOCOM '09)*, pp. 73–81, April 2009.

[19] M. Wang, L. Xu, and B. Ramamurthy, "Linear programming models for multi-channel P2P streaming systems," in *Proceedings of the IEEE Conference on Computer Communications (INFOCOM '10)*, 2010.

[20] C. Zhao, X. Lin, and C. Wu, "The streaming capacity of sparsely-connected P2P systems with distributed control," in *Proceedings of the IEEE Conference on Computer Communications (INFOCOM '11)*, pp. 1449–1457, 2011.

[21] R. J. Vanderbei, *Linear Programming: Foundations and Extensions*, Springer, 2nd edition, 2001.

[22] D. Palomar and M. Chiang, "A tutorial on decomposition methods and distributed network resource allocation," *IEEE Journal on Selected Areas in Communications*, vol. 24, no. 8, pp. 1439–1451, 2006.

[23] S. Boyd and L. Vandenberghe, *Convex Optimization*, Cambridge University Press, 2004.

[24] D. P. Bertsekas, A. Nedic, and A. E. Ozdaglar, *Convex Analysis and Optimization*, Athena Scientific, 2003.

20

LDPC FEC Code Extension for Unequal Error Protection in DVB-T2 System: Design and Evaluation

Lukasz Kondrad,[1] Imed Bouazizi,[2] and Moncef Gabbouj[1]

[1] *Tampere University of Technology, Department of Signal Processing, P.O. Box 553, Tampere 33720, Finland*
[2] *Huawei Technologies Ltd., European Research Center, Riesstraße 25, Munich 80992, Germany*

Correspondence should be addressed to Lukasz Kondrad, lukasz.kondrad@tut.fi

Academic Editor: Manzur Murshed

The Digital Video Broadcasting organisation has recently introduced the second generation of terrestrial broadcast transmission standards, DVB-T2. The newly introduced tools ensure significant gain in performance of DVB-T2 compared to the first generation variant of the standard. One of these tools is the new physical layer concatenated forward error correction code. The inner among the concatenated codes is the Low-Density Parity Check code. The paper proposes a method to extend this code so varying coding strength inside one physical layer pipe of DVB-T2 is enabled in a backward compatible way. As consequence, unequal error protection transmission scheme at a physical layer of DVB-T2 can be efficiently deployed. The paper provides a step-by-step description of the design procedure of the extension. Moreover, the modification to the processing chain and the framing structure of DVB-T2, that ensures backward compatibility to the legacy system, is provided. The proposed method is evaluated under AWGN channel and TU6 channel. Experiments performed on four different video sequences show significant improvements in quality of experience when the proposed extension is used to achieve UEP transmission.

1. Introduction

Unequal error protection (UEP) is a well-known technique in multimedia communication used to selectively enhance robustness of transmitted data. The main idea behind UEP is to assign the amount of the protection data based on the relative importance of the protected data to the overall presentation. Scalable media streams [1, 2] inherently contain data with different levels of importance. Thus, they present an ideal use case for UEP transmission schemes. For example, a base layer data of a H.264/SVC video stream is typically FEC coded at a higher protection level compared to an enhancement layer (EL) data of the same stream. This is due to the fact that an error-free enhancement layer data is of no use to an H.264/SVC decoder, if the corresponding base layer (BL) data was corrupted during transmission.

By using a UEP transmission scheme jointly with scalable multimedia encoders, graceful quality degradation can be achieved. Thus, a system that supports UEP transmission schemes allow for flexible quality of service configuration.

A user with good reception conditions is able to consume a full quality service, while a user with bad reception conditions is still able to consume the service but at a lower quality (lower frame rate, smaller resolution, or lower fidelity). In a system that does not support UEP transmission schemes only one level of service quality is possible. As consequence, a strict tradeoff between bandwidth utilization and robustness of a transmitted date has to be made.

Graceful degradation, which can be provided by employing a UEP transmission scheme, is a desired solution in broadcast transmission systems. This was recognised by DVB [3], an international consortium which develops standards for broadcast transmission. The system support for a UEP transmission scheme is one of the commercial requirements for the second generation of the DVB standard for handheld devices [4]. Moreover, DVB adopted H.264/SVC as one of the video codecs used for broadcast services [5]. However, none of the existing DVB standards natively supports UEP transmission of scalable media.

DVB-T2 [6] could benefit from a method that would allow a UEP transmission scheme. The DVB-T2 system was designed to provide service-specific robustness, which could be used to implement a UEP transmission scheme for scalable media transmission. However, constraints imposed by the DVB-T2 standard make a straightforward use of the service-specific robustness for a UEP transmission scheme limited. This is mainly due to the fact that DVB-T2 receivers are forced to decode only a single data physical layer pipe (PLP) at any point in time. Thus, different layers of a scalable media cannot be transmitted over separate PLPs. Furthermore, FEC code rate manipulation in one PLP cannot be done with sufficient flexibility, hence a UEP transmission scheme cannot be applied.

A UEP transmission scheme could be applied on the upper layers by deploying one of the FEC techniques described in [7]. For example, a UEP transmission scheme on layers above the physical layer was proved to be beneficial when applied to DVB-H transmission system [8, 9]. However, due to the nature of the physical layer FEC code defined in DVB-T2, the upper layer FEC would require operation on large data portions in order to be effective. This would lead to higher system latency and would have a significant impact on a channel zapping delay. Furthermore, introducing additional redundancy at the upper layers may not be efficient from a bandwidth utilization point of view.

This paper describes the design of LDPC code extension that is applicable to the native DVB-T2 LDPC codes. The proposed extension overcomes the limitation of the DVB-T2 system and allows flexible service component-specific robustness at the physical layer of DVB-T2 in a backwards compatible way. By using the proposed extension, varying coding strength inside one PLP of the DVB-T2 system is possible. As a result, the UEP transmission scheme can be implemented and integrated in the DVB-T2 system in an effective and cost-efficient manner. This paper extends the work introduced in [10] by providing a detailed design, additional extensions, and an extensive performance evaluation. In addition, a feasible use case for the extension, that is, a UEP transmission scheme, is presented and benefits of such use case when compared to standard DVB-T2 transmission scheme are thoroughly evaluated.

The remainder of the paper is organised as follows. In the next section an insight into LDPC codes is given. Section 3 describes the framing structure and LDPC codes specified by the DVB-T2 system. The design of the proposed extension and its impact on the processing chain of the DVB-T2 standard are discussed in Section 4. Simulation results demonstrating the performance of the proposed method over AWGN and TU6 channels are presented in Section 5. In Section 6 the use of the extension to provide UEP in DVB-T2 transmission system is presented. Finally, Section 7 concludes the paper.

2. Low-Density Parity Check Code

The Low Density Parity Check (LDPC) code family [11, 12] is among the better performing error correction coding technologies among modern channel coding schemes. For the last decade, more sophisticated classes of LDPC codes have been developed by members of the research community, each offering advances in one area or another. It was shown that LDPC codes can compete with turbo codes of the same length [13, 14].

An LDPC code is a linear block code characterised by a sparse m by n parity check matrix H. A matrix is said to be sparse if fewer than half of the elements are nonzero. Such a parity check matrix corresponds to a code with a design rate $r = (n - m)/n$, assuming all rows of the matrix are independent.

Using an LDPC code, a block of k information bits can be encoded in a code word of size n, where $k = n - m$. For the encoding procedure, typically a generator matrix G is determined based on a parity matrix H, where $HG = 0$. The generator matrix G does not necessarily have to be a sparse matrix, which can increase the complexity of the encoding procedure. However, some of the LDPC code families allow encoding based on a parity check matrix H, and hence reduce the complexity of the encoding process [15]. One of such codes is the extended irregular repeat-accumulate (eIRA) family of LDPC codes [16]. eIRA codes are discussed in more details in Section 3.

An iterative message-passing decoding algorithm based on the concept of belief propagation [17] is generally utilized to decode an LDPC code. The details of such a decoding algorithm can be found in [18]. If the Tanner graph [19] does not have any cycles, such message passing algorithms compute exact probabilities [17]. Otherwise, the decoding algorithm computes only approximate solutions, yet provides an effective decoding capability [20].

LDPC codes can be divided into two groups, regular and irregular LDPC codes. A code is called regular if all degrees of the variable nodes are equal and also all degrees of the check nodes are equal. In an irregular code each variable node and each check node can have different degrees assigned. In this paper, we will work with irregular LDPC codes. For the theoretical analysis such codes can be represented by the pair of degree distribution polynomials $(\lambda(x), \rho(x))$ and the length of the code n.

$$\lambda(x) := \sum_{i=2}^{d_v} \lambda_i x^{i-1},$$

$$\rho(x) := \sum_{i=2}^{d_c} \rho_i x^{i-1}, \tag{1}$$

where λ_i is the fraction of edges in the Tanner graph connected to degree-i variable nodes, ρ_i is the fraction of edges connected to degree-i check nodes, and $\lambda(1) = \rho(1) = 1$. d_v and d_c denote the maximum degree for variable nodes and check nodes, respectively. The degree distribution pair can be used to predict a decoding threshold for the LDPC code.

3. DVB-T2

This section provides a brief introduction to the DVB-T2 system and is divided into two parts. Section 3.1 provides an overview of a DVB-T2 processing chain. Section 3.2 gives a

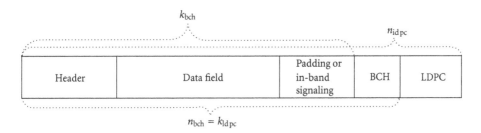

FIGURE 1: FEC frame structure in the DVB-T2 system.

deeper insight into the LDPC codes specified by the DVB-T2 standard.

3.1. Background. The DVB-T2 physical layer data channel is divided into logical entities called the physical layer pipe (PLP). Each PLP carries one logical data stream. An example of such a logical data stream would be an audio-visual multimedia stream along with the associated signalling information. The PLP architecture is designed to be flexible. Arbitrary adjustments to robustness and capacity of each PLP can be easily done. Each PLP's processing chain consists of four modules: Input Processing, Bit Interleaved Coding and Modulation (BICM), Frame Builder, and Modulator. The task of input processing module is to map the input data into Base Band (BB) frames. A BB frame comprises BB header, data field carrying the input data, optional in-band signalling, and padding, if necessary. Each BB frame is k_{bch} bits long and the size of BB frame does not change over time in a given PLP. BB frames are then passed to the BICM module. Among other things, the BICM module is handling FEC encoding, where a serial concatenation of two binary linear FEC codes is used: a Bose-Chaudhuri-Hocquenghem (BCH) code [21] as the outer code and a LDPC code as the inner code. By appending the FEC parity bits at the end of the BB frame an FEC frame is created (Figure 1). The FEC frame is characterised by a fixed size n_{ldpc} (16200 bits or 64800 bits) irrespective of the used FEC code rate. The desired code rate is achieved by setting appropriate size of the BB frame, that is, k_{bch} value. After the FEC frame is created, a frame builder module maps it to a physical layer frame. The physical layer frame is then interleaved and mapped to OFDM symbols. The last module, the Modulator, is responsible for modulation and transmission.

3.2. FEC Codes. The DVB-T2 system was designed to operate in the presence of high levels of noise and interference. It can be said that choosing the proper FEC code was one of the key components to achieve good performance by the terrestrial system. The DVB group opted for the use of a well-established and verified LDPC code supported by an additional BCH code. The BCH code was deployed to eliminate long error floors typical for LDPC codes at low error rates.

The LDPC codes deployed in the DVB-T2 system belong to the eIRA codes subclass [16] and are characterised by low-complexity encoding and shorter error-rate floors compared

to other irregular LDPC codes. The parity check matrix of a eIRA code is constrained to be in the form:

$$H = [H_1 H_2], \qquad (2)$$

where H_1 is an m by k sparse matrix and H_2 is an m by m staircase lower triangular matrix.

The form of the matrix H_2 was designed to avoid degree two cycles in the Tanner graph representation. Additionally, the characteristic of the H_2 matrix allows efficient encoding. A generator matrix G of an eIRA code can be expressed as

$$G = \left[I H_1^T H_2^{-T} \right], \qquad (3)$$

where matrix H_2^{-T} corresponds to a differential encoder whose transfer function is $1/(1 \oplus D)$. In the transfer function $\oplus$ denotes exclusive or operation and D stands for a 1 bit register. Based on this, the FEC encoding in DVB-T2 can be performed in two steps. First, the output of the BCH encoder is multiplied by a sparse matrix H_1^T producing an intermediate result. Secondly, the intermediate result is differentially encoded by a H_2^{-T} matrix generating the parity bits, which are combined with the output of the BCH encoder into a systematic code word.

To make the encoding of LDPC codes in DVB-T2 more efficient, matrix H_1 was designed to be in a quasicyclic form. Such a representation allows implementation of an encoder with shift register circuits [22], as well as reducing the memory storage requirements. Matrix H_1 is divided into $k_{ldpc}/360$ groups. In each group all columns have the same degree distribution dv_g. The positions of ones in columns are given for the first column in each group. For the remaining 359 columns the position of ones in each group is calculated in reference to the first column of the group using (Algorithm 1) where r_{ji} is the position of jth one in the ith column from the group and Q is a code rate dependent constant specified by the DVB-T2 standard.

LDPC decoding in DVB-T2 is based on a standard iterative exchange of information among variable nodes and check nodes, as described in Section 2.

4. The Proposed Code Extension Method

The DVB-T2 system provides limited possibilities to manipulate code rates in the FEC encoding subsystem. This paper proposes a method which allows service-component-specific robustness at the physical layer of DVB-T2 in a backwards

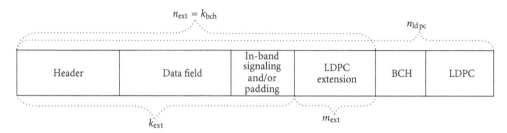

FIGURE 2: Structure of FEC frame carrying additional LDPC parity bits.

```
(1) for i = 1 to 359 do
(2)     for j = 1 to dv_g do
(3)         rji ← (r_{j0} + i × Q) mod (m)
(4)     end for
(5) end for
```

ALGORITHM 1

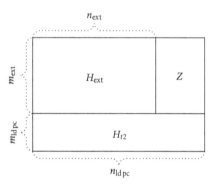

FIGURE 3: The structure of a combined parity check matrix H_{com}.

compatible way and the same overcomes the limitation. The design of the LDPC code extension is split into two steps. First, in Section 4.1, the question of how to introduce additional parity using a framing structure of the DVB-T2 system is answered. In Section 4.2 the design procedure of the extension FEC code matrix is given.

4.1. Concept. Pruning is one of the methods used for constructing variable-rate LDPC codes. The method changes code rate by eliminating variable nodes in the bipartite Tanner graph, which in turn modifies the check degree of connected check nodes. We employ the idea to change the code rates of the native DVB-T2 LDPC codes.

We propose the following modification to the processing chain and the framing structure of the DVB-T2 system. The supplementary LDPC encoder, which calculates the additional repair bits, is placed between the Input Processing module and the BICM module in the PLP processing chain. The supplementary LDPC encoder calculates m_{ext} parity bits over the first k_{ext} bits of a BB frame created by the Input Processing module. An extension parity check matrix H_{ext} is used to calculate those m_{ext} parity bits. The parity check matrix H_{ext} is designed in the way that $n_{ext} = k_{ext} + m_{ext}$ is always smaller than or equal to size of a BB frame equal to k_{bch}. The Input Preprocessor module, aware that the extension is used, decreases the size of Data Field in each BB frame that at least m_{ext} padding bits are present in each BB frame. As consequence, the m_{ext} repair bits generated by the LDPC extension encoder can be placed over the last m_{ext} padding bits of the BB frame. Such processed BB frame is then passed to the BICM module. The BICM module operates according to the DVB-T2 standard. The structure of the modified FEC frame is presented in Figure 2. A receiver that supports the proposed extension uses the extension parity bits and the native DVB-T2 LDPC parity bits together. The receiver creates a combined parity check matrix H_{com}

as presented on Figure 3. 3 is composed with H_{ext}, which is the parity check matrix used by the supplementary LDPC encoder, Z matrix, which is a zero matrix, and H_{t2}, which is the parity check matrix of the native DVB-T2 LDPC code. A legacy receiver treats the m_{ext} repair bits of the FEC frame as padding bits of BB frame and operates according to the DVB-T2 standard. Due to this the backward compatibility to the legacy DVB-T2 system is ensured.

4.2. Design. In this subsection a step-by-step description of the design of H_{ext} matrix is presented. The proposed method may not provide optimal results. In the H_{com} matrix, the parity check matrix H_{t2} and the zero matrix Z are given. Therefore, the goal is to find the degree distribution for the parity matrix H_{ext} that results in favourable error correction performance for the extended DVB-T2 LDPC code. Additionally, the parity matrix H_{ext} should meet the following two requirements.

First, the parity matrix H_{ext} should be divisible into Q number of groups having the exact amount of columns, where all columns in the group have the same degree. This ensures that the H_{ext} matrix will be in a quasicyclic form which results in low complexity encoding.

It is a known issue [16] that during the decoding process of an LDPC code, the log-likelihood ratio [18] of low degree variable nodes converges slower than that of the variable nodes with higher degrees. On the other hand, high degree check nodes are not desired in LDPC codes, since the more variables are involved in a check node, the more probable the check is to fail [13]. Therefore, to balance between those two trade-offs, low degree variable nodes are assigned to the

---

(1) Assign degree 1 to the last m_{ext} columns of the H_{ext} matrix
(2) Assign arbitrary degrees to each of the Q groups of the H_{ext} matrix.
(3) Calculate a degree distribution of the combined parity matrix H_{com}
(4) Calculate a decoding threshold for a given degree distribution of H_{com}

ALGORITHM 2

TABLE 1: The parameters of the extension matrix H_{ext} for the three tested use cases.

	k_{ext}	n_{ext}	Q
3/5 $\rightarrow$ 1/3	5400	9360	26
3/4 $\rightarrow$ 1/2	7200	11520	32
4/5 $\rightarrow$ 2/3	10800	12240	34

rows of a parity matrix corresponding to redundant parity bits. As a result, assigning a degree equal to one to the last m_{ext} columns of the parity matrix H_{ext} becomes the second constraint.

Taking into account the above-mentioned constraints, Algorithm 2 in conjunction with a numerical optimization algorithm, for example, Differential Evolution [23], can be used to determine the favourable degree distributions of the H_{com} matrix.

To calculate the degree distribution of the combined parity matrix H_{com} (4) can be used

$$\lambda_i = \frac{E_{d_v^i}}{E},$$
$$\rho_i = \frac{E_{d_c^i}}{E}. \qquad (4)$$

In these equations E is the number of all edges in a Tanner graph representation of the matrix H_{com}. $E_{d_v^i}$ and $E_{d_c^i}$ represent the number of all edges outgoing from variable nodes and check nodes with degree i, respectively. To test the theoretical decoding threshold of the combined parity matrix H_{com}, the density evolution technique was employed [24]. An alternative method, which is not discussed in this paper, to find a favorable H_{com} matrix structure is to use the extrinsic information transfer (EXIT) chart technique [25, 26].

After finding the favourable degree distribution of H_{com}, the next step is to create the parity matrix H_{ext}. Due to the fact that H_{t2} and Z are known, and we know how many ones are in each group of H_{ext}, we can calculate the degree distribution of H_{ext}. In order to create H_{ext} based on its degree distribution we use protograph expansion technique [27]. A protograph is a small graph which by copy and permute technique is utilised to create a larger graph. If a target matrix is to have dimension m_t by n_t then the protograph dimension shall be $m_p = m_t/q$ and $n_p = n_t/q$, where q is the periodicity of the target matrix. When the protograph is copied q times, edges of individual replicas need to be permuted among q replicas. However, the permutation of the edges has to follow some constraints so the derived matrix would preserve decoding threshold properties of the protograph and would have a quasicyclic structure. For example, if a variable node vn_i is connected to a check node cn_j in the protograph, the variable node vn_j in a replica can only connect to one of the q replicas of the check node cn_j. The periodicity of H_{ext} is the same as in H_{t2}, that means q is equal to 360 in our case. Based on the degree distribution of H_{ext} we create the protograph by using a progressive edge-growth technique [28]. Next, by copy and permute technique combined with Algorithm 1, a protograph is expanded to H_{ext}. Additionally, to improve decoding performance of the code, permutation selection is carried out in such a way that at least length 4 cycles in the combined parity matrix H_{com} are not present [13].

5. Evaluation of the Proposed Extended Codes

In order to evaluate the LDPC code extension method proposed in Section 4, three extensions to the native DVB-T2 codes have been designed. The native DVB-T2 LDPC codes with code rates 3/5, 3/4, and 4/5 were extended to produce code rates 1/3, 1/2, and 2/3, respectively. Through the paper, these three extended DVB-T2 LDPC codes are referred to as 3/5 $\rightarrow$ 1/3, 3/4 $\rightarrow$ 1/2, and 4/5 $\rightarrow$ 2/3. The parameters of the extension matrix H_{ext} for the extended DVB-T2 LDPC codes are presented in Table 1. Additionally, Table 2 presents the positions of ones in the first column of a group, which in conjunction with Algorithm 1 from Section 3 allows to build the H_{ext} matrices used during the evaluation process. The value of Q that is required by the algorithm is given in Table 1.

The extended codes were implemented in a DVB-T2 physical layer simulator. The proper functioning of the DVB-T2 simulator was verified by comparing its performance results to the results presented in the DVB-T2 Implementation Guidelines [29]. Using the simulator, a set of simulations was performed to evaluate the extended DVB-T2 LDPC codes. In all simulations, maximum duration T2 frames (250 ms) comprising short FEC frames (16200 bits long) were used. The modulation parameters were set to 16 QAM, 8k FFT size, and 1/4 guard interval. P1 not-boosted pilot pattern was used, and constellation rotation was not applied. The simulations were conducted on two transmission channel models: an additive white Gaussian noise (AWGN) channel model and a TU6 80 Hz channel model [30], which accurately represents a moving receiver. The results considered were obtained from a transmission of 1800 FEC blocks. Error calculations were performed by averaging the residual error rates after FEC frame decoding process.

Figures 4, 5, and 6 present the obtained results. In each of these figures, the results for both the native (to be extended) DVB-T2 LDPC codes as well as the extended DVB-T2 LDPC codes, are plotted. Based on the obtained results, it can be observed that the proposed LDPC extension improves performance of the native DVB-T2 LDPC codes.

TABLE 2: Addresses of parity bit accumulators for H_{ext}.

(a) 3/5 → 1/3		(b) 3/4 → 1/2		(c) 4/5 → 2/3
528	3556	1092	964	152
1134	1978	2869	3646	1381
3093	2681	1478	3369	6
587	2755	2907	29	1115
512	3736	2598	1663	1172
3505	2034	3944	11	1245
2673	3856	1992	1833	122
496	2978	1981	3318	575
3258	3090	1382	3382	372
751	1688	2031	152	1149
59	1285	760	3115	618
528	1772	2033	659	1307
2257	3129	1464	2623	260
1653	2108	817	3183	377
3656	3548	1046	3959	210
2145		1156	3297	195
3554		809	1246	1248
200		390	2480	833
3193		2940	2354	790
1324		1825	2776	211
907		3320		1224
3251		1713		893
1382		3490		502
657		3263		739
119		1620		576
3772		925		109
		3398		346
		4083		179
		1408		264
		2885		345
		1890		598
		3595		71
				1296
				1357

TABLE 3: Bit rate [KBPS] of base layer (BL) and cumulative bit rate of base layer and enhancement layer (BL + EL) for four tested sequences.

	City	Crew	Harbour	Soccer
BL	313,8	306,7	331,2	300,0
BL + EL	1010,2	991,2	961,9	1075,8

TABLE 4: Comparison of SNR value [dB] when BER 10^{-4} for Base Layer protection in UEP and EEP cases.

	AWGN			TU6		
	EEP	UEP	Delta	EEP	UEP	Delta
Scenario 1	5.5	4.8	0.7	8.2	7.5	0.7
Scenario 2	9.3	6.7	2.5	12.8	9.5	3.3
Scenario 3	10.5	9.7	0.8	14.6	13.7	0.9

code rate of the UEP transmission scheme. For example, bit rates of BL and EL for four sequences from Section 6 are presented in Table 3. As a result, for the calculation a BL to EL ratio was assumed to be 3/7. Three scenarios of UEP for the three extensions were analysed. In Scenario 1, the EL is protected by the native DVB-T2 LDPC code with the code rate 3/5 and the BL is protected by the extended DVB-T2 code 3/5 → 1/3. The resulting average code rate, which would correspond to code rate of EEP transmission, is approximately 1/2. In Scenario 2, the EL is protected by the native DVB-T2 LDPC code with the code rate 3/4 and the BL is protected by the extended DVB-T2 code 3/4 → 1/2. The resulting average code rate, which would correspond to code rate of EEP transmission, is approximately 2/3. In Scenario 3, the EL is protected by the native DVB-T2 LDPC code with the code rate 4/5 and the BL is protected by the extended DVB-T2 code 4/5 → 2/3. The resulting average code rate, which would correspond to code rate of EEP transmission, is approximately 3/4. The performance of the native DVB-T2 LDPC code at the calculated average code rates is also plotted in Figures 4, 5, and 6. Scalable codecs such as H.264/SVC produce bit-streams which is partitioned into layers that form a hierarchy. Thus, in order for a particular layer to be useful to the decoder, all layers it depends on also need to be available. In other words, if a scalable encoder produces one base layer and one enhancement layer in order for an enhancement layer to be useful in decoding, the base layer needs to be available to the decoder. Therefore, it is important to compare the results of UEP and EEP transmission schemes for base layer protection perspective. The significant performance gap between the native DVB-T2 LDPC code at the calculated average code rate, which corresponds to the BL and EL protection in the EEP transmission scheme, and that of the extended DVB-T2 LDPC code, which corresponds to the BL protection in the UEP transmission scheme, can be clearly observed. The improvement for the BL protection when the extension is used to deploy the UEP transmission scheme are summarized in Table 4 and amount up to more than 3 dB

Therefore, due to the extensions the limitation of DVB-T2 can be overcome and means to implement a UEP transmission scheme at the physical layer of DVB-T2 in backward compatible way are provided.

In a UEP transmission scheme, data, based on its importance, is divided into two or more protection levels. Next, each protection level has assigned different robustness, for example, by using different FEC code rates. In a EEP transmission scheme a single protection level is assigned to all transmitted data regardless of its importance. The comparison between the UEP transmission scheme and the EEP transmission scheme, under the constraint of an equal level of available bandwidth and thus using the same amount of protection data ensures fairness for the evaluation of the proposed extension. The two-protection-level UEP scheme from Section 6 was used to calculate the resulting average

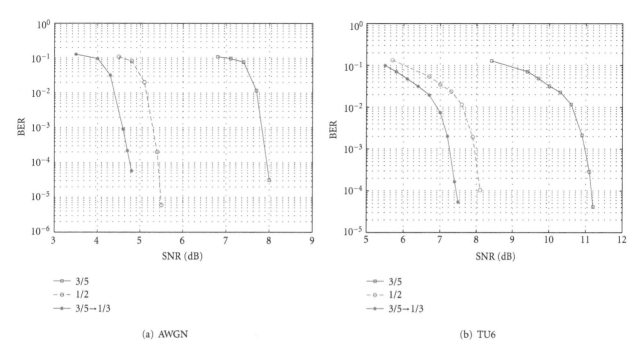

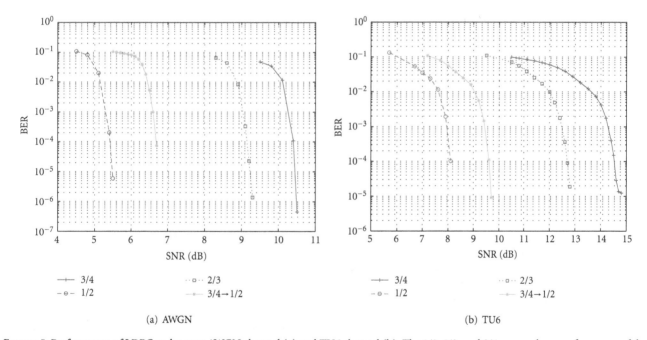

FIGURE 4: Performance of LDPC codes over AWGN channel (a) and TU6 channel (b). The 3/5 and 1/2 curves show performance of the native DVB-T2 LDPC codes with the corresponding code rates. The 3/5 → 1/3 curve shows performance of the native DVB-T2 LDPC with code rate 3/5 extended to the code rate 1/3 using the proposed method.

FIGURE 5: Performance of LDPC codes over AWGN channel (a) and TU6 channel (b). The 1/2, 2/3, and 3/4 curves show performance of the native DVB-T2 LDPC codes with the corresponding code rates. The 3/4 → 1/2 curve shows performance of the native DVB-T2 LDPC code with code rate 3/4 extended to the code rate 1/2 using the proposed method.

in Scenario 2. The gain can be reflected in practical quality improvements for the user which is showed in Section 6.

Figures 5 and 6, additionally, plot simulation results for the native DVB-T2 LDPC codes that provide the same amount of repair data as the extended DVB-T2 LDPC codes. For example, the native DVB-T2 code 1/2 is equivalent to

the extended code 3/4 → 1/2. It should be noted that the DVB-T2 standard does not specify code rate 1/3. It can be observed that the results achieved by the extended DVB-T2 LDPC codes slightly underperform compared to the respective native DVB-T2 LDPC codes. For convenience, performance of the native and the extended codes, for

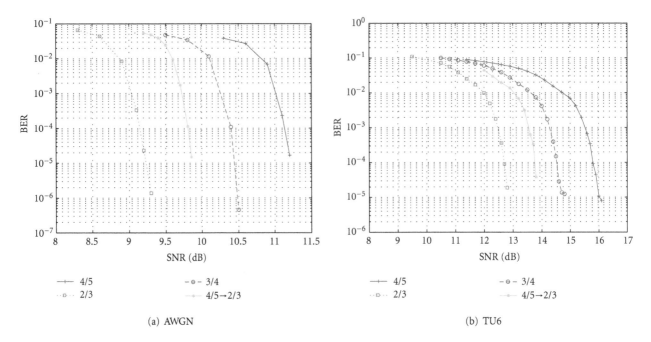

FIGURE 6: Performance of LDPC codes over AWGN channel (a) and TU6 channel (b). The 2/3, 3/4, and 4/5 curves show performance of the native DVB-T2 LDPC codes with corresponding code rates. The 3/4 → 1/2 curve shows performance of the native DVB-T2 LDPC code with the code rate 4/5 extended to code rate 2/3 using the proposed method.

TABLE 5: Comparison of the SNR value [dB] when BER 10^{-4} for the native and extended DVB-T2 codes.

	1/2			2/3		
	Native	Extended	Delta	Native	Extended	Delta
AWGN	5.5	6.7	−1.2	9.2	9.7	−0.5
TU6	8.2	9.5	−1.3	12.7	13.7	−1.0

residual BER 10^{-4}, are presented in Table 5. The extended codes performance is weakened due to constraints which are imposed by the backward-compatibility requirement. The matrix H_{com} must contain the original code rate matrix H_{t2}. Therefore, the purpose of the extended codes is not to replace native DVB-T2 codes but to enable varying FEC protection for data transmitted over one PLP in a backward-compatible way. In other words the extended codes should be used only when a UEP transmission scheme is considered. If a EEP transmission scheme is deployed then the native codes should be utilized.

6. Use Case for the Proposed Extended Codes

The main use case for the proposed extension is to allow UEP transmission over DVB-T2 system in a backward-compatible mode. Figure 7 depicts partial high level block diagram of PLP processing chain, when the proposed extension is used to enable UEP transmission scheme. The Input Preprocessor module splits incoming data to high level protection and low level protection streams. Low level protection stream is processed by input processor in accordance with the standard, and BB frames k_{bch} bits long are formed. For the

high level protection stream, the input processor creates BB frames also k_{bch} bits long. The k_{bch} value depends on the code rate chosen for the given PLP. However, in case of high level BB frames input processor ensure that cumulative size of BB header, data, and in-band signalling does not exceed k_{ext} bits. The remaining space of the high level BB frame is filled with padding. The high level BB frames are next passed to the extension FEC encoder. The encoder calculate m_{ext} parity bits from the first k_{ext} bits of the high level BB frame. Next, the m_{ext} parity bits are placed over padding bits and form integral part of the high level BB frame. Such formed low and high level BB frames are multiplexed together and passed to BICM module. The BICM module operates according to the DVB-T2 standard. Both types of BB frames are encoded using the same native DVB-T2 FEC code. To ensure that receiver is able to differentiate between FEC frames, with the low level of protection and with the high level of protection, additional L1 signalling would be required. Legacy receiver processes high level and low level BB frames in the same way. For a receiver with the support of the extension low level BB frames are also processed in the standard way. However, for the decoding of the high level BB frames the combined matrix H_{com}, Figure 3, is used.

We showed in Section 5 that the proposed extensions strengthen the performance of the native DVB-T2 LDPC codes. We also mentioned that the main use case for the proposed LDPC extensions is to enable varying FEC protection for a data transmitted over one PLP in a backward-compatible way. In other words, the aim is to enable UEP of a service at physical layer of DVB-T2. Therefore, we present now the gain, in practical quality improvements from the user perspective, which can be achieved by employing UEP

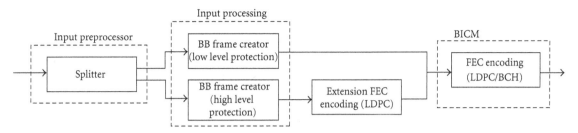

FIGURE 7: Partial high level block diagram of PLP processing chain when the proposed extension is used to enable UEP transmission scheme.

TABLE 6: Average PSNR [DB] value of luminance component of the four tested sequences for the high quality video (BL + EL) and the base quality video up-scaled to the high quality video dimension.

	City	Crew	Harbour	Soccer
BL + EL	33,7	34,3	29,9	33,6
up-scaled BL	28,0	32,3	27,0	30,8

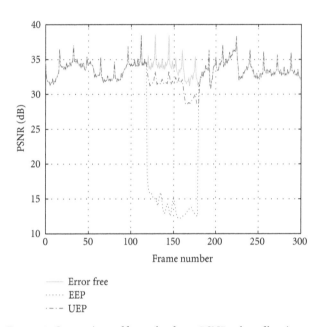

FIGURE 8: Comparison of frame-by-frame PSNR value of luminance component between UEP scheme and EEP scheme when two-second long transmission error is encountered. For reference PSNR value of luminance component in error-free transmission is also depicted.

compared to EEP. For this purpose, we used four different video sequences, City, Crew, Harbour, and Soccer (the video sequences are publicly available). Each sequence was encoded and decoded using the H.264/SVC reference software [29]. The base layer (BL) has CIF (352 × 288) resolution and a frame rate of 15 fps. The enhancement layer (EL) has 4CIF (704 × 576) resolution and a frame rate of 30 fps. The resulting bit rates of encoded sequences are presented in Table 3. The PSNR values for the BL and EL are displayed in Table 6. In the UEP scheme, EL of H.264/SVC video streams were assigned to low protection level, that is, the native DVB-T2 LDPC code with code rate 3/4, and the BL of those H.264/SVC video streams were assigned to high level protection, that is, the extended DVB-T2 LDPC code with cde rate 3/4 → 1/2. This is equivalent to Scenario 2 from Section 5. In the EEP scheme, which uses the same amount of bandwidth as the foregoing UEP scheme, BL and EL of those H.264/SVC video streams were assigned to the same protection level, that is, the native DVB-T2 LDPC cdeo with code rate 2/3.

At the receiver, the following error concealment algorithms were assumed. In both the EEP and in UEP cases, whenever both BL and EL are corrupted, that is, a picture cannot be decoded, the most recent correctly decoded picture is frozen. However, in the UEP case, when EL is corrupted but BL is still error-free, then the BL picture is up-scaled to the full EL resolution and it replaces the corresponding EL picture. Table 6 provides the average PSNR value when the whole BL is up-scaled.

Next, the following scenario was assumed. For a certain period of time, SNR value of the received signal at the mobile receiver drops to a level in which the codes protecting EL in the UEP transmission scheme and both layers in the EEP transmission scheme are not able to provide an error-free signal. This may happen due to mobility of a receiver. However, the code extended by the proposed method protecting BL in the UEP transmission scheme is strong enough to successfully decode the signal. Based on Table 4, it can be said that the signal strength drops to SNR value between 6.7 dB and 9.3 dB in AWGN channel and 9.5 dB and 12.8 dB in TU6 channel. Figure 8 depicts a video quality of the Soccer sequence for the UEP case and the EEP case, when such a drop in the received signal strength lasts 2 seconds. As it can be observed, the PSNR curve for the UEP case shows acceptable video quality during the degradation phase, whereas for the EEP case, the video quality is completely unacceptable during that period. Moreover, it should be noted that in the UEP case, the user receives continuous video with a lower quality and a lower frame rate while, in the EEP case, the user experiences a 2-second-long frame freeze. Table 7 presents the average PSNR values for each tested sequence for three error duration periods: 0.5, 1, and 2 seconds. The values presented in Table 7 clearly show a better video service is achieved when the proposed extension method is utilized to provide the UEP transmission scheme.

TABLE 7: Average PSNR [DB] of luminance component for the UEP case and the EEP case depending on error duration [s].

		City	Crew	Harbour	Soccer
0.5 [s]	UEP	33.5079	34.2212	29.8656	33.5280
	EEP	32.8645	33.5622	29.4930	32.6144
1.0 [s]	UEP	33.3123	34.1905	29.7793	33.4293
	EEP	32.0403	32.8139	28.8789	31.5801
2.0 [s]	UEP	32.9317	34.1255	29.6094	33.2984
	EEP	30.4126	31.1425	27.5265	29.5853

7. Conclusions

In this paper, a method to extend the LDPC codes of the DVB-T2 system was proposed. The method was introduced to overcome the limitations imposed by the DVB-T2 standard and to enable varying FEC protection for data transmitted over a single PLP. Using the proposed extension, it becomes possible to adjust the protection level of the native DVB-T2 LDPC codes BB frame by BB frame. Consequently, services transmitted using a single PLP are enabled to have different levels of error protection that may be used at the service component level. The paper also discussed the adaptation of the proposed LDPC extension method in the DVB-T2 framing structure to ensure backwards compatibility to the legacy receivers. Moreover, a step-by-step description of the design procedure of the LDPC extension was provided. The procedure should make extension of any of the native DVB-T2 LDPC codes relatively simple. The simulation results provide evidence of the benefits of deploying the proposed LDPC code extension in the DVB-T2 environment. The results have shown that with the same bit budget, due to the use of the LDPC extension, the UEP transmission scheme can be implemented and playback continuity at the receiver side in adverse channel conditions can be significantly improved. Consequently, better user experience in DVB-T2 transmission system can be ensured.

Abbreviations

AWGN: Additive White Gaussian Noise
BB: Base Band
BCH: Bose-Chaudhuri-Hocquenghem
BER: Bit Error Rate
BICM: Bit Interleaved Coding and Modulation
BL: Base Layer
CIF: Common Intermediate Format
DVB: Digital Video Broadcasting
DVB-T2: DVB 2nd Generation Terrestrial
EEP: Equal Error Protection
eIRA: extended Irregular Repeat-Accumulate
EL: Enhancement Layer
EXIT: EXtrinsic Information Transfer
FEC: Forward Error Correction
LDPC: Low-Density Parity Check
PLP: Physical Layer Pipe
PSNR: Peak Signal-to Noise-Ratio

SNR: Signal-to-Noise Ratio
SVC: Scalable Video Coding
UEP: Unequal Error Protection.

Acknowledgments

This work was partially supported by Nokia and the Academy of Finland, Project no. 129657 (Finnish Centre of Excellence program 2006–2011).

References

[1] International Telecommunication Union, *Frame Error Robust Narrowband and Wideband Embedded Variable Bit-Rate Coding of Speech and Audio from 8-32 kbit/s*, Telecommunication Standardization Sector of ITU, Geneva, Switzerland, 2008.

[2] International Telecommunication Union, *Advance Video Coding for Generic Audiovisual Services*, Telecommunication Standardization Sector of ITU, Geneva, Switzerland, 2007.

[3] Digital Video Broadcasting (DVB), http://dvb.org/.

[4] Digital Video Broadcasting (DVB), "Commercial Requirements for NGH," DVB Document CMNGH0015, June 2009.

[5] European Telecommunications Standards Institute (ETSI), "Specification for the use of Video and Audio Coding in DVB services delivered directly over IP protocols," TS 102 005, March 2010.

[6] European Telecommunications Standards Institute (ETSI), "Digital Video Broadcasting (DVB): frame structure channel coding and modulation for a second generation digital terrestrial television broadcasting system (DVB-T2)," TS 102 005, March 2010.

[7] Digital Video Broadcasting (DVB), "Upper Layer Forward Error Correction in DVB," DVB Document A148, March 2010.

[8] I. Bouazizi, L. Kondrad, M. Hannuksela, and M. Gabbouj, "Efficient FEC protection of scalable media streams in DVB-H," in *Proceedings of the 58th Annual IEEE Broadcast Symposium*, pp. 1–6, October 2008.

[9] M. M. Hannuksela, V. K. M. Vadakital, and S. Jumisko-Pyykkö, "Comparison of error protection methods for audio-video broadcast over DVB-H," *EURASIP Journal on Advances in Signal Processing*, vol. 2007, Article ID 71801, 12 pages, 2007.

[10] L. Kondrad, I. Bouazizi, and M. Gabbouj, "LDPC fec code extension for unequal error protection in 2ND generation DVB systems," in *Proceedings of the IEEE International Conference on Multimedia and Expo (ICME '10)*, pp. 504–509, July 2010.

[11] R. G. Gallager, "Low density parity-check odes," *IRE Transactions on Information Theory*, vol. 8, no. 1, pp. 21–28, 1962.

[12] D. MacKay and R. Neal, "Good codes based on very sparse matrices," in *Cryptography and Coding*, C. Boyd, Ed., vol. 1025 of *Lecture Notes in Computer Science*, pp. 100–111, Springer, Berlin, Germany, 1995.

[13] T. J. Richardson, M. A. Shokrollahi, and R. L. Urbanke, "Design of capacity-approaching irregular low-density parity-check codes," *IEEE Transactions on Information Theory*, vol. 47, no. 2, pp. 619–637, 2001.

[14] M. G. Luby, M. Mitzenmacher, M. A. Shokrollahi, and D. A. Spielman, "Improved low-density parity-check codes using irregular graphs," *IEEE Transactions on Information Theory*, vol. 47, no. 2, pp. 585–598, 2001.

[15] T. J. Richardson and R. L. Urbanke, "Efficient encoding of low-density parity-check codes," *IEEE Transactions on Information Theory*, vol. 47, no. 2, pp. 638–656, 2001.

[16] M. Yang, W. E. Ryan, and Y. Li, "Design of efficiently encodable moderate-length high-rate irregular LDPC codes," *IEEE Transactions on Communications*, vol. 52, no. 4, pp. 564–571, 2004.

[17] J. Pearl, *Probabilistic Reasoning in Intelligent Systems: Networks of Plausible Inference*, Morgan Kauffmann, San Francisco, Calif, USA, 1988.

[18] T. K. Moon, *Error Correction Coding: Mathematical Methods and Algorithms*, Wiley-Interscience, 2005.

[19] R. M. Tanner, "A recursive approach to low complexity codes," *IEEE Transactions on Information Theory*, vol. 27, no. 5, pp. 533–547, 1981.

[20] Y. Weiss, "Correctness of local probability propagation in graphical models with loops," *Neural Computation*, vol. 12, no. 1, pp. 1–41, 2000.

[21] R. C. Bose and D. K. Ray-Chaudhuri, "On a class of error correcting binary group codes," *Information and Control*, vol. 3, no. 1, pp. 68–79, 1960.

[22] Z. Li, L. Chen, L. Zeng, S. Lin, and W. H. Fong, "Efficient encoding of quasi-cyclic low-density parity-check codes," *IEEE Transactions on Communications*, vol. 54, no. 1, pp. 71–81, 2006.

[23] R. Storn and K. Price, "Differential evolution a simple and efficient heuristic for global optimization over continuous spaces," *Journal of Global Optimization*, vol. 11, no. 4, pp. 341–359, 1997.

[24] T. J. Richardson and R. L. Urbanke, "The capacity of low-density parity-check codes under message-passing decoding," *IEEE Transactions on Information Theory*, vol. 47, no. 2, pp. 599–618, 2001.

[25] S. T. Brink, "Convergence behavior of iteratively decoded parallel concatenated codes," *IEEE Transactions on Communications*, vol. 49, no. 10, pp. 1727–1737, 2001.

[26] S. ten Brink and G. Kramer, "Design of repeat-accumulate codes for iterative detection and decoding," *IEEE Transactions on Signal Processing*, vol. 51, no. 11, pp. 2764–2772, 2003.

[27] J. Thorpe, "Low-density parity-check (LDPC) codes constructed from protographs," Tech. Rep. JPL INP, 2003.

[28] X. Y. Hu, E. Eleftheriou, and D. M. Arnold, "Progressive edge-growth tanner graphs," in *Proceedings of the IEEE Global Telecommunicatins Conference (GLOBECOM '01)*, vol. 2, pp. 995–1001, November 2001.

[29] European Telecommunications Standards Institute (ETSI), "Digital Video Broadcasting (DVB): implementation guidelines for a second generation digital terrestrial television broadcasting system (DVB-T2)," TS 102 831, February 2009.

[30] "Digital Land Mobile Radio Communications—COST 207," Tech. Rep., Commission of the European Communities, Luxemburg, 1989.

Permissions

The contributors of this book come from diverse backgrounds, making this book a truly international effort. This book will bring forth new frontiers with its revolutionizing research information and detailed analysis of the nascent developments around the world.

We would like to thank all the contributing authors for lending their expertise to make the book truly unique. They have played a crucial role in the development of this book. Without their invaluable contributions this book wouldn't have been possible. They have made vital efforts to compile up to date information on the varied aspects of this subject to make this book a valuable addition to the collection of many professionals and students.

This book was conceptualized with the vision of imparting up-to-date information and advanced data in this field. To ensure the same, a matchless editorial board was set up. Every individual on the board went through rigorous rounds of assessment to prove their worth. After which they invested a large part of their time researching and compiling the most relevant data for our readers. Conferences and sessions were held from time to time between the editorial board and the contributing authors to present the data in the most comprehensible form. The editorial team has worked tirelessly to provide valuable and valid information to help people across the globe.

Every chapter published in this book has been scrutinized by our experts. Their significance has been extensively debated. The topics covered herein carry significant findings which will fuel the growth of the discipline. They may even be implemented as practical applications or may be referred to as a beginning point for another development. Chapters in this book were first published by Hindawi Publishing Corporation; hereby published with permission under the Creative Commons Attribution License or equivalent.

The editorial board has been involved in producing this book since its inception. They have spent rigorous hours researching and exploring the diverse topics which have resulted in the successful publishing of this book. They have passed on their knowledge of decades through this book. To expedite this challenging task, the publisher supported the team at every step. A small team of assistant editors was also appointed to further simplify the editing procedure and attain best results for the readers.

Our editorial team has been hand-picked from every corner of the world. Their multi-ethnicity adds dynamic inputs to the discussions which result in innovative outcomes. These outcomes are then further discussed with the researchers and contributors who give their valuable feedback and opinion regarding the same. The feedback is then collaborated with the researches and they are edited in a comprehensive manner to aid the understanding of the subject.

Apart from the editorial board, the designing team has also invested a significant amount of their time in understanding the subject and creating the most relevant covers. They scrutinized every image to scout for the most suitable representation of the subject and create an appropriate cover for the book.

The publishing team has been involved in this book since its early stages. They were actively engaged in every process, be it collecting the data, connecting with the contributors or procuring relevant information. The team has been an ardent support to the editorial, designing and production team. Their endless efforts to recruit the best for this project, has resulted in the accomplishment of this book. They are a veteran in the field of academics and their pool of knowledge is as vast as their experience in printing. Their expertise and guidance has proved useful at every step. Their uncompromising quality standards have made this book an exceptional effort. Their encouragement from time to time has been an inspiration for everyone.

The publisher and the editorial board hope that this book will prove to be a valuable piece of knowledge for researchers, students, practitioners and scholars across the globe.

List of Contributors

Sajid Nazir, Vladimir Stanković and Ivan Andonović
Department of Electronic and Electrical Engineering, University of Strathclyde, Glasgow G1 1XW, UK

Dejan Vukobratović
Department of Power, Electronics and Communication Engineering, University of Novi Sad, 21000 Novi Sad, Serbia

Dario Vieira
LRIE Lab, ´ Ecole d'Ing´enieur des Technologies de l'Information et de la Communication (EFREI), 94800 Villejuif, France

Cesar A. V. Melo
Department of Computing Science, Federal University of Amazonas, 69077-000 Manaus, AM, Brazil

Yacine Ghamri-Doudane
Ecole Nationale Sup´erieure d'Informatique pours l'Industrie et l'Entreprise (ENSIIE), 91025 Evry, France
LIGM Lab, Universit´e Paris-Est, 75420 Champs-sur-Marne, France

Kai-Chun Liang and Hsiang-Fu Yu
Department of Computer Science, National Taipei University of Education, Taipei 106, Taiwan

Chih-ChaoWen and Cheng-ShongWu
Department of Electrical Engineering, National Chung Cheng University, Chia-Yi 62102, Taiwan

Francisco Utray
Spanish Centre of Captioning and Audio Description (CESyA), Avenida de Gregorio Peces-Barba 1, 28918 Madrid, Spain
Research Group TECMERIN, Journalism and Audiovisual Communication Department, Universidad Carlos III de Madrid, C/Madrid 126, 28903 Getafe, Madrid, Spain

Mercedes de Castro
Spanish Centre of Captioning and Audio Description (CESyA), Avenida de Gregorio Peces-Barba 1, 28918 Madrid, Spain
Telematics Department, Universidad Carlos III de Madrid, Avenida de la Universidad 30, 28911 Legan´es, Madrid, Spain

Lourdes Moreno
Computer Science Department, Universidad Carlos III de Madrid, Avenida de la Universidad 30, 28911 Legan´es, Madrid, Spain

Belén Ruiz-Mezcua
Spanish Centre of Captioning and Audio Description (CESyA), Avenida de Gregorio Peces-Barba 1, 28918 Madrid, Spain
Computer Science Department, Universidad Carlos III de Madrid, Avenida de la Universidad 30, 28911 Legan´es, Madrid, Spain

Monchai Lertsutthiwong, Thinh Nguyen and Bechir Hamdaoui
School of EECS, Oregon State University, Corvallis, OR 97331, USA

Zeng-Yuan Yang and Li-Ming Tseng
Department of Computer Science and Information Engineering, National Central University, Jhongli 32001, Taiwan

Yi-Ming Chen
Department of Information Management, National Central University, Jhongli 32001, Taiwan

Wafa Ben Hassen and Meriem Afif
Mediatron: Research Unit on Radio Communication and Multimedia Networks, Higher School of Communication of Tunis (Sup'com), Carthage University, Cit'e Technologique des Communications, Route de Raoued Km 3.5, 2083 El Ghazala, Ariana, Tunisia

Chenghao Liu and Moncef Gabbouj
Department of Signal Processing, Tampere University of Technology, 33720 Tampere, Finland

Miska M. Hannuksela
Nokia Research Center, 33720 Tampere, Finland

Tamás Jursonovics
Deutsche Telekom AG — Products & Innovation, T-Online-Allee 1, 64295 Darmstadt, Germany

Sándor Imre
Department of Telecommunications, Budapest University of Technology, Budapest, Hungary

Tsao-TaWei
Department of Computer Science and Information Engineering, Ming Chuan University, No. 5, Deming Road., Guishan Township, Taoyuan County 333, Taiwan
Technical Division, Develop Department, YES Information Incorporated, Xinyi District, Taipei 110, Taiwan

Chia-HuiWang
Department of Computer Science and Information Engineering, Ming Chuan University, No. 5, Deming Road., Guishan Township, Taoyuan County 333, Taiwan

Yu-Hsien Chu
Technical Division, Develop Department, YES Information Incorporated, Xinyi District, Taipei 110, Taiwan
Department of Engineering Science and Ocean Engineering, National Taiwan University, Taipei 106, Taiwan

Ray-I Chang
Department of Engineering Science and Ocean Engineering, National Taiwan University, Taipei 106, Taiwan

Ioannis G. Fraimis and Stavros A. Kotsopoulos
Wireless Telecommunications Laboratory (WTL), Department of Electrical and Computer Engineering, University of Patras, 26500 Rio, Greece

Carolina Blanch Perez del Notario, Rogier Baert and Maja D'Hondt
SSET Department of IMEC, Kapeldreef 75, 3001 Leuven, Belgium

Ying-Nan Chen
Department of Computer Science and Information Engineering, National Central University, Chung-Li 32054, Taiwan

Chi-Huang Shih, Yeong-Yuh Xu and Yao-TienWang
Department of Computer Science and Information Engineering, HungKuang University, Taichung 433, Taiwan

Emilie Dumont and Georges Quénot
UJF-Grenoble 1/UPMF-Grenoble 2/Grenoble INP, CNRS, LIG UMR 5217, 38041 Grenoble, France

Yuanlong Cao and Jianfeng Guan
State Key Laboratory of Networking and Switching Technology, Beijing University of Posts and Telecommunications, Beijing 100876, China

Changqiao Xu
State Key Laboratory of Networking and Switching Technology, Beijing University of Posts and Telecommunications, Beijing 100876, China
Institute of Sensing Technology and Business, Beijing University of Posts and Telecommunications, Jiangsu, Wuxi 214028, China

Hongke Zhang
State Key Laboratory of Networking and Switching Technology, Beijing University of Posts and Telecommunications, Beijing 100876, China
National Engineering Laboratory for Next Generation Internet Interconnection Devices, Beijing Jiaotong University, Beijing 100044, China

Huang Shyh-Fang
Department of Information Communication, MingDao University, Changhua 52345, Taiwan

Yifeng He and Ling Guan
Department of Electrical and Computer Engineering, Ryerson University, Toronto, ON, Canada M5B2K3

Lukasz Kondrad and Moncef Gabbouj
Tampere University of Technology, Department of Signal Processing, P.O. Box 553, Tampere 33720, Finland

Imed Bouazizi
Huawei Technologies Ltd., European Research Center, Riesstraße 25, Munich 80992, Germany

Printed in the USA
CPSIA information can be obtained
at www.ICGtesting.com
JSHW051438221024
72173JS00006B/1504